THE VERNACULAR ARISTOTLE

This book explores the ways in which Aristotle's legacy was appropriated and reshaped by vernacular readers in Medieval and Renaissance Italy. It considers translation in a broad sense, looking at commentaries, compendia, rewritings and abridgments alongside vernacular versions of Aristotle's works. Translation is thus taken as quintessential to the very notion of reception, with a focus on the dynamics – cultural, social, material – that informed the appropriation and reshaping of the 'master of those who know' on the part of vernacular readers between 1250 and 1500. By looking at the proactive and transformative nature of reception, this book challenges traditional narratives about the period and identifies the theory and practice of translation as a liminal space that facilitated the interaction between lay readers and the academic context while fostering the legitimation of the vernacular as a language suitable for philosophical discourse.

EUGENIO REFINI is Assistant Professor of Italian Studies at New York University. His interests include Renaissance poetics, rhetoric and drama; reception of antiquity and translation studies; and the intersections of music and literature. His publications include a monograph on Alessandro Piccolomini (*Per via d'annotationi: le glosse inedite di Alessandro Piccolomini all'Ars Poetica di Orazio*, 2009) and several articles and book chapters on Ludovico Ariosto, Torquato Tasso, Latin Humanism and the musical culture of early modern Italy.

CLASSICS AFTER ANTIQUITY

Editors
Alastair Blanshard
University of Queensland
Shane Butler
Johns Hopkins University
Emily Greenwood
Yale University

Classics after Antiquity presents innovative contributions in the field of Classical Reception Studies. Each volume explores the methods and motives of those who, coming after and going after antiquity, have entered into a contest with and for the legacies of the ancient world. The series aims to unsettle, to provoke debate, and to stimulate a re-evaluation of assumptions about the relationship between Greek and Roman classical pasts and modern histories.

Other titles in the series

Afterlives of the Roman Poets: Biofiction and the Reception of Latin Poetry
Nora Goldschmidt
ISBN: 978-1-107-18025-3

The Perpetual Immigrant and the Limits of Athenian Democracy
Demetra Kasimis
ISBN: 978-1-107-05243-7

Borges' Classics: Global Encounters with the Graeco-Roman Past
Laura Jensen
ISBN: 978-1-108-41840-9

*Classical Victorians: Scholars, Scoundrels and Generals in
Pursuit of Antiquity*
Edmund Richardson
ISBN: 978-1-107-02677-3

*Modernism and Homer: The Odysseys of H. D., James Joyce,
Osip Mandelstam, and Ezra Pound*
Leah Culligan Flack
ISBN: 978-1-107-10803-5

THE VERNACULAR ARISTOTLE

Translation as Reception in Medieval and Renaissance Italy

EUGENIO REFINI

New York University

CAMBRIDGE UNIVERSITY PRESS

CAMBRIDGE
UNIVERSITY PRESS

University Printing House, Cambridge CB2 8BS, United Kingdom

One Liberty Plaza, 20th Floor, New York, NY 10006, USA

477 Williamstown Road, Port Melbourne, VIC 3207, Australia

314–321, 3rd Floor, Plot 3, Splendor Forum, Jasola District Centre, New Delhi – 110025, India

79 Anson Road, #06-04/06, Singapore 079906

Cambridge University Press is part of the University of Cambridge.

It furthers the University's mission by disseminating knowledge in the pursuit of
education, learning, and research at the highest international levels of excellence.

www.cambridge.org
Information on this title: www.cambridge.org/9781108481816
DOI: 10.1017/9781108693684

© Eugenio Refini 2020

First published 2020

Printed in the United Kingdom by TJ International Ltd. Padstow Cornwall

A catalogue record for this publication is available from the British Library.

ISBN 978-1-108-48181-6 Hardback

To my parents,
Miranda and Marcello

Contents

Figures

Series Editors' Preface

The Latin roots of *tradition* and *translation* (respectively, *trado* and *transfero*) share not only a prefix (*trans-*) but also the same basic spatiotemporal metaphors. Both, in other words, ask us to imagine a process by which something is moved from point A to point B. That the thing being moved has (or is) 'value' is further suggested by other English words derived from both ('trade', 'transfer', etc.), to say nothing of the deeper root of *trado*: *do*, 'I give'. This last verb lurks at the very heart of older notions of 'the classical tradition' as not just a 'gift' of those clever and talented Greeks and Romans, but a hulking inheritance to which subsequent ages supposedly owed both care and respect. Such notions now seem quaint (or even morally or politically suspect), supplanted by more supple accounts of 'classical reception' that emphasise the agency of person or age 'receiving' this supposed gift – a gift that, on close inspection, is revealed to be as much a product of said person or age as it is an intact legacy from the past. But what of 'translation', especially when the movement in question is from Greek or Latin? Can and should we similarly upend the hypothesis of ancient value 'transferred' to the present, in order to recover the creative work of translators and their readers in creating that very value?

This question animates Eugenio Refini's *The Vernacular Aristotle: Translation as Reception in Medieval and Renaissance Italy*. As his title makes clear, 'point A' in this study is Aristotle, who by the later Middle Ages was such an authority that he could be cited, simpliciter, as 'the Philosopher'. But if Aristotle is in some ways an exemplary figure from (and for) the classical canon, in others he is problematic. His oeuvre is vast and varied and covers an astonishing range of subjects, albeit with conclusions that are not always consistent between this or that work. This is partly the result of the origins of his texts, with most of the surviving *Corpus Arisotelicum* seemingly comprising lecture notes rather than finished treatises. The analysis is dense and minute, often mired in technical vocabulary, some of it given specialised meanings by Aristotle himself. And then, of course, there is the fact that he wrote in Greek. That was not in itself a problem for his contemporaries, but it was already a significant mediating factor for medieval readers who knew him only in Latin translation. Later, as Latin too began to yield to the vernacular, the Philosopher slipped, for many, even further out of reach.

One might suppose, therefore, that the proliferating translations of Aristotle into the vernacular in the late medieval and early modern period represent nothing more than an effort to rescue his works from a linguistic dead end, preserving their value as an ongoing gift to posterity. This, indeed, was part of the stated intent of his translators. But as Refini's probing portrait reveals, the story is far more complex. On one hand, as translators grappled with the text and their task, their work inevitably became one of interpretation as much as one of translation. (Here too, as Refini points out, there lurks a pun, in that *interpres* is the Latin word for 'translator'.) On the other, far from being destined only for a 'lower', Latinless audience of non-specialists, their translations circled back to inform 'higher' work of Aristotelian exegesis and new philosophy still conducted in Latin. Vernacular translation, in other words, was an integral part of Aristotelian reception throughout the period in question.

This fact is interesting in its own right, revising a crucial chapter in the reception of a major classical author and shedding new light on late medieval and early modern philosophical thought more generally – and not just in 'academic' philosophical circles. But Refini's book offers even more: namely, a model for the study of what his introduction labels 'translation as reception'. His case studies, organised around specific projects of translation, provide close analysis not just of the resulting texts but of the physical books in which they circulated and the readers through whose hands (and sometimes, under whose annotating pens) they passed. The dynamism of Aristotle's late medieval and early modern life, in Refini's colourful reconstruction, embraces not just abstract concepts and rebarbative terminology, but a messy world of books, printers, merchants, patrons and a remarkably varied cast of readers. Reception in such scenarios is often double or triple, while seemingly linear movements like tradition, translation and transmission are shown to trace geometries of extraordinary complexity.

Acknowledgements

The idea to write this book came to my mind towards the end of my time as a post-doctoral research fellow at the University of Warwick within the AHRC-funded project 'Vernacular Aristotelianism in Renaissance Italy' (2010–13). Having had the wonderful opportunity to do extensive research in libraries and archives in Europe and North America, the materials accumulated proved too many to be analysed and discussed as part of the project's immediate outcomes. Thanks to another productive period of research as Ahmanson Fellow at Villa I Tatti, The Harvard University Center for Italian Renaissance Studies (2013–14), the project of a monograph on the vernacular reception of Aristotle in late medieval and Renaissance Italy developed further and – as is typical of research projects conducted on the hills of Vincigliata – changed significantly. Increasingly concerned with the interaction of reception and translation, the project's rationale benefited enormously from the following leg of my academic journey, Johns Hopkins University, where the productive dialogue with colleagues across the humanities led to the final shape of the book.

My colleagues directly involved in the AHRC project have been crucial to this book and I cannot thank them enough for their intellectual generosity and continuous support: David A. Lines, Simon Gilson, Jill Kraye, Luca Bianchi and Grace Allen. It has been a privilege to have them as interlocutors – a privilege only matched by our ongoing conversations. Other people at Warwick have contributed in many ways to my research during three unforgettable years in the UK. I think, in particular, of my colleagues in Italian Studies and in the Centre for the Study of the Renaissance: Serena Bassi, Paul Botley, Emma Campbell, Giacomo Comiati, Alessio Cotugno, Ingrid De Smet, Rocco Di Dio, Peter Mack, Loredana Polezzi, Alexander Russell, Sara Trevisan, Christiania Whitehead. Much gratitude I owe to Jayne Brown, whose heartwarming and helpful presence made my everyday routine on the Warwick campus particularly enjoyable and productive.

I wish to thank the entire community at Villa I Tatti as well as the Ahmanson Foundation, which, during my year in Florence, generously supported my research. In particular, I am grateful to Lino Pertile and Anna Bensted for making me cope with my nostalgia for the Midlands since the very beginning of my stay at the Villa; Jonathan Nelson, Michael Rocke, Allen Grieco and Margaret Haines for the many enlightening conversations over coffee, lunch and tea; my co-fellows and the visiting professors, without whom this book would hardly be what it is: Rossend Arqués, Nicholas Baker, Davide Baldi, Karen-edis Barzman, Katherine Bentz, Robert Black, Francesca Borgo, Elena Calvillo, Angela Capodivacca, Angelo Cattaneo, Roger Crum, Vanessa De Cruz Medina, Maria Deprano, Guy Geltner, Raúl González Arévalo, Gerard González Germain, John Henderson, Tamar Herzig, Árni Ingólfsson, Elizabeth Kassler-Taub, Noriko Kotani, Elizabeth Lagresa, Marika Leino, Giordano Mastrocola, Emily Michelson, Morgan Ng, Stephen Orgel, Neslihan Şenocak, Daniel Stein Kokin, Miriam Szocs, Miguel Taín Guzmán, Koichi Toyama, Carl Villis, Gur Zak. I am sure they will not mind if I give one of them – Cecilia Muratori – special credit, not only for her invaluable help as a scholar, but also for her precious friendship, certainly one of the two most significant relationships built during my year in Florence.

Since my arrival at Johns Hopkins in 2014, I have been constantly exposed to a variety of stimuli that, coming from different disciplines, have been affecting significantly my work well beyond this specific project. I wish to thank Christopher S. Celenza for his generosity and for reminding me that 'humanism' is not a historical category to be taken for granted; and I wish to thank Walter Stephens for his generosity and for reminding me that all historical categories are potentially fake. Much of my gratitude goes to Shane Butler for his continuous support and for making me feel (somewhat too generously) a half-classicist. I also thank Laura Di Bianco, whose outside view has helped me look at my own work from a refreshing distance; Stephen Campbell, who showed me that 'vernacularisation' applies to art history too; Sara Miglietti, whose insightful reading of an early draft of my introduction is but the peak of a much deeper (and deeply appreciated) commitment to our friendship and scholarly collaboration; Gabrielle Spiegel and all the participants of the Andrew W. Mellon Seminar for their challenging comments on the first chapter of this book; Sharon Achinstein for her insightful reading of the same chapter and for her continuous advice. An important contribution – both intellectual and material – to this work came from the Special Collections in the Sheridan Libraries and from the Charles Singleton Center for the Study of Pre-Modern Europe. By thanking Earle Havens and Lawrence Principe, I extend my gratitude to all the colleagues and members of staff that have facilitated my work. I also wish to thank all the members of the Cenacolo Italiano di Baltimora, who gave me invaluable feedback on early drafts of my chapters, as well as the graduate students in the Italian PhD program at JHU who have been a constant source of inspiration during the final stages of my research.

Many other friends and colleagues have been, consciously or unconsciously, of great importance to the development of this project: Annalisa Andreoni, Albert R. Ascoli, Bryan Brazeau, William Caferro, Maurizio Campanelli, Alberto Casadei, Claudio Ciociola, Rita Copeland, Alison Cornish, Virginia Cox, Eva Del Soldato, Luca D'Onghia, Consuelo Dutschke, William Egginton, Nicola Gardini, Paul Gehl, Sonia Gentili, Jessica Goethals, Marco Guardo, Amey Hutchins, Victoria Kirkham, Valentina Lepri, John McClucas, Martin McLaughlin, Maria Luisa Meneghetti, Silvia Montiglio, Paola Nasti, April Oettinger, Katrin Pahl, Fiammetta Papi, Stephen Parkin, Anna Pegoretti, Lorenzo Pericolo, John Pollack, Leonardo Proietti, Anna Laura Puliafito, Matteo Residori, Brian Richardson, Roberta Ricc_, Jessica Richardson, Andrea Rizzi, Claudia Rossignoli, Marco Sgarbi, Harry Sieber, Eleonora Stoppino, Claudia Tardelli, Franco Tomasi, Troy Tower, Jane Tylus, Juan Miguel Valero Moreno, David Wallace, Bernadette Wegenstein, Neil Weijer, Susan Forscher Weiss, Michael Wyatt, Massimo Zaggia.

Along with the anonymous readers, whose remarks have been of great help while revising my manuscript, I wish to acknowledge the continuous support of the series editors and of all those at Cambridge University Press who have assisted me during the production of the book.

These acknowledgements would not be complete without mentioning a few very special individuals: my parents, Miranda and Marcello, and my brother, Tommaso, who, in the distance, are always there; Lina Bolzoni, who encourages me every step of the way; Maude Vanhaelen, whose generosity as both friend and scholar goes far beyond her thorough feedback on my work; Laura Maria Castelli, whose Aristotelian expertise is not the only reason for my gratitude; and Davide Daolmi, *you know, darling, why.*

Notes on the Text

Sections of Chapters 2, 3 and 5 re-elaborate and expand three previous publications: 'Aristotile in parlare materno: Vernacular Readings of the *Ethics* in the Quattrocento', *I Tatti Studies* Vol. 16 (2013): 311–41; 'Shifting Identities: Jacopo Campora's *De immortalitate anime* from Manuscript to Print', in *Remembering the Middle Ages in Early Modern Italy*, ed. Lorenzo Pericolo and Jessica Richardson. Turnhout, Brepols, 2015: 67–80; 'By imitating our nurses: Latin and Vernacular in the Renaissance', in *The Routledge History of the Renaissance*, ed. William Caferro. London, Routledge, 2017: 46–61.

Introduction
Translation as Reception

Two kinds of images populate this book: images of cultural authority, such as the portrayal of the philosopher Aristotle enthroned, and images of cultural debasement, such as the depiction of the philosopher Aristotle mounted and thus reduced to servitude by the courtesan Phyllis. While they belong to different and independent iconographic traditions, the first kind functions as the premise of the second, which, in turn, reverses the assumptions embodied by the first. One celebrates Aristotle as an outstanding cultural authority, while the other shows him deprived of his authoritative status and transformed into a common man vulnerable to the tricks of life. The two images, both very popular in the Middle Ages and the Renaissance, are emblematic of the dynamics that informed the reception of Aristotle in the period, particularly where vernacular translation is concerned. Indeed, the fall of the philosopher from his chair captures the gradual appropriation of Aristotle's legacy on the part of the new reading publics that shaped the vernacular cultures of Europe between the age of Dante and the advent of print.[1]

As Erich Auerbach argues, lay readers from the period's aristocratic and mercantile elites catalysed the production and consumption of vernacular literatures.[2] While Auerbach's theory remains compelling, more can be said, and indeed needs to be said, about the ways in which readers engaged (or aspired to engage) in the making of vernacular literature. The primary contention of this book is that, between 1250 and 1500, translation

---

[1] For the notion of 'reading public', see the recent discussion of the term in Miglietti and Parker (2016). For details about the two iconographies of Aristotle (enthroned and mounted by the courtesan), see Chapter 1.

[2] Auerbach (1965); beyond Auerbach's reflection on the formation of vernacular audiences in medieval Europe, invaluable insights into the social dimension of vernacular literature and its circulation in the Middle Ages are those by Monfrin (1963, 1964).

offered vernacular audiences a particularly productive space for interaction with both the medieval academic tradition and humanist scholarship. Translation was not only concerned with the appropriation of values but also with the gradual establishment of linguistic tools able to express and communicate those values. Accordingly, through the practice of translation, a prominent place was given to the ethical dimension of language and its uses.

Translation is taken here and throughout the book in the broad meaning of the original Latin *translatio*, a meaning (or rather a cluster of meanings) that the vernacular cultures of medieval and early modern Europe inherited from antiquity.[3] With its focus on the idea of transference, the term entails processes of transformation, adaptation and reshaping – the same processes that are at the core of reception in its many forms. A further, implicit contention of the book, then, is that translation is not only a form of reception (and so forms a crucial subfield in the broader area of reception studies) but that it is a necessary precondition of reception.[4] One could even say that, no matter what media are involved in the process, there is no reception without translation and vice versa. Or, to put it in Rita Copeland's terms, the process of displacement entailed by translation is always set in motion by a moment of receptiveness.[5] If an act of translation is responsible for shaping a given image of Aristotle, this is only possible because of the way in which the translator has received the conceptual elements that constitute the image itself, including pre-existing iconographic traditions, iconology, as well as the variety of narratives that relate to these.[6] At the same time, the very act of receiving an object (either textual or visual)

---

[3] The broad meaning of the term *translatio* is suggested by the etymology of the word as described by, among others, Isidore of Seville and, closer to the period that is examined here, Huguccio of Pisa; see Cecchini and Arbizzoni (2004), s.v. 'translatio'. On the reception of the classical notion of *translatio* in the Latin Middle Ages, see Chiesa (1987); for a discussion of the notion of translation between Latinate and vernacular cultures in the Medieval period, see Copeland (1991); for a special focus on the Italian case, Dionisotti (1967), Folena (1991), Gehl (1994) and Cornish (2011). State-of-the-art collections of essays on early modern cultures of translation are Newman and Tylus (2015) and Den Haan, Hosington, Pade and Wegener (2018); a recent discussion of vernacular translation in fifteenth-century Italy is Rizzi (2017).

[4] For recent developments in the area of reception studies, stemming from the seminal contribution of Martindale (1993), see Hardwick (2003), Martindale and Thomas (2006), Porter (2008) and Butler (2016).

[5] Copeland (1991: 35): 'the translator performs an act of aggressive interpretation so as to lay open his language and usage to receive a formative influence. We might recall here the paradox in imitation theory whereby the copy both stamps its impress upon the model and receives that model's impress upon its own features … In a sense, translation asks for a similar moment of appreciative desire and receptiveness.'

[6] For the distinction between iconography and iconology, see Panofsky (1955), Gombrich (1972) and Taylor (2008).

inevitably entails an act of translation. What might sound like an inconclusive circle involving translation and reception proves instead a productive way to rethink the relationship between the two. Indeed, the impasse is broken when one considers both translation and reception as intimately related to interpretation (a relationship that, as we shall see, is embedded in the medieval etymology of the Latin word for translator: *interpres*).[7] By including interpretation in the analysis, it is possible to shed light on the peculiar way in which translation and reception relate to each other. In fact, translation and reception, both involved with interpretation, can only be distinguished from one another artificially. Nevertheless, as the case studies discussed in this book show, they do not entirely coincide.[8] Rather, by regarding them as informing one another, I shall offer an interpretive model in which translation fulfils its function through reception and reception contributes actively to the translation process.

If this book will take 'translation' in its broad sense, including forms of adaptation, abridgment and rewriting, 'reception' will first and foremost be taken in its literal meaning (i.e., *to receive* something), with a special focus on the materiality of the reception process. Yet, by receiving an object (textual, visual, or a combination of the two) the reader/observer is involved in a complex process in which the object is not simply 'received': rather, it is brought to life. To be more precise, this is a process in which the object is described, retold, eventually translated into one of its possible lives.[9] Indeed, the ways in which cultural objects are received (i.e., constructed as objects of interpretation) depend on the context of reception, which is defined by factors as diverse as chronology, geography, politics, society, gender and, not least, language, all factors that are key not only to reception but also to translation.[10] Enhancing the gap that separates any form of reception from its apparent object, these factors challenge the utopian desire to recover the past that is at the core of traditional ideas about translation.[11] From this point of view, the understanding of reception central

---

[7] On the relationship between translation and interpretation, see Martindale (1993: 86–94).

[8] A similar point about the mutual (but only partial) overlapping of translation and reception has been made recently with regards to contemporary literary translation; see, for instance, Zhou (2013) and D'Egidio (2015).

[9] For the idea that reception is key in making the meaning(s) of a text, see Martindale's reassessment of Jauss' theory in Martindale (1993 11–13); cf. Martindale (2006: 4–5).

[10] As suggested by Stanley Fish in a statement that captures many arguments entailed by reception theory, linguistic and textual facts are not the objects of interpretation, but their product; in the same vein, Fish stressed the role of 'institutional' contexts in the production of meaning. See Fish (1980).

[11] On the utopian dimension of translation, Venuti (2012: 11–31).

to recent developments in reception studies performs a corrective action on enduring but untenable tropes of faithfulness in translation and the recovery of an alleged 'original'.[12] At the same time, reception offers a manageable grid to tackle the scepticism that, in the aftermath of Walter Benjamin's famed essay on the translator's task, has informed modern conceptions about translation and its impossibility.[13] Indeed, if Charles Martindale is right in suggesting that any object from the past, any study of which necessarily constitutes an act of reception, is elusive, the same can be said about translation.[14] In attempting to reconstitute an object across contexts, translation faces the unattainability of the object itself, which, by being translated, becomes a different one.

Translation, therefore, materialises the difficulties and epistemological ambiguities entailed by reception in two ways.[15] First, the translator receives what he or she constructs as a 'source' and then acts as a medium between that source and a new audience. In this respect, the medieval etymology of the Latin term for 'translator', *interpres*, is instructive. As suggested by the combination of the preposition *inter* ('between') and the word *praes* (which, according to the medieval etymological interpretation, means 'mediator' but also 'rich in spoils'), the act of linguistic mediation can be described as a way to move riches (i.e., words) from one language to another.[16] The point was made explicitly by etymologist Huguccio of Pisa at the beginning of the thirteenth century:

> *Pres* ('mediator') is compounded [i.e., forms compound words] if it is taken as *dives* ('rich'), such as in *interpres*. *Interpres* is someone who knows several languages, that is, someone who explains a language by means of another or transfers one language into another; and they have this name because they mediate between one language and another; or [one could say that the word *interpres*] is based on *pres*, which means 'rich', because translators enrich languages by transferring words from one language into another.[17]

---

[12] Faithfulness and fidelity are the most common criteria evoked in discourses about translation throughout the ages. On their problematic status, see Hurtado Albir (1990), Venuti (2000; 2017: 14, 18, 30).

[13] For the text of Benjamin's essay *The Task of the Translator* (1923) and relevant bibliography, see Venuti (2000: 15–23).

[14] For a discussion of translation within his wider reflection on reception, see, in particular, Martindale (1993: 75–100).

[15] On the epistemological challenges posed by reception, see Butler (2016).

[16] The medieval etymology of the word *praes* differs from the currently accepted one, which goes back to the Sanskrit *prath* (= to spread abroad). I wish to thank one of the anonymous reviewers for highlighting this point.

[17] Cecchini and Arbizzoni (2004), s.v. 'interpres': 'Pres componitur, secundum quod accipitur pro dives, hic et hec *interpres -tis*, et dicitur interpres qui diversa genera linguarum novit, scilicet qui unam linguam exponit per aliam vel unam linguam transfert in aliam, et dicitur sic quia mediator

The triangular relationship involving the source, the translator and the target language is not simple after all. In fact, the translator's work is the result of a process of reception that, while cutting through previous layers of reception, is necessarily influenced by them. As Martindale stresses, 'the translated text is already an interpretation … since translation depends on prior reading practices'.[18] Consequently, the translator's targeted audience receives a 'translated' object that is not simply the product of the translator's own reading of the source but the result of earlier processes of reception (what Martindale himself calls 'chain of receptions') that translation inevitably assimilates.[19] Yet, as I aim to show in this book, it is exactly the progressive overlay of 'prior reading practices' as well as the networks of such reading practices (prior, contemporary and future) that contribute to making translation an elusive goal.

Second, the mutually determinant nature of translation and reception affects the way in which the source is received by and through the translator's work, as well as the way in which a given translation is received by its immediate and later audiences.[20] Thus, translation is not a simple act of reception, but it becomes essential to the reception process as a whole. Considering translation accordingly, not as a synonym but as an analogous term for reception, I aim in this book to stress the role that reading practices play in translation, particularly in contexts in which the readership takes an active part in facilitating and shaping the process of translation, as well as in promoting the translation's dissemination. In fact, as I have done regarding the concept of translation, I shall take 'reading' too in a broad sense, ranging from commissioning and owning a book to taking notes in the margins or even selecting material to copy into a miscellaneous notebook.[21] Similar forms of active reception are fuelled by translation and, in turn, nourish translation, creating the linguistic conditions for the appropriation, adaptation and (re)construction of the past.

The vernacular reception of Aristotle, whose philosophical authority reigned unparalleled from the mid-twelfth century to the threshold of modernity, is a case in point. Latin translations of Aristotle's works made

---

est inter unam loquelam et aliam; vel componitur a pres quod est dives, quia interpretes ditant loquelam, transferentes vocabula de una loquela in aliam.' On the Latin terminology of translation (*translatio, interpretatio, traductio*), with a special focus on its medieval and early modern legacy, see Folena (1991).

[18] Martindale (1993: 13).
[19] *Ibid.*: 29.
[20] For a stimulating discussion of 'how to read a translation', see Venuti (2012: 109–15).
[21] Classical studies on the history of reading are Iser (1978), Eco (1979), Fish (1980), Darnton (1990), Chartier (1994), Grafton (1997) and Blair (2010).

between 1150 and 1250, the corpus known today as 'Aristoteles Latinus', turned the philosopher into the supreme embodiment of pagan wisdom. Aristotle appeared in this capacity in painting and sculpture across the Middle Ages and the early modern period, while his works became the backbone of university education, providing Europe with a system of knowledge that would last for centuries.[22] Though hindered at first by the ecclesiastical authorities because of controversial statements on topics like the immortality of the soul and the eternity of the world, Aristotle's thought became one of the pillars of Christian culture, thanks to the interpretive effort of philosophers such as Albert the Great and Thomas Aquinas, who reconciled his thought to the principles of Christian theology. In academic contexts in this period, Aristotle spoke Latin, and he would continue to speak Latin for a long time, either the 'rough' Latin of the scholastics or, starting around 1400, the 'polished' classicising Latin of the humanists. The new wave of Latin translations of Aristotle's works promoted by early fifteenth-century intellectuals such as Leonardo Bruni challenged the scholastic approach to language, particularly its lack of expertise in classical style, but did not question the priority of Latin as the language of knowledge par excellence.[23]

At the same time, Aristotle's *auctoritas* had been seeping through lay culture, where Latin was gradually making room for the vernacular and the vernacular was finding ways to acquire the status of a literary and philosophical language. (Here and throughout the book I will prefer the Latin *auctoritas*, to be understood as 'authoritative and supposedly reliable source', over the ambiguous and potentially misleading English equivalent 'authority'.)[24] Two contexts are particularly indicative of this transformation: the court and the city-state. In both, though in different ways, translation worked as an intermediary between Latinate academic discourses (both scholastic and, later, humanist) and their reception on the part of vernacular consumers.[25] Either perceived as an inevitable alternative

---

[22] For an introduction to the recovery of Aristotle in the medieval West, see Dod (1982), Lohr (1982) and Brams (2003). On the establishment of Aristotle as the core of the university curriculum, see Lines (2002); for a general overview on medieval universities across Europe, see Janin (2008); with a focus on Italian universities in the Renaissance, Grendler (2002).

[23] Recent discussions of humanist opinions on the status of the vernacular vis-à-vis Latin are Maxson (2013) and Rizzi (2013). For further details, see Chapter 4 in this book.

[24] For the problems entailed by the notion of 'authority', see Kojève's seminal study of 1942, now Kojève (2004); more specifically on the culture of the Middle Ages and the Renaissance, see Von Leyden (1958) and Brownlee and Stephens (1989).

[25] On the mediation between academic practices and vernacular cultures facilitated by translation in conjunction with a renewed interest in the inventive function of rhetoric, see Copeland (1991).

or boisterously promoted as a positive tool to reach out to a larger number of readers, the 'vernacularisation of Latin literature', as convincingly argued by Alison Cornish, was not so much an importation of something foreign as a shift in register and social class – from the clergy to the court or, in Italy, to the semi-literate well-off citizens of the city-states for whom written and oral eloquence in the vernacular had practical, political, commercial and ethical purposes'.[26] A few examples will illuminate this shift.

When the Prior General of the Augustinian Hermits, Giles of Rome (c. 1245–1316), was asked by the king of France Philip III to write a government handbook for the dauphin (the future King Philip IV), the renowned commentator of Aristotle reworked the *Ethics* and the *Politics* into one of the most popular mirrors of princes in history.[27] In 1280, when the *De regimine principum* was published, one would never have expected a prestigious scholar like Giles to stoop to writing a philosophical treatise in the vernacular. And yet, within less than two years, the king commissioned from Henry de Gauchi a translation of the text into the dauphin's mother tongue. The king's request suggests that the royal household was not at all insensitive to the advantages of reading in one's own language. The dedicatee had excellent Latin, as stated by French poet Jean de Meun in his translation of Boethius' *Consolatio Philosophiae*, also written for Philip IV, but the very fact that the translation was commissioned suggests that he would have found a vernacular version easier to read.[28] The translator's justification of his work, where the translation is presented as a mere gesture of courtesy for the prince, reiterates a common prejudice about linguistic hierarchies, according to which the vulgar tongue submits to the prestige of Latin. At the same time, it witnesses the progressive legitimation of the vernacular, which, through translation, was appropriating themes and discussions usually restricted to the Latinate elites. In this respect, the case of Giles' *De regimine principum* is exemplary: the original Latin version circulated widely among Latinate readers across Europe, but a concurrent and broad circulation of the text was made possible by vernacular translation.[29]

---

[26] Cornish (2011: 3); see also Gehl (1994) for a discussion of the notion of cultural hierarchy entailed by medieval theories and practices of translation.

[27] For an overview of the life, career and production of Giles of Rome, see Briggs and Eardley (2016); on the *De regimine principum* specifically and its wide circulation, Briggs (1999a).

[28] Jean de Meun's statement is discussed in Copeland (1991: 134).

[29] On the vernacular reception of Giles' treatise, which was translated into several languages beyond French, see Briggs (1999a); of particular interest is the 1288 Italian version of the text, which was translated from Gauchi's French; cf. Papi (2015, 2016).

In the 1280s, Philip IV's amour-propre still required vernacular translations made for him to be excused. Within less than a century, things had changed considerably. One of his successors, Charles V, asked philosopher Nicole Oresme to provide the royal library with a French translation of Aristotle's main works of moral philosophy (*Nicomachean Ethics*, *Economics*, *Politics*).[30] Oresme's gigantic enterprise, completed in the early 1370s, had a limited circulation, with the beautifully illuminated copies of the Aristotelian translations functioning more as tokens of cultural prestige and political power than as books actually to be read.[31] Still, the king's desire to make Aristotle speak French was rich in political and ideological implications. The vernacular frame of the gift strengthened the status of French not only as the language of the nation but also as a language suitable for philosophy and thus a language that could equal the prestige of Latin. Furthermore, by receiving Aristotle's works in his own mother tongue, the ruler put himself in the position that had been Alexander the Great's, who had Aristotle as his mentor. The translator stood as proxy for the author/teacher, while the patron adopted the role of the ancient ruler/student.

The gratifying and self-celebratory analogy with Alexander the Great built on Alexander's relationship to Aristotle, which occupied much space in the broad tradition of narratives about the life and deeds of the ancient king.[32] Among them, the pseudo-Aristotelian *Secret of Secrets* held a special place.[33] The spurious work, allegedly sent by the philosopher to the young ruler, covered a variety of subjects, most of which pertained to morals, politics and government, including a very popular section on physiognomy, which had a successful life of its own. The text, more rudimentary than Aristotle's genuine philosophical treatises and far removed from their speculative heights, was probably written in Arabic in the tenth century and translated into Latin in the mid-twelfth century, becoming very popular across Europe through various vernacular translations.[34] While the beautifully illuminated Aristotle produced for Charles V did not leave the king's library, the *Secret of Secrets* made it through much broader communities of readers who would read it along works of moral conduct and

---

[30] More in general on Oresme's contribution to late medieval theory and practice of translation, see Lusignan (1986: 154–66; 1988).

[31] A detailed reconstruction of Oresme's endeavour in the light of the illuminated manuscripts of his Aristotelian translations made for the royal library is provided by Sherman (1995).

[32] For an overview of the medieval literary representations of Alexander, see Stock (2016).

[33] See Grignaschi (1980), Ryan and Schmitt (1982) and Williams (2003b).

[34] Translations of the *Secret of Secrets* appeared in several vernaculars; for a discussion of the circulation of the text in the Romance area, see Cecioni (1889), Milani (2001), Rapisarda (2001), Williams (2003a), Zamuner (2005), Carré and Cifuentes (2010) and Lines (2019).

Christian devotion. It circulated as a repository of words of wisdom that, although often hardly related to genuine Aristotelian thought, contributed to the popular reception of the philosopher as an emblem of knowledge and intellectual authority.[35]

A similar and possibly wider contribution to the vernacular reception of Aristotle came from a text that shared several analogies with the *Secret of Secrets*: the anonymous Arabic compendium of the *Nicomachean Ethics*, which was translated into Latin by Herman the German around 1240 under the title *Summa Alexandrinorum*.[36] Soon translated into Italian by Taddeo Alderotti, a Florentine professor of medicine based at the University of Bologna, the compendium (commonly known as *L'Etica d'Aristotele*, 'Aristotle's Ethics'), was incorporated into Brunetto Latini's *Tresor* (c. 1260), one of the most popular encyclopaedias of the Middle Ages.[37] The *Tresor*, written in French during Brunetto's exile in France and translated into Italian shortly thereafter, was pivotal to the vernacular dissemination of a Christianised version of Aristotle's moral philosophy, and it was widely read well into the Renaissance. By presenting moral, political and rhetorical instructions as precious gems in a treasure chest, Brunetto shaped his translation project according to the commercial frame of mind peculiar to the mercantile culture of his time. The author of the *Tresor* thus fulfilled the function of the translator as described, as we have seen, by Huguccio of Pisa, according to whom the action performed by the *interpres* is accompanied by the transfer of 'valuable' words from one language to another, with the consequent enrichment of the target language.[38] When Brunetto, in the opening of the *Tresor*, compares knowledge to money and highlights that without money no transaction between men would be possible, he reveals that the work's primary scope is to outline practical principles for social interaction.[39] The *Tresor*, with the compendium of Aristotle's *Ethics* at its core, is not a simple collection of precious teachings but a statement about the role of language in any form of negotiation. With its focus on language and knowledge as tools for mediation, the *Tresor* executes the very function of vernacular translation. Theoretical and practical philosophy

---

[35] Some examples of this process will be discussed in Chapter 4.

[36] This work and its vernacular dissemination will be discussed in detail in Chapter 2.

[37] See Bolton Holloway (1993), Beltrami (2007) and Cornish (2011: 126–57).

[38] Similar ideas about translation were not new; for their presence in classical theories of translation (Cicero in particular), see chapter 4 in McElduff (2013).

[39] Beltrami (2007: 4): 'Et si come sens deniers n'auroit nulle moieneté entre les heuvres des genz, qui adreçast les uns contre les autres, ausresi ne puet nus hom [s]avoir des autres choses pleinement se il ne set ceste premiere partie don livre.'

along with rhetoric are made available to vernacular readers as instruments to construct and consolidate communal life.

Despite the pattern outlined by the successful circulation and reception of works such as Brunetto Latini's *Tresor*, the development of vernacular literature, especially philosophical prose, was far from linear. Latin remained the preferred option for the international circulation of texts and ideas, and its use was powerfully revamped by humanism, the rise of which doubly complicated the relationship between Latin and vernacular.[40] On one hand, humanism vigorously reinstated the cultural prominence of Latin (i.e., the classical Latin of the ancients), thus challenging the use of both medieval Latin and the vernacular; on the other hand, humanism, thanks to the renewed knowledge of Greek, shaped itself as the one and only intermediary able to recover the classical past and translate it effectively into the present.[41] The frictions produced by the humanists' approach to antiquity vis-à-vis scholasticism and, to a great extent, vernacular culture are particularly visible in the history of the reception of Aristotle, whose legacy was claimed by all parties.[42] Examples of similar dynamics include, among others, Leonardo Bruni's own effort to make Aristotle a flagship authority of humanism, a cultural project that, as this book shows, did have important – though not uncontested – effects on vernacular culture.[43] Within such a picture, vernacular translation performed a mediation not only between past and present but also between the various players involved in the cultural and linguistic conflicts of the time.

As these few examples indicate, making Aristotle speak in the vernacular meant negotiating between academic prestige and the preoccupations of lay readers normally excluded from the Latinate consumption of knowledge. Vernacular translations of Aristotle in the period entailed inevitable processes of transformation that, in different ways, made the philosopher's teachings at once more accessible and more relevant to people's lives. The appropriation of the philosopher on the part of the vernacular audience came through the linguistic 'domestication' of academic knowledge (this was the case of Giles' *De regimine principum* and, as we shall see in this book, of several translations of Aristotle's works made between 1250 and 1500). But the process of appropriation was also fuelled from below, so to

---

[40] On the long history of Latin as a language of knowledge, see Waquet (2002).
[41] For a wide discussion of the issues entailed by the humanist approach to antiquity, see Celenza (2018). On the ways in which humanists shaped their intellectual mission, see Baker (2015).
[42] See Schmitt (1983), Lanza (1989), Kraye (1993), Witt (2000), Lines (2002) and Blum (2012).
[43] For a discussion of these aspects, see Chapters 3 and 4 in this book.

speak, by the concurrent and widespread circulation of texts that offered simplified versions of Aristotelian philosophy, even if they were only partially or loosely related to Aristotle's genuine thought (e.g., the *Secret of Secrets* and the *Summa Alexandrinorum*). In these cases, the 'domestication', which was conceptual in the first place, preceded the vernacular rewriting, making similar texts particularly successful with readers outside the erudite and academic circles.

Translation thus operates at two different levels: intra-lingual (when the source is adapted, reshaped and/or simplified within the same linguistic or cultural context) and inter-lingual (when the scope of the rewriting is primarily linguistic).[44] When considered as parts of the reception process, these two kinds of translation – which Charles Briggs has proposed to label 'vulgarisation' (intra-lingual) and 'vernacularisation' (inter-lingual) – are interrelated; and yet, as this book shows, they do not exhaust all the possibilities entailed by translation.[45] One could argue that Giles of Rome himself, while moving within an all-Latin context, was 'vulgarising' Aristotle's *Ethics* and *Politics*, which he knew through the Latin versions circulating in medieval universities and religious *studia*. As a matter of fact, by selecting and repackaging ideas taken from Aristotle, Giles was making them more accessible to a supposedly Latinate reader who had no interest in the scholarly approach needed to access the sources directly. 'Vulgarisation' leads instead to 'vernacularisation' when, because of concurrent linguistic gaps, a Latin text needs to be brought into the vernacular in order to be received by its non-Latinate (or poorly Latinate) reader. This model of translation (which was commonly known in Italy by the term 'volgarizzamento') tends to work better for the vernacular appropriation of Latin texts that are already the result of some sort of intellectual filtering.[46] Accordingly, the 'vernacularisation' of works that come straight from the scholarly context into the vernacular, without having been previously simplified, is not as successful. Even if the linguistic gap is bridged, those works remain arduous for readers unfamiliar with philosophical jargon – a situation that, by the way, would only change in the sixteenth and seventeenth centuries,

---

[44] The distinction between inter-lingual and intra-lingual is outlined by Roman Jakobson in his 'On linguistics aspects of translation' (1959); for a recent edition of Jakobson's essay, see Venuti (2000: 113–18). For more recent discussions of the two concepts, see Ernst-August Gutt in Venuti (2000: 376–96) and Korning Zethsen (2009).

[45] See Briggs (2003). See the discussion of these categories in Cornish (2011: 3). See also Buridant (1983: 119) and Folena (1991). On the hierarchical dimension implicit in the medieval practice of vernacular translation, see Segre (1993).

[46] On the term 'volgarizzamento' and its uses, see Folena (1991) and Cornish (2011).

when vernacular translation would combine with the systematic enhancement of the vernacular as a language capable of philosophical and scientific
sophistication.[47]

As with all artificial distinctions, the one between 'vulgarisation' and
'vernacularisation' is far from unproblematic. I prefer to think in terms of
tension between different perspectives on translation as a tool for philosophical dissemination. By reading this tension in translation practice
through the filter of the reception of Aristotle, I propose to reassess the place
of vernacular translation in a period often described in the simplistic terms
of sharp contrasts between cultures (e.g., scholasticism vs. humanism) and
languages (e.g., Latin vs. vernacular, classical Latin vs. medieval Latin).
To this purpose, I am considering chronological limits that challenge traditional narratives about medieval and Renaissance cultures. By looking at
the vernacular reception of Aristotle between the age of Dante and the late
fifteenth century (that is, by looking at a chronological span that combines
periods usually addressed separately), I do not wish to take part in the
long-lasting debate about change and continuity in the transition from the
Middle Ages to the early modern period. In the wake of Eugenio Garin's
and Paul Oskar Kristeller's seminal studies on this topic, many scholars
have offered abundant reasons to support either side of the controversy.[48]
Indeed, my own analysis incidentally and unsurprisingly shows that the
way in which Aristotle was received, translated, adapted and transformed
in the period was characterised by elements of both continuity and change.
Rather, the focus of this study, which attempts to overcome the strict
dichotomy of continuity and change, is a different one: namely, a focus
on the contagious nature of vernacular translation within the process of
Aristotelian reception. As the case studies discussed in this book suggest,
not only was the translation of Aristotle pivotal to the many ways in which
the philosopher was received and appropriated by vernacular readership,
but it also had consequences that affected Latin (and, to some extent,
Greek). This apparently paradoxical statement becomes less so when one
thinks of translation not simply as the production of lexical equivalence
but as an attempt fully to receive a text, that is, to read and, eventually, to
interpret it.[49] If we accept the idea that a text's meaning is unstable, always

---

[47] The point is made, with particular regards to the case of the reception of Aristotle, in the various
      essays included in Lines and Refini (2015) and Bianchi, Gilson and Kraye (2017).
[48] For a compelling outline of these problems, see Black (2001: 12–21).
[49] See Martindale (1993: 84–6), for a discussion of translation as a 'problem in semiotics' rather than as
      a matter of simple 'word for word lexical equivalence'.

'realised at the point of reception', as Martindale puts it, then translation fully reveals its interpretive nature.[50] As such, the translation process does not produce a stable, definitive 'text'; rather, it produces an 'ever-widening fan of translations', which projects a variety of interpretations back onto the unattainable original.[51]

Pushing similar considerations one step further, in this book I argue that the potentially unlimited interpretive nature of translation lies in the productive interaction of the players involved in the reception process: translators and their readers.[52] Instead of simply considering translators as authors of translations and readers as their receivers, I propose to see both translators and readers as integral parts of the translation process. This approach is based on a twofold assumption: translators are readers as much as readers are translators. Despite its somewhat tautological nature, the idea of reception as the interaction of translators and readers is particularly productive when one considers historical periods in which approaches to the classical tradition are characterised by trends that are at once distinct and conflicting. If understood as a form of proactive reception involving both translators and readers, translation offers a frame within which to rethink the notion of 'tradition' itself as a continuous and ever-changing process of appropriation. On one hand, the various interpretive layers that pile up between the texts and their later readings – and which constitute the 'tradition' – seem to increase the distance (or cultural difference) between the texts themselves and their later readers. On the other hand, as this book aims to show, it is within this distance (or space of difference) that multiple uses of the past are produced.

The images of cultural authority and the images of cultural debasement that populate this book share the 'space of difference' created by the productive interplay of translation and reception. As argued in Chapter 1, visual topoi of debasement (such as the 'mounted Aristotle') provide a fruitful standpoint from which to look at the gradual emancipation of the vernacular. More precisely, the chapter proposes to read the popular anecdote of Aristotle mounted and bridled by the courtesan Phyllis as relevant

---

[50] *Ibid.*: 3. For further reflection of the idea that meaning is always realised at the point of reception, see Batstone (2006).

[51] Martindale (1993: 100); see also Batstone (2006: 19) for an effective statement about the elusive power of the text, not only vis-à-vis the maker, but also vis-à-vis the (ever-changing) receiver.

[52] A similar point is made, though moving from a different approach, by Rizzi (2017), who studies vernacular translators in fifteenth-century Italy following three main axes (scribal culture, authority, agency).

to the interaction of Latin academic practices and vernacular culture. By building on the idea that the taming of the philosopher in the anecdote stages the conflict between the 'artificial' culture of academic learning and concurrent ideas about nature, I argue that some versions of the story (e.g., the thirteenth-century *Lai d'Aristote*) relate to the late medieval reflection on the ethical worth of the mother tongue. To this end, I compare the iconography of the mounted Aristotle to the depiction of Grammar, whose 'bilingual' status mirrors the ambiguous place that the vernacular holds vis-à-vis Latin in the age of Dante, Petrarch and Boccaccio. The chapter then looks at other spaces, textual and visual, for the translation of the philosophical ideals embodied by Aristotle. In different ways, both the novella tradition (as exemplified by the *Novellino* and the *Decameron*) and the visual display of civic values (as witnessed by painted cycles such as those in San Gimignano, Siena and Asciano) shed light on the ways in which the appropriation of Aristotle shaped the new vernacular societies while also being part of wider discussions about linguistic difference.

Dante Alighieri's contribution to the establishment of the vernacular as a language of knowledge along with his critique of contemporaneous vernacular translation, both discussed in Chapter 2, offer yet another perspective on the multifaceted process through which vernacular culture appropriated and, in a sense, tamed Aristotle's authority. The chapter situates Dante's portrayal of Aristotle within the poet's broader reflection on language. Taking the appearance of Aristotle in the *Divine Comedy* as a starting point, I show that Dante's notion of language cannot be understood without looking at his discussion of the relations between Latin and the vernacular, particularly in the *Convivio*. From this point of view, Dante's harsh criticism of Taddeo Alderotti's Italian translation of the *Summa Alexandrinorum* invites us to reconsider the failure of the *Convivio* itself, which did not foster the cultural revolution that Dante sought. By exploring the textual transmission of Taddeo's translation between 1300 and 1500, the final section of the chapter enlightens its relevance to the vernacular reading communities that found forms of cultural and social legitimation in works of this kind.

The implications of vernacular translation, especially when considered against the background of the uneasy relationships between scholasticism and humanism, are best demonstrated by the reception of the *Nicomachean Ethics* in the fifteenth century, which is at the core of Chapters 3 and 4, focused on Venetian and Florentine examples respectively. There I show that, when considering the role of vernacular readers in reshaping Aristotle's teachings, vernacular translation appears not simply as a combination of continuity and change but as an active promoter of such a combination. Chapter 3 concentrates on translations commissioned by members of the Giustiniani family in Venice: as aristocrats deeply involved in mercantile activities, the Giustiniani were the prototype of the vernacular readership interested in supporting social status and wealth through cultural legitimation. The chapter first analyses the earliest Italian translation of the *Nicomachean Ethics*, authored around 1430 by the Augustinian theologian Antonio Colombella at the behest of Pancrazio Giustiniani. Based on the medieval Latin version of the *Ethics*, Colombella's translation can be read as an attempt to adapt the traditional academic study of Aristotle to the needs of vernacular readers. Of particular interest is the translator's prologue, which offers unprecedented insights into contemporary translation practice and theory. The other text analysed in this chapter is the annotated translation of the pseudo-Aristotelian treatise *On Virtues and Vices* by the Dominican Lazzaro Gallinera, who dedicated it to Pancrazio Giustiniani's son-in-law, Bernardo, in the 1460s. The work testifies to the permeability between scholastic traditions and new humanist trends; it also gives us some indication as to how a challenging text like the *Ethics* could be adapted to a lay readership. The chapter includes a discussion of Benedetto Cotrugli's *Libro de l'arte della mercatura* (1458) and the mercantile milieu into which forms of patronage such as the Giustiniani's belonged.

Chapter 4 brings us from Venice to Florence. Here I study the variety of reading practices that characterised the vernacular reception of Aristotle amidst the controversies between 'traditionalists' and 'humanists'. Instead of highlighting the hiatus between cultures, as most scholarly narratives do, the chapter examines the role played by vernacular translation as a facilitator for the interaction of different perspectives. Along with discussions of key figures such as Domenico Da Prato and Leonardo Bruni, I explore the proactive role played by readers and patrons in shaping the boundaries of philosophical culture in the vernacular. To this purpose, special attention is given to the compositional strategies deployed by cultivated merchants in *zibaldoni* (notebooks) such as Giovanni Rucellai's, where conflicts of cultures were resolved under the aegis of the layman's curiosity. Similar preoccupations inform the manuscript transmission of Bernardo Nuti's Italian translation of Aristotle's *Nicomachean Ethics* (c. 1460), which I also discuss in the chapter. Extant manuscript copies of Nuti's version (which was based on Leonardo Bruni's 'humanist' translation of the *Ethics*) have much to tell us about the social, ideological and, to some extent, political patterns that characterised the reception of Aristotle's moral philosophy in the period.

At the same time, as shown in Chapter 5, reception and translation reveal their interconnection when considered as part of a transformative act. This is particularly evident in the case of loose translations such as compendia and abridgments, which, through their own reception, are continuously transformed into new texts. The chapter thus offers a different insight into the ways in which Aristotle was read and adapted in the fourteenth and fifteenth centuries, particularly when the philosopher's legacy is combined with the reception of other authors, producing fascinating forms of cultural hybridism. In order to map this phenomenon, I look at the vernacular afterlife of Luca Mannelli's Latin *Compendium moralis philosophiae* (c. 1350) and the multifaceted textual transmission of Jacopo Campora's vernacular dialogue *De immortalitate animae* (c. 1430). Both compendia were written by members of the Dominican order with typically scholastic backgrounds and were not particularly innovative in their philosophical content. However, their interest lies in the various ways in which they were disseminated, reshaped, repackaged and marketed. By tracing the transformation of the two works, the chapter documents the broad implications entailed by the proactive nature of vernacular reading practices in late medieval and Renaissance Italy.

When we think about reception as a 'two-way relationship between the source text or culture and the new work and receiving culture', to quote Lorna Hardwick, or, in James Porter's words, as a series of 'dynamic processes that flow in two directions at once, both forward and backward', then the relevance of translation to reception, caught in a threefold relationship involving past, present and future, becomes evident.[53] Translators (whether active translators or 'simple' readers) move within those three poles. By doing so, they challenge notions of linearity commonly associated with the idea of tradition and invite us to think about reception as constantly in the making. As Aristotle's case suggests, the process is open-ended, involving different languages and cultures as well as different layers of language and culture within the same linguistic domain. Through the various steps of the process, which can hardly be disentangled, the Philosopher acquires different shapes. Seated on a professorial chair or ridiculed by a witty courtesan, Aristotle is read, translated, transformed and appropriated, giving shape to the multiple meanings that his reception creates over time.

[53] See Hardwick (2003: 4) and Porter (2008: 474).

CHAPTER I

Taming the Philosopher

Triumphs of Love

An old man with a long beard being ridden by a beautiful woman who has mastered both bridle and whip: this image, which might look like an irreverent cross-section of domestic life, in fact enjoyed a widespread popularity in medieval and early modern art. A number of objects, including paintings, sculptures, miniatures and birth trays, bear witness to the fortune of this image, the ironic appropriation of which is primarily due to the identity of the male character. Either represented on its own or, as is frequently the case, as part of wider compositions, the scene stages an apocryphal episode from the life of Aristotle. Told and retold by many authors in different languages, the story of the philosopher who, after chastising Alexander the Great for his sexual intemperance, is ridden by a beautiful courtesan (commonly known by the name of Phyllis) was interpreted as either a misogynist tale or a cautionary encomium of Love, whom not even the wisest man on earth is able to resist.[1]

Although Petrarch in his *Triumph of Love* did not mention the episode, the image and the text soon joined fortunes.[2] Not only did Aristotle and the courtesan appear in paintings inspired by Petrarch's *Triumphs* – as in the *trionfi* painted by Giovanni di Ser Giovanni ('Lo Scheggia') in the 1460s and now in the Pinacoteca of Siena, among others – but they were also frequently included in illustrations of the poet's work.[3] In 1442, for instance, the Florentine miniaturist Apollonio di Giovanni made the

---

[1] On the episode of Aristotle and Phyllis and its reception in medieval culture, see Storost (1955, 1956), De Cesare (1956, 1957), Herrmann (1991) and Smith (1995: 66–102).

[2] For accounts of the various representations of the episode in the figurative arts, see Marsilli (1984) and Smith (1995: 103–201) (the use of the image in relation to the illustration of Petrarch's *Triumphi* is discussed *ibid.*: 193–6); more recently, Meneghetti (2015: 27, 337, 150–1).

[3] Cavazzini (1999: 84–8). Other examples include five painted salvers connected to the workshop of Florentine painter Apollonio di Giovanni; see Jacobson-Schutte (1980: 479–83). The birth tray preserved at the Victoria and Albert Museum in London is mentioned by Smith (1995: 195).

taming of the Philosopher a key feature of his rendition of the Triumph of Love in one of the most beautifully illuminated manuscripts of Petrarch's *Triumphs*, now preserved in the Biblioteca Laurenziana in Florence.[4] While Petrarch evokes several dozens of followers of the irresistible god, Apollonio's full-page illustration of the *Triumph of Love* [Figure 1.1] selects four *exempla* to symbolise the overwhelming power of lust: Samson and Delilah, Hercules and Omphale, Vergil awaiting his would-be lover in a basket, and Aristotle and the courtesan. (Of these, only Samson and Hercules were actually part of Petrarch's poem.)[5] On one hand, Apollonio's selection of the two heroes (Samson and Hercules) reminds us that the power of Love is stronger than physical vigour; on the other, the poet and the philosopher stand for the weakness of wisdom when confronted by the inescapable force of Love.

The courtesan's riding of Aristotle found its way through the tradition that singled out the dangers of falling in love and, in particular, the dangers of dealing with women, as suggested by the emblematic illustration of the episode in two manuscripts of Brunetto Latini's famous encyclopaedia, the *Tresor*, written during the author's exile in France (c. 1260). In both manuscripts (one now in Carpentras [Figure 1.2] and the other in Karlsruhe) the anecdote is illustrated in detail, with the various moments of the story being framed as part of a narrative sequence.[6]

Brunetto's mention of the episode of the mounted Aristotle in book 2 of the *Tresor* is very brief, in a chapter devoted to the dangers of women.[7] Yet, in these manuscripts, the image is strategically placed at the beginning of

---

[4] Florence, Biblioteca Medicea Laurenziana, MS Strozzi 174, fol. 19r, treated in Callmann (1974: 58). Jacobson-Schutte (1980: 482–8) connects this illustration of the *Triumphi* to Apollonio's painted salvers, discussed in Callmann (1974: 58–9).

[5] Samson is mentioned in *Triumphus Cupidinis* 3.49–51: 'Poco dinanzi a lei vedi Sampsone, / vie più forte che saggio, che per ciance / in grembo a la nemica il capo pone' (Pacca and Paolino 1996: 144; 'Closely beyond her, Samson you may see, / Stronger than he is wise, who foolishly / Laid low his head upon a hostile lap', transl. Wilkins). Hercules is given in *Triumphus Cupidinis* 1.124–25: 'Colui ch'è seco, è quel possente e forte / Hercole, ch'Amor prese' (Pacca and Paolino 1996: 82; 'With him is Hercules: for all his strength / Love captured him', transl. Wilkins). For a discussion of the ways in which characters such as Vergil and Aristotle entered the figurative afterlife of Petrarch's *Triumphi*, see Smith (1995: 137–90).

[6] See Carpentras, Bibliothèque Inguimbertine, MS 269, fol. 108r; and Karlsruhe, Landesbibliothek, MS 391, fol. 115r. For a discussion of the Carpentras manuscript, see Roux (2008: 21–2). Both images are also briefly discussed in Roux (2009: 90–4, 181–2).

[7] Brunetto Latini, *Tresor* 2.106.1. See the passage (in which Aristotle's wisdom is matched with Merlin's) in the critical edition Beltrami (2007: 580–2): 'Mes il avient maintes fois que il n'ont nul povoir de soi meisme, ainces abandonent et cuer et cors a l'amor d'une feme; et en cest maniere perdent il lor sens, si que il ne voient gote … Neis Aristotes, li tres saiges philosophes, et Merlin furent deceus par femes, selonc que les estoires racontent' ('But it often happens that these people have no power over themselvs; rather they abandon themselves body and soul to the love of a

Figure 1.1 Apollonio di Giovanni, *Trionfo d'Amore*, c. 1442
Florence, Biblioteca Medicea Laurenziana, ms. Strozzi 174, fol. 19*r*

Figure 1.2 Aristotle and Phyllis, from Brunetto Latini, *Tresor*,
Carpentras, Bibliothèque Inguimbertine, ms. 269, fol. 108r

book 2, thus opening the section of the *Tresor* entitled *L'Ethique d'Aristote* that contained Brunetto's French translation of a widely successful compendium of Aristotle's *Nichomachean Ethics*, the *Summa Alexandrinorum*, which had been circulating in Latin and Italian since the mid-thirteenth century.[8] As observed by Brigitte Roux, the format of the image is unusual and, by far, more complex than the decoration of illuminated initial letters typical for texts of this kind.[9] Given the context, it is difficult to interpret this visual occurrence as an ironic statement about the moral authority of Aristotle, who is, after all, the supposed *auctor* of this section of the *Tresor*, of which Brunetto Latini is but the translator. The image instead invites the reader to consider the ways in which moral teachings are put into practice when expressed to a new audience. Thus it also seems to gesture towards a moral code where authoritative prescriptions are adapted to the expectations of Brunetto's lay readers – a feature that, as we shall see, relates to the aims of vernacular translation.

The Song of Nature

Even if the detailed representation of the anecdote in the two manuscripts of the *Tresor* brings the episode of Aristotle and the courtesan to the forefront, most textual allusions to the legend, including Brunetto's, tend to focus only on the simplistic equation between love and the loss of self-control. A more articulate set of patterns, though, informs some rewritings of the episode that, at least in part, seem to challenge its commonly accepted meaning. Among these, the famous *Lai d'Aristote* stands out.[10] Written in France in the first half of the thirteenth century and commonly attributed to Henri d'Andeli (though the authorship has been recently questioned), the poem represents the anecdote according to the ideals of courtly love (*fin' amor*).[11] The *Lai* is not meant to warn against the dangers of love but instead to lay claim to the power of Nature. As such, this is not

woman; in this way they lose their sense, so that they become blind … Even Aristotle the great philosopher and Merlin were deceived by a woman, according to what history tells us', transl. Barrette and Baldwin 1993: 15c–1).

[8] On the conflation of sources in the second book of Brunetto's *Tresor*, see Beltrami (2007: XVII–XIX). For a discussion of the translations of the *Summa Alexandrinorum*, see Chapter 2 in this book.

[9] Roux (2008: 21–2).

[10] The reference edition of the text is Delbouille (1951). Recent editions of the text, with rich introductions and a retrospective bibliography, are those by Infurna (2005) and Brook and Burgess (2011). My quotations from the text (simply indicated as *Lai*) come from Infurna's edition. Unless indicated otherwise, English translations of the passages quoted are mine.

[11] For a thorough discussion of the authorship, which goes beyond our scope here, see Brook and Burgess (2011: 9–38), where the poem is attributed to one Henri de Valenciennes.

only a poem on love, but is foremost a reflection on the conflict between nature and learning, a conflict that, as we shall see, finds its definition in the characterisation of Aristotle. While the poet uses the term 'nature', he does not use the word 'learning'. I adopt the term here to signify the cultural paradigm embodied by Aristotle, as well as the idea of moral education as a means to dominate instincts that the period regarded as products of nature rather than culture.

The plot of the *Lai d'Aristote* is easily recounted.[12] Alexander the Great, who is in love with a beautiful Indian woman (the name of Phyllis does not appear in this version of the story), has begun devoting more time and energy to her than to the administration of his kingdom. His tutor Aristotle, worried by the metamorphosis of his pupil into a veritable *fins amis* ('courtly lover'), speaks out to the king and encourages him to go back to his duties.[13] Alexander is at pains to follow Aristotle's advice, but, as he acknowledges to his beloved, he finds it very difficult to leave her. Eventually, the king realises that his fault did not lie in loving her but in renouncing love.[14] The woman, now poised to take the lead in the narrative, finds a way to punish Aristotle and, with Alexander's consent, puts her plan into action. By exploiting her beauty and trusting the power of Love, she manages to seduce the old philosopher. She walks next to his window, singing to him and wearing only a shirt.[15] Aristotle's infatuation is inevitable but not immediate and his punishment is only complete when, after some hesitation, he agrees to be ridden by the woman without knowing that Alexander is observing the scene. When the king shows up and criticises Aristotle for his undignified behaviour, the philosopher is

---

[12] The work's influences and possible imitations have been the object of several studies: Delbouille (1951: 53–6), Infurna (2005: 9–37), Brook and Burgess (2011: 9–38).

[13] The lexicon of *fin' amor* is explicit in the depiction of Alexander, as in *Lai* 97–103: 'Amors qui tot prant et enbrace / Et tot aërt et tot enlace / L'avoit ja si en braies mis / Qu'il ert devenuz fins amis, / Dont il ne se repentoit mie, / Quar il avoit trouvee amie / Si bele com a souhaidier' ('Love, which takes hold of and embraces so much, / And seizes and ensnares everything, / Had held him in such bondage / That he had become a true lover, / For which he had no regrets, / Since he had found a beloved / As beautiful as any he could wish for'; transl. Brook and Burgess 2011: 53). As for the characterisation of Aristotle, the philosopher's alleged wisdom is highlighted at the beginning of his speech to the king in *Lai* 159–60: 'Aristote, qui tot savoit / Quanqu'an droite clergie avoit' ('Aristotle, who knew everything / That appertained to true learning'; transl. Brook and Burgess 2011: 55).

[14] *Lai* 236–9: 'Neporquant bien sai qu'ai mespris / Quant por aus desfis ainc en mi / La volonté de fin ami, / Mais ge doutai despit et honte' ('However, I know that it was my mistake / to follow their words and, / due to my fear of scorn and shame, / to silence the desire of a true lover').

[15] *Lai* 281–302: 'Lors s'est en pure sa chemise / El vergier desoz la tor mise, / En un bliaut inde gouté / ... / S'en vait escorçant son bliaut, / Chantant basset, non mie halt' ('Clad just in her chemise, / She entered the garden beneath the tower, / In a blue, spotted tunic, / ... / Raising her tunic as she moved / And singing in a low voice, not loudly'; transl. Brook and Burgess 2011: 59).

forced to admit that any attempt to avoid the force of love and desire is useless.

At the core of Henri's poem lies the attempt to legitimise the idea that nature (i.e., natural instincts) is crucial to human conduct. A motif that recurs throughout the *Lai* is the opposition between 'nature' (as embodied by the beautiful courtesan) and learning (as represented by Aristotle), an opposition that, as suggested by Natalie Zemon Davis, mirrors the historical/psychic opposition of female vs. male, sexual passion vs. 'dry sterile philosophy'.[16] While this motif provides a key to understanding the poem and suggests a fruitful feminist deconstruction of the anecdote, the recurrent opposition also offers a window on a wider ethical discussion concerned with language and its uses.[17] Indeed, Henri's retelling of the story stages a provocative contest between different visions of the world reflected in different ideas on language. Not only does the poet (through the voice of the courtesan) highlight the primacy of nature over learning, but he also stresses the opposition between the courtesan's communicative skills and the philosopher's. Aristotle's command of dialectic and grammar, the very source of his alleged wisdom, proves useless when challenged by personified Nature.[18] Very different from the allegorical and somewhat abstract personification of Nature described by Alain of Lille's late twelfth-century poem *De planctu Naturae*, Nature is embodied here by the courtesan herself,[19] whose beauty easily turns the philosopher away from his books.[20] Charmed by the clever seductress, Aristotle realises that his devotion to

---

[16] Davis (1975: 136).

[17] The most recent and exhaustive discussion of the episode of the mounted Aristotle in light of the female/male opposition is Smith (1995: 66–102).

[18] The weakness of grammar and dialectic vis-à-vis nature is highlighted by the courtesan's speech to Alexander in *Lai* 250–9: 'Ne ja vers moi ne li vaudra / Dïaletique ne gramaire, / Se par moi Nature nel maire, / Puis que ge m'en sui aramie, / Donc saura il trop d'escremie / Et si le parcevroiz demain. / Sire rois, or vos levez main / Si verroiz Nature apointier / Au maistre por lui despointier / De son sens et de sa clergie' ('He will not find any help in Dialectic and Grammar; he will prove a valiant warrior – you will see his valour tomorrow – if Nature, when she will be fighting against him, will not let me tame him. My lord, wake up early, and you will see Nature attacking your master in order to deprive him of all his wisdom and knowledge').

[19] Alain of Lille's allegorical description of Natura in the *Plaint of Nature* is certainly one of the most elaborate personifications in the medieval tradition. While Alain's Nature is characterised by traits of physical beauty, the description in *De planctu Naturae* (Sheridan 1980: 73–105) leans towards a kind of allegorical writing from which a text like the *Lai d'Aristote* distances itself. Henri's description of the courtesan, by contrast, is solely focused on the physical beauty of the woman but her relation to Nature is made explicit by the narrator in *Lai* 288–9: 'Bien li ot Nature floré / Son cler vis de lis et de rose' ('Nature had decked / Her fair countenance with lilies and roses'; transl. Brook and Burgess 2011: 59).

[20] *Lai* 322–5: 'Levez est, si siet a ses livres. / Voit la dame aler et venir; / El cuer li met un souvenir / Tel que ses livres li fait clorre' ('Aristotle rose and sat at his books; / He saw the fair one coming

study was in vain: once eager to acquire the world's knowledge, he has now lost all of his learning. Dialectic and grammar, which stand for the speculative tools embodied by Aristotle, are defeated by earthlier yearnings – more precisely, by the physical beauty of the courtesan and the charming beauty of her singing. In fact, pretending to be unaware of Aristotle's presence, the courtesan seduces the old philosopher by singing strophes from love songs (three *rondeaux* and a stanza from a *chanson de toile*).[21] On one hand, the insertion of strophic forms into the structure of the *Lai* produces an effect of realism, since the device is used frequently in French medieval poetry to let the audience 'hear' the same singing that the character is hearing within the fiction of the narrative.[22] On the other hand, the performance of the courtesan promotes love poetry as a form of language that persuades even the most stubborn philosopher more effectively than any rational argument.

As argued by Dante Alighieri in the second book of his *De vulgari eloquentia* (c. 1304), love poetry is quintessentially vernacular (where 'vernacular' refers to one's mother tongue in opposition to languages learned artificially by means of grammatical rules). Indeed, according to Dante, love joins well-being (*salus*) and virtue (*virtus*) as the subjects most suitable for poetical composition in the vernacular.[23] Love poetry is thus presented as the ideal expression of one's first (i.e., 'natural') language, the language unconsciously acquired by babies in their cradle that, according to a

---

[21] and going, / And this stimulated thoughts in his heart, / Such that they made him close his books'; transl. Brook and Burgess 2011: 60).

[21] For details on these lyrical inserts, see Delbouille (1951: 21–9), Infurna (2005: 28–32) and Brook and Burgess (2011: 30–3).

[22] On the practice of poetic quotation in medieval poetry, though mostly of the troubadours, see Kay (2013).

[23] Dante, *De vulgari eloquentia* 2.2.7 (here and throughout the book, I quote from the edition Tavoni 2011 and use Botterill's 1996 English translation): 'Sed disserendum est, que maxima sint. Et primo in eo quod est utile: in quo, si callide consideremus intentum omnium querentium utilitatem, nil aliud quam salutem inveniemus. Secundo, in eo quod est delectabile: in quo dicimus illud esse maxime delectabile quod per preciosissimum obiectum appetitus delectat; hoc autem venus est. Tertio, in eo quod est honestum; in quo nemo dubitat esse virtutem. Quare hec tria, Salus videlicet, Venus et Virtus, apparent esse illa magnalia que sint maxime pertractanda, hoc est ea que maxime sunt ad ista, ut armorum probitas, amoris accensio, et directio voluntatis' ('But we must discuss what these things of greatest importance may be. To begin with what is useful: here, if we carefully ponder the goal of all those who seek what is useful, we will find that it is nothing other than their own well-being. Secondly, what is pleasurable: here I say that what is most pleasurable is what is the most highly valued object of our desires; and this is love. Thirdly, what is good: and here no-one will doubt that the most important thing is virtue. So these three things, well-being, love, and virtue, appear to be those most important subjects that are to be treated in the loftiest style; or at least this is true of the themes most closely associated with them, prowess in arms, ardour in love, and control of one's own will').

well-established commonplace, men and women learn from their mothers and wet-nurses.[24] When considering Henri's version of the Aristotle anecdote from the standpoint of language, the apocryphal episode acquires deeper implications. Regardless of Henri's putative parody of university scholars, what matters in his retelling of the story is the fact that the language of philosophy and academic rhetoric is defeated by the 'vernacular' voice of the courtesan.[25] Aristotle speaks French in the poem, of course, but the reference to his knowledge of grammar and dialectic, the primary tools of philosophical inquiry, alludes to the Latinate world of scholars and university professors who spent most of their time studying and interpreting the works of the Philosopher. Indeed, any scholar's curriculum would have had at its core grammar and dialectic, which, alongside rhetoric, formed the *trivium*, the preliminary step to any further education.[26] Yet the status of the three arts of discourse (grammar, dialectic and rhetoric) becomes ambiguous in the long process of transition that accompanies the rise of vernacular cultures, for they are not simply concerned with a particular subject matter but instead with language and communication itself. While grammar ('grammatica'), in particular, remains a synonym for Latin (language and literature) for a long time, the need to reconsider the meaning of 'mother tongue' becomes pressing when the vernacular establishes itself and is progressively acknowledged as the language naturally spoken by people.

Vulgarising Grammar

Indicative of this conflict is the allegorical representation of grammar as a nursing woman in many medieval pictorial cycles of *artes liberales*. As Gary

---

[24] A key formulation of this concept once again comes from Dante's *De vulgari eloquentia* 1.1.2: 'vulgarem locutionem appellamus eam qua infantes assuefiunt ab assistentibus cum primitus distinguere voces incipiunt; vel, quod brevius dici potest, vulgarem locutionem asserimus sine omni regula nutricem imitantes accipimus' ('I call "vernacular language" that which infants acquire from those around them when they first begin to distinguish sounds; or, to put it more succinctly, I declare that vernacular language is that which we learn without any formal instruction, by imitating our nurses').

[25] The idea that the author aimed to parody the scholars of the Sorbonne has been proposed by Delbouille (1951: 20, 58). Smith (1595: 69–70) suggests that a similar reading of the *Lai* was indeed possible, as indicated by Matheolus' *Lamentations*, where it is said that 'Aristotle's humiliation proves that women are more powerful than the *Perihermeneias*, the *Elench*, the *Prior* and *Posterior Analytics*, mathematics and logic.'

[26] For an overview of the liberal arts in the Middle Ages, see Wagner (1983). The most complete discussion of the liberal arts in the medieval period is Martianus Capella's *De nuptiis Mercurii et Philologiae*; see Stahl and Burge (1971–77).

P. Cestaro argues in his study of Dante and the 'grammar of the nursing body', the motif encapsulates profound questions about the status of language and its acquisition, including dynamics of reward and punishment.[27] Here I would like to connect such dynamics to the evolving status of the vernacular. Usually associated with the ancient grammarian Priscian, the allegory of grammar points to Latin as the normative language one should acquire before embarking on further education. Concurrent developments within the vernacular context, however, challenge the previously uncontested priority of Latin in language learning, as suggested by the numerous vernacular grammars that were produced across Europe in the period.[28] The tension in the field of grammar between Latin and the vernacular was particularly strong in Italy, where the legacy of Latinity had deep roots. In fact, while vernacular grammars appeared in other areas of Europe as early as in the thirteenth century, the first Italian grammar, Leon Battista Alberti's *Grammatichetta*, did not appear until 1443.[29]

An instructive example of this friction is found in the *Canzone delle virtù e delle scienze* ('Song of Virtues and Sciences'), composed by Bolognese amanuensis Bartolomeo de' Bartoli around 1355 and dedicated to Bruzio Visconti, the son of the lord of Milan and a noted bibliophile.[30] In the beautifully decorated Chantilly Codex, the *Canzone* combines stanzas of poetry in Italian with explanatory rubrics in Latin and a set of illustrations. The bilingual nature of Bartolomeo's project is made explicit in the Latin title of the work: 'Incipit Cantica ad gloriam et honorem magnifici militis domini Brutii … in qua tractantur de virtutibus et scientiis vulgarizatis'.[31] The first part of the *canzone*, devoted to the virtues, opens under the aegis of prophets (Moses, Ezekiel, John the Evangelist) and the Church Fathers (Augustine, Ambrose, Paul, Gregory, Jerome). The second part, which describes the sciences (the liberal arts), instead opens with the

---

[27] Cestaro (2003: 9–48); the author offers a compelling discussion of the status of grammar within medieval theories of language, Dante's in particular. On the iconography of the liberal arts, see Katzenellenbogen (1961) and Verdier (1969). A more recent and detailed study focused on medieval culture is Stolz (2004); on grammar, see *ibid.*: 58–9 and, for the examples of the iconography of grammar considered here: figures 1 (Herrad von Hohenburg, *Hortus deliciarum*), 24 (Alain of Lille, *Anticlaudianus*) and 116 (the panegyric of Robert of Anjou).

[28] On the rise of vernacular grammars in medieval Europe, see Percival (1975); on the teaching of grammar, with a focus on Tuscany, Black (2007). For a wider discussion of the legacy of classical grammar and rhetoric and its role in the development of vernacular literatures, see Copeland (1991).

[29] Patota (1996), Poggi Salani (2001), Manni (2007) and Celenza (2018: 131–2).

[30] Bartolomeo's *Canzone* is witnessed in a beautifully illuminated codex now at Chantilly, Bibliothèque du Chateau, MS 599; for an edition of the text, with introduction and facsimile of the original, see Dorez (1904).

[31] *Ibid.*: 21.

representation of Lady Philosophy seated above the universe, surrounded by four philosophers: Aristotle, 'the one who seeks true knowledge'; Plato, 'the one who transcends nature'; Socrates, who 'chastises men's vices'; and Seneca, 'the moral one'.[32] The stanzas of the poem, in which virtues and sciences are individually described and accompanied by visual depictions, take on the function of presenting the topic in the vernacular. In contrast the Latin rubrics are based on Augustine's writings and embody the erudite component of the work. But the vernacular overrides the Latin in the envois concluding the two sections of the *canzone*. In both cases, the previous stanzas are summarised in diagrams that include scaled-down images and reiterative verses in Italian [Figure 1.3].[33]

Within this structure, which epitomises the difference between linguistic layers, the visual and verbal illustration of grammar in the twelfth stanza is of particular interest [Figure 1.4]. Grammar is represented as a seated woman, nursing a boy who holds a small board inscribed with the Latin alphabet (a so-called 'abecedario'). The image translates the nursing activity of grammar described in the accompanying stanza, which recounts that, through her milk, the boy acquires the knowledge of language ('el senno litterale') that is the fountain of all wisdom and eloquence.[34] Another detail of the image, though, warrants our attention. The woman holds a whip with her left hand, the eloquent symbol of her teaching duties, which, as suggested by Alain of Lille's description of grammar, include forms of corrective punishment:

> While the child still sighs at the breasts of his nursing mother, this food feeds him and the one who cannot yet take solids is nourished by liquid ... She increases the severity of one of her hands with a whip with which she punishes the faults which youth in its way absorbs. Thus by blows she makes the milk more bitter, by the milk she makes the blows more mild. In one and the same action she is father and mother.[35]

[32] *Ibid.*: 24, 36.

[33] *Ibid.*: 34–5, 51.

[34] *Ibid.*: 38: 'Bella, gentile, legiadra è Gramaticha. / È questa gioven che cum la mamilla / Al fantulin istilla / El senno litterale, ond'el cognosse / Più per quel lacte e posse / Perfecto fare et haver sapientia; / Ch'ella d'ogne eloquentia / Altrui ce dà de l'ideoma el fructo. / ... / Né posse al mondo ben senza lei vivere' ('Grammar is beautiful, noble and elegant. She is this young woman who – through her breast – instills the child with the knowledge of letters; her milk makes him more knowledgeable, hence he learns how to make himself good and acquire wisdom. She offers the fruit of all eloquence ... It is impossible to live in peace and happiness without her'; my transl.). The same passage from the *canzone* is briefly discussed in Cestaro (2003: 47–8). For the relevance of the image to later periods, see Sanson (2011).

[35] For the passage from the second book of Alain of Lille's *Anticlaudianus*, see Copeland and Sluiter (2009: 523); and cf. Cestaro (2003: 41–2). Cf. Ziolkowski (1985) for a discussion of grammar in Alain's poetry. On the connection between flogging and the teaching of grammar, see Ong (1971: 124–6).

Figure 1.3 Diagram of the Liberal Arts, from Bartolomeo de' Bartoli, *Canzone delle virtù e delle scienze*, Chantilly, Bibliotèque du Château, ms. 599 (c. 1355)

Figure 1.4 Grammar, from Bartolomeo de' Bartoli, *Canzone delle virtù e delle scienze*, Chantilly, Bibliotèque du Château, ms. 599 (c. 1355)

Yet, while grammar in Alain of Lille refers only to the study and production of Latin texts, Bartolomeo's allegory projects the nursing and teaching functions of grammar onto the vernacular world. As indicated by her own address to the audience in the recapitulatory diagram, grammar mediates between past and present, between Latin and the newly born vernaculars: 'D'ogne vulgare altrui fructo ve porgho / E d'ogne litteral senno i['] m'acorgho'.[36] She offers the fruit of the vulgar tongue and she also knows how to grasp the 'literal sense' ('litteral senno') of a text, where the meaning of 'literal' hangs in the balance between Latin and the vernacular, the two linguistic fields that Bartolomeo's grammar embodies. In a way, while endorsing the traditional arrangement of the liberal arts as they were codified by the Latin Middle Ages, the *Canzone delle virtù e delle scienze* bears witness to a turning point in the history of the emancipation of the vernacular from the cultural privilege of Latin.[37]

In its linguistically hybrid shape, Bartolomeo's poem performs a translating function that is both declared in the title of the work ('de virtutibus et scientiis vulgarizatis') and made explicit when the arts of discourse are directly concerned. Indeed, the vernacular stanzas on grammar, dialectic and rhetoric not only claim the importance of those three arts in their own right, but also stress their relevance to the vulgar tongue. The status of the three *artes sermocinales* is in fact deeply affected by the shift of focus from Latin to the vernacular that informs the process of translation. While these arts were conceived and codified for the production of Latin texts, they are now transferred to a vernacular context.[38] This process, best witnessed in Italy in the linguistic thoughts of Dante, Petrarch and Boccaccio, was neither easy nor unchallenged. Within it, grammar held the most ambiguous position: on one hand, grammar stood for the language moulded by grammatical rules (i.e., Latin) as opposed to the irregular and unstable vernaculars; the iconographic tradition, on the other hand, proposes grammar as the embodiment of the nursing function of language that was nonetheless commonplace in the genealogical legitimisation of the vernacular (often described as the 'mother tongue' that, as recalled above, we acquire spontaneously from mothers and nurses).[39]

Cestaro (2003: 20–2) discusses the iconography of the whip in relation to Martianus Capella's portrayal of Lady Grammar in the *De nuptiis Mercurii et Philologiae*.

[36] Dorez (1904: 34). For the diagram, see Figure 1.3.

[37] See the insightful remarks on the relation between grammar and the bilingualism that characterises the period in Gehl (1993: 26–7, 78–9, 233–5) and Gehl (1994).

[38] The most compelling discussion of this process to date remains Copeland (1991). See also Copeland and Sluiter (2009) for an overview of the status of grammar in medieval culture.

[39] See Dante's statement in *De vulgari eloquentia*, 1.1.2. On the complex relations between Latin and the vernacular in the late Middle Ages and the early Renaissance, see Tavoni (1984), Campanelli (2014)

The first tradition, which views Latin as a grammar stabilised by teachable rules, is embodied by the grammar that, in conjunction with dialectic, failed to help Aristotle resist the courtesan according to the author of the *Lai d'Aristote*. Despite his renowned skills in the arts of discourse, Aristotle, whom Bartolomeo de' Bartoli defined as the philosopher 'who seeks true knowledge', surrenders easily to the enticement of sexual desire in the form of a female figure. The whip, a traditional attribute of grammar, is here the instrument with which the courtesan tames the philosopher.[40] Along with the bridle, the whip emblematises the debasement to which Aristotle is compelled. His humiliation, though, marks the expression of a moral code that, in the French poem, is legitimised by the reference to Nature, a figure that similarly validates the use of the vernacular. This situation contrasts Aristotle's presumed intellectual superiority and the allegedly spontaneous vernacular shrewdness of the courtesan, whose skills are pictured as conforming to the laws of Nature.[41]

A similar opposition informs a short retelling of the episode in the *canzone* that opens 'Sovente in me pensando come amore' ('Thinking often to myself about love'), attributed to the early fifteenth-century Florentine poet Antonio di Meglio.[42] The poem is one of many texts that, in the footsteps of Petrarch's *Triumphs*, stigmatise the power of Love by recalling examples of the god's famous victims. There, Aristotle appears alongside wise men such as Vergil and Solomon. Instead of simply alluding to the anecdote of the courtesan, though, the poet frames it in terms relevant to discussions of language: 'Aristotile, un huom di tanta copia, / Odi vulgariçar ch'una donçella / Fu che gli mise sella / E cavalcòl come un fantin la canna' ('You hear stories about Aristotle, a man of great *copia* and how once a young lady saddled and rode him like a boy does his stick [horse]').[43] The poet recalls Aristotle's 'copia', which refers to the classical notion of *copia verborum et rerum*, the abundance of words and subject matter acquired through education in the liberal arts – the same

---

and Refini (2017). For an enlightening account of the role played by Boccaccio in establishing the *volgare* as the backbone of the modern literary tradition, which includes, in different ways, Dante and Petrarch, see Eisner (2013).

[40] Roux (2009: 182) highlights the 'attributs magistraux' in illustrations of Aristotle's courtesan, but does not propose any connection with the iconography of grammar.

[41] As a matter of fact, the courtesan is neither naïve nor spontaneous. All that matters in the *Lai d'Aristote* is that she performs the role of the spontaneous and unaware seductress, thus embodying an idea of nature that, while different from the cultural function performed by Aristotle, is indeed a cultural construct.

[42] De Cesare (1956: 210–11).

[43] *Ibid.*: 211.

meaning this word exhibits in the final envoi of Bartolomeo de' Bartoli's *Canzone delle virtù e delle scienze*, where the poet highlights the 'copia' (literally, 'abundance') of wisdom that informs the poem.[44] At the same time, though, the use of the verb *vulgarizzare* refers to the wide dissemination of this episode, popularised by both texts and images in the late Middle Ages. The phrasing of this *canzone* is of particular interest, for it stresses the vernacular twist acquired by the moral anecdote. One might say that it is thanks to the courtesan that Aristotle is removed from his philosophical and rhetorical dryness, and brought back to the real world of the vernacular, where Love is not evil but a 'natural' component of life.

The pertinence of the opposition between Latin and vernacular as a mirror of the related opposition between 'artificial' learning and Nature is confirmed by a playful reference to Aristotle and the courtesan in a later work by the sixteenth-century writer Girolamo Ruscelli (1518–66). In his satirical poem *Delle lodi del fuso* ('Eulogy of the spindle'), based entirely on sexual innuendos, Ruscelli uses Aristotle's encounter with the courtesan to restore the supposedly natural order that his own philosophy had subverted.[45] Accustomed to teaching young male pupils – a veiled allusion to the philosopher's inclination to pederasty – Aristotle is not familiar with the 'distaff' and, by analogy, his punishment must be to have the young lady mount him like a horse.[46] Ruscelli's allusion to the anecdote echoes the long literary tradition, particularly abundant in the Renaissance, that targeted pedants, scholars and schoolteachers (usually stigmatised as pederasts) for their misuse of Latin. The jargon spoken by these characters in many sixteenth-century comic plays, a mixture of Latin and vernacular phrases created especially to be ridiculed, captures the disconnect between what was meant to be 'natural' and what was meant to be 'artificial', a disconnect that was also at the core of contemporary debates on language and its uses.[47]

---

[44] Dorez (1904: 45).

[45] The passage from Ruscelli's poem is mentioned by De Cesare (1956: 233–4).

[46] *Ibid.*: 233–4: 'Aristotil, che ognuno sa quanto fusse / Saggio, nella vecchiezza ad imparare / Di filare, e di torcer si condusse. / Ma perché troppo bene adoperare / Non sapea la conocchia, ch'era usato / Insegnar sol fanciulli, e disputare, / N'era severamente gastigato / Dalla maestra, e lo faceva sovente / Camminar brancoloni ed insellato' ('Aristotle, whose wisdom is known to everybody, in old age attempted to learn how to spin and twist. Yet, as someone who was only used to teach boys and to dispute, he was not expert in handling the distaff; for this reason, he was harshly chastised by his mistress, who often bridled him and made him crawl'; my transl.).

[47] For a discussion of the figure of the *pedante* in Renaissance comedy, see Staüble (1991).

The Moral of the Story

But let us return to the period prior to the canonisation of the vernacular that was accomplished by Pietro Bembo's writings on language in the early sixteenth century and profoundly altered the relationship between Latin and Italian. Between 1250 and 1500, the episode of the mounted philosopher inspired other uses relevant to the development of forms of culture (both textual and visual) that can be usefully labelled 'vernacular' and that contributed to the broader 'translation' of moral teachings based primarily on the Aristotelian golden mean. This is the case of the appearance of the anecdote on the walls of public and semi-public spaces such as the town hall in San Gimignano [Figure 1.5] or the Bishop's Palace at Colle Val d'Elsa.[48] As C. Jean Campbell argues in her study of the early fourteenth-century frescoes in the Palazzo Comunale at San Gimignano, the episode of Aristotle and the courtesan painted in the Camera del Podestà is part of a wider cycle of images better understood in the light of contemporaneous vernacular literature.[49]

In what remains today of a once rich series of scenes, the anecdote of Aristotle is accompanied by the parable of the prodigal son and, on another wall, by the famous scenes in the bedchamber (in one, a man and a woman bathing and, in another, the same two characters in bed). One of the most remarkable cycles of medieval Italian secular painting, the frescoes at San Gimignano raise questions about their function and purpose. While this is not the place to reconsider a topic that has been the object of extensive study, the combination of Aristotle and the courtesan with scenes of everyday life is worth highlighting here. Along with themes of prodigality and avarice (both relevant to the function performed by the city's administrator), the illustration of the philosopher's subjection to the courtesan opens a window onto the conflict between 'natural' inclinations and reason. The taming of the philosopher is represented here under the vigilant gaze of Alexander and his wife, according to a version of the anecdote similar to the one told by storyteller Giovanni

---

[48] The frescos in San Gimignano have been studied in detail by Campbell (1997); cf., more recently, Meneghetti (2015: 227–9); the less famous cycle of Colle Val d'Elsa is discussed by Petrioli (1996: 215–21).

[49] Campbell (1997: 197): 'Like the *Decameron*, the decorations of San Gimignano's Communal Palace were conceived in what might be called a vernacular spirit, a spirit that was, by definition, concerned with the experience of life and language in this world.'

Figure 1.5 Memmo di Filippuccio, *Aristotle and Phyllis* (c. 1300),
San Gimignano, Palazzo Pubblico, Camera del Podestà

Sercambi (1347–1424) in his *Novelle*.[50] This version gives the anecdote a
more contemporary flair and has the king's wife, Orsina, who had been

---

[50] See the text of the novella in Sinicropi (1995: 448–59); and *ibid.*: 459–63, for a detailed account of
its sources and influences. For a discussion of Sercambi's collection of *novelle*, see Salwa (1991).

the direct target of Aristotle's criticism, commission his punishment. Though the archetype for this version of the story can only be identified with difficulty, the fresco it resembles is nonetheless consistent with a literary tradition exemplified at its best by Giovanni Boccaccio's *Decameron* (c. 1350), one that was quite concerned with discussions of ethics, social values and behaviour. This literary tradition was one of the most productive expressions of the new vernacular society that, in many ways, was appropriating and reshaping discourses usually produced within the narrower circles of scholars and men of learning. The relevance of Aristotle to this process is self-evident, for he embodied the philosophical and scientific inheritance of the classical past that lay at the core of medieval culture. Considered within such a framework, the anecdote of Aristotle's debasement can thus be read as an emblem for the multifaceted transition that made philosophy more easily accessible to wider audiences almost solely conversant in the vernacular.

The novella tradition, even before Boccaccio, offers instructive examples of this process, which can in fact be described in terms of translation. Aristotle appears, for instance, as the main character in the sixty-eighth novella of the *Novellino*, the most important collection of short stories before the *Decameron*, assembled by an anonymous compiler towards the end of the thirteenth century.[51] In the novella entitled 'D'una quistione che fece un giovane ad Aristotile' ('Of a question that a young man proposed to Aristotle'), one of Aristotle's pupils asks about the misbehaviour of an old man whom he has seen 'doing wanton follies' – a situation that, by the way, recalls Aristotle's own sexual intemperance in the anecdote of the courtesan, where the moral of the story was underscored by the philosopher's old age.[52] Aristotle replies by providing an abridged version of a key concept derived from the *Nicomachean Ethics*. Since reason fades away as people age, thereby making them more susceptible to natural

---

[51] For the text of the novella, see the critical edition by Conte (2001: 116–17). For a critical introduction to the *Novellino*, see Conte (2001: xv–xxviii).

[52] *Ibid.*: 116–17: 'Aristotile fue grande filosofo. Un giorno venne a·llui un giovane con una nuova domanda, dicendo così: "Eh, maestro: i' ho veduto cosa che molto mi dispiace all'animo mio: ch'io vidi un vecchio di grandissimo tempo fare laide mattezze: onde, se la vecchiezza n'ha colpa, io m'accordo di voler morire giovane anziché invecchiare e matteggiare. Onde per Dio, maestro, metteteci consiglio, se essere può" ' ('Aristotle was a great philosopher. There came to him one day a young man with a singular question – "Master, he said, I have seen a thing which much displeases my mind. I have seen an old man ripe in years doing wanton follies. Now if the cause of such things be age, I have decided to die young. Therefore for the love of God give me counsel, if you can" '; transl. Storer 1925: 160).

instincts, the only way to control them is to cultivate good behaviour at a young age:

> I cannot do other than tell you that when the nature of man grows old, the good natural heat changes into weakness, while the reasonable virtue fails and alters. For your instruction I will teach you what I can. Do so that in your youth you practice all beautiful pleasant and honest things, and guard yourself from indulging in what is contrary to them; so when you are old, you will live without evil, not from nature or from reason, but owing to the long pleasant and noble habit you have formed.[53]

Here the philosophical concept of *habitus* ('usanza', habit), central to the second book of the *Nicomachean Ethics*, is expressed through an exemplum that illustrates the notion in a very effective way. In fact, the same concept is to be found in countless contemporary texts, from the *Letters* of Guittone d'Arezzo to Brunetto's *Tresor* and Dante's *Convivio*.[54]

As the *Novellino* itself suggests, however, the idea of bringing the philosophical tradition into the vernacular was not unchallenged. The famous story told in the seventy-eighth novella is enlightening in this regard, as demonstrated by Alison Cornish in her study of vernacular translation in

---

[53] Transl. Storer (1925: 161); cf. the original in Conte (2001: 117): 'Io non posso consigliare che, invecchiando, la natura non muti in debolezza: il buono calore naturale se verrae meno, la virtù ragionevole è manca. Ma per la tua bella provedenza io t'aprenderò com'io potrò. Farai così: che, nella tua giovenezza, che tu usarai tutte le belle et oneste cose e le piacevoli, e dal lor contrario ti guarderai al postutto. Quando serai vecchio, non per natura né per ragione viverai con nettezza, ma per la tua bella, piacevole e lunga usanza ch'avrai fatta.'

[54] See Aristotle's discussion of the notion of 'habit' in *Nichomachean Ethics* 1103a 20–1103b 25. For a complete list of sources that rephrase the same concept in the novella, see Conte (2001: 360–1). See also Guittone d'Arezzo, *Lettere* 21.7; and Latini, *Tesoretto* 1656–64. Of particular interest are the phrasings in *Tresor* 2.10.1; see Beltrami (2007: 344): 'La vertu de l'entendement est engendree et escreue on l'ome par doctrine et par enseignement, et por ce li covient esperience et lonc tens. La vertu de moralité naist et croist par *bon us* et honeste, car ele n'est pas en nos par nature, a ce que chose naturel ne puet estre muee de sa nature par usage contraire ... Et ja soit ce que ceste vertu ne soit en nos par nature, certes la puissance d'aprendre la est en nos par nature, et li compliment est en nos par *usaige*' ('The virtue of understanding is born and increases in man through doctrine and instruction, and for this long experience is needed. The virtue of morality is born and increases by good and honest use, for it is not in us naturally, because a natural thing cannot be changed in its contrary usage ... and although this virtue is not in us by nature, certainly the power to learn it is in us by nature, and its perfection is in us through usage'; transl. Barrette and Baldwin 1993: 150–1). See also Dante, *Convivio* 4.21.14 (here and throughout the book I quote from the edition Fioravanti 2014 and use Lansing's 1990 English translation): 'E però vuole santo Augustino, e ancora Aristotile nel secondo dell'Etica, che l'uomo s'ausi a ben fare e a rifrenare le sue passioni, acciò che questo tallo che detto è, per buona consuetudine induri e rifermisi nella sua rettitudine, sì che possa fruttificare, e del suo frutto uscire la dolcezza dell'umana felicità' ('Therefore St. Augustine asserts, as does Aristotle in the second book of the *Ethics*, that one should make a habit of doing well and of restraining one's passions in order that this sprout of which we spoke may grow strong through good habit and be strengthened in its uprightness, so that it may bear fruit and from this fruit bring forth the sweetness of human happiness').

the age of Dante.[55] The protagonist of the novella is a philosopher 'who was much given to vulgarising science, to please some lords and other persons'.[56] This statement pictures a vernacular readership not dissimilar from the one outlined by Dante in the *Convivio*, where the author declares to be addressing 'noble persons ... princes, barons, knights and many other noble people, not only men but women, of which there are many in this language who know only the vernacular and are not learned'.[57] According to the novella, in a vision one night, the philosopher sees the Goddesses of Science 'in the form of beautiful women, in a bawdy house'.[58] When they are asked the reason for their presence, they reply: 'You are he who makes [us] to be here.'[59] Once awake, the philosopher decides to give up 'vulgarising' science, concluding that 'not all things are adapted to all persons'.[60] The story stages a long-lasting bias that will haunt vernacular translation well into the early modern period: namely, that translating philosophy or science into the vernacular implies debasing their status. The degrading function associated with vernacular translation is combined with a misogynist perception of the vernacular in order to argue that, once they are brought into the vulgar tongue, philosophy and science become prostitutes: beautiful, approachable and seductive but dangerous and misleading.

This bias, in a way, takes us back to the connection between gender and language, which was at the core of the rewriting of the anecdote of Aristotle and the courtesan in the *Lai d'Aristote*.[61] Even without formal training in grammar and dialectic, the courtesan is capable of destroying the philosopher's arguments. In so doing, she challenges the effectiveness of a rhetorical and moral code that, rather than acknowledging the rights of Nature, demeans them in favour of artificially constructed behaviour.

---

[55] Cornish (2011: 32–3). For other useful remarks about this novella, see Del Soldato and Rizzi (2013: 240–1). The text of the novella can be read in Conte (2001: 131–2).

[56] Storer (1925: 177); Conte (2001 131) 'Fue uno filosofo, lo quale era molto cortese di volgarizzare la scienzia a' signori, per cortesia, e ad altre genti.'

[57] Dante, *Convivio*, 1.9.5; the passage will be discussed further in Chapter 2.

[58] Storer (1925: 178); Conte (2001: 131): 'Una notte li venne in visione che li parea vedere le dee della scienzia a guisa di belle donne: e stavano al bordello e davansi a chi le volea.'

[59] Storer (1925: 178); Conte (2001: 131): ' "Che è questo? Non siete voi le dee della scienzia?" Et elle rispuosero: "Certo sì". "Com'è ciò? voi siete al bordello?" Et elle rispuosero: "Ben è vero: perché tu se' quelli che vi ci fai stare!" '

[60] Storer (1925: 178); Conte (2001: 132): 'Isvegliossi, e pensossi che volgarizzare la scienzia si era menomare la deitade. Ritràsesine e pentési fortemente. E sappiate che tutte le cose non sono licite a ogni persona.'

[61] On the gendered treatment of language and, in particular, the vernacular, see, among others, Ong (1971); Cornish (2000).

The Vernacular Ethics of Storytelling

Despite important differences in genre and purpose, these sources combine debates on ethics with discussions of language. Such combination is crucial to the establishment of the vernacular as an instrument capable of both performing actions and voicing the motivations behind them. Boccaccio's *Decameron* is one of the clearest examples of this dynamic. If the *Novellino* elaborates debates over language, translation and the challenges entailed by both, Boccaccio's masterwork brings the discussion to an unprecedented level of awareness and self-reflection. The author's attempt to outline a moral philosophy based on the observation and description of human behaviour provides the reader with a gallery of exempla that display moral flexibility and challenge the idea of a fixed ethics. Boccaccio's positive opinion of the ethical value of the vernacular is unquestionable:[62] by addressing his 'beloved women' in both the preface and the conclusions of the *Decameron*, the author transforms the gendered trope that mythologises the connection between women and the vernacular into a systematic framework within which he can draw a linguistic manifesto.[63]

In the conclusion to the *Decameron*, in which Boccaccio defends himself from the possible allegation of immorality raised by some of the stories, the author focuses on the social context he is addressing and on the intellectual profile of his addressees. The author explains that the *novelle* are not meant to be read at church or in the schools of philosophers ('scuole de' filosofanti'), clearly distinguishing his intended readers from readers with some sort of philosophical training. The phrasing, in fact, recalls Dante's autobiographical reference in the *Convivio* to the religious schools and philosophical disputations he attended.[64] As the author himself maintains,

---

[62] Boccaccio's acquaintance with Aristotle, more specifically, with the *Ethics* and Thomas Aquinas' commentary thereof, has been the object of several studies that have highlighted the Aristotelian patterns informing Boccaccio's moral and political reflection; see Flasch (1995), Kirkham (1995), Bausi (1999), Barsella (2012) and Ellero (2012, 2014). Boccaccio's notion of 'ethics' has most recently been detailed by Migiel (2015).

[63] The bibliography on Boccaccio's advocacy of the vernacular is vast but see, among others, Bruni (1990), Forni (1996) and Eisner (2013). For the ethical value embedded in Boccaccio's defence of the vernacular, see Hastings (1975), Mazzotta (1986) and Kirkham (1993). On the notion of *cortesia* in Boccaccio's works, see Olson (2014).

[64] Branca (1976: 960): 'Appresso assai ben si può cognoscere queste cose non nella chiesa, delle cui cose e con animi e con vocaboli onestissimi si convien dire, quantunque nelle sue istorie d'altramenti fatte che le scritte da me si truovino assai; né ancora nelle *scuole de' filosofanti* dove l'onestà non meno che in altra parte è richesta, dette sono; *né tra cherici né tra filosofi* in alcun luogo ma ne' giardini, in luogo di sollazzo, tra persone giovani benché mature e non pieghevoli per novelle, in tempo nel quale andar con le brache in capo per iscampo di sé era alli più onesti non disdicevole, dette sono'; (Rebhorn 2013: 342): 'Moreover, it is perfectly clear that these stories were not told in

the *Decameron* does not address clerks and scholars but, rather, young, honest people who wish to amuse themselves without deviating from the path of virtue. The lack of scholarly training and philosophical education that Boccaccio expects of his addressees is stressed later, in the conclusion, in which he justifies the length of certain stories by explaining that the women for whom he is writing did not study in Athens, Bologna, or Paris: unprepared for the concise statements typical of philosophical literature, his readers will profit from lengthier and more detailed accounts.[65] However, Boccaccio by no means implies that women are incapable of philosophical reasoning. In his later commentary on Dante's *Divine Comedy*, he will go as far as to affirm that the presence of several women among the 'holy spirits' in Limbo suggests that women can engage in philosophical arguments even if they are not afforded formal training. Indeed, their virtuous behaviour and the fulfilment of the duties demanded of them (including the education of children) stem from a profound philosophical knowledge that is as good as the expertise of professors, represented by the tripartite core of Aristotelian philosophy, namely, ethics, politics and economics:

> This is also the case for the women who live chastely and honestly and pursue their domestic duties in an intelligent and organized fashion, for *without the teachings of philosophy* such a life would be impossible. We must recognize that the reading and studying of philosophy is not something confined to universities, schools, and disputations. It can oftentimes be learned within the hearts of men and women. In her room, a wise woman may contemplate her position and her nature. From this contemplation, she may conclude that her honour derives above all else from her chastity, the love of her husband, her feminine seriousness, thriftiness, and her attention

a church, about whose affairs we should speak with the greatest reverence both in our hearts and in our words, although one can find many things in its sacred stories that go well beyond what you encounter in mine. Nor were they rehearsed either in *the schools of philosophy* where decency is required no less than anywhere else, or in any locale frequented by *clergymen and philosophers*. Rather, they were told in gardens, places designed for pleasure, among people who were young, but sufficiently mature so as not to be led astray by stories, and at a time when it was acceptable for even the most virtuous to go about with their breeches on their heads if they thought it would preserve their lives'). See also Dante, *Convivio*, 2.12.7: 'E da questo imaginare cominciai ad andare là dov'ella si dimostrava veracemente, cioè *nelle scuole delli religiosi e alle disputazioni delli filosofanti*' ('I began to go where she was truly revealed, namely to the *schools of the religious orders* and to the *disputations held by the philosophers*'; emphasis mine). For a discussion of the term 'filosofanti', see Pegoretti (2015).

[65] Branca (1976: 963): 'E oltre a questo, per ciò che né a Atene né a Bologna o a Parigi alcuna di voi non va a studiare, più distesamente parlar vi si conviene che a quegli che hanno negli studii gl'ingegni assottigliati' (Rebhorn 2013: 344: 'And besides, since none of you is going to be a student in Athens or Bologna or Paris, I need to speak to you here at greater length than to those whose wits have been sharpened by their studies').

to the family. She may also conclude that it is her responsibility vigilantly to
safeguard and to watch over the things that her husband, who works outside
the house, has earned and brought home. It is her duty diligently to raise
the children, to instruct them, and to teach them manners … What more is
taught by philosophers in schools than what she teaches in ethics, politics,
and economics? Nothing at all. Women who have acted and who act wor-
thily according to their station in life, therefore, shall be seated alongside
philosophers, for they will have earned praise and enduring fame.[66]

Boccaccio's statements recall his earlier characterisation of the audience of
the *Decameron*, further highlighting the difference between his vernacular
readers and the learned men who dictate the boundaries of literate culture.
As Boccaccio's conclusions suggest, the issues of language, style and subject
matter are deeply intertwined with the vernacular poetics that informs the
Decameron.

   Beyond the many *novelle* that echo and articulate in various ways the
issues at stake in the conclusions, the author's own voice makes a crucial
point in the introduction to day four of the *Decameron*, in what is perhaps Boccaccio's most outspoken declaration of the relationship of his vernacular storytelling to the conflict between nature and learning. As is well
known, the author there tells his own novella in order to defend himself
from those who accuse him of an excessive inclination towards women.[67]
This short text raises questions about the legitimacy of an educational
model based on the rejection of nature (a model that, incidentally, is no
different from the one stigmatised by the *Lai d'Aristote*). After the death
of his beloved wife, Filippo Balducci decides to devote the rest of his life

---

[66] Papio (2009: 251). See the original passage in Padoan (1994: 279): 'Così ancora le donne, le quali
castamente e onestamente vivono e i loro offici domestici discretamente e con ordine fanno, sanza
filosofica dimostrazione non gli fanno. E dobbiamo credere non sempre nelle catedre, non sempre
nelle scuole, non sempre nelle disputazioni leggersi e intendersi filosofia: ella si legge spessissimamente
ne' petti delli uomini e delle donne. Sarà la savia donna nella sua camera, e penserà al suo stato, alla
sua qualità: e di questo pensiero trarrà l'onor suo, oltre ad ogni altra cosa, consistere nella pudicizia,
nell'amor del marito, nella gravità donnesca, nella parsimonia, nella cura famigliare; trarrà ancora
di questo pensiero apartenersi a lei di guardare e di servare con ogni vigilanzia quello che il marito,
faticando di fuori, acquisterà e recherà in casa, d'allevare con diligenzia i figliuoli, d'ammaestrargli,
di costumargli, e similmente intorno alle cose oportune dar ordine a' servi, e all'altre cose simili.
Che il filosofo leggerà più a costei nella scuola, che nella sua etica, che nella politica, che nella
iconomica le dimosterrà? Niuna cosa. Dunque quelle, che così hanno adoperato e adoperano, non
indegnamente, secondo il grado loro, co' filosafi sederanno, di laude e di fama perpetua degne.'
[67] Branca (1976: 346–9). For a discussion of the novella, often read as the staging of the conflict
between nature and reason, see Sanguineti (1982), Fedi (1987), Baratto (1993: 56–7), Wallace
(1991: 48–52), Forni (1996: 50–1) and Candido (2015–16). More recent studies – Best (2006), Picone
(2008) and Baxter (2013) – have focused on the linguistic implications of the novella, highlighting
the role of metaphorical language as it relates to sexual repression and contemporary debates on
sexual language.

to the service of God and retires to an isolated place outside Florence, where he and his son both live as hermits. Once the boy reaches the age of eighteen, without ever being aware of women, the two men visit Florence. While the father is confident that his son's morally inflexible education will protect him from the dangers of society, the young man bumps into a group of women for the first time in his life and cannot resist his desire. Though he is warned that they are 'evil' ('mala cosa'), the son wants to know what they are.[68] Filippo's reply, based on a wilful misuse of language that has been aptly described as 'an act of linguistic deflection', unveils the pointlessness of the criticism that Boccaccio himself faces:[69] 'In order to avoid awakening some less than useful desire from among his son's carnal appetites, the father was unwilling to give them their proper name – that is, women – and answered instead: "They're called goslings"'.[70] The son forgets everything else and begs his father to bring one of the 'goslings' with them so that he can 'take care of feeding it'.[71] Filippo's misuse of language produces his son's accidental double entendre, which leads the father to acknowledge that 'his wits were no match for Nature' and so 'he regretted that he had ever brought his son to Florence'.[72] If Boccaccio's tale of the goslings has usually (and rightly) been interpreted as a defence of the author's fondness for women, the legitimacy of which depends on nature, Filippo's use of language invites us to consider the linguistic implications of the story. Recent scholarship has connected the novella to Boccaccio's wider reflections on the relation between sexual language and sexual acts.[73] But Filippo's reply to his son's question can also be read as an example of bad translation, a misleading and artificial manipulation of language that, as the denouement of the plot suggests, is challenged and defeated by the

[68] Branca (1976: 348): 'per avventura si scontrarono in una brigata di belle giovani donne e ornate, che da un paio di nozze venieno: le quali come il giovane vide, così domandò il padre che cosa quelle fossero. A cui il padre disse: – Figliuol mio, bassa gli occhi in terra, non le guatare, ch'elle son mala cosa. Disse allora il figliuolo. – O come si chiamano?' (Rebhorn 2013: 118: 'by chance they came upon a company of beautiful, well-dressed young women who were returning from a wedding somewhere. As soon as the boy saw them, he asked his father what they were. "My son," replied his father, "keep your eyes on the ground and don't look at them, for they are evil." "Oh," asked his son, "what are they called?"'.

[69] Baxter (2013: 815–16).

[70] Rebhorn (2013: 118). Cf. Branca (1976: 118): 'Il padre, per non destare nel concupiscibile appetito del giovane alcuno inchinevole disiderio men che utile, non le volle nominare per lo proprio nome, cioè femine, ma disse: – Elle si chiamano papere.'

[71] Rebhorn (2013: 118). Cf. Branca (1976: 349): 'Deh! se vi cal di me, fate che noi ce ne meniamo una colà sù di queste papere, e io le darè beccare.'

[72] Rebhorn (2013: 118–19). Cf. Branca (1976: 349): 'e sentì incontanente più aver di forza la natura che il suo ingegno; e pentessi d'avelo menato a Firenze'.

[73] The most complete and compelling discussion of the topic is offered by Baxter (2013).

boy's natural instincts. In fact, while the son does not have the instruments to question his father's reply, he is capable of using language to his favour by sticking to the literal meaning of the metaphor.[74]

Boccaccio's Filippo and Henri's Aristotle share a similar experience: they both face a defeat caused by their reluctance to acknowledge the power of nature. Furthermore, both anecdotes deal with language, in that they both offer a reflection on the various ways in which a moral and behavioural code is imposed through language and subverted by language. They also entail acts of translation and transference of values aimed to soften the rigour of Aristotle's and Filippo's teachings: the philosopher's command of grammar and dialectic, like Filippo's linguistic alteration, eventually surrenders to Nature, whose allegedly naïve language claims to establish a direct connection between words and things. The courtesan's song in the *Lai d'Aristote* and the young man's double entendre about feeding the goslings in Boccaccio's novella are not only the emblem of the language of nature, but also the symbol of the process of appropriation and reshaping through which the vernacular world incorporates and reconstitutes discourses about ethics.

'I, Aristotle, who arranged all moral virtues'

Appropriation and reshaping do not necessarily entail the kind of debasement experienced by Aristotle in the anecdote of the courtesan. If the mounted philosopher is a successful commonplace in poetry, iconography and storytelling, its fortune owes to its being a subversion of another successful trope: the common portrayal of Aristotle as an undisputed philosophical *auctoritas*. This is particularly true when the 'Philosopher' is singled out as the personification of the world's knowledge – for instance, in Dante's depiction of Aristotle in Limbo, as we shall see in Chapter 2 – or as the embodiment of the political ideals foundational to effectively ruled states. Aristotle does not appear in Ambrogio Lorenzetti's *Allegoria ed effetti del Buono e del Cattivo Governo* ('Allegory and Effects of Good and Bad Government', 1338–39) in the Sala de' Nove in the Palazzo Pubblico in Siena, but the cycle is nonetheless significantly informed by the philosopher's teachings.[75] Representing one of the earliest and most ambitious uses of

---

[74] Wallace (1991: 48–52), highlights Filippo Balducci's linguistic function throughout the novella, since it is the father who *names* things in order to explain them to his son.

[75] The bibliography on the possible sources for Lorenzetti's frescos and their cultural implications is wide but see, among others, Rubinstein (1958), Skinner (1986, 1999 and 2002: 39–117), Donato (1988: 1116–32; 1997: 363–76; 2003). While Rubinstein, followed by most scholars, argues for the Aristotelian inspiration of the cycle, Skinner has proposed the Ciceronian tradition as a key source

vernacular inscriptions within a figurative cycle, Lorenzetti's frescoes can moreover be usefully described as a project of translation involving words and images. Indeed, the cycle testifies to an unprecedented attempt to represent political ideas filtered through the medieval reception of classical learning. As suggested by several scholars, the use of inscriptions to complement the meaning of the paintings – a feature that Lorenzetti's frescoes share with Simone Martini's *Maestà* ('Virgin Enthroned', 1315) painted on the wall of the room adjacent to them in the Palazzo Pubblico – marks a turning point in the emancipation of the vernacular.[76] This process goes hand in hand with a marked increase in vernacular translation, which occurs in various forms throughout the fourteenth century.[77]

While Aristotle is not the only author concerned with this process, his role within it is nonetheless critical, for the philosopher, among other sources, inspired the iconographic program of Lorenzetti's frescoes, particularly the praise of the Common Good ('Bene comune') that is at its core. As indicated by Maria Monica Donato's study of political iconography in late medieval art, the relevance of the Aristotelian thread to Lorenzetti's allegory is confirmed *ex post facto* by the cycle of illustrious men painted by Taddeo di Bartolo between 1408 and 1414 in the adjoining hall called *anticappella* ('antechapel').[78] Taddeo's portrayal of Aristotle serves as the keystone to the entire composition, both as a sign of political knowledge and as the incarnation of philosophical authority. In evident dialogue with Lorenzetti's precedent, Aristotle points towards the famous men of the past as examples, both positive and negative, of the fundamental role of civic harmony. As suggested by the many inscriptions that frame the cycle, Aristotle's lesson is clear: without harmony, the city collapses. As recalled above, the inscriptions in both Lorenzetti's *Allegory* and Martini's *Virgin Enthroned* favoured the vernacular, a linguistic choice that exhibits the same ideological implications behind the 1309 translation of the city's statute in the vernacular.[79] Taddeo's cycle instead opts for a bilingual option that outlines a clear linguistic hierarchy strongly

for Lorenzetti's frescos. As suggested by Donato, the Aristotelian and Ciceronian perspectives converge when understood as experiencing a revival, at least within the vernacular context, through works like Brunetto's *Tresor*.

[76] See Donato (1988: 1116–32) and Brugnolo (1997: 316–27).

[77] For an overview of the tradition of the *volgarizzamenti*, see Dionisotti (1967), Folena (1991) and Cornish (2011).

[78] On the cycle by Taddeo di Bartolo, see Rubinstein (1958: 189–207) and Donato (1988: 1117–24, 1154–57).

[79] The Sienese *costituto* was first written in Latin but was translated into Italian at the behest of the city's officials shortly thereafter. It was ruled that one copy of the constitution always be available to the citizens 'in volgare di lettera grossa, bene leggibile et bene formata, in buone carte pecorine …

influenced by the humanist inspiration of the work. Depicted in the garb of a university professor from Taddeo's time, Aristotle addresses the audience in Latin, speaking from his chair [Figure 1.6].[80]

Two Latin inscriptions aim to voice the philosopher's address to his audience. In the first, after having presented himself as a 'student of the causes of things', Aristotle points towards the examples offered by the illustrious men depicted as part of the cycle.[81] In the second inscription, Aristotle mentions his own name ('Magnus Aristoteles ego sum') and refers to his own capacity to inspire virtuous actions.[82] The two Latin inscriptions, which illustrate the meaning of the frescoes by installing the *auctoritas* of the philosopher, feature classically stylised hexameters explicitly imitating Vergil's verse.[83] Yet (and this is where, once again, translation emerges as key to the process I am describing), Taddeo's cycle includes a vernacular sonnet, which summarises the paintings and makes them accessible to observers unschooled in Latin.[84] The choice to have Aristotle speak Latin is connected to the humanist ideals animating the

---

acciocché le povare persone et altre persone che non sanno grammatica, et li altri, e' quali vorranno, possano esso vedere et copia inde trarre et avere a loro volontà' ('in the vernacular, written in large script, easily readable and well shaped, on good quality parchment … so that the poor and those who do not read Latin, and all the others that wish to, can see it and copy it in order to have it at their disposal'); see the text in Lisini (1903: D. I, rub. 134). For an overview of the document and its context, see Giordano and Piccinni (2013) and, more recently, Tylus (2015: 8, 21, 162).

[80] Guerrini (2004: 72–5) recalls that Aristotle is a steady presence in Sienese art, starting with Giovanni Pisano's statue of the philosopher made for the façade of the cathedral; for more details on the iconographic presence of Aristotle in Sienese art, see Guerrini (2003).

[81] Donato (1988: 1155): 'Ille ego, qui rerum causas scrutatus et artes / Publica res docui surgat quibus omnis [in] astra / Exemplum civile tuum, preclara senarum / Urbs, tibi monstro viros, quorum vestigia sacra / Dum sequeris foris atque domi tua Gloria [cre]scet / Libertasque tuos semper servabit honor[es]' ('I am the one who, having explored the causes of things and their making, taught how a State rises towards the heavens: as your civic example, illustrious city of Siena, I show you these men: as long as you follow their sacred footsteps, your glory will increase both in your homeland and abroad, and liberty will always be honoured').

[82] *Ibid.*: 'Magnus Aristoteles ego sum, qui carmine seno, / Est etenim perfectus, duxit ad actum / Quos virtus tibi signo viros, quibus atque superne / Res crevit Romana potens, celosque subivit' ('I am the great Aristotle, the one who, in hexameters – which is, in fact, a perfect kind of verse – point towards the men, whom virtue led to action; thanks to them, Rome increased its power and reached the heavens'). On the relevance of Aristotle to the cycle of illustrious men, see the synthesis offered by Rubinstein (1958: 194): 'It was only fitting that Aristotle should have been chosen to serve as guide to the antechapel; for he provides the link between the philosophical allegory of the Sala de' Nove with its Aristotelian theme and the historical *exempla* of the antechapel. He still appears as the prime teacher of civic philosophy.'

[83] On the Virgilian echo that informs the hexameters, see Guerrini (2003: 37).

[84] For useful remarks on the bilingual dimension of Taddeo di Bartolo's cycle, see Donato (1997: 370–1). As noted by Rubinstein (1958: 193), the Italian sonnet was 'evidently for the benefit of those councillors who might find the Latin hexameters [of Aristotle's inscriptions] too difficult'.

Figure 1.6 Taddeo di Bartolo, Aristotle, Cycle of Illustrious Men (1408–14), Siena, Palazzo Pubblico, Anticappella

cycle and reinstates to some extent the cultural priority of Latin over the vernacular. In contrast, the Italian sonnet functions as a negotiating medium and bridges the gap between viewers who are literate in Latin and those who are not.

A thematically similar cycle painted a few years earlier on the walls of the so-called *Sala di Aristotele* ('Aristotle's hall') at Casa Corboli in Asciano effects a balance between the two linguistic components that instead privileges the vernacular.[85] Completed in the last quarter of the fourteenth century, the anonymous and badly damaged frescoes revolve around the depiction of the cardinal virtues and identify Aristotle as the one who first arranged them. Appearing at the centre of a rather complex composition, Aristotle is depicted as an old man with a long beard, framed by allegories of the cardinal virtues and relevant *exempla* [Figure 1.7].[86]

As is the case with Taddeo di Bartolo's Aristotle, the philosopher holds a scroll that gives him voice. Here, in a context apparently untouched by the dawn of humanism, Aristotle speaks in Italian verses. The scroll reads: 'I, Aristotle, who arranged all the moral virtues, wish for no one to live unrestrained. In fact, men should foster the practice of virtue by imitating those who …'[87] The passage breaks off abruptly, but Aristotle's self-presentation is clear: the philosopher's organisation of the moral virtues, which refers to Aristotle's systematic treatment of virtue in the *Nicomachean Ethics*, provides men and women with a behavioural guide that discourages excess. In the statement 'I wish for no one to live unrestrained', the Italian 'disfrenato' (literally, 'unbridled') draws on the metaphorical lexicon that was at the core of the anecdote of Aristotle mounted and bridled by the courtesan. The idea of controlling one's own instincts is closely connected to the notions of self-restraint and moderation that lay at the core of Aristotle's moral philosophy, especially in its simplified version for readers with no formal education in the discipline. The same connections are evoked in the Asciano frescoes by other inscriptions that turn the cycle into a proper compendium of Aristotelian teachings filtered through Christian values. One sententious pronouncement summarising the message of the cycle, for instance, highlights the importance of moderation and modesty to the welfare of both individuals and society. The first sentence, 'Orgoglio non dura' ('Pride lasts not'), alludes to the pitfalls of pride and to the benefits of humility, a Christian virtue absent from Aristotle's system but redefined by Thomas Aquinas, who gave the Christian concept of humility towards God a civic and earthly flair consistent with Aristotelian morality.[88] The second sentence in the inscription, 'misura non chala' ('moderation wanes not'), refers instead to the Aristotelian concept of μετριότης (in

---

[85] For a thorough study of the cycle at Asciano, see Donato (1988) and, more recently, the discussion of the iconographic program in Wartenberg (2015: 175–238).

[86] Aristotle is surrounded by representations of the virtues (Prudence, Justice, Force, Temperance), each in turn accompanied by one visual example. See the detailed description of the cycle in Donato (1988: 1141–8).

[87] *Ibid.*: 1152: 'Io Aristotile che le vertù morali / conposi tutte con modo ordinato / amo che niun viva disfrenato / ne … ma a le vertù spanda l'ali / prendendo asenpro a quelli che …'.

[88] A recent overview of humility in Thomas Aquinas can be seen in Overmeyer (2015).

Figure 1.7 Anonymous, Aristotle and the cardinal virtues (c. 1375–1400), Asciano, Casa Corboli

Latin, *medietas*), the site of the fulfilment of virtue, which, in Aristotelian terms, is not opposed to vice but situated between two extremes, that is, excess and lack.[89]

The same contamination of sources informs the articulation of the four cardinal virtues surrounding Aristotle as well as other illustrations in the cycle, such as the judgement of Solomon, the dream of Nebuchadnezzar and the wheel of Barlaam.[90] While Aristotle's scroll mentions the 'moral virtues' – as the philosopher defines them in the *Ethics* – the four virtues that appear next to him are immediately recognisable as the 'cardinal virtues' (Prudence, Justice, Force and Temperance) that, through Cicero and Thomas Aquinas, had superseded and assimilated Aristotle's moral virtues. The process of assimilation can be taken as a very good example of the ways in which the basic principles of Aristotle's moral philosophy were adapted by Christian doctrine through the Latin philosophical tradition. While the priority of Justice among the virtues harkens to Aristotle's *Ethics*, the importance of Prudence (which was an intellectual virtue for the Greek philosopher, not a moral one) is the product of Cicero's elaboration of Aristotelian moral thought. All these philosophical threads converge in the inscriptions that give voice to the virtues themselves. In fact, in the Asciano cycle, Aristotle is not the only 'speaking' character, for the personified virtues also explicitly address the viewers. As indicated by Donato's study of the extant textual fragments in the frescoes, each virtue was assigned a stanza from the anonymous *canzone Increata virtù dal sommo cielo* ('Uncreated virtue from the highest heaven').[91] The *canzone* is devoted to the Virtues' lament of political discord, a theme consistent with the political motif of the frescoes in both Asciano and Siena. In a later manuscript copy of the *canzone*, the text was curiously attributed to Dante Alighieri, despite being wholly unrelated to his poetic corpus. Filippo Benci (1419–75) transcribed the text along with other *canzoni* in a miscellaneous manuscript that had belonged to Antonio Pucci,[92] one of the *zibaldoni* ('notebooks') that, as we shall see in the following chapters, offer useful insights into the readership targeted by vernacular translation. *Increata virtù* can be read both as a political statement and as a compendium of the virtues primarily modelled

---

[89] Donato (1988: 1147–8).

[90] For details about the depiction of the judgment of Solomon, see *ibid*.: 1205–14; on Nebuchadnezzar's dream, see *ibid*.: 1222–34; and on the wheel of Barlaam, see *ibid*.: 1235–64.

[91] The *canzone* is discussed *ibid*.: 1179–203; the text of the *canzone* is witnessed in its entirety in MS Florence, Biblioteca Medicea Laurenziana, Laur. Tempi 2, fols. 88*v*–90*r*.

[92] See Varvaro (1957) and Tanturli (1978: 206).

on Aquinas' interpretation of Aristotle. In that respect, it is very similar in tone to Franco Sacchetti's political *canzone* composed in the aftermath of the Ciompi revolt of 1378, itself a poem rich in allusions to Aristotle's ethical and political lexicon.[93] The excerpts from the *canzone* in the Asciano cycle perform the same translating function that characterises the political frescoes in Siena. But while Taddeo di Bartolo's cycle in Siena stands at the intersection of medieval traditions and new humanist trends, the cycle at Asciano presents itself as a genuinely vernacular project closer to the ideals that had inspired Lorenzetti's allegorical masterpiece.[94]

Quite dissimilar in their purposes, the courtesan's song in the *Lai d'Aristote* and the *canzone* of the Virtues in the Asciano cycle nonetheless embody two interrelated functions of the vernacular: namely, those that Dante described in the *De vulgari eloquentia*.[95] Within his articulate defence of the vernacular, Dante defines the *canzone* as the poetic form that is most effective at revealing the expressive potential of the mother tongue. As recalled earlier in this chapter, Dante considered that viable topics for vernacular poets included love and virtue: it can be argued that the courtesan's song illustrates the power of language to express love, whereas the *canzone* at Asciano treats virtue by means of exempla. In both cases, Aristotle, the philosopher par excellence, who for thinkers of the time constituted the highest *auctoritas* of classical antiquity as well as the repository of all knowledge, is made more accessible to an audience that, as Erich Auerbach brilliantly observed, catalysed the new vernacular cultures of Europe.[96] While the appropriation of Aristotle implies various simplifications of his philosophical legacy, it also fosters the selection and appropriation of specific aspects of the Aristotelian tradition that are so relevant to those involved in the nascent vernacular turn. The sixty-eighth novella in the *Novellino*, discussed above, perfectly exemplifies the abridgment that Aristotle's lexicon and ideas face when translated *into* the vernacular *for* vernacular

---

[93] Donato (1988: 1186–7) highlights the similarities between the two poems.
[94] *Ibid.*: 1155–7.
[95] Dante, *De vulgari eloquentia* 2.2.7.
[96] See Auerbach (1965). The definition of a literary public in Auerbach's essay captures the main implications of the phenomenon described here, particularly the fact that the vulgarisation process does not envision a full democratisation of knowledge and culture. In fact, as Auerbach suggests, the very notion of 'literary public' applies to a rather small group of people, 'a social group corresponding to what in modern times is termed the literary public in contrast on the one hand to the great mass of the uneducated and on the other hand to those who made literature and learning their profession' (239). On the notion of 'reading public' in the medieval period, with a particular focus on the production of vernacular literature, see Monfrin (1963, 1964).

audiences. The reduction of Aristotle's notion of *habitus* into a short and rhetorically effective exemplum is far removed from the complexities of the topic as it is discussed in the *Nicomachean Ethics*, but nonetheless manages to capture and express one version of Aristotle's moral philosophy, which the author feels is more apt for his audience. The Aristotelian celebration of virtue and moderation in the painted cycles in Siena and Asciano similarly abridges a nuanced discussion to adapt it to the needs of the time. As such, these forms of translation are effective in making the notions accessible to people traditionally excluded from the consumption of Aristotle's works; they also relate these ideas to contemporary debates over ethics and politics. As I indicate in the next chapter, this process of adaptation explains the wide circulation of vernacular works on moral philosophy, such as Taddeo Alderotti's translation of the *Summa Alexandrinorum*, which Dante criticised in the *Convivio*. By comparing Dante's perspective on issues of language and translation with the popularity of Alderotti's work, it is possible to better recognise the readership that the 'taming' of Aristotle sought to address.

CHAPTER 2

The Master of Those Who Know (and Those Who Don't)

Aristotle in Limbo

While the image of Aristotle ridden by the courtesan offers an ironic portrayal of Alexander's teacher, Dante Alighieri's depiction of Aristotle in Limbo sitting silently, surrounded by his fellow philosophers, restores the intellectual prestige of the 'master of those who know'.[1] Despite obvious differences, the two images share similar preoccupations about the ways in which the philosopher's teachings are brought to lay men and women outside the circles of scholars and clergymen who had exclusive access to the highest levels of culture. But if the author of the *Lai d'Aristote*, with his earlier rewriting of the anecdote of the mounted Aristotle, uses the philosopher's debasement to tame the inflexibility of the moral code extracted from Aristotelian texts, Dante undertakes a project that is perhaps more demanding: that of legitimising in ethical terms the practice of making Aristotle's knowledge available to a vernacular audience. The tension between the philosopher's arguments and the courtesan's song that informs the *Lai d'Aristote* enables a broader discussion, with higher stakes about the need to create linguistic and communicative tools that could make Aristotle conversant with the vernacular.

In Dante's universe, Limbo is the place that best represents antiquity as well as the porous mechanisms of its reception.[2] Indeed, Limbo, the home of virtuous non-Christians and unbaptised infants, is a very peculiar space. It is removed from the harshness of the underworld and, considering the company of souls condemned to stay there, it proves almost pleasant.[3] The soul of the Latin poet Vergil, Dante's guide throughout Hell and Purgatory,

---

[1] Dante, *Inferno*, 4.130–32 (here and thereafter, quotations from Dante's *Divine Comedy* come from Chiavacci Leonardi 1991–97 and English translations come from Hollander 2000, 2003, 2007): 'Poi ch'innalzai un poco più le ciglia, / vidi 'l maestro di color che sanno / seder tra filosofica famiglia' ('When I raised my eyes a little higher, / I saw the master of those who know, / sitting among his philosophic kindred').

[2] On the interaction of translation and reception, see my introduction to this book.

[3] The bibliography on Limbo is too vast to be summarised here but see at least the relevant entry in the *Enciclopedia dantesca*: Montanari (1971). For a recent discussion of Limbo in Dante's *Divine Comedy*,

resides in Limbo because he lived before the revelation of Christ. Limbo is also the place where Dante runs into the other classical poets whom he venerates as poetic models: Homer, Horace, Ovid and Lucan.[4] Dante, with customary modesty, is happy to proclaim himself 'sixth among such intellects' ('sesto tra cotanto senno'), and is ever happier to congratulate himself for not having to join his masters in Limbo after death.[5] But the great poets of the past are not the only inhabitants of Limbo: indeed, the castle where the 'honorable souls' ('spiriti magni') are confined is, so to speak, a multidisciplinary location.[6] The great spirits who embodied virtue before the Christian revelation include heroic and historic figures of various religions and philosophers both male and female, as Giovanni Boccaccio highlights in his commentary on the *Divine Comedy*.[7] Standing out among them, Aristotle is simply referred as 'the Philosopher'. The 'master of those who know' – the most influential philosophical voice of the classical past and an *auctoritas* enduring far beyond the age of Dante, the great thinker whose works were considered the summa of knowledge – need not even be named explicitly.

In the famous Holkham manuscript, an illuminated copy of the *Comedy* made in northern Italy during the third quarter of the fourteenth century now at the Bodleian Library, the iconographic attributes that distinguish the soul of Aristotle from the other souls, all portrayed naked, are his beard and a red hat that recalls the features of academic caps. These attributes conflate the image of the philosopher as a venerable elder with that of the philosopher as a professor [Figure 2.1].[8]

Curiously, the same two attributes characterise the portrayal of Vergil in the illuminations of the same manuscript, in which he also wears a red gown and a purple cloak.[9] The iconography of both Vergil and Aristotle follow common prototypes of the Middle Ages. On one hand, the portrayal of Vergil as a bearded adult (quite different from the depiction of

---

    with a special focus on the theological problems raised by its the pagan residents, see Grzybowski (2015: 111–19).

[4] Dante, *Inferno* 4.85–90.

[5] *Ibid.* 4.102. The importance of this episode has been discussed by, among others, Barolini (1984) and, more recently, Ascoli (2008: 68, 195, 313).

[6] Dante, *Inferno* 4.119.

[7] See the discussion of Boccaccio's presentation of the relationship between women and philosophy in Padoan (1994: 279) and Papio (2009: 251), and in Chapter 1 in this book.

[8] Oxford, Bodleian Library, MS Holkham misc. 48, fol. 7. On the codex, see Rotili (1972: 53–6, 72–7) and De La Mare (1982: 333–4); on the iconography of Limbo in illuminated manuscripts of the *Divine Comedy*, see Brieger, Meiss and Singleton (1969: 121–2, plates 67–78).

[9] The visual characterisation of Vergil is consistent throughout the miniatures in the Holkham Hall manuscript; see, for a clear example, the illustration of canto 2, fol. 2.

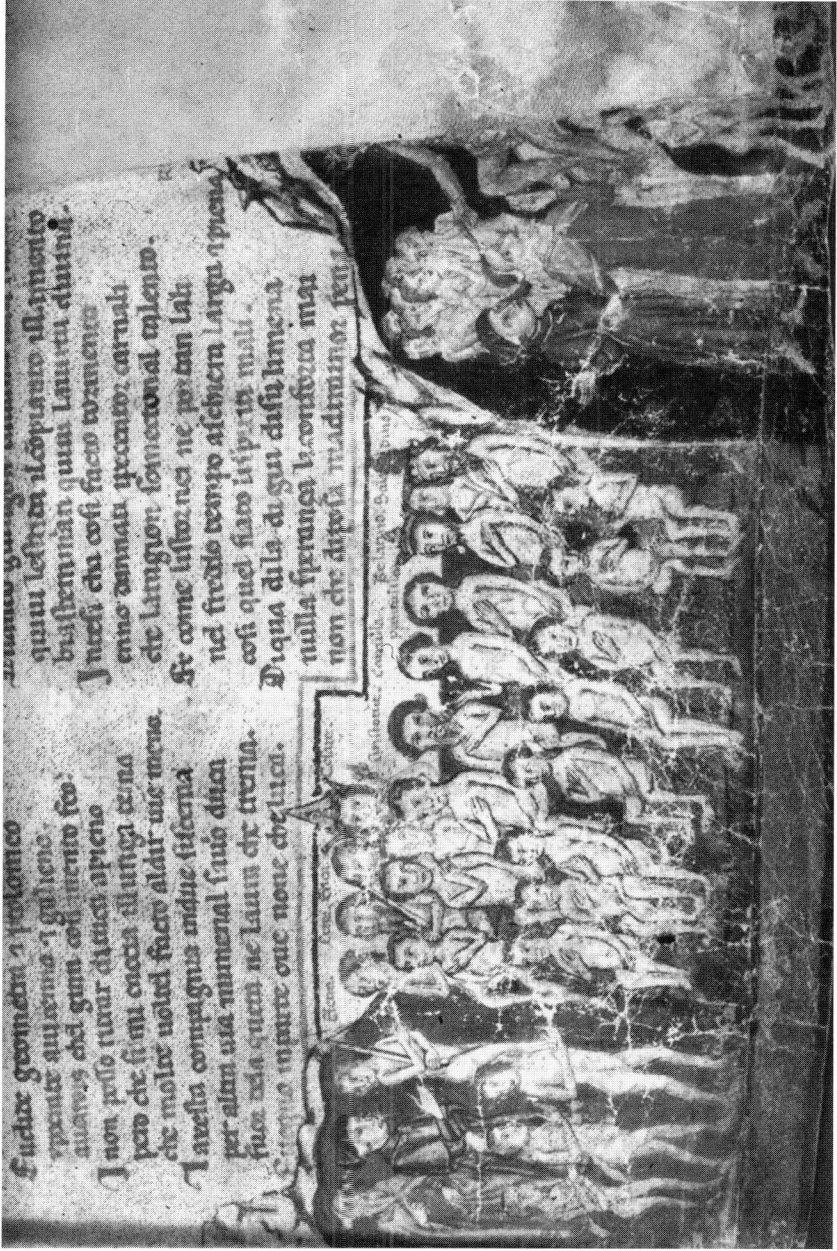

Figure 2.1 Dante, *Commedia*, the Holy Spirits in Limbo. Oxford, Bodleian Library, ms. Holkham misc. 48, p. 7

53

him in his adolescence that had persisted since late antiquity) recalls his identification with a magician.[10] On the other hand, while Aristotle's beard is commonplace in his iconography, the academic cap echoes traditional representations of the philosopher as a scholar, which we find in countless medieval and Renaissance manuscripts of his works.

The two figurations coexist in pictorial representations of the philosopher such as the 'Aristotelian' cycles in Siena and Asciano discussed in Chapter 1. As examples of the process of cultural appropriation that made classical figures more familiar to their medieval readers, the depictions of both Aristotle and Vergil in the Holkham *Comedy* accidentally stress the interconnection between the two characters: these are not only 'honorable souls', but also Dante's guides, although in different ways. While the illuminator's choices do not say much about the relationship of Aristotle and Vergil proposed by the poem, they do offer their own commentary.[11] Though difficult to render through the basic and almost naïve composition of the illustration that packs all the figures in Dante's Limbo tightly next to one another, the observer notices Aristotle's prominent position in the philosopher's likeness to Vergil, a characterisation that invites us to reflect on the functions that the two figures perform in the poem.[12]

Much has been said about the relationship between the pilgrim Dante and his guide Vergil, who, more than a simple chaperone, provides Dante with a model that is at once poetic and philosophical.[13] Dante's familiarity with Vergil and his works must therefore be read as a dialogue that goes far beyond the practice of poetic imitation. A well-known example of Dante's relation to Vergil is the identification of his own work vis-à-vis his model: before reaching Heaven, where the *Comedy* can at last be defined a 'poema sacro' ('sacred poem'), Dante refers to his own work as 'la mia comedìa' ('my comedy'), in respectful contrast to Vergil's poem, the *Aeneid*, which Vergil – through the voice of Dante – calls 'la mia tragedìa' ('my tragedy').[14] Within the fiction of the conversation between the two poets, Dante does not miss the chance to have his deep knowledge of Vergil's

---

[10] For the characterisation of Vergil as a magician, see the second part of Comparetti (1997), and more recently Petrucci (2007).

[11] For a first approach to the wide corpus of illuminated manuscripts of the *Divine Comedy*, see Brieger, Meiss and Singleton (1969); on the illustrations of the poem as a form of commentary, see Battaglia Ricci (2001, 2008) and Zanichelli (2006).

[12] It is worth mentioning that the prominence of Aristotle's position in Limbo is stressed in later illustrations of the scene such as Johannes Stradanus' 1587 cycle; see Biagi (1892).

[13] Ascoli (2008: 301–56).

[14] Dante, *Paradiso*, 25.1; *Inferno*, 21.2; and 20.113. See Casadei (2013: 15–43).

poetry assessed by Vergil himself: 'ben lo sai tu che la sai tutta quanta' ('you know that well enough, who know the whole [of the *Aeneid*]').[15]

Vergil, however, is not the only *auctor* singled out as one of Dante's main sources of inspiration. The other is Aristotle.[16] As with Vergil, Dante's acquaintance with Aristotle's works is suggested by the abundance of Aristotelian sources in the text and by explicit allusions to the poet's own study of Aristotle's works.[17] In canto 11 of *Inferno*, Vergil calls on Dante's Aristotelian education to solve two questions about the moral structure of Hell: the pilgrim is invited to think of what the *Ethics* say about the three main vices and how the *Physics* presents the relationship between human art and nature.[18] The use of the possessive adjective ('la *tua* Etica', 'la *tua* Fisica') is meant to stress Dante's familiarity with two of the philosophical and scientific sources that most contributed to the shaping of his own intellectual project.

As several scholars have observed, while Vergil's mention of the *Physics* is perfectly consistent with the argument developed in the passage, his reference to the *Ethics* is problematic, particularly with regards to the tripartite division of vices according to which the architecture of Hell is

---

[15] Dante, *Inferno*, 20.114. As observed by Francesco da Buti in his commentary on Dante's *Divine Comedy*, the poet here does not display immodesty, since he is not boasting but rather he is telling the truth about his thorough knowledge of Vergil's works: '*Ben lo sai tu*; Dante, che l'alta Tragedia lo nomina così, *che la sai tutta quanta*; ecco che l'autore si dà lodo di sapere tutto l'Eneida di Virgilio che, benchè finga che parli Virgilio, le parole sono pur di Dante; onde molti vorrebbon riprender l'autore che non fece bene ad inducere Virgilio che lodasse la sua opera e lodasse Dante. Et a questo si può rispondere che, quando l'uomo parla per la verità e non per fine di loda, è licito a ciascuno manifestare e dire le sue buone opere' ('*You know that well enough*; Dante, whom the high Tragedy names this way, *who know the whole*; here the author praises himself for his knowledge of Virg's *Aeneid*; indeed, even if he makes Virgil speak, those words are Dante's; for this reason, many would criticise the author for introducing Virgil and making him praise his [i.e. Dante's] work as well as Dante himself. This remark can be replied by saying that when someone speaks the truth and not in order to praise oneself, it is appropriate if they showcase their good works'); I am quoting from Claudia Tardelli's forthcoming edition of Buti's commentary.

[16] On the reasons behind Dante's choice of Vergil rather than Aristotle as his main guide, see the still useful remarks by Comparetti (1997, 256–76).

[17] An overview of the presence of Aristotle in the *Comedy* is offered by De Matteis (1970); for thorough discussions of the ways in which Dante translates passages from the medieval Latin versions of Aristotle into his own works, see Groppi (1966) and Chiamenti (1995).

[18] See Dante, *Inferno*, 11.79–83: 'Non ti rimembra di quelle parole / con le quai la tua Etica pertratta / le tre disposizion che 'l ciel non vole: / incontenenza, malizia e la matta / bestialitade?' ('Do you not recall the words / your *Ethics* uses to expound / the three dispositions Heaven opposes, / incontinence, malice, and mad brutishness'? See also 11.101–4: 'e se tu ben la tua Fisica note, / tu troverai, non dopo molte carte, / che l'arte vostra quella, quanto pote, / segue, come 'l maestro fa 'l discente' ('And, if you study well your *Physics*, / you will find, after not too many pages, / that human toil, as far as it is able, / follows nature, as the pupil does his master').

conceived.[19] If the three terms mentioned by Vergil with respect to the *Ethics* ('incontenenza, malizia e la matta / bestialitade') recall Aristotle's phrasing in the medieval Latin version that Dante would have known ('circa more fugiendorum tres sunt species, malitia, incontinentia et bestialitas'), the real meaning of the third, 'matta bestialitade', is not clear.[20] While Aristotle's *bestialitas* refers to some exceptionally cruel transgression, Dante's 'bestialitade' is likely to refer to the sin of violence, which is punished in the following section of Hell. Therefore, Vergil's allusion to the *Ethics* not only testifies to Dante's Aristotelian expertise, but also exhibits Dante's ability to *translate* Aristotle so as to make classical teachings cohere with the needs of Christian doctrine.

Thanks to its prestigious inhabitants, Limbo proves a veritable goldmine of pre-Christian virtue and knowledge; however, to be mined by Dante's vernacular readers, this self-contained space needs to be brought across, in other words transferred and adapted to a different cultural frame. From this point of view, Dante's project performs the translating function referenced in the previous chapter. As indicated by the early commentators of the *Divine Comedy* as well as its modern editors, the number of classical passages Dante appropriates and reuses is impressive.[21] Aristotle's works (specifically, the Aristotle transmitted by the medieval commentators) feature prominently among them. As Sonia Gentili and Alison Cornish among others stress,[22] however, Dante does not fashion a mere patchwork of Aristotelian quotations translated into the vernacular, but envisions a project that surpasses the translation practices related to the coeval tradition of *volgarizzamenti* ('vernacular translations') of the classics. Indeed, the adaptation at work in the *Comedy* is based on a creative notion of translation that favours the expressive, communicative and poetic potential of the target language. In order to fully grasp Dante's perspective on language and translation, let us first turn to his linguistic reflection and then to his explicit criticism of the translation practices of his time. My argument will be twofold: I will show that Dante's ideas can provide a useful theoretical framework in which to inscribe medieval practices of translation; at the same time, however, the examination of Taddeo Alderotti's Italian translation of the compendium of the *Ethics* known as the *Summa*

[19] For a discussion of the philosophical and theological implications of Dante's reading of Aristotle, see Nardi (1955: 193–207), Mazzoni (1985) and Freccero (1986: 79–90).
[20] Aristotle, *Ethics*, 7.1, 1145a: 'Let us next begin a fresh part of the subject by laying down that the states of moral character to be avoided are of three kinds – Vice, Unrestraint, and Bestiality' (transl. Rackham).
[21] A detailed list of Dante's 'translations' is in Chiamenti (1995).
[22] Gentili (2005: 127–66); Cornish (2011: 126–59).

Alexandrinorum (the manuscript tradition of which will be discussed in the final part of this chapter) strongly suggests that what Dante dismissed as bad translation practices enjoyed a wide dissemination and level of consumption that far exceeded Dante's expectations.

Assessing the Vernacular

While the *Divine Comedy* embodies the ultimate and barely imitable outcome of Dante's linguistic experimentation, the poet's ideas on language and translation had already come to light in previous writings, the *Convivio* ('The Banquet' from 1304 to 1307) and *De vulgari eloquentia* ('On Vernacular Eloquence' from 1304 to 1305). The domestication of Aristotle's philosophical legacy is particularly central to the *Convivio*, often seen as Dante's attempt to write a philosophical encyclopaedia in the vernacular that would challenge the status of Latinate culture.[23] Dante's opinion on the relationship between Latin and the vernacular differed from the most typical approaches of his time. Instead of focusing solely on the assumption of an insuperable qualitative divide between the two, Dante views language through a double lens: he does discuss the ethical and political role of linguistic choices within his own historical context, but also situates his analysis within a larger reflection on the philosophy of language. At the core of both perspectives, respectively represented by the *Convivio* and *De vulgari eloquentia*, is the conscious claim that the vernacular, as opposed to Latin, is the medium that is most natural to humankind.[24] For Dante, the vernacular, the language that we acquire 'by imitating our nurses', deserves both our fullest appreciation and our pledge to enhance its beauty.[25]

Dante's ideas resounded widely in the Renaissance debate concerning the relationship between Latin and the vernacular, particularly in the sixteenth century when the debate influenced concurrent discussions on the actual nature and features of the vernacular, traditionally referred to as *la questione della lingua* ('the controversy on language').[26] In fact, one conflict fed the other and the rise of humanism in the fifteenth century

---

[23] For an introduction to the *Convivio*, see Ascoli (2007); see in particular 52–55 and 62–63 for remarks on Dante's integration of Aristotle. The most exhaustive discussion of Dante's *Convivio* today, with special attention given to its philosophical components, is Fioravanti (2014: 49–51), who rejects the interpretation of the work as an encyclopaedia; Fioravanti stresses instead Dante's attempt to develop a form of vernacular communication based on coeval academic models.

[24] For an overview of Dante's reflection on language, see Fortuna, Gragnolati and Trabant (2010), Tavoni (2013) and, within a discussion of Renaissance culture, Celenza (2018: 4).

[25] Dante, *De vulgari eloquentia* 1.1.2.

[26] A detailed introduction to the *questione della lingua* is found in Marazzini (1993). For a wider discussion of the role played by Dante's writings in the Renaissance debate on language and, specifically,

certainly complicated their relationship. The opposition between Latin and the vernacular that is implicit in Dante's defence of the vulgar tongue transformed into a much larger controversy after the rebirth of classical Latin in Italy. Walking 'in the footsteps of the ancients', most humanists harshly criticised both medieval Latin (which they considered a corruption of Cicero's language) and the vernacular (labelled the language of the illiterates).[27] Yet, paradoxically, Latinate humanism contributed to the progressive appreciation of the vernacular. It was indeed only by challenging common assumptions about the inferiority of the vernacular that the advocates of the *volgare* managed to legitimise its status and use. Also, most of their arguments were built on the same ideas that Dante championed in the early fourteenth century, particularly the notions of naturalism and the vernacular's potential to be a highly sophisticated medium for literature and philosophy.[28]

If it is misleading to read Dante's reflections on language through the lens of later developments in the field, it is undeniable that Dante distanced himself from approaches to the topic that were common in his own time. As Alison Cornish convincingly argues, Dante's approach to translation is to challenge the ideology behind contemporaneous *volgarizzamenti*, which he criticises for their failure to truly commit to develop the vernacular into a proper literary language.[29] Dante's implicit argument is that the *volgarizzamenti* of his time are conceived as merely instrumental and limit their scope to a form of translation that is not concerned with forging and ennobling the *volgare*. In contrast, he argues in both theory and practice that the vernacular can be more than a mere tool for non-Latinate readers. As one would expect, Dante's discussion always concerns the relationship between the vernacular and Latin. In this respect, Dante's argument in the *Convivio* is subtle: while acknowledging the superiority of Latin in terms of nobility, virtue and beauty, Dante provides a philosophical legitimation for his use of the vulgar tongue. Dante presents the *Convivio* as a commentary on his own vernacular *canzoni*, and this justifies in his eyes the use of the vernacular language: indeed, an exposition of the *canzoni* in Latin

---

on the relationship between Latin and Italian, see Refini (2017: 47–50); for a reassessment of the debate within the development of humanist culture, see Celenza (2018: 384–400).

[27] Witt (2000); for a discussion of the somewhat ambiguous position of humanists such as Leonardo Bruni on the status of the vernacular vis-à-vis Latin, see Chapter 4 in this book.

[28] See Mazzocco (1993) and Celenza (2009). Further discussion of this aspect will be offered in Chapter 4.

[29] Cornish (2011: 126–57).

would inevitably create a disproportionate relationship between the text and the critique.[30]

This argument, which is built on logical reasoning, is followed by remarks that lead to a more intuitive reassessment of the cultural values of the vernacular. The vernacular, Dante first explains, speaks to a much larger audience than Latin, which implies that the transmission of knowledge through the vulgar tongue will have a wider impact on society, thereby leading more people to science and virtue.[31] The use of the vulgar tongue, the *Convivo* goes on to argue, is justified by the natural affection we feel for it.[32] While Dante outlines a very personal experience, his arguments invite readers to extrapolate a model applicable to all from this individual account: it is through their conversation in the vernacular, Dante argues, that his parents met, interacted and ultimately enabled his birth. Likewise, it is in the vernacular that Dante began his education. In fact, he first encountered Latin through the vernacular, which thus prepared him for higher forms of knowledge.[33] For these reasons, Dante feels a natural inclination to foster the growth of his mother tongue by ensuring it had the same stability typical of 'grammatical' languages such as Latin.

However, as shown recently by Gianfranco Fioravanti and Maria Luisa Ardizzone, among others, Dante's project goes beyond a generic discussion of language.[34] The commitment to fulfil the expressive potential of the *volgare* corresponds to an agenda in which the transmission of knowledge is fundamental to the 'structural' function that the ruling class is expected to possess in society. Such an agenda is expressed – characteristically, for Dante – in a strictly Aristotelian lexicon that addresses the intersections of language, ethics and politics. Given these social implications, a thorough understanding of the *Convivio* depends on the identification of the work's audience. After criticising the numerous scholars who 'do not acquire learning for its own use but only insofar as through it they may gain money or honor', Dante specifies that he is writing for

> those who because of the world's wicked neglect of good have left literature to those who have changed it from a lady into a whore; and these noble

---

[30] Dante, *Convivio* 1.5.6–7.
[31] *Ibid.* 1.9.2–5.
[32] *Ibid.* 1.10.
[33] *Ibid.* 1.12. Dante's reconstruction of the didactic function exerted by the vernacular within his own education is consistent with the well-documented intermingling of Latin and the vernacular in the teaching practice of Latin in late medieval Florence; see, in particular, Gehl (1993).
[34] Fioravanti (2014: 53); Ardizzone (2016).

persons comprise princes, barons, knights, and many other noble people, not only men but women, of which there are many in this language who know only the vernacular and are not learned.[35]

There are undeniable political undertones in this statement: Dante is here targeting the aristocracy of his time, which stands accused of causing the cultural and political decline of Italy. In doing so, he brings the discussion on language from a purely theoretical context to present-day reality.

From a slightly different perspective, the account of the vernacular in the *De vulgari eloquentia* adds yet another layer to Dante's discussion. The *Convivio*, despite its innovative outcomes, shares the traditional idea of a qualitative divide between Latin and the vernacular. By contrast, the *De vulgari eloquentia* reassesses the relationship between them by affirming the natural and chronological priority of the vernacular.[36] Here Dante offers a largely inaccurate history of the language that allows him to defend the superiority of the vernacular over Latin. According to him, Latin was an artificial language created in order to cope with the progressive and unavoidable evolution of the natural ones. This idea remained central throughout the fifteenth and the sixteenth centuries in discussions about the relationship between Latin and the vernacular. The critical assumption that a form of diglossia occurred as early as in antiquity, where a grammatical Latin coexisted with a non-grammatical language no different from the vernacular of Dante, would later be used by certain humanists to support the priority of Latin.[37] However, Dante's views were quite different: instead of opposing the grammatical Latin to a non-grammatical vernacular, he defended the idea that the vernacular was not only more natural to humankind, but that it could acquire the status of a grammatical language. It is in fact through *art* (i.e., through the obedience and manipulation of artistic rules) that a 'natural' language like Italian (i.e., a language spontaneously learned by children at their youngest age) can be granted the status of the so-called *locutiones regulatae* (i.e., languages structured according to grammatical rules).

---

[35] Dante, *Convivio* 1.9.5: 'coloro che per malvagia disusanza del mondo hanno lasciata la litteratura a coloro che l'hanno fatta di donna meretrice; e questi nobili sono principi, baroni, cavalieri, e molt'altra nobile gente, non solamente maschi ma femmine, che sono molti e molte in questa lingua, volgari e non litterati'.

[36] Dante, *De vulgari eloquentia* 1.1.1–3 and 1.9.6–11. Dante's well-known reassessment of the values of the vernacular culminates in *Paradiso* 26.124–32 with the speech by Adam, the first man, who explains that his language was indeed a vernacular, meaning a natural language subject to change and evolution. For a discussion of Dante's Adam, see Corrado (2010).

[37] Tavoni (1984).

Even if it is true that, by endeavouring to identify an 'ideal' Italian vernacular, Dante quickly retreats from the 'natural' to the 'artificial', his premise is nonetheless revolutionary, and doubly so.[38] First, he consciously applies the notion of eloquence to the *volgare*, acknowledging that vernacular eloquence is 'necessary to everyone – for not only men, but also women and children strive to acquire it, as far as nature allows'.[39] As such, vernacular eloquence demands development, so that speakers can benefit from their communication skills. Second, and perhaps more importantly, Dante provides a definition of *vulgaris locutio* that uses the opposition between nature and art to argue that the vernacular is superior to Latin, precisely because it is natural to mankind. (As we have seen in Chapter 1, the same opposition was central to the *Lai d'Aristote* and Boccaccio's reflection on language, particularly in the novella of Filippo Balducci.) Dante thus identifies 'vernacular language' as

> that which infants acquire from those around them when they first begin to distinguish sounds; or, to put it more succinctly, I declare that vernacular language is that which we learn without *any formal instruction*, by imitating our nurses. There also exists another kind of language, at one remove from us, which the Romans called grammar ['grammatica'] … Few, however, achieve complete fluency in it, since knowledge of its rules and theory can only be developed through dedication to a lengthy course of study. Of these two kinds of language, the more noble is the vernacular: first, because it was the language originally used by the human race; second, because the whole world employs it, though with different pronunciations and using different words; and third because *it is natural to us, while the other is, in contrast, artificial* [emphasis mine].[40]

Thus *grammatica* is the result of 'formal instruction' and is therefore limited to those who enjoy the opportunity to study it, whereas the vernacular is the language to which we are all naturally exposed. This makes the

---

[38] For a recent discussion of the relationship between art and nature in Dante's works, see O'Connell and Petrie (2013).

[39] Dante, *De vulgari eloquentia* 1.1.1: 'talem scilicet eloquentiam penitus omnibus necessariam videamus, cum ad eam non tantum viri sed etiam mulieres et parvuli nitantur, in quantum natura permictit'.

[40] *Ibid.* 1.1.2–4: 'vulgarem locutionem appellamus eam quam infantes adsuefiunt ab adsistentibus, cum primitus distinguere voces incipiunt; vel quod brevius dici potest, vulgarem locutionem asserimus, quam sine omni regula, nutricem mitantes, accipimus. Est et inde alia locutio secundaria nobis, quam Romani gramaticam vocaverunt … [A]d habitum vero huius pauci perveniunt, quia non nisi per spatium temporis et studii assiduitatem regulamur et doctrinamur in illa. Harum quoque duarum nobilior est vulgaris: tum quia prima fuit humano generi usitata; tum quia totus orbis ipsa perfruitur, licet in diversas prolationes et vocabula sit divisa; tum quia naturalis est nobis, cum illa potius artificialis existat.'

vernacular more *nobile* (which, in this context, means essential to human nature) than the *grammatica*. As has been noted before, this argument seems to contradict what Dante said in the *Convivio*, where he recognised the superiority of Latin. However, this contradiction is only apparent and should instead be understood as a shift of emphasis reflecting the universal tension between natural language and the artifice needed to make any language eloquent. The nobility of the vernacular is in fact grounded in ontology (that is, in its being the 'natural' linguistic option for any speaker), an argument that preserves regulated languages like Latin as models in the establishment and progressive refinement of vernacular literacy itself. Despite the convolution of the argument, Dante's effort to reflect critically on the uses of the vernacular and provide a theory of the vernacular language marks a turning point in the history of the relationship between Latin and the vernacular. Dante is also the first to put his theory into practice by producing a fully developed work of vernacular literature, the *Divine Comedy*, which at once incorporates classical models and supersedes them by making use of the vernacular as a sophisticated, complex literary language.

'All men by nature desire to know'

Without diminishing the strictly linguistic aspects of Dante's reflection on language, the element of it that is most relevant to this study is its ethical dimension, developed throughout the *Convivio* explicitly under the aegis of Aristotle.[41] The philosopher is in fact the primary inspiration behind the work, not only in its subject matter, but also, and more importantly, in its intellectual premises and purpose. If, in the *Divine Comedy*, Aristotle is named 'the master of those who know', the *Convivio* opens by recalling that knowledge is indeed naturally desired by all human beings: 'As the Philosopher says at the beginning of the *First Philosophy*, all men by nature desire to know.'[42] The statement is a literal quotation from the very beginning of Aristotle's *Metaphysics* ('All men by nature desire to know').[43] As has been duly noted by modern students of the *Convivio*, the same quotation was a commonplace in the scholastic Aristotelian commentary tradition.[44]

---

[41] For a recent discussion of the philosophical frame of Dante's *Convivio*, including its Aristotelian components, see Ardizzone (2016).
[42] Dante, *Convivio* I.I.I: 'Sì come dice lo Filosofo nel principio della Prima Filosofia, tutti li uomini naturalmente desiderano di sapere.'
[43] Aristotle, *Metaphysics* 980a 21.
[44] See the references collected by Fioravanti (2014: 93–5).

Worth highlighting, however, is Dante's translation of a commonplacing Latin academic practice into his vernacular writing. He thus embarks on a project that goes well beyond contemporary ideas about translation (e.g., the ones that informed the practice of *volgarizzamento*) and entails an attempt to create a linguistic space for scientific and philosophical literature in the vernacular. In fact, if it is true that everyone instinctively desires knowledge, it is just as true that knowledge cannot be acquired without language.

In the situation described by Dante at the beginning of the *Convivio*, though, knowledge is possessed by a small group of people, the privileged diners seated 'at the table where the bread of the angels is eaten'.[45] Dante explains that 'many are, however, deprived of this most noble perfection by various causes within and outside of man which remove him from the habit of knowledge'.[46] Internal causes (or *impedimenta*, as per the lexicon of scholastic philosophy) include both bodily imperfections that impede learning and that are therefore excusable as well as defects of the soul – namely, wickedness – that deserve reproach. External causes can involve domestic and civic responsibilities, excusable due to their necessity but also reprehensible indolence, often caused by environmental factors. Dante is not saying anything new: the *impedimenta* argument was another commonplace in the medieval exegesis of Aristotle. However, what is new are the linguistic implications of the argument.[47] Indeed, by applying the argument to the vernacular language and culture in general, Dante reveals the linguistic gap between literate readers and 'illiterate' speakers without access to the exclusive world of Latinate learning.

Though Dante does not sit at the 'blessed table', he does see himself, after having 'fled the pasture of the common herd', gathering up 'a part of what falls to the feet of those who do sit there'.[48] Remembering 'the unfortunate life' lived by those he left behind and being 'moved by compassion', the speaker of the *Convivio* wishes to share with his vernacular readers the 'meal' he has set aside: this 'meal' is a series of *canzoni* about love and virtue, two of the topics that are indicated as viable for vernacular poetry

---

[45] Dante, *Convivio* i.i.7: 'Oh beati quelli pochi che seggiono a quella mensa dove lo pane delli angeli si manuca!'

[46] *Ibid.* i.i.2: 'Veramente da questa nobilissima perfezione molti sono privati per diverse cagioni, che dentro a l'uomo e di fuori da esso lui rimovono da l'abito di scienza.'

[47] For examples of other uses of the *impedimenta* argument in the Aristotelian commentary tradition, see Fioravanti (2014: 95–7).

[48] Dante, *Convivio* i.i.10: 'E io adunque, che non seggio alla beata mensa, ma, fuggito della pastura del vulgo, a' piedi di coloro che seggiono ricolgo di quello che da loro cade.'

in the *De vulgari eloquentia*, as we saw in Chapter 1.[49] Dante is thus ready 'to set their table' and 'present to all men a banquet' of meat and bread.[50] The metaphor casts the text of Dante's own *canzoni* as the meat of the banquet, while the bread is the author's own commentary. In that respect, Dante acts as the intermediary between the crumbs of knowledge he has gathered from the learned men and the would-be diners that constitute his non-Latinate audience.

Upon further inspection, Dante's mediation proves double, for he translates classical knowledge into his vernacular poetry and, at the same time, unveils its meaning through his own vernacular commentary. Indeed, as the author himself says, while the appeal of the *canzoni* derives in part from their poetic beauty, the reader's grasp of their philosophical content requires a further process of translation in a non-lyrical form (where 'translation' means 'cultural translation'). Dante's project of vulgarisation thus proves much more ambitious than the typical *volgarizzamenti* of his time. While *volgarizzamenti* aimed to reproduce (or, in other words, to stand for) the texts that they were translating, the *Convivio* provides its readers with the original text of the *canzoni* and a line-by-line explanation that appropriates and replaces the sources of Dante's knowledge. This is not to say that Dante has little concern with acknowledging his sources. In fact, evidence suggests that he is particularly careful to declare the *auctoritates* on which he bases his arguments. What Dante is operating here is a form of transfer that sets him apart from contemporaneous *volgarizzamenti*. Rather than merely transferring knowledge from one language to another, the process enacted by Dante effectively creates a new linguistic space for the transmission of knowledge.

It would be anachronistic to talk of a democratisation of culture here. However, the scope of Dante's project is revolutionary, for it stresses the ethical and political implications of the Aristotelian statement that people naturally desire to know. It is important at this point to have a closer look at Dante's targeted audience in the *Convivio*, for, as we will see, this gives us some insight into the political and ethical implications of his linguistic project.[51] According to Dante, the noble men and women who have

---

[49] *Ibid.* 1.1.10: 'conosco la misera vita di quelli che dietro m'ho lasciati, per la dolcezza ch'io sento in quello che a poco a poco ricolgo, misericordievolmente mosso, non me dimenticando, per li miseri alcuna cosa ho riservata'. Compare *De vulgari eloquentia* 2.2.7.

[50] Dante, *Convivio* 1.1.11: 'intendo fare un generale convivio di ciò ch'i' ho loro mostrato, e di quello pane ch'è mestiere a così fatta vivanda, senza lo quale da loro non potrebbe essere mangiata'.

[51] *Ibid.* 1.9.5.

been invited to regain control over culture should commit themselves to making the treasures of knowledge fruitful once more, for the material and intellectual avarice of scholars has made them of little use. As Dante himself suggests, the primary benefit envisioned by this work is that its noble readers will be led 'to knowledge and virtue'. (Dante will return to nobility in the fourth book of the *Convivio*, which is comprised entirely of a thorough discussion of the concept.)[52] The realisation of this potential is not the acquisition of knowledge per se but, first and foremost, the restoration of a social and political lay elite able to apply philosophical teachings for the good of the wider community they have been called to lead.[53] A project of this kind, as part of the author's broader political reflection, makes Dante a 'master of those who know' in his own right, thus highlighting his function as a mediator.

This project recalls various assumptions about the education of the ruling classes addressed by Giles of Rome (c. 1245–1316) in his treatise *De regimine principum* ('On the Rule of Princes') only a few decades before the composition of the *Convivio*.[54] As I have recalled in my introduction to this study, the work was written in Latin for the young prince Philip of France, the future king Philip the Fair, between 1277 and 1280. The treatise was soon widely read throughout Europe, and hundreds of manuscript copies confirm its reception well beyond the boundaries of Latinate culture. In fact, by 1282, Giles' treatise was already translated into French and, not long after, into Italian: the earliest Italian translation (a Sienese manuscript indicated as a possible source for Lorenzetti's frescoes in the Palazzo Pubblico) bears the date 1288.[55] The circulation of vernacular editions of *De regimine principum* was not as wide as that of its Latin counterpart, but it nonetheless indicates the relevance of Giles' own thoughts about the language skills of his intended audience. In a fascinating chapter on the role of the liberal arts in education for rulers-in-training, Giles explains that, while it is advisable for a prince to master

---

[52] *Ibid.* 1.9.7: 'Lo dono veramente di questo comento è la sentenza de le canzoni a le quali fatto è, la qual massimamente intende inducere li uomini a scienza e a vertù, sì come si vedrà per lo pelago del loro trattato.'

[53] Boccaccio betrays a similar concern with morality and, specifically, the restoration of society in Aristotelian terms; see, most recently, Migiel (2015).

[54] On Giles' *De regimine principum*, one of the most successful political treatises of the European Middle Ages, see Kempshall (1999) and Briggs (1999).

[55] Rubinstein (1958: 183). The Italian translation of Giles' *De regimine principum* has been the object of thorough study in recent years; see Papi (2015, 2016a); and Fiammetta Papi's recent critical edition *Il 'Libro del Governamento dei re e de' principi'* (2016b).

all seven disciplines (grammar, logic, rhetoric, music, arithmetic, geometry and astronomy), such a study would demand much energy and time. Princes should thus focus on the arts most vital to their future obligations as rulers: moral philosophy, divided according to the Aristotelian tradition into ethics, economics and politics. To be able to rule over their subjects, rulers must be well versed in the government of themselves and their families. Even if the ideal 'mirrors of princes' should include a good knowledge of the liberal arts, Giles acknowledges that future rulers have little time for liberal education, introducing an argument about domestic and civic responsibility that, as we have seen, Dante will endorse in the *Convivio*, more precisely in his discussion of the *impedimenta* that prevent men from learning.[56]

Assuming that moral philosophy comes first, Giles suggests that a prince with time constraints should be content with merely a basic understanding of the liberal arts. That said, if a young nobleman is poor in grammar and lacks sufficient Latin, he may recur to vernacular translations to acquire his philosophical instruction:

> If it happens that the sons of the noblemen do not have any Latin, they need to have the moral sciences translated into French or Italian, or into any other language so as to let them learn how to rule over themselves and others.[57]

Giles' statement clearly illustrates a situation that was far from sporadic, a situation in which even cultivated elites were gradually preferring to read in their mother tongue rather than in Latin.[58] In other words, vernacular translations served the needs of a social class that, as outlined by Dante in the *Convivio*, was becoming increasingly more distant from the realm of Latin learning. It should be noted, however, that Giles considered this process of vernacularisation as an inevitable compromise dictated by the social needs of his time. For Dante, in contrast, the vernacular translation and appropriation of culture is a necessary process to ensure happiness, virtue and political harmony.

---

[56] This argument is absolutely commonplace in the tradition of compendia, not only in the Middle Ages but also in later periods, as was recently pointed out by Lines (2015).

[57] My translation; I am referring to the passage in the 1288 Italian translation of the *De regimine principum*; see the text in Papi (2016b: 442): 'Et sed elli aviene che i filliuoli dei gentili uomini no(n) sapessero gramaticha, ellino debbono avere le sciençe morali volghariçate o in fra[n]ciesco o in latino o i(n)n alchuno altro linguagio acciò ch'ellino sieno ssufficientem(en)te entrodocti a ssap(er) e ghovernare loro (e)d altrui.'

[58] On the specific case of the vernacular dissemination of Giles of Rome's *De regimine principum*, see my introduction 7–11.

Disfiguring the Philosopher

The vernacularisation of moral philosophy mentioned by Giles as a possible shortcut for those unable to undertake the study of Latin is similar to the kind of vernacularisation Dante criticises in the *Convivio* when referring to the translation of the *Ethics* by Taddeo Alderotti, a Florentine professor of medicine at the University of Bologna.[59] There Dante explains that one of his reasons for not choosing Latin for the commentary on his *canzoni* was the fear that it would have been poorly translated into the vernacular by someone else, clearly alluding to the poor quality of coeval *volgarizzamenti*:

> Thinking, therefore, that the desire to understand these *canzoni* would have induced some unlearned person to have the Latin commentary translated into the vernacular, and fearing that the vernacular might have been set down by someone who would have made it seem offensive, as did the one who translated [*transmutò*] the *Ethics* from Latin – and that was Thaddeus the Hippocratist – I arranged to set it down, trusting in myself more than in another.[60]

According to Dante, the translator disfigured the Latin text of the *Ethics* by translating it into a linguistically poor form of vernacular. The statement has been of the utmost interest to modern scholars, because it attests to the early reception of Taddeo Alderotti's vernacular translation of the *Summa Alexandrinorum*, possibly the most popular compendium of Aristotle's *Ethics* and one that circulated through the late Middle Ages and well into the early modern period. Translated into Latin by Herman the German in the 1240s from a now lost Arabic version, the *Summa* was itself translated into Italian by Alderotti around 1260 and circulated under the title *L'Etica d'Aristotile* ('Aristotle's Ethics'). As mentioned in Chapter 1, the text reappeared in French as part of Brunetto Latini's *Tresor*, written during the author's exile in France between 1260 and 1266 (more precisely, Brunetto's French version of the *Summa*, entitled *L'Ethique d'Aristote*, appears at the beginning of book 2 of the *Tresor*). Upon its translation into Italian soon after, the *Tresor* further intermingled with the manuscript transmission of Alderotti's version of the *Summa* and contributed to the vernacular

---

[59] On Alderotti's biography and scholarly profile, see Belloni and Vergnano (1960) and Siraisi (1981).
[60] Dante, *Convivio*, 1.10.10 'Onde, pensando che lo desiderio d'intendere queste canzoni, [a] alcuno illitterato avrebbe fatto lo comento latino transmutare in volgare, e temendo che 'l volgare non fosse stato posto per alcuno che l'avesse laido fatto parere, come fece quelli che transmutò lo latino dell'Etica – ciò fue Taddeo ipocratista –, providi a ponere lui, fidandomi di me di più che d'un altro.'

spread of Aristotelian ethics that informed the civic culture of the Italian communes.[61]

Dante's phrasing ('as did the one who translated the *Ethics* from Latin – and that was Thaddeus the Hippocratist') is somewhat ambiguous: it seems to suggest that Taddeo Alderotti translated Aristotle's *Nicomachean Ethics*. Given Dante's familiarity with Aristotle's treatise through the Latin version circulating in the Middle Ages, he could not have possibly considered Alderotti's as a straightforward translation of Aristotle's *Nicomachean Ethics*: in fact, Alderotti's text is much shorter than the *Ethics* and it omits many speculative sections of Aristotle's treatise, thus making it more legible than the original. This apparent inconsistency might suggest that Dante did not realise that Alderotti was translating from Herman's Latin version of the *Summa* (i.e., a compendium of Aristotle's *Ethics*) rather than from a proper Latin translation of Aristotle's treatise. Dante's negative judgement thus seems to be based not only on the style of Alderotti's text, but also on its character in general. After all, as remarked by Sonia Gentili, the quality of Taddeo Alderotti's translation, when compared to its original source, is not bad at all, and the translator even refers to Aristotle's *Ethics* directly when the text of the *Summa* is problematic.[62] What Dante criticises is instead the very rationale of Alderotti's work, the idea itself of transferring a given text into another language with no ambition to enhance the target idiom. While the asperities of Aristotle's *Ethics* are doubly 'tamed' by Taddeo's version of the *Summa* – the *Ethics* is shortened and, through translation, its language is made familiar to the vernacular audience – Dante challenges the strategy of domestication that informs the *volgarizzamento*. Of course, it would be misleading to argue that Dante's implicit ideas on translation reveal a philological approach to the past, where the translator aims to go back to the supposed 'original'.[63] Rather, what distinguishes his project from the translation practices of his time, usually aimed at bringing the source text into their present, is his focus on the creative processes of appropriation. Dante does not simply aim to make Aristotle available to the vernacular audience, but rather attempts to provide his non-Latinate readers with the tools to enrich their own language and culture.

Dante's approach to the problem of translation, however, remains exceptional. While the unfinished *Convivio* did not manage to reach

---

[61] Gentili (2005: 41–9). Cf. Chapter 1, 18–21.
[62] Gentili (2015).
[63] On the problematic nature of similar tropes about translation, see my introduction to this book, particularly 4 and 13.

Dante's intended audience ('princes, barons, knights and many other noble people, not only men but women'), the vernacular compendium of the *Ethics* that Dante despised in fact proved extremely successful, as suggested by its abundant and complex textual tradition. As indicated by Concetto Marchesi in his still invaluable contributions on the Latin and vernacular circulation of Aristotle's *Ethics* in the Middle Ages, the dissemination of Taddeo Alderotti's translation of the *Summa* cannot be properly acknowledged without considering its contamination by the transmission of Brunetto's *Tresor*, both the original French text and its later Italian version commonly known as the *Tesoro volgare*.[64] As Sonia Gentili has recently and convincingly reconstructed, the most likely relationship between these texts suggests the chronological priority of Alderotti's Italian translation of the *Summa Alexandrinorum*, which would thus be the source of Brunetto Latini's French version.[65] Yet, Gentili points out, both Alderotti and Latini take a rather flexible approach to the practice of translation, not opposed to the intermingling of different sources.

The relationship between the two vernacular versions of the compendium (Italian and French) is further complicated by the fact that Alderotti's text reappears as part of the anonymous late thirteenth-century Italian translation of the *Tresor* long attributed to Bono Giamboni. The complexity of the manuscript tradition of Brunetto's *Tresor*, which, both in French and in Italian, includes complete and incomplete versions as well as indirect witnesses, forms two main channels along which the vernacular translation of the *Summa* is transmitted. The first channel is the group of forty-five manuscripts that present the *Summa* autonomously, fourteen of which attribute the translation to 'magistro Taddeo' (i.e., Taddeo Alderotti). The second track comprises manuscripts where the text is related to Brunetto Latini, either in copies of the *Tesoro volgare* or in the thirty or so manuscripts in which the standalone *Summa* is presented as a part of (or an extract from) the *Tesoro*. The interconnection between the two tracks is confirmed by some witnesses of the second group that preserve Taddeo's name in the colophon at the end of the *Ethics* section.

With such an intricate textual transmission, further complicated by the production of several printed editions from the late fifteenth century onwards, many philological questions remain open, and the production of a critical edition based on the whole of the tradition seems beyond reach,

[64] Marchesi (1904).
[65] Gentili (2005: 27–49); the argument s further substantiated in Gentili (2015).

at least for the moment.[66] The study of the manuscript tradition nonetheless offers valuable insights into the success of the *Summa*. As I will show in the next section of this chapter, study of the material history of this text and investigations of the many traces left by scribes, illuminators, patrons and owners offer a sense of the reading public who consumed works of this kind. They also contribute to better situate Dante's somewhat exceptional position in the history of vernacular translation. Indeed, given that Dante shapes his own ideas about language and translation in the *Convivio* as a criticism of works such as Taddeo Alderotti's, the circulation of the vernacular *Summa* helps assess the actual reading preferences and habits of the vernacular audience that Dante himself was targeting.

An Aristotelian Bestseller and its Readers

Over more than two centuries, dozens of copies of Taddeo's translation of the *Summa Alexandrinorum* were made, thus providing us with an extraordinary range of materials to explore: my own list of witnesses currently counts seventy-five manuscripts. Spanning from approximately 1300 to 1568, when the text came to be printed under the name of Brunetto Latini, the textual transmission of the *Summa* challenges common assumptions about the allegedly linear development of humanism.[67] A typical product of medieval culture, the work passed through a variety of audiences and, as we shall see, proved particularly successful in contexts that underwent the humanist turn, intermingling with the Renaissance rediscovery of the 'true' Aristotle.

Notable among the earliest copies of Alderotti's translation of the *Summa Alexandrinorum* is MS Banco Rari 220, now in the Biblioteca Nazionale Centrale in Florence. Copied in 1339 by a scribe named 'Sander', the volume was commissioned by Giovanni di Messer Lapo Arnolfi.[68] Arnolfi

---

[66] As a matter of fact, Sonia Gentili's forthcoming edition of Taddeo's compendium is based on a single manuscript. On this editorial choice, see Gentili (2015). The text of the compendium was printed twice in the sixteenth century, first in 1538 as part of an Aristotelian collection edited by the understudied Giovanni Manenti (this edition also included the *Secret of Secrets* and the *Physiognomy*) and then in the 1568 printing by Jean de Tournes in Lyon, which attributed the text to Brunetto Latini and dedicated it to the Florentine aristocrat Vincenzo Magalotti. See Manenti (1538) and Latini (1568). For biography on Manenti, see Pattini (2007).

[67] In the edition Latini (1568), the work is given as a compendium of the *Ethics* authored by Brunetto, not as a translation.

[68] On Florence, Biblioteca Nazionale Centrale, MS Banco Rari 220, dated 1339, see Marchesi (1903: 65), Kristeller (1963–1997 vol. 1: 176), Bertelli (2002: 113), Gentili (2005: 32) and Pelle, Russo, Speranzi and Zamponi (2011: 59–60). Details about the scribe and its patron and owner are on fol. 22*v*: 'Sander me scrissit // Giovanni di messere Lapo Arnolfi lo fece scrivere. Conpiesi di scrivere

belonged to the Florentine aristocracy and took an active part in the civic life of the city (his family was also actively involved in banking).[69] His name is recorded as the 'gonfaloniere di giustizia' from 1332 to 1333, just a few years before the manuscript was produced; the name of Giovanni Arnolfi reappears in 1346 among the four patricians elected to join a judicial review commission.[70] Written in *littera textualis* ('bookhand') and elegantly decorated, the manuscript is the prototype of the philosophical volumes that members of the Florentine elite sought for their private libraries. The codex includes no other works: the *Summa* is meant to stand on its own as a sort of epitome of the values that, at least in theory, informed the culture and political views of the ruling class.

Other copies of Alderotti's work follow the same pattern as Arnolfi's. When manuscripts do not make any mention of scribes and owners, features such as format and script can give us precious information about the provenance of the piece: this is the case, among others, of MS Codex 273 at the University of Pennsylvania,[71] and MS Ashb. 955 at the Biblioteca Medicea Laurenziana in Florence, both copies written in *littera textualis* and decorated.[72] In spite of occasional misleading or even erroneous information about the text – as is the case with MS Pal. 634 of the Biblioteca Nazionale of Florence, where the translation is attributed to a Giovanni Minorita[73] – material details such as script and ductus suggest that most of these copies come from similar contexts, thus illuminating the social dimension of the text's circulation.

Manuscripts of both the standalone vernacular *Summa* (usually bearing the title *Etica d'Aristotile*) and Brunetto Latini's *Tesoro volgare* produced in the decades around 1300, for instance, are frequently copied in *littera textualis*. One scribe, the Pisan Bondì Testari, copied out the *Tesoro* during

---

martedì dì XXII di giugno anno MCCCXXXVIIII°' ('Sander wrote me // Giovanni of messere Lapo Arnolfi had him write. Writing was finished on Tuesday, June 22nd 1339'). Another copy of the work written by the same scribe is Florence, Biblioteca Nazionale Centrale, MS Magl. XII.57, from the fourteenth century; the note 'Sander me scrissit' ('Sander wrote me') appears here on fol. 26r. On this manuscript see Marchesi (1903: 65), Bertelli (2002: 133) and Gentili (2005: 32).

[69] Brucker (1962: 126–7).

[70] Rodolico (1955: 175), Brucker (1962: 107), Najemy (1982: 161) and Pelle, Russo, Speranzi and Zamponi (2011: 60).

[71] On Philadelphia, University of Pennsylvania Library, MS Codex 273, dated to before 1356, see Zacour and Hirsch (1965: 98). Curiously, MS Codex 273 includes a list of the electors who vote for the emperor, an addition totally unrelated to the *Summa* that also appears in MS Magl. XII.57 and thus seems to indicate a relationship between the two manuscripts.

[72] On Florence, Biblioteca Medicea Laurenziana, MS Laur. Ashb. 955, from the fourteenth century, see Cecioni (1889: 73) and Marchesi (1903: 65).

[73] On Florence, Biblioteca Nazionale Centrale, MS Pal. 634, from the fourteenth century, see Gentile (1889–99 vol. 2: 202–3) and Bertelli (2002: 162).

his stay in Genoa as a prisoner after the Battle of Meloria, when Pisa was defeated by the Republic of Genoa. This beautiful codex (MS Plut. 42.23 now in the Biblioteca Medicea Laurenziana), decorated with illuminated initials, is clearly a deluxe product and is consistent with the rather common execution of scribal work from prison.[74] The layout of this kind of volume, usually arranged in two columns, as well as the large format, recall the features of contemporaneous university books (the so-called *libri da banco*),[75] exemplified by MS 1538 of the Biblioteca Riccardiana of Florence, copied by Berto de' Bianchi in the early fourteenth century.[76] As pointed out by scholars of medieval miniatures, the decoration of this manuscript conforms to the illuminations produced in Bologna, and the script has also been connected to Bolognese scribal culture. Explicit reference to the university context, furthermore, is found in the colophon of one of the many vernacular works included in Berto's manuscript compilation.[77] The name 'Bertus de Blanchis' also appears in a document from 1332 to 1333 related to the University of Bologna, seemingly confirming the link between the manuscript and the milieu of the local university, a detail that indicates the osmosis between the Latinate world of scholarship and vernacular reading practices.[78]

MS Ricc. 1538 is a varied miscellany of vernacular works, including several *volgarizzamenti*.[79] The *Ethics* here features alongside the *Fatti dei*

---

[74] On Florence, Biblioteca Medicea Laurenziana, MS Plut. 42.23, datable to between 1287–99, see Marchesi (1903: 70–1), Bertelli (2008: 231–2; 2011: 66, 101). Bondì's name appears at fol. 147r: 'Bondì pisano mi scrisse / Dio lo benedisse, / Testario sopranome. / Dio lo chavi di Gienova di pregione, / (e) allui (e) a li autri che vi sono, / (e) da Dio abiano benisione. Amen, amen' ('Bondì of Pisa wrote me, / God blessed him, / Testario [is] his nickname. / May God free him from prison in Genoa / both himself and the others who are there, / may they be blessed by God. Amen, amen'). On the decoration of the manuscript, see Roux (2009: 102). On the practice of copying manuscripts in prison, see Meneghetti (1992) and Cursi (2009); for particular reference to Genoa and Bondì Testari, see Cambi (2015: 159–60).

[75] Petrucci (1969).

[76] On Florence, Biblioteca Riccardiana, MS Ricc. 1538, from the fourteenth century, see Marchesi (1903: 66), Morpurgo (1900: 533–8), Muzzioli (1954: 135), *Mostra di codici romanzi*, 177–9, figure 23, Lazzi (2001: 183–6, figures 45–6), Bertelli (2008: 244–5) and De Robertis and Miriello (2006: 15–16). Berto de' Bianchi's explicit reads: 'Explicit auctoris opus hic finisque laboris. Finito dito opus dominus Bertus de Blanchis a chi Dio li dia vita e honore e grandeça e buono stato, a lui e tutta la soa familia. E gran vita e lunga vita. Bo(logna).'

[77] Morpurgo (1900: 536). The manuscript includes *Il libro di Cato* with a vernacular commentary, the explicit to which reads 'Explicit liber Catonis cum expositionibus vulgaribus compositis in studio Boneniensis. Dei gracias. Amen.'

[78] Rodolico (1898: 287).

[79] The *ex libris* of the Mellini family can be read in MS Ricc. 1538, fol. 111r: 'Questo libro si è di Giovanni di Domenico di Piero di Francesco di Duccio di Giovanni d'Antonio di Bernardo Mellini e chi lo achata lo renda.' The same folio bears the family's coat of arms and the motto 'Fede et amore'.

Romani ('Deeds of the Romans'), a translation of Cicero's oration *Pro Marcello* attributed to Brunetto Latini, some excerpts from the pseudo-Aristotelian *Secreta secretorum* ('Secret of Secrets'), the *Formula honestae vitae* ('Rules for an Honest Life') by Martin of Braga, the *Fiore di retorica* ('Flower of Rhetoric') by Guidotto of Bologna, Sallust's *Bellum Iugurtinum* ('Jugurthine War') translated by Bartholomew of San Concordio, as well as excerpts from the Bible and several hagiographies.[80] If all the witnesses of the vernacular *Summa* contribute to tell its multifaceted textual history, miscellanies such as Ricc. 1538 prove particularly helpful in situating the work within the cluster of writings that vernacular readers would have consumed.

Outside of the university classroom where professors and scholars studied the Latin Aristotle – though not altogether detached from it, as suggested by the case of Berto's Bolognese manuscript – Taddeo's vernacular translation of the *Summa* was read along with works of historiography, moral philosophy and Christian doctrine forming the cultural backbone for the vernacular audience. Since in many cases texts tended to circulate together as part of miscellanies, attempts to follow their transmission provide useful information about the interests of readers. For instance, Alderotti's version of the *Summa* is frequently compiled alongside not only other portions of the *Tesoro volgare* and other works by Brunetto Latini but also with the pseudo-Aristotelian *Secret of Secrets*, the moral subject matter of which finds obvious resonance with the philosophical popularisation fostered by the *Summa* itself.[81]

An example of such juxtaposition is MS Yates Thompson 28 of the British Library, copied in *littera textualis* by Bartolomeo di Lorenzo of Figline in 1425, which includes an Italian version of the *Secret of Secrets*, along with excerpts from the ethical and political sections of the *Tesoro volgare*.[82] Also, as is the case with MS Ricc. 1538, MS Yates Thompson 28 is extensively decorated, a material feature that points towards the wealthy milieu that these luxury objects addressed. Even when lacking illustrations,

---

[80] For a complete list of the works included in the miscellany, see Morpurgo (1900: 533–8).

[81] Bibliography on the *Secret of Secrets* is vast, given its wide circulation not only in Latin but also in various European vernaculars, as indicated by Ryan and Schmitt (1982) and Williams (1994, 2003a). On its European circulation, see Grignaschi (1980) and Zamuner (2005). On the Italian versions, see Cecioni (1889), Perrone (2001), Rapisarda (2001) and Milani (2001, 2006). See my introduction to the present study, 8–9.

[82] London, British Library, MS Yates Thompson 28, dated 1425, fol. 143*v*: 'Questo libro e scripto dimano di fere bartolomeo di lorenco da fighine compvito adi xvj dimarco Mccccxxv'. The manuscript also includes the *Secret of Secrets* (fols. 1*r*–43*r*), the *Tesoro* (fols. 43*v*–130*v*), and miscellaneous texts (fols. 130*v*–143*v*); see Watson (1979: vol. 1: 82–3 and plate 376 in vol. 2) and Natali (2012: 77).

the copies of the *Summa* in *textualis*, often embellished by basic decorations such as illuminated initials, seem to indicate the same context of well-off lay readers who consumed other vernacular bestsellers. MS It. 2593 at the Biblioteca Universitaria in Bologna, for instance, was copied around 1400 by Paolo di Duccio Tosi, the scribe of several vernacular manuscripts, including copies of Dante's *Divine Comedy*.[83]

This kind of readership is further illuminated by, among other manuscripts, MS Cerchi 844 of the Archivio di Stato in Florence, written in *textualis* around 1400 and belonging to Bindaccio di Michele de' Cerchi (1450–1510).[84] As with the aforementioned Giovanni Arnolfi, the biography of Bindaccio de' Cerchi reveals a reading public that, throughout the fifteenth century and well into the sixteenth century, appreciated works such as Alderotti's. Like many Florentine aristocrats, Bindaccio spent his youth in mercantile activities, but also became involved in local politics. As suggested by a book of *ricordanze* that he wrote in his later years, Bindaccio was an enemy of the Medici family and a fierce opponent of Savonarola.[85] Along with his own writings, Bindaccio transcribed several *volgarizzamenti* with content similar to the miscellanies mentioned above. The fact that Bindaccio's library included a copy of Alderotti's compendium confirms the consistency of the cultural and social patterns that characterised the circulation of the work and, more precisely, its reception within the circle of aristocrats and affluent merchants.

But while manuscripts such as Ricc. 1538 and Yates Thompson 28 are precious objects wrought by professional or semi-professional scribes, Bindaccio's miscellany marks a new chapter in the history of vernacular culture between the later Middle Ages and the early Renaissance: the rise of individuals copying texts for their own personal use. The *littera textualis*, the standard for professional scribes and popular in scholarly contexts, gives way to cursive scripts of notarial or mercantile origin (the so-called 'mercantesca'), hands typical of the cultivated laity who found fulfilment in exercising the *vita activa* while also pursuing some forms of education.[86]

---

[83] On Bologna, Biblioteca Universitaria, MS 2593, from around 1400, see Frati (1909–23: 1923: 107; 1916: 193–4). For an overview of the activity of Paolo di Duccio Tosi, see Boschi Rotiroti (2015).

[84] Florence, Archivio di Stato, MS Cerchi 844, from around 1400, fol. 1r: 'Questo libro è di Bindaccio di Michele de Cerchi'. For details about Bindaccio and the Cerchi family, see Malanima (1979), Goldthwaite (1985), Black (2007: 109, 171, 637, 649), Goldthwaite (2009: 54, 410, 415–19) and Kirshner (2015: 119, 123, 128).

[85] For a detailed description of Bindaccio's *libro di ricordanze* (Florence, Biblioteca Riccardiana, MS 1105), see Morpurgo (1900: 122–7).

[86] The social and cultural implications of scripts and handwriting are discussed by Petrucci (1995: 169–235); see also Gehl (1993: 37–8).

Though somewhat difficult to circumscribe, this broader context witnesses the fortune of Alderotti's translation among readers who likely received basic education in Latin that was insufficient to read demanding works such as the Latin Aristotle.

As indicated by Robert Black, among others, Florence presents an invaluable case in the history of vernacular education because the republic's unique literary culture and social dynamics are amply documented.[87] The wealth of extant documents related to the textual culture of the city in the late Middle Ages and the Renaissance constitutes a corpus rich enough to support certain generalisations. In addition, historians of translation profit from the peculiar social and political structure of the city in the period. By balancing an energetic bourgeoisie and a vigorously protective aristocracy, Florentine society favoured the production and consumption of works in the vernacular, works that offered a key to understanding and describing present-day reality.[88] Along with works by Dante and Boccaccio, *volgarizzamenti* such as Alderotti's played a major role in the elaboration of vernacular discussions about contemporary politics. Such a process can only be understood by situating it within the rebirth of classical rhetoric in medieval Italy, which, as Virginia Cox argues, catalysed civic humanism.[89] Without underestimating the pivotal role of humanists like Coluccio Salutati and, more so, Leonardo Bruni in the establishment of a new 'philological' approach to the past, it is fair to argue that the late medieval appropriation of classical philosophy and rhetoric was central to the development and legitimation of vernacular culture. It is within this framework that Alderotti's version of the *Summa* found its way into a readership beyond the narrow circles of scholars and students with direct access to Latin translations of Aristotle's *Nicomachean Ethics*.[90]

The numerous copies of Alderotti's *Etica* written in cursive scripts with mercantile features thus offer useful insights on the communities of its readers. Interestingly, many such manuscripts tell family stories, thus witnessing the somewhat common preoccupation with the establishment

---

[87] On the specific situation of education and schooling in Florence, see Black (2001, 2007). See also the outline of education in Florence by Grendler (1989: 71–8).

[88] For an overview of Florentine society and culture in the early Renaissance, see Brucker (1962, 1998a).

[89] See Cox (2003, 2006). On the reception of Cicero's rhetoric throughout the medieval period, with insights into both Latinate and vernacular contexts, see Cox and Ward (2006).

[90] On the role played by Brunetto Latini within the progressive establishment of the vernacular as a language suitable for rhetorical, moral and political purposes, see Bolton Holloway (1993). Brunetto's experience as a translator and, even more relevant to my purposes, as the translator of Cicero's orations, is most recently discussed by Lorenzi (2013).

of reading traditions that, in a way, vouched for the moral assessment of one's family and lineage. One example, MS Laur. Gaddi 83, now in the Biblioteca Medicea Laurenziana in Florence, is a mid-fourteenth-century copy of Brunetto Latini's *Tesoro*, which belonged to the 'sons of Giovanni di Ser Andrea di Michele Benci', a Florentine citizen who was a 'lanaiuolo', a member of the 'Arte della lana'.[91] The wool guild of Florence, one of the most powerful guilds in the *Arti Maggiori* ('Major Trades'), enjoyed close connections to the administration of the commune.[92] Of particular note is the ownership inscription, which focuses on Giovanni's sons and stresses that the book is a tool for their education and a constant reminder of the moral values that the family aims to perpetuate. A very similar situation is the one outlined by the many notes of possession found in another codex in the same library, MS Laur. Plut. 89 sup. 110.[93] Written in 1451 in an elegant humanist cursive hand, the manuscript belonged to several members of the Bencivenni family, which, as recalled by a 1488 note of possession, was part of the *Arte dei medici e speziali* ('Guild of Doctors and Apothecaries'), another major guild in Florence.[94] One signator is Iacopo di Piero Bencivenni, who describes himself as 'ciptadino fiorentino speziale a piè del Ponte Vecchio', perhaps the same Iacopo di Piero who obtained the title of count palatine from Pope Leo X in 1515.[95] The manuscript, again, evokes the Florentine elite and the important role books played in the life of the families.

In the cases when the scribe is also the owner, the relevance of a given text to the culture of the family is even stronger. A particular interest in Aristotle's *Ethics* informs the scribal activity of Bonaccorso di Filippo Adimari, a member of a prestigious aristocratic family in Florence heavily involved in art patronage throughout the fifteenth century.[96] Bonaccorso's

91 See the fifteenth-century owner's note in Florence, Biblioteca Medicea Laurenziana, MS Laur. Gaddi 83, from the mid-fourteenth century, fol. 11r: 'Questo libro si chiama texoro di maestro Brunetto Latino fiorentino, ed è de' figliuoli di Giovanni di ser Andrea di Michele Benci Lanaiuolo cittadino fiorentino, chi lo truova lo renda.' The verso of the same folio includes a moral sonnet beginning 'Qual sorte mi conciesse o quale istella'. See Marchesi (1903: 70), Mascheroni (1969: 498–9), Bolton Holloway (1986: 28 n.17; 1993: 525), Bertelli (2008: 236–7; 2011: 107).
92 Specifically on the 'arte della lana', see Hoshino (1980). On Florentine guilds more broadly, see Staley (1906), Doren (1940), Brucker (1998a: 90–105) and Brucker (1998b: 65–108).
93 Florence, Biblioteca Medicea Laurenziana, MS Plut. 89 sup. 110, fifteenth century; the ownership inscription appears at fol. 42. Marchesi (1903: 66–7).
94 On the Arte dei Medici e Speziali, see the classic study by Ciasca (1927).
95 Florence, Archivio di Stato, Famiglia Bencivenni, fasc. 542.
96 The Adimari family is mentioned by Dante as a 'proud and insolent race' in *Paradiso* 16.115; members such as Filippo Argenti and Tegghiano d'Aldobrando are also remembered in *Inferno* 8.31 and 16.41, respectively. The artistic patronage of the Adimari family is best embodied by the famous 'Cassone Adimari' (from around 1450), now in the Gallerie dell'Accademia in Florence and currently attributed to Giovanni di Ser Giovanni ('Lo Scheggia'); see Bellosi and Haines (1999).

activity as a scribe is noteworthy for the light it sheds on the deliberate development of Florentine vernacular culture in a time usually (and rightfully) described as the triumph of Latin humanism. But the importance of translation to the experience of vernacular readership is hard to overstate: most of the many manuscripts that Bonaccorso transcribed both for his own perusal and for that of others (either on commission or as gifts) are, in fact, vernacular translations of Latin works, from Cicero's *Tusculanae disputationes* and *De officis* to the histories of Sallust and Livy.[97] Bonaccorso's activity testifies to widespread mediation between Latin and the vernacular that surpassed the usual preference given to the classics: not only did he copy out translations of classical authors, but also transcribed translations of contemporaneous Latin works such as those by Leonardo Bruni.[98] If Giuliano Tanturli's detailed reconstruction of the trends characterising the production of vernacular texts in fifteenth-century Florence offers invaluable remarks on the effects of the cultural hegemony of Latin vis-à-vis vernacular culture, a closer look at the same documentation suggests that the phenomenon is better understood in terms of interaction.[99]

The successful reception of Taddeo Alderotti's translation of the *Summa* in fifteenth-century Florence is strong evidence of such interaction, especially in the case of Bonaccorso di Filippo Adimari. His copy was written in 1445 'a uso e stança di sé e di suoi amici' ('for the use and ownership of himself and his friends'), a statement commonly used to refer to forms of shared consumption of the book.[100] What makes Bonaccorso's production particularly relevant, though, is the fact that, almost twenty years after copying the compendium of the *Ethics*, he also copied out a vernacular

[97] Several manuscripts copied by Bonaccorso di Filippo Adimari are relevant to this study. First, Florence, Biblioteca Riccardiana, MS Ricc. 1601, which includes a copy of Donato degli Albanzani's translation of Petrarch's *Life of Julius Caesar*, written in 1458; see Morpurgo (1900: 168) and De Robertis and Miriello (2006: 56). Second, MS Ricc. 1603, a miscellaneous collection copied in 1464 that contains vernacular translations of Cicero's *De amicitia*, *De senectute*, and his orations, the *De quattuor virtutibus* of Pseudo-Seneca, as well as letters by Leonardo Bruni; see Morpurgo (1900: 581–2). A third manuscript, a copy of a translation of Cicero's *De officiis* written by Bonaccorso for Giovanni Spinelli in 1485, is Florence, Biblioteca Medicea Laurenziana, MS Laur. Plut. 76.75. On Bonaccorso's undated copy of Livy, see Dalmazzo (1845: LIV). On his 1453 copy of Sallust, see *Catalogue Wellesley*, 22n187. On his 1459 copy of Bartolomeo di San Concordio, see Manni (1734: 9–10).
[98] On Bonaccorso's copies of Leonardo Bruni's works, see Maxson (2014: 78–9).
[99] Tanturli (1988).
[100] Florence, Biblioteca Nazionale Centrale, MS Pal. 729, dated 1445, fol. 45: 'Finito è libro chiamato l'Eticha d'Aristotile a dì xxv d'ottobre mille quatrocento quarantacinque, per le mani di Bonaccorso di Filippo Adimari da Firençe a uso e stança di sé e di suoi amici'. See Gentile (1889–1899 vol. 2: 268), Marchesi (1903: 68); Bénédictins du Bouveret (1965–82: 2297) and Bianchi (2003: 51–2 and plate 33).

translation of Leonardo Bruni's 'new' Latin version of the *Nicomachean Ethics*. This translation was prepared in the 1460s by the humanist and schoolteacher Bernardo Nuti, a close friend of Marsilio Ficino and (as will be discussed in Chapter 4) a key player in the interaction that further blurred the boundaries between Latin humanism and vernacular culture. Adimari's copy of Nuti's translation of the *Ethics* was meant to be read by friends and family members too. This particular example suggests that Bonaccorso's literary taste, possibly influenced by contemporary humanist culture, developed throughout the twenty years that separate the two manuscripts; it also indicates that the relationship between Latin humanism and vernacular culture is not as clear-cut as it has often been described, and that vernacular translation functions as a powerful liaison between the two.

The case of Bonaccorso di Filippo Adimari indicates one shift informing vernacular culture in mid-fifteenth-century Florence. Even more relevant to this shift is the scribal activity of several members of the Benci family in the fifteenth century, possibly the clearest example of the interaction between Latin humanism and vernacular culture in Renaissance Florence. Tanturli's pioneering study of the 'Benci copisti' – particularly Tommaso, Filippo and Giovanni, sons of Lorenzo di Giovanni di Taddeo – brilliantly recreates the process of production and consumption of vernacular literature in a context dominated by humanist culture.[101] Collectors of various genres, the Benci family made transcriptions for their own use in miscellanies, literally inscribing themselves into the tradition of *zibaldoni* and *libri di ricordi*, typical products of mercantile societies in medieval and early modern scribal culture.[102] Tanturli demonstrates the significance of the inclusion of *volgarizzamenti* in the Benci miscellanies and Alderotti's translation of the *Summa Alexandrinorum* appears among them more than once. Entitled the *Fioretti dell'Eticha d'Aristotile* ('Little Flowers of Aristotle's *Ethics*'), the text is included in MS 1585 of the Biblioteca Riccardiana (where, unsurprisingly, it accompanies the *Secret of Secrets*) as well as in MS A.IX.28 of the Biblioteca Universitaria in Genova.[103]

The scribal activity of the Benci and, in particular, the place of Tommaso (1427–70) between vernacular culture and the most innovative fringes

---

[101] Tanturli (1978).

[102] On the scribal activities of the Florentine bourgeoisie, particularly the merchant classes, see the classical study by Bec (1967). On the 'libri di ricordanze', see Ciappelli (1989).

[103] On Florence, Biblioteca Riccardiana, MS Ricc. 1585, from the fifteenth century, see Morpurgo (1900: 569), Marchesi (1903: 69) and Tanturli (1978: 210, 251, 293). Genova, Biblioteca Universitaria, MS A.IX.28, from the fifteenth century, is mentioned by Tanturli (1978: 210).

of humanism are somewhat exceptional but not without parallel. Other examples confirm the productive role of translation as a powerful tool to break down the boundaries between Latin and vernacular cultures, such as MS II.I.71 in the Biblioteca Nazionale in Florence, a voluminous miscellany compiled by Antonio da Filicaia in 1490.[104] A typical member of the mercantile elite, Filicaia held several positions in the administration of the city: he served as consul for his guild, the Arte della lana, first in 1462 and again in 1471 and 1490, as well as 'castellano' of the fortress of Sant'Agnese in Pisa in 1467, 'priore' in 1485, and from 1511 to 1512, captain of the infantry.[105] Throughout his career, Filicaia kept personal records and copied texts for himself and close acquaintants, mostly wide-ranging vernacular miscellanies.

Filicaia's manuscripts are particularly precious for their colophons, in which the scribe left remarkable traces of his experience as both copyist and reader. He usually refers to the fact that the manuscripts were copied for his own reading and for the benefit of his descendants, a trope that we have met earlier in this chapter. But what makes Filicaia's colophons especially relevant is the scribe's perspective on the moral value of the texts at hand. Such is the case of the statement at the end of Filicaia's copy of Alderotti's translation of the *Summa* in MS II.I.71:

> Copied by myself, Antonio di Piero di Nicolaio di Manetto da Filicaia and completed on this day, February 2nd, 1490, so it may be a lesson and doctrine in living well in virtue and good habits for those who will come after me and so I am comforted that this book and many others written out by me to similar ends will all be kept and reread often and may they be fruitful for whoever prepares to read them, forever in the honor and praise of God the most powerful.[106]

Filicaia's colophon, written almost two centuries after Dante's criticism of Taddeo Alderotti's translation sheds light on the nonetheless successful reception of the text. Despite not being a translation of the original *Ethics*, the *Etica d'Aristotile* is valued as a guidebook for living virtuously. To

---

[104] On Florence, Biblioteca Nazionale Centrale, MS II.I.71, dated 1490, see Mazzatinti (1898: 31) and Bianco (2003: 237).

[105] Bianco (2003: 238–9).

[106] Florence, Biblioteca Nazionale Centrale, MS II.I.71, fol. 156: 'Copiata per me Antonio di Piero di Nicolaio di Manetto da Ffilichaia e ffinita quessto di due di febbraio anno 1490 perché sia insegniamento e dottrina di bene vivere in virtù e buoni cosstumi di chi verrà dopo me et però quessto libro e molti altri schritti per me a ssimile effetto conforto che sieno tutti conservati e spesse volte riletti e pigline buoni frutti chi in essi studierà di leggierli sempre a onore e laulde dello omnipotente Iddio.' See Bianco (2003: 240).

perform this pedagogical function, the text must be kept in the home and read several times so readers may appropriate its teachings.

Surely, the early circulation of Alderotti's work differs significantly from its reception in the mid-fifteenth century and onward, which was affected by the spread of humanist culture, as we have seen. Filicaia's miscellany illustrates this difference well. On one hand, this *zibaldone* is consistent with earlier examples of vernacular miscellanies where Alderotti's version of the *Summa* appears alongside other *volgarizzamenti* of both classical works of moral philosophy and Christian doctrine. On the other hand, it stands out as the only known compilation to include the vernacular translation of that supreme emblem of refined humanist culture: the *Pymander*, Marsilio Ficino's Latin version of the *Corpus Hermeticum*.[107] The text chosen for Filicaia's miscellany, an Italian translation of Ficino by Tommaso Benci (1427–70) dedicated to Florentine merchant Francesco di Nerone, represents one of the most advanced developments of vernacularisation, one that mirrors patterns of cultural appropriation typical of Latin humanism.[108] The wealthy, merchant-class Benci dedicates his vernacular *Pimandro* to a fellow merchant: in so doing, Benci stresses that, although professional duties can impede merchants from studying, vernacular translations like the *Pimandro* will make philosophy accessible to those 'non dotti della latina lingua' ('non conversant with Latin') who have nonetheless expressed their desire to read it.[109] By including Benci's *Pimandro* in his miscellany, Filicaia shows that translation is indeed a space where works as diverse as Alderotti's 'medieval' version of the *Summa Alexandrinorum* and Ficino's 'humanist' rendering of the *Pymander* can live side by side as witnesses to the productive interaction of cultural contexts.

Beyond the Bestseller

The outline sketched above suggests that the afterlife of Taddeo Alderotti's translation of the *Summa Alexandrinorum* far exceeded Dante's judgement.

---

[107] The *Pymander* is part of the *Corpus Hermeticum*, printed in a Latin translation by Marsilio Ficino in 1471. 'Confilosofo' to Ficino, like his brother Giovanni Benci, Tommaso translated the *Pymander* into Italian in 1463, just a few months after Ficino's Latin version was completed. Benci's *Pimandro* circulated in manuscript and was printed in Florence in 1545 by the printer Torrentino. See Purnell (1977) and Gentile and Gilly (1999).

[108] The text of Benci's preface is in Kristeller (1937: 99–101). Though the printed edition from 1545 bears the dedication to Francesco di Nerone, it is important to remember that earlier manuscripts addressed the same dedication to various friends of Benci's, all from the mercantile class; see Ragni (1966).

[109] Kristeller (1937: 99).

As the textual tradition shows, one of the reasons for the successful reception of the *Summa* was certainly its association with Brunetto Latini's encyclopaedic work. But the significant number of manuscripts where the *Summa* appears independently from the *Tesoro* confirms the view that, for most vernacular readers throughout the later Middle Ages and the Renaissance, Alderotti's text was considered as the vernacular substitute for Aristotle's *Ethics*. Much shorter than the original, the abridged version of the treatise responded to the intellectual needs of a new social and economic class rather than being addressed to scholars and university students, an aspect that certainly contributed to its success. In fact, the case of Alderotti's translation is by no means unique. Other compendia of the *Ethics* existed – including at least two other Italian translations of the *Summa Alexandrinorum* published outside the Taddeo/Brunetto tradition – evidencing the fortune similar abridgments enjoyed with varied vernacular readers and illuminating the contexts in which such works were produced.

A further example, illustrated by MS It. II.72 now in the Biblioteca Marciana in Venice, seems to be the result of a connection with university teaching, a connection that we have already seen in relation to Berto de Bianchi's Bolognese codex.[110] Written on parchment in the fourteenth century and with illuminations in the French style, this manuscript is of particular interest not only because it witnesses a different translation of the *Summa*, but also for the frame provided by its incipit and explicit. First, the title of the work refers explicitly to the original source, thus avoiding the confusion entailed by the title *Etica d'Aristotile* used in the versions by Alderotti and Brunetto:

> Here begins the summa of the sages of Alexandria, which they drew from the book of Aristotle called *The Book of Customs*. Book one on the goal of virtue, which is called beatitude: first brought from Arabic into Latin and [from] Latin into Tuscan. For the honor of God and with prayers for friends and their welfare.[111]

The incipit describes the work for what it is: a translation of the *Summa Alexandrinorum*, that is a selection of materials from Aristotle's *Ethics*,

---

[110] Venice, Biblioteca Nazionale Marciana, MS It. II.72 [4838], from the fourteenth century. For bibliography on this manuscript, still lacking extensive study, see the note in Morelli (1776: 50–1); and a more detailed description in Frati and Segarizzi (1909–1911 vol. 1: 241–2).

[111] Venice, Biblioteca Nazionale Marciana, MS It. II.72, fol. 1r: '[Q]ui komincia la somma de li savi d'Alexandria la quale alles[ero] de li:ro d'Aristotile e detto libro di kostumanza. Libro primo [de] fine de la vertù lo quale è apellato beatitudi[ne]: [trans]lato prima d'arabbico in latino e d'[arabbico in] latino en toscano. A l'onore de dio [e] a preghiera deli amici e per lo bene d'essi.'

here referenced by the common alternate title *Libro di costumanza* (*Book of Morality*). As the title indicates, the original *Summa Alexandrinorum*, translated first from Arabic into Latin (the source text referenced here is in fact Herman the German's Latin version of the *Summa*) has been translated from Latin into the Tuscan vernacular.

If the incipit ends with commonplace mention of the 'amici' (friends) who requested the translation and who will benefit from reading the book, the colophon also provides some information on the translator:

> Here ends the summa of the philosophers of Alexandria, which are sayings called *Of Morality* chosen from Aristotle's book. And this book was brought [*traslato*] from Latin into Tuscan as best as the scholar who transmitted it could. For the honor of God and with prayers for friends and for the welfare of whose who through these lectures could become better, may it please God. Be well.[112]

While the translator is not named, he is defined as a 'scolaio', a word that in other *volgarizzamenti* from the period refer to students, suggesting another connection between the practice of vernacular translation and the scholastic and academic worlds.[113] What is visible here is the very process of mediation translators performed between academic discourse and vernacular culture.[114]

Even if the identity of the 'scolaio' who translated the *Summa* remains unknown, the mention of his occupation refers to the academic contexts. A similar situation is evoked by another vernacular translation of the *Summa* witnessed by four manuscripts, two of which are attributed to a Nicolò Anglico, likely active in the first half of the fourteenth century.[115] While the compiler's identity and the site of production remain largely mysterious, the manuscript copies do contextualise the translation and its circulation. The two manuscripts bearing the name Nicolò Anglico belong to different periods. MS Chig. M.VIII.162 at the Vatican is a fourteenth-century manuscript written in a *littera textualis* that, alongside the *Etica d'Aristotile* 'reducta in volgare per maestro Nicholo Anglico' ('brought into the vernacular by Master Nicolò Anglico'), also includes one of the

---

[112] *Ibid.*: fol. 78*v*: 'Qui a fine la somma de li filosofi d'Alexandria. Le quali sono sentenze electe del libro d'Aristotile appellate di kostumanza. E fu traslato questo libro di latino in toscano sì kome fare seppe alkuno scolaio ke di ciò si tramise. All'onore de Dio e da preghiera de li amici e per lo bene di koloro che per kotali sermoni potessero divenire megliori et a Dio piacia. Valete.'

[113] Cornish (2011: 32).

[114] Such a process is described in Copeland (1991).

[115] This compendium also awaits thorough study, only conceivable once a future critical edition of the text can reconstruct the relations between the various witnesses. A recent inquiry into the manuscript transmission of the compendium is Scarpino (2015).

earliest translations of Aristotle's *Rhetoric*, also attributed to Anglico in its explicit: 'Questo ene lo fine de la Rethorica d'Aristotile reducta in vulgare dal maestro Nicholao Anglico' ('This is the end of Aristotle's *Rhetoric* brought into the vernacular by Master Nicolò Anglico').[116] The second manuscript to mention Anglico is a Neapolitan humanist copy of the same text, now MS CF 1.8 of the Biblioteca dei Girolamini in Naples, dated 1466.[117] Two additional manuscripts, each produced in the fourteenth century (MS It. II.2 of the Marciana and MS Cicogna 1474 of the Correr Museum in Venice), witness the Italian translation of the Latin *Summa* without mentioning the name of Anglico.[118]

Nicolò Anglico has been tentatively identified with a scribe active at the Neapolitan court in the 1330s, but his relevance to this study is that the oldest reference to him labels him a 'maestro'.[119] Indeed, MS Chig. M.VIII.162, in which the *Rhetoric* follows the abridged version of the *Ethics*, points towards a scholarly context that, while typically concerned with Latin versions of those works, was progressively opening its boundaries to the vernacular. Written in two rubricated columns and decorated with illuminated initials (including the depiction of Aristotle on the first page), this large-format manuscript is consistent with the form of other books related to university teaching. As such, the Vatican manuscript documents a moment in the history of the text that was shaped by dynamics similar to those informing the early circulation of Taddeo Alderotti's translation of the *Summa*.[120] These were books most probably planned to circulate outside the universities and yet remained connected, through their translators, formats and layouts, to the Latinate world of academia.

While not as successful as Alderotti's, the translation putatively attributed to Anglico did enjoy a degree of circulation, as suggested by the extant copies. If manuscripts Cicogna 1474 and Marc. It. II.2 exhibit the trends seen with respect to Alderotti's translation, the copy at the Gerolamini

---

[116] Vatican City, Biblioteca Apostolica Vaticana, MS Chig. M.VIII.162, from the thirteenth century; see Scarpino (2015: 724–6). The compendium of the *Ethics* occupies fols. 1r–16v, the translation of Aristotle's *Rhetoric* fols. 20r–83v.

[117] Naples, Biblioteca Statale Oratoriana dei Girolamini, MS CF 1.8, dated 1466, see Scarpino (2015: 717–21).

[118] Venice, Biblioteca Nazionale Marciana, MS It. II.2 [4326], from the fourteenth century; see Frati and Segarizzi (1909–11: 192–5) and Scarpino (2015: 721–2). On Venice, Biblioteca del Museo Correr, MS Cicogna 1474, from the fourteenth century, see Fulin (1872: 104), Benedetti (1988: 136), Caracciolo Aricò (2008: 105) and Scarpino (2015: 722–4).

[119] The translator's identity is discussed by Scarpino (2015).

[120] See, for example, the aforementioned case of the early fourteenth-century Bolognese copy of the *Ethics* produced by Berto de' Bianchi, now MS Florence, Biblioteca Riccardiana, Ricc. 1538; see above, 72.

sheds light onto another form of circulation. Copied in 1466 by the scribe Gian Marco Cinico, a calligrapher at the service of the king of Naples, Ferrante of Aragon, and probably decorated by Cola Rapicano, the manuscript is a typical humanist book produced for an aristocratic library. The manuscript was in fact dedicated to the duchess of Andria, Maria Donata Orsini, and wife of the fourth duke of Andria, Pirro del Balzo.[121] The history told by the production of this manuscript is of great interest: not only does it reflect the contemporaneous aristocratic taste for expensive books, but it also witnesses the *longue durée* of the cultural pattern outlined, in different ways, by both Giles of Rome and Dante. As the fortune of Giles' *De regimine principum* suggests, vernacular translations of works of moral philosophy proved particularly useful to rulers and politicians lacking a solid command of Latin. But, as Dante exemplifies in the *Convivio*, it is equally vital that the men and women of the elites snatch culture and learning out of the hands of professional scholars who have transformed these intellectual pursuits into sources of profit.

The 'humanist' reshaping of Anglico's translation of the *Summa* in the copy dedicated to the duchess of Andria in 1466 is not an isolated case of cultural transfer. As I have shown, Alderotti's own translation enjoyed great success with wealthy merchants and patricians: it also figured in the libraries of prominent political leaders (the kind of readership that, by the way, Dante was targeting in the *Convivio*). A beautifully decorated copy of Alderotti's work, for instance, was produced in the 1460s for the duke of Milan, Francesco I Sforza, by the scribe Fabrizio Elfiteo.[122] The first folio of the manuscript features beautiful decorations that refer to its Milanese orbit, such as the coat of arms held by two angels on the upper section of the folio and by the mottos 'Merito et tempore' ('with merit and time') and 'A bon droit' ('with good reason'). The explicit reference to Aristotle's dedication of the *Ethics* to his son Nicomachus – the title of the work reads 'L'Ethica de Aristotele ad Nicomacho suo figliuolo' ('The Ethics of Aristotle to his son Nicomachus') – introduces an element typically absent from copies of Taddeo's translation of the *Summa*, which, as we have seen, use the simpler title *L'Etica d'Aristotile*. The mention of Nicomachus, from the title of Aristotle's *Nicomachean Ethics*, can be interpreted as a gesture to claim some classical flair, at least superficially. (But it is also likely to show

---

[121] Details regarding this manuscript are in Scarpino (2015: 717–21).

[122] Milan, Biblioteca Ambrosiana, MS C 21 inf., from around 1460; see Marchesi (1903: 7, 9, 66), Kristeller (1963–1997 vol. 1: 319, vol. 2: 534), Pellegrin (1969: 55) and, for further bibliography, Zaggia (2007: 377).

an awareness that there were other works of Aristotle's moral philosophy such as the *Eudemian Ethics*, so that it was necessary to specify.)[123] The Sforza copy represents a stage of the circulation of Alderotti's translation in which the reception of the *Summa* intermingles with vernacular readers newly interested in the complete version of Aristotle's *Nicomachean Ethics*. As we shall see in Chapters 3 and 4, the emergence of direct translations of the *Ethics* in the fifteenth century is the result of cultural stimuli with quite different origins. Indeed, the vernacular discovery of the 'original' *Ethics* was a result of the 'humanist' revival of Aristotle championed by scholars like Leonardo Bruni, treated in Chapter 4, but it also reveals the dedication to the vernacular dissemination of philosophy shared by members of religious orders from the more traditional academic establishment. Those orders are at the core of the following chapter. By focusing on the patronage of the aristocratic Giustiniani family in fifteenth-century Venice (yet another example of the vernacular elite addressed by Dante in the *Convivio*), I will show that the earliest Italian translations of Aristotle's *Nicomachean Ethics* and the pseudo-Aristotelian treatise *On Virtues and Vices* were the products of the interaction between wealthy laymen and academics trained within the scholastic tradition. Yet far from being impervious to concurrent developments in humanism, the examples I will explore indicate that vernacular translation merged long-established academic practices with new trends in the study of the classical past.

---

[123] To this category, which can be defined loosely as 'humanist', belongs a similar codex made in the fifteenth century for the Bentivoglio family, now Rome, Biblioteca Nazionale Centrale, MS Vittorio Emanuele 725; see Frati (1906: 194).

CHAPTER 3

Family Business
Readying the Ethics for the Layman

Overlooking the Piazza

The Venetian lay interest in all things Aristotelian has a long history. Accordingly, the philosopher's visual presence in the city of Venice is significant. Even before Paolo Veronese sumptuously depicted Aristotle in the Salone Sansoviniano of the Biblioteca Marciana, the philosopher had already twice appeared in an iconic public space near the library: the colonnade of the Palazzo Ducale facing Piazza San Marco. In the beautifully carved capitals of the colonnade, Aristotle is first presented as the emblem of dialectic, with a Latin inscription describing him as 'Aristoteles dialecticus' [c. 1350, Figure 3.1], in an image that recalls the Latinate cycles of the *artes liberales* treated in Chapter 1.[1]

In the capital of Justice from around 1450, which John Ruskin esteemed the most beautiful of the entire series, Aristotle is instead identified by a vernacular inscription. This personification of Justice is accompanied by examples of good government and figures of lawgivers, and 'Aristotile che diè lege' ('Aristotle who declares laws', in Ruskin's translation) appears on the right side, dominating the others in a position of prominence [Figure 3.2].[2]

Holding his *Constitution of the Athenians*, the philosopher is presented here as the emblem of lawmaking.[3] But the connection between Aristotle and the theme of justice is also granted by the central role that the discussion of political virtue plays in his moral system, particularly in the *Nicomachean Ethics*.

---

[1] See Manno (1999) for a detailed discussion of the capitals. On the figure of 'Aristoteles dialecticus', part of a series of wise men that represent the liberal arts, see *ibid.*: 123–5.

[2] See *ibid.*: 69–77; and Ruskin (2007: 364).

[3] On the importance of the work within the Aristotelian political corpus, as well as its authorship, which might in fact owe to one of Aristotle's disciples, see Rhodes (1981).

Figure 3.1 'Aristoteles Dialecticus', sculpted capital, Venice, Palazzo Ducale, c. 1340–55

Figure 3.2 'Aristotele che diè lege', sculpted capital, Venice, Palazzo Ducale, c. 1450

If this connection, already seen in both Siena and Asciano, is typical in the political iconographic tradition, the Venetian capital is also intriguing for its linguistic presentation. As a matter of fact, the inscriptions open the allegorical cycle to the vernacular world, thus amplifying the visual translation performed by the sculptures.[4] Justice is not simply illustrated through visual examples, but the meaning of the images is instead made explicit in the native language of the audience. In this regard, the use of the vernacular in the inscription acquires an ideological status no different from that which informed the vernacular translation of the Sienese constitution of 1309.[5] The idea that Justice speaks the language of the citizens corresponds to the rhetorical gestures that city-states like Siena and Venice performed to cast themselves as examples of good government.[6] At the same time, these examples of public display aimed to affect the citizens, inducing them to build and share common moral codes. Political propaganda and other forms of civic promotion thus merge with some of the functions more broadly performed by translation. These alignments are particularly evident in vernacular translations that combined ethical subject matter and the ethical value entailed by the very use of the mother tongue.

Once again, the reception of Aristotle offers a useful lens through which the friction between the use of language and the outline of shared morals can be examined, especially in lay contexts. In this respect, a striking example is found in Petrarch's invective *De sui ipsius et multorum ignorantia* ('On His Own Ignorance and That of Many Others'), composed towards the end of his time in Venice (1362–67).[7] The work offers useful insights into Petrarch's intellectual autobiography and sheds light on the more conservative components of the Aristotelian cult that informed Venetian lay culture in that period. While Petrarch's discussion is not concerned with the opposition between Latin and the vernacular, it is nonetheless useful to understand the characteristic ways in which Aristotle's moral philosophy was first translated into the vernacular. By focusing on a cultural and linguistic conflict internal to the Latinate world, Petrarch's invective also

---

[4] The linguistic implications of the vernacular inscriptions in the capital vis-à-vis the earlier Latin inscriptions were highlighted by Ruskin (2007: 364): 'Note, by the by, the pure Venetian dialect used in this capital, instead of the Latin in the more ancient ones.'

[5] See Chapter 1, 43.

[6] On the Aristotelianism that informs the political culture of the Venetian Republic in the Middle Ages and the Renaissance (especially on the circulation of ideas taken from Aristotle's *Politics*), see Dibello (2015).

[7] For the text of the invective, see Marsh (2004). For an introduction to Petrarch's *De ignorantia*, see Kennedy (2009).

allows us to grasp the premises of similar discussions that, through translation, became relevant to the production of vernacular texts as well, as the case studies in this chapter will demonstrate.

Petrarch's targets are four of his Venetian friends (a soldier, a merchant, a nobleman and a physician), all of whom present themselves as following in Aristotle's venerable footsteps. The four had attacked Petrarch's presumed lack of philosophical knowledge, had criticised his penchant for eloquence, and had exhibited a resentment stemming primarily from his critique of the authoritative idea of knowledge that the medieval interpreters, in Petrarch's opinion, identified with Aristotle. Yet in the somewhat paradoxical and ironic apology of his own ignorance, Petrarch shows that the issue at stake is not Aristotle's philosophy but, instead, blind allegiance to the philosopher, which can only perpetuate sterile learning and can never make knowledge truly productive. Whereas Dante had not dared challenge Aristotle's *auctoritas*, Petrarch is not intimidated by the 'master of those who know'. Though it would be wrong to describe Petrarch as anti-Aristotelian, it is no secret that he had a clear preference for Plato, whom he considered, alongside Augustine, the pagan philosopher who most approximated Christian truth.[8] Plato's primacy is made explicit in Petrarch's *Triumphi*, which deliberately rewrites Dante's portrayal of the ancient philosophers in Limbo. In the *Triumphus Famae* ('Triumph of Fame'), Petrarch describes Plato as the philosopher 'who of them all came closest to the goal / Where to by Heaven's grace man may attain'; Aristotle, who comes next, is instead celebrated simply for his 'high intellect'.[9] Petrarch is hardly lessening the importance of Aristotle's philosophical legacy, but instead suggests – here and also more clearly in the *De ignorantia* – that, although Aristotle should be certainly considered an extraordinarily knowledgeable human being, he was still a mortal.[10] Aristotle contributed widely to the advancement of knowledge, but he also made mistakes, so, while he should not be chastised, he should not be idolised either.

Petrarch's critique of his 'Aristotelian' friends is twofold. On one hand, by building an argument relevant to the reception of classical authors, he places his Christian faith before his veneration of the ancients. Accordingly, while he respects Aristotle's legacy, he privileges the Christian tradition

---

[8] On Petrarch's preference for Plato, see Kraye (1993: 16–19); and Fenzi (2008: 63). On Petrarch's role in the birth of the humanist movement, see among others Witt (2000: 230–91) and Celenza (2017).
[9] Petrarch, *Triumphus Famae III*, 4–7 (transl. Wilkins), in Pacca and Paolino (1996: 433–4): 'e vidi Plato, / che 'n quella schiera andò più presso al segno / al qual aggiunge cui dal cielo è dato; / Aristotele poi, pien d'alto ingegno'.
[10] Bianchi (1994).

when theology and, to some extent, secular morality are concerned. On the other hand, Petrarch protests the notion of *auctoritas* at the core of his friends' approach to the transmission of knowledge, disapproving of the scholastics' use of Aristotle and their tendency to hypostatise the philosopher. A third, crucial concern that runs across the invective and that, in a way, encompasses the author's other arguments is Petrarch's advocacy of eloquence and, more generally, his treatment of the communicative and performative functions of language.

One of the main flaws Petrarch identifies in the Aristotelian tradition is its lack of interest in the implementation of virtue. Petrarch argues that the real purpose of moral education is to practice virtue and not just to be knowledgeable about virtue. Pivotal to such an achievement is, in his opinion, good use of language. In this framework, eloquence does not wholly consist of a refined style inspired by the literary models of the past, but instead primarily concerns disseminating philosophical teachings and inciting students to behave in accordance with them. Scholarship has already acknowledged that this attitude is what situates Petrarch at the forefront of humanism and distinguishes him from the academic traditions of his own time.[11] If knowledge is what his friends praise – knowledge as a pursuit detached from the real practice of virtue – then Petrarch prefers to be considered 'unlearned': 'illiteratus', the same word commonly used to describe those without Latin.[12] He thus outlines a distinction between 'learned' and 'unlearned' people within the context of Latinate culture. The argument is subtle and suggests that Petrarch's primary concern is not the use of one language versus another (e.g., Latin vs. Italian), but instead the very conception of language. Petrarch defends eloquence as a tool for the critical appropriation of knowledge against a less flexible use of language based on an uncritical acceptance of the *auctoritas* principle.

Even if Petrarch's discussion refers to an entirely Latin context, the core of his argument applies to both intra-linguistic and inter-linguistic relations. More specifically, issues of translation and textual interpretation surface in his critique of the linguistic deformation that, in Petrarch's opinion, characterises the transmission of Aristotle in the Latin Middle Ages. If

---

[11] See Witt (2000: 230–91) and Kirkham and Maggi (2009); for a recent account of Petrarch's place within the cultural and ideological transition that informed the fourteenth century, see Celenza (2017).

[12] Marsh (2004: 342–3): 'Ego autem nitar semper et optabo illiteratus dici, dum vir bonus aut non malus sim, ut vel sic quiescam: fesso nil dulcius est quiete' ('Still, I shall always strive and hope to be called unlearned, so long as I am good or at least not bad; and so long as this brings me rest, for nothing is sweeter to the weary than rest').

Petrarch does not approve of the philosopher's style, this is not the fault of Aristotle but instead of the poor Latin translations available at that time:

> Now, I admit that I take no great pleasure in the style of the famous man, as it comes down to us. But before I was condemned on a charge of ignorance, I learned from Greek witnesses and from Cicero's writings that Aristotle's personal style was sweet, copious, and ornate. Yet because of the coarseness or the envy of his translators, the text of Aristotle has come down to us so harsh and rough that it scarcely charms the ear or sticks in the memory. This is why it is often easier for the speaker and more pleasant for the listener to express Aristotle's thought in words different from his own.[13]

His perspective on the shabby translations of Aristotle resembles the attitude that would later inform Leonardo Bruni's humanist project of new Latin translations capable of restoring the philosopher's eloquence from the perversions of the medieval translators.[14] They believed these rough, older translations of Aristotle could only disseminate sterile erudition and that the transmission of Aristotle's philosophical legacy could only be effective if rephrased in a correct and eloquent Latin. In fact, Petrarch directly experienced the limitations of the Latin versions of Aristotle's works, the *Ethics* in particular, for even if they made him more learned, he says, they failed to have any effect on his will.[15]

Petrarch's criticism of the translators coheres with his harsh remarks on the commentators of Aristotle, who were also responsible for the deformation of the text. By targeting the practice of commenting upon authoritative sources, which was a main feature of academic culture in the Middle Ages, Petrarch challenges the very core of the education system of his time:

> There are people who dare not write anything of their own. In their desire to write, they turn to expounding the works of others ... From

[13] *Ibid.*: 312–13: 'Equidem fateor me stilo viri illius, qualis est nobis, non admodum delectari, quamvis eum in sermone proprio et dulcem et copiosum et ornatum fuisse, Grecis testibus et Tullio auctore, didicerim, antequam ignorantie sententia condemnarer. Sed interpretum ruditate vel invidia ad nos durus scaberque pervenit, ut nec ad plenum mulcere aures possit, nec herere memorie; quo fit ut interdum Aristotilis mentem non illius, sed suis verbis exprimere et audienti gratius et promptius sit loquenti.'

[14] On Bruni's translations, see Chapter 4, 75–8.

[15] Marsh (2004: 314–15): 'Aristotilis libros legi, quosdam etiam audivi, et antequam hec tanta detegeretur ignorantia, intelligere aliquid visus eram, doctiorque his forsitan nonnunquam, sed non – qua decuit – melior factus ad me redii, et sepe mecum et quandoque cum aliis questus sum illud rebus non impleri, quod in primo *Ethicorum* philosophus idem ipse prefatus est, eam scilicet philosophie partem disci, non ut sciamus, sed ut boni fiamus' ('I have read all of Aristotle's books on ethics, and have heard lectures on some of them. Indeed, before my great ignorance was discovered, I seemed to understand some of his teaching. At times they perhaps made me more learned, but never a better person, as was proper. I often complained to myself and sometimes to others that the goal announced by the philosopher in Book One of his *Ethics* is not realized in fact – namely, that we study this branch of philosophy not in order to know, but in order to become good').

this, they seek praise which they cannot hope to win on their own or with others' help, but only by praising authors and books in their chosen field – and by praising them impetuously, immoderately, and always with great hyperbole. Our age in particular offers a multitude of people who expound others' works or, should I say, who devastate them?[16]

By attacking the commentators of Aristotle, Petrarch is attacking a long-established academic practice that, in his opinion, is of no service to the text or the audience. Rather than committing to the proper dissemination of knowledge, commentators perform an activity that is not only unrelated to actual learning but also primarily self-referential, far from the activities philosophy ought to perform. With his invective *De ignorantia*, Petrarch is thus proposing an approach to the classical past in direct conflict with the dominant academic culture of his time. He is at once taming the inflexibility of the legacy as championed by the Scholastics while also identifying the performative function of language as the tool with which virtue can be attained. By prioritising Christian revelation over pagan philosophy, Petrarch tames Aristotle's *auctoritas*, but the obscurity of the language spoken by the Aristotle of the Scholastics is also tamed by the philosophical task Petrarch confers on language. As this chapter will demonstrate, Petrarch's criticism finds relevance well beyond the boundaries of Latin culture and resonates with the vernacular reception of Aristotle at the time of the humanist turn.

The mechanisms outlined in Petrarch's invective – in particular the way in which academic discussions of ethics and language reflected concurrent developments within the vernacular world – can be usefully explored in the context of Venetian manuscript culture. The decades between the representation of 'Aristoteles dialecticus' in the mid-fourteenth century and the 'Aristotile che diè lege' in the mid-fifteenth century were crucial in the development of a specific lay readership that tended to combine the prestige of an aristocratic heritage with large-scale mercantile activities. Two of Petrarch's 'Aristotelian' friends addressed in the invective belonged to this class of wealthy, socially influential and, in most cases, politically powerful men: the merchant Tommaso Talenti and the nobleman Zaccaria

---

[16] *Ibid.*: 322–3: 'Sunt qui nichil per seipsos scribere audeant et, scribendi avidi, alienorum expositores operum fiant … et hinc laudem querant, quam nec per se sperant posse assequi, nec per alios, nisi illos in primis et illorum libros, hoc est subiectum cui incubuere, laudaverint, animose id ipsum, et immodice, ac multa semper yperbole. Quanta vero sit multitudo – aliena dicam exponentium, an aliena vastantium? – hac presertim tempestate.'

Contarini. Both were well educated in Latin, as far as we can understand from the invective, and represented a social class that, in Petrarch's time, legitimised its cultural status by sharing the forms of knowledge set forth by the academic establishment.[17] Though Talenti and Contarini were able to engage a scholar of Petrarch's stature in a Latin conversation, the same cannot be said of many of their peers, especially those whose commitments were not primarily focused on learning. While cultivated patricians and high-ranking merchants did usually receive some measure of Latin education, they lacked the proficiency and the time to confront classical sources directly. For most of these readers, language was an instrument of negotiation; hence their preference for the vernacular and, more specifically, their interest in translations of texts that could legitimise their professional and civic status.

The unique social and economic structures of Venice distinguished its aristocrats, usually involved with mercantile businesses, from those of other cities, who were generally landowners. As Niccolò Machiavelli would observe at the beginning of the sixteenth century, picturing a situation that had remained basically unchanged, 'the Gentlemen in that Republic [i.e., Venice] are more so in name than in fact, as they do not have great incomes from possessions, their riches being founded on commerce and movable property'. Having neither extensive estates such as castles nor jurisdiction over other men, Machiavelli continued, 'that name of Gentleman is [in them] a name of dignity and reputation, without being based on those things on which men are called Gentlemen in other Cities'.[18] Indeed, the concepts of 'dignity' and 'reputation' were both chief preoccupations of Venetian aristocrats involved in mercantile activities, especially when the legitimation of their wealth and moral profile through culture were concerned.

---

[17] For an overview of schooling and education in medieval and Renaissance Venice, see Grendler (1989: 42–70); more precisely, on the specifics of mercantile education, see *ibid.*: 306–29.

[18] Machiavelli, *Discorsi sulla prima deca di Tito Livio* 1.55, transl. Walker and Richardson in Crick (2003: 247–8). For the original passage, see Vivanti (2000: 120–1): 'i gentiluomini in quella Republica sono più in nome che in fatto; perché loro non hanno grandi entrate di possessioni, sendo le loro ricchezze grandi fondate in sulla mercanzia e cose mobili, e di più, nessuno di loro tiene castella, o ha alcuna iurisdizione sopra gli uomini: ma quel nome di gentiluomo in loro è nome di degnità e di riputazione, sanza essere fondato sopra alcuna di quelle cose che fa che nell'altre città si chiamano i gentiluomini'. The dual status of Venitian patricians, involved with both political offices and mercantile affairs, has been poignantly outlined by Luzzatto (1961: 33). A standardised feature of Venetian society between the fourteenth and fifteenth centuries, the involvement of patricians in trade and commerce that Machiavelli describes tends to decrease during the sixteenth century. For a detailed account of this shift, see Tucci (1973: 346–78).

To consider this process of legitimation in light of developments in the vernacular reception of Aristotle in the period, this chapter explores two case studies of the patronage related to the Venetian branch of the illustrious Giustiniani family in the fifteenth century: the first complete Italian version of the *Nicomachean Ethics*, translated from Latin in the 1430s by the Augustinian friar Antonio Colombella of Recanati at the behest of the merchant and nobleman Pancrazio Giustiniani, and the annotated translation of the pseudo-Aristotelian treatise *On Virtues and Vices*, published by the Dominican theologian Lazzaro Gallineta of Padua in the 1460s and dedicated to Pancrazio's son-in-law, Bernardo. The unusual quantity of paratextual materials that frame the two works reveal Colombella's and Gallineta's ideas about translation as a process aimed at the dissemination of philosophical knowledge – a fundamentally moral knowledge – among a lay audience of patrician and mercantile stock. At the same time, the two examples offer invaluable insights into the kind of readers who actively partook in the processes of translation and reception of Aristotle. A further case in point is offered by statements about the education of merchants such as those found in Benedetto Cotrugli's *Libro de l'arte de la mercatura* ('Book on the Art of Trade', 1458), discussed towards the close of this chapter. Each of these works demonstrates in its own way that Petrarch's preoccupation with the use of language and the efficacy of moral teachings was also central to the vernacular production and consumption of philosophical works a century later.

Conversation Piece

A stylishly dressed gentleman listens to a friar who converses with him in an elegant miniature [Figure 3.3] that opens the dedication copy of Antonio Colombella's Italian translation of the *Nicomachean Ethics*. As the manuscript (now in Modena, Biblioteca Estense Universitaria, MS Ital. 279) announces, the work was completed by Colombella for Pancrazio Giustiniani, whose coat of arms stands out on the lower border of the decoration that frames the first folio.[19] The depiction of the conversation

---

[19] Modena, Biblioteca Estense Universitaria, MS Ital. 279 [alpha.P.5.6]. The dedicatee, Pancrazio Giustiniani, is mentioned by the translator in the prologue ('mesere Pancrati Iustiniani de la illustrissima terra di Venegia', fol. 1*v*) and in the afterword ('Onde ad me basta avere satisfacto ad voi, messere Pancrati, che di questa fatica ne sete stato cagione', fol. 172*r–v*). The coat of arms of the Giustiniani family appears on fol. 1*r*. For a description of the manuscript, see Fava and Salmi (1950: 119–20). A transcription of Colombella's prologue and afterword (along with a passage from the text of Colombella's translation of the *Ethics*) was provided by Giovanni Galvani (see it in Galvani 1894: 77–81). More recently, both texts are edited in Refini (2013: 335–41).

Figure 3.3 Modena, Biblioteca Estense Universitaria, MS Ital. 279 [alpha.P.5.6], fol. 1r

between the theologian and the patrician represents visually the process of translation and reception embodied by Colombella's work: while both preface and miniature, in a way, give voice to the translator rather than to the reader, the project as a whole also witnesses the active role of the patron, whose desire to own the *Ethics* in his mother tongue sheds light on the cultural transformations that informed vernacular readership in the early fifteenth century. More precisely, the manuscript illuminates the cultural space in which vernacular translation created connections not only between Latinate authors and non-Latinate readers, but also between the various cultural trends associated with each. Before investigating the fluid situation witnessed by Colombella's translation, let us dwell for a moment on the actors involved in this conversation.

Apparently, the author of the translation and the dedicatee did not meet in Venice, since, as far as we know, Colombella never visited the city.[20] An Augustinian friar from Recanati, Colombella was trained at the Florentine convent of Santo Spirito before moving to Paris in 1419 to be a lector at the Studium Generale. He studied theology, obtained his degree there in 1424 and remained in Paris until 1432. After short-term duties in Tournai and Basel, where he held important conciliar offices on behalf of the Augustinian order, Colombella was offered a chair of theology at the university of Leuven, where he lived from 1434 to 1441.[21] During his time in Flanders, Antonio joined his colleagues from the Augustinian convent of Bruges in an attempt to move the newly founded university of Leuven there.[22] Despite the strong support of the dukes of Brabant, the attempt failed and Antonio was forced to relinquish his chair. He later moved to Rome, where he lived in the convent of Sant'Agostino and in 1447, thanks to his personal relations with Pope Nicholas V, he was made bishop of Senigallia.[23] After a quarrel with Sigismondo Pandolfo Malatesta, lord of Rimini, Antonio moved to Ancona in 1456 and resided there until his death in 1466.

Much less is known about Pancrazio Giustiniani and, in particular, the circumstances around his commissioning of the undated translation of the *Ethics*. Nonetheless, several clues allow us to make a plausible hypothesis about the chronological and geographical context that led to Antonio's

---

[20] For a biography of Antonio Colombella, see Alonso (1982).
[21] See Reusens (1881–1903: vol. 1: 192 and 2:39, 41–2, 45–74, 156, 158, 161ff.).
[22] De Jongh (1911: 37, 39, 87ff.).
[23] Alonso (1977: 197–222).

translation. The decoration of the manuscript, particularly the miniature representing the translator and the dedicatee, has been stylistically linked to the Swiss painter Jean Bapteur, active in Italy, Switzerland and France during the 1430s and 1440s.[24] This chronology coheres with the identification of the dedicatee as one of the two members of the Giustiniani family who, in the first half of the century, were both named Pancrazio: Pancrazio, son of Orsato, and the eponymous son of Pancrazio's brother Marco.[25] Since very little is known about these two, it is difficult to establish connections between either of them and Antonio Colombella. Fortunately, the younger Pancrazio wrote several letters to his father Marco between 1429 and 1430 from Bruges, where he was living as a member of the community revolving around the Morosini family.[26]

The length of the younger Pancrazio's stay in Flanders is uncertain, but it is known that Colombella, during his time in Leuven, had a strong relationship with Bruges, where he was in touch with the local Italian community.[27] Assuming that Pancrazio stayed in Bruges or had contacts in the town during the 1430s, it is plausible that he met Colombella there. The fact that Colombella's ecclesiastic title does not appear in the manuscript – the translator simply introduces himself as 'maestro' and a member of the Augustinian order ('me, maestro Antonio da Ricanati de l'ordine di Sancto Agostino') – suggests that the translation was finished before 1447, when Antonio was made bishop.[28] While the translation is extremely important in itself, particularly for its attempt to give Aristotle a vernacular voice at a time when the merits of Italian vis-à-vis Latin could not be taken for granted, what will be of particular interest to the present study is the translator's attempt at framing the text and guiding the vernacular reader through the reading.

---

[24] Fava and Salmi (1950: 119–20).

[25] In 1423, the elder Pancrazio married one of the daughters of Giovanni di Pietro Emo. His nephew Pancrazio, son of Marco Giustiniani, married Isabella di Francesco di Federico Cornaro in 1424 and was a member of the Quarantia Criminal, one of the Venetian institutions in charge of the management of justice; see Litta (1819–64: vol. 18 (1840), table 5). For a history of the Giustiniani family, with details about both Pancrazios, see Hopf (1859). See Refini (2013: 341) for a summary of the Giustiniani genealogy, based on Litta.

[26] The letters, preserved in Antonio Morosini's diary, treat several topics of contemporary history, including details about the action brought against Joan of Arc; see Nanetti (2010). For a reassessment of biographical details about Pancrazio, see the appendix to Dorez and Lefèvre-Pontalis (1898–1902 vol. 4: 300–5).

[27] For an overview of Italian mercantile communities based outside Italy, see Tanzini and Tognetti (2012).

[28] Refini (2013: 336).

Accessing the *Nicomachean Ethics* in the Vernacular

There is no record that Colombella knew of Leonardo Bruni's new Latin translation of the *Nicomachean Ethics*, which Bruni dedicated to Pope Martin V in 1417, but given the resonance of Bruni's achievement across Europe, it would be no surprise if he did. Still, Colombella translated Aristotle's treatise from Robert Grosseteste's Latin version, as revised by William of Moerbeke. Colombella's choice was certainly consistent with his scholastic training, but it can also be read as a statement about the value of the Aristotelian corpus studied in universities and in schools of the religious orders. Indeed, in translating the *Ethics*, Colombella follows his source closely: his vernacular text repeats syntactic and lexical features from the Latin Aristotle, in the attempt to offer the reader an inter-lingual replica of the source text. Nevertheless, he does attempt to aid the reader, intervening where needed to unpack the obscurity of his Latin source. For instance, as we will see below, he adopts a particular way of dealing with Grosseteste's method of transliterating Greek words, a method that was heavily criticised by Bruni. While a scholar like Colombella would likely have endorsed Alfonso de Cartagena's critique of Bruni's humanist version of the *Ethics*, the practice of vernacular translation offered him the opportunity to comment explicitly on a textual tradition that he found problematic.[29] In fact, Colombella's preface not only introduces vernacular readers to the *Ethics*, thus rehearsing the function typically performed in the Latin commentary tradition by the *accessus ad textum* ('introduction to the text'), but it also addresses issues of translation.[30]

Colombella's prologue to Pancrazio Giustiniani opens with a reference to the notion of nobility. By recalling a passage from Seneca's *Epistles*, Colombella reminds his reader that 'nobility is virtue' or rather 'freedom from vices.'[31] He develops his argument with an explicit allusion to a passage from the fourth book of Aristotle's *Politics*, which states that nobility consists of the union between virtue and wealth. This passage, which Dante also quotes in the *Convivio*, does not imply that wealth

---

[29] On the so-called '*Ethics* controversy' between Leonardo Bruni and Alfonso de Cartagena, see Griffiths, Hankins and Thompson (1987: 201–8), Baldassarri (2003: 93–103), Botley (2004: 41–62) and Valero Moreno (2015).

[30] The manuscript is articulated as follows: (a) the translator's prologue to the dedicatee, fols. 1r–2v; (b) a life of Aristotle, fols. 2v–3v; (c) Aristotle's *Nicomachean Ethics*, fols. 5r–171v; (d) the translator's afterword, addressed to the dedicatee, fols. 171v–172v; and (e) paragraph indexes with relevant rubrics at the beginning of each book.

[31] Modena, Biblioteca Estense Universitaria, MS Ital. 279, fol. 1r. The translator is probably referencing Seneca, *Epistles* 5.3 where the topic of nobility is discussed.

supports nobility – for Aristotle himself maintains elsewhere that virtue, not wealth, is what makes people illustrious – but that it can, when properly employed, make virtue stand out.[32] Colombella then describes his dedicatee as an excellent example of nobility, whose noble origins harken back to the emperor Justinian. The present translation of the *Ethics*, he continues, was hotly solicited by Pancrazio himself and will strengthen the young Venetian's noble nature. But the translator does not conceal his concerns about the difficulty of translating the Aristotelian treatise into the dedicatee's mother tongue ('parlare materno'). Rather, knowing that other translators had struggled before him, Colombella agreed to embark on the translation only for the sake of his friendship with Pancrazio.[33] Beyond reproducing the well-established topos of authorial modesty, here he also refers to the real challenge of translating the *Ethics*, an issue he will address later in the prologue and at further length in the afterword.

Colombella then proceeds to summarise moral philosophy, the contents of Aristotle's *Ethics* and the interrelated notions of happiness and virtue. Evoking the tripartite character of Aristotle's moral philosophy, a commonplace in the exegetical tradition, Colombella argues for three different kinds of virtue in mortals. As a 'rational animal' ('animale ragionevole'), one needs 'moral virtue' ('morale virtù') to distinguish oneself from beasts; as a 'family-oriented animal' ('animale familiare et domestico'), one requires 'virtues pertaining to the administration of the household' ('virtù dispensative et yconomiche'); finally, as a social animal, one must have 'political virtues' ('virtù civile et politiche').[34] It is worth noting that the domains of economics and politics are markedly interrelated in Colombella's account. The label 'animale familiare et domestico' in fact refers to both the private sphere of the house, concerned with relations between family members (parents, wife, sons, servants), and the collective sphere of society, which refers to the management of public relations (citizens, foreigners, peers and members of superior or inferior ranks).[35] Only

---

[32] *Ibid.*: 'determina Aristotile nel quarto de la Politica che gentilezza è virtù congiunta con antiche ricchezze' ('In *Politics*, book 4, Aristotle determines that nobility is virtue in conjunction with old wealth'). See Aristotle, *Politics* 4.8, 1294a 21–2. See also Dante, *Convivio* 4.3.6: 'Federigo di Soave … domandato che fosse gentilezza, rispuose ch'era antica ricchezza e belli costumi' ('Frederick of Swabia … when asked what nobility was, replied that it was ancestral wealth and fine manners'); and cf. Dante, *Monarchia* 2.3.4: 'Est enim nobilitas virtus et divitie antique, iuxta Phylosophum in Politicis'.

[33] Modena, Biblioteca Estense Universitaria, MS Ital. 279, fol. 1*v*.

[34] *Ibid.*: fol. 2*r*.

[35] On the interplay of ethics, economics and politics within the Aristotelian exegetical tradition, see Weijers (1988), Lafleur and Carrier (1995: 406) and Lines (2005: 11–12). For similar articulations of Aristotle's moral philosophy, see among others Costa (2008: 174–5), with relevant references

when completely liberated from vice and passions and completely focused on the exercise of reason can mortals turn to the divine in order to attain the highest level of happiness accorded to human beings. The three kinds of virtue correspond directly to divisions in Aristotle's moral corpus and the way moral philosophy was taught at the university: the *Nicomachean Ethics* and the *Magna Moralia* deal with the self, while the *Economics* treats the family and the *Politics* considers society as a whole.[36]

After this summary, Colombella turns to the difficulty of his task as a translator. Several Latin translators (e.g., Jerome) had discussed this topic, but only a few medieval ones had provided readers with explicit and conscious remarks on their task.[37] Colombella first articulates the difference between Aristotle's 'way of speaking' and 'ours', by which he means the difference between Aristotle's writing style (as Colombella would have known it through the Latin of the medieval version) and the elements peculiar to the Italian tongue: 'Since Aristotle's way of speaking is very meticulous ("scrupoloso") and most dissimilar to ours, by trying to get as close as I can to it, I will sometimes use his exact words, at other times I will use his sense and, more often, I will follow both.'[38] Colombella identifies meticulousness as an element peculiar to Aristotle's style and his use of the adjective 'scrupoloso' refers to a specific way of developing arguments and sentences that he will later posit as central to philosophical language.[39]

The distinction between 'words' ('parole') and 'sense' ('senso') nonetheless situates his remarks within the enduring debate over *verbum de verbo* and *ad sensum* translations, suggesting a compromise that accounts for the uniqueness in the source text and adopts a flexible approach to the text itself, as the translator follows both words and sense. The translator's compromise, as he soon reveals, aims to respect the source text while promoting eloquence: he sees as one of the translator's key duties that of establishing the true meaning of the text ('Sempre servando la verità del texto') while also recommending that translators preserve the elegance of

---

to Eustratius as a main source for such tripartite subdivision of moral philosophy; and Costa (2010: 109–10, 129–30). Colombella will summarise again the subdivision of moral philosophy when explaining the title of the *Ethics*; see below.

[36] Modena, Biblioteca Estense Universitaria, MS Ital. 279, fol. 2r–v.

[37] See Folena (1991) and Cornish (2011).

[38] Modena, Biblioteca Estense Universitaria, MS Ital. 279, fol. 2v: 'Et perché el dire d'Aristotile è scrupoloso molto et molto strano dal modo del parlare nostro, accostandomi al suo parlare quanto potrò, alcuna volta dirò le sue proprie parole, alcuna volta el senso, et le più de le volte l'uno et l'altro.'

[39] The relevance of the adjective to philosophical language is confirmed by its employment in related early Italian sources. See *Legenda aurea*, 129, for example, where the term refers to the study of philosophy and logic: 'con scrupoloso studio siamo andati per questi sillogismi de' filosofi' (Levasti 1924–26 vol. 3: 1139); 'with meticulous study we have gone through these syllogisms of philosophers'.

the language into which the text is translated ('la elegantia de la loquela nostra').[40] Echoing Jerome's arguments for preserving the distinctive feel of the target language, Colombella's use of the word 'elegantia' reveals his concern for matters of style and confirms his awareness of the notion of *proprietas linguarum*.[41]

To preempt criticism, Colombella returns to these issues in the afterword as well. As regards the opposition between *verbum de verbo* and *ad sensum* translation, Colombella further explains that translations demand a certain degree of flexibility:

> I must confess that on many occasions I had to give the sense, for the words given in their original order would be so odd that they would not be intelligible. Many times I have added a noun or an adjective. Often I have explained some specific terms in order to make the sense consistent; and often I have lengthened [a sentence], replaced antecedents with relative pronouns, and replaced *et* with *vel* and *vel* with *et*.[42]

Colombella's advocacy of translating the understood meaning behind the words is also illustrated later in the afterword, when he imagines the readers' responses to certain problematic passages: 'in a few cases I had to make explicit a sentence about which Aristotle keeps silent, leaving to the expert reader [the duty to supply it]: nonetheless, if a sentence is omitted, the surrounding portion of the text will be incomplete'.[43] By making explicit what the author leaves unspoken, the translator discloses the truly exegetical nature of his endeavour.

---

[40] Modena, Biblioteca Estense Universitaria, MS Ital. 279, fol. 2*v*.

[41] For Jerome's statements on *elegantia* and *proprietas*, see Chiesa (1987: 15–19). Compare the prologue to Thomas Aquinas', *Contra errores Graecorum*, where he writes that translators should be able to change their 'way of speaking' according to the rules and properties of the language into which a text is translated: 'Unde ad officium boni translatoris pertinet ut ea quae sunt Catholicae fidei transferens, servet sententiam, mutet autem modum loquendi secundum proprietatem linguae in quam transfert. Apparet enim quod si ea quae litteraliter in Latino dicuntur, vulgariter exponantur, indecens erit expositio, si semper verbum ex verbo sumatur' ('It is, therefore, the task of the good translator, when translating material dealing with the Catholic faith, to preserve the meaning, but to adapt the mode of expression so that it is in harmony with the idiom of the language into which he is translating. For obviously, when anything spoken in a literary fashion in Latin is explained in common parlance, the explanation will be inept if it is simply word for word', transl. Fehlner).

[42] Modena, Biblioteca Estense Universitaria, MS Ital. 279, fol. 171*v*: 'confesso che m'è stato necessità dire molte volte la sentenza, però che le parole così proprio come stanno sarebbono sì strane che non farebbono intelligentia. Et molte volte ho aggiunto el substantivo o vero l'aiectivo, et spesso dichiarato alcun termine acciò che la sentenza meglio consuone, et spesso ho allungato et messo el relativo per l'antecedente, et per *vel*, et *vel* per *et*.'

[43] *Ibid.*: 'È stato ancor bisogno in alcuno luogo dire una sentenza che Aristotile tace, lassandola al perito lectore: et se ella non se dicesse sarebbe el texto vicino tronco.'

This attitude, which recalls some of the topoi central to the contemporary debate on translation, continues a tradition already well established in the vernacular context. Bartholomew of San Concordio (1262–1347), for instance, opened his translation of Sallust's *Bellum Catilinae* ('Conspiracy of Catiline') by pointing out the need to reshape the text in order to make it suitable to the vernacular tongue; in other words, he sought to provide a text that could be easily understood by readers unacquainted with the peculiarities of the Latin language.[44] Gentile da Foligno (c. 1272–1348) was also aware of the differences between Latin ('gramatica') and the vernacular when he produced a translation of the devotional treatise *Scala Paradisi* ('Ladder of Paradise') chiefly focused on the transmission of its 'sententia'.[45] In his version of Livy, however, Giovanni Boccaccio advocated helping vernacular readers to understand and enjoy a text through translations informed by exegetical intentions. Boccaccio used the term 'esposizione', which recasts translation as explanation, and stated that his readers would have difficulty reading a strictly word-for-word rendition.[46]

The clearest example of Colombella's approach to his source text is his clarification of those philosophical terms that in the Grosseteste-Moerbeke version of the *Ethics* had only been transliterated from Greek into Latin

[44] Puoti (1843: 3–4): 'sì mi brigherò di recarlo al volgare, benchè malagevolmente far si possa, per la gravezza del libro, e perché le parole e il modo volgare non rispondono in tutto alla lettera; anzi conviene ispesse fiate d'una parola per lettera dirne più in volgare, e non saranno però così proprie. Anche alle fiate si conviene uscir alquanto delle parole per isponere la sententia e per poter parlare più chiaro ed aperto' ('I will do my best to bring it into the vernacular, even if this is a difficult task due to the gravity of the book and to the fact that vernacular words and style do not correspond precisely to the Latin ones; on the contrary, oftentimes, one Latin word requires multiple vernacular ones, which will not be as specific. Also, one often needs to leave the words somewhat to explain the sense and speak more clearly and openly').

[45] De Luca (1954: 3): 'non intendo di seguitare al tutto l'ordine delle parole del libro, scritte in gramatica, però che in questo modo non si dichiara bene, per la molta differenzia che è dal parlare in volgare al gramaticale; ma intendo di ponere le sentenzie delle parti e de' paragrafi del libro … più chiaro ch'io potrò' ('I do not aim to follow closely the order of words in the book as they are in Latin; this would not let me explain the text well due to the great difference between Latin and the vernacular; but I plan to offer the sense of the sections and paragraphs of the book to the best of my ability').

[46] Pizzorno (1842–45 vol. 5: 10–11): 'Né è mio intendimento nella sposizione … seguire strettamente per tutto la lettera dell'Autore: perocché, ciò facendo, non veggio che io al fine intento potessi venire acconciamente, il quale è di voler fare chiaro a' non intendenti la intenzione di T. Livio. Perciocché non in un luogo uno, ma in molti esso sì precisamente scrive, che se sole le sue parole, senza più, si ponesseno, si rimarebbe tronco il volgare a coloro, dico, i quali non sono di troppo sottile avvedimento, che così pocc ne intenderebbero volgarizzato, come per lettera' ('In my exposition, I will not follow closely the words of the Author: if I did that, I would not get to the desired outcome, which is to make Livy's intention clear to the unlearned. The reason for this is that in many places he writes in such a meaningful way that, should I leave the words as they are with nothing more, the vernacular phrasing would remain truncated, especially to those who are not skilled; as such, they would not understand it better than if they were reading it in Latin'). See also Folena (1991: 41–2). For similar ideas in Latin works, see in particular the case of Niccolò Tignosi's fifteenth-century commentary on the *Ethics* in Lines (2001: 35–42; 2002: 185–214).

without being given a proper translation. As my following chapter will recall, the issue lay at the core of Leonardo Bruni's criticism of the Latin medieval translations of Aristotle, which he accused of being unable to provide Latin equivalents to Greek terms. If Colombella, still respectful of the scholastic tradition, keeps the transliterated terms in his vernacular translation, he also commits to a systematic process of explanation through gloss. The translator thus compromises between the obscurity of the academic lexicon and the interpretive needs of his vernacular reader. Cacophonous words such as 'eutrapelo' (from 'eutrapelos', 'skilled in conversation') and 'bomolocho' (from 'bomolochos', 'scold') – just to stick to the examples pointed out by Bruni in the preface to his own translation of the *Ethics* – are duly explained with Italian equivalents ('dolce o gratioso', 'morditore'), which complete the translator's task.[47]

Colombella's reflection, however, is not restricted to general matters of translation, but also touches on philological methods. After having demonstrated his practice of expanding the text when the content is insufficient, Colombella recalls that the Latin version of Aristotle's text is corrupt in several passages and that the appearance of contradictory terms in different manuscripts can lead to conflicting interpretations.[48] Here, Colombella emphasises the translator's role in producing meaning, which, he explains, is the task also carried out by the 'expositori' (commentators).[49] The term 'expositori' refers to the exegetical practice of the *expositio*, a systematic rephrasing of the source aimed at explaining it. Indeed, the translator's reference to the commentators here is polemical, for interpreters never ceased to debate the meaning of controversial Aristotelian terms, which, depending on their context, may have disparate (and sometimes peculiar) meanings that often differ from the standard definition. Rather than address these discrepancies, commentators tended to champion interpretations that not only differed from what today's readers understand as the correct definition of the text, but were often in conflict with it.

---

[47] See the passage in *Ethica Nicomachea* (recensio recognita) 2.6, 08a25, in Gauthier (1974: 406): 'Circa delectabile autem quod quidem in ludo, medius quidem *eutrapelos*, et disposicio *eutrapelia*. Superhabundancia autem, *bomolochia*, et qui habet eam *bomolochos*.' Compare Colombella's translation in Modena, Biblioteca Estense Universitaria, MS Ital. 279, fol. 27v: 'Circa il dilecto nelle cose iocose, colui che è nel mezzo in Greco si dice *eutrapelo*, et la virtù *eutrapelia*; el latino li dice dolce o gratioso; et la soprabondanza in Greco *bomolochia* e colui che l'ha *bomolocho*; in latino si può dire morditore.' For Bruni's comments on these terms, see Chapter 4 of this book, 172–3.

[48] Modena, Biblioteca Estense Universitaria, MS Ital. 279, fols. 171v–172r: 'Truovasi anche li più de texti incorrepti et uno discorda dall'altro in molti termini donde se ne possono trare diversi intellecti' ('Most passages are incorrect and one is not consistent with the other in the use of several terms, which causes different understandings').

[49] *Ibid.*: fol. 172r.

When the text is fatally obscure, the only way for the translator to prevent the translation from being unduly interpretive is an abstruse word-for-word translation, a method that recalls Nicole Oresme's approach to the obscurity of Aristotle's *Ethics* in his French translation.[50] In such moments Colombella refers directly to the commentary tradition: 'the reader who wishes to understand those obscure passages is very welcome to turn to the commentators'.[51]

For Colombella, the presence of obscure and difficult passages is not due to any neglect of rhetorical elegance on Aristotle's part, for Aristotle's style did not pursue elegance (but is praiseworthy for other reasons).[52] In response to harsh criticisms of Aristotle's style such as Petrarch's, Colombella elaborates a defense based on the distinction of registers peculiar to different intellectual fields. Aristotle's style ('modo') cannot be translated rhetorically: the 'ornato rethorico piano et aperto' ('rhetorical style, clear and open') is peculiar to authors such as Cicero, Seneca and Macrobius, whose rhetorical qualities match the literary ambitions behind their production. Rather than follow a rhetorical mode, Aristotle's style aims to communicate logical procedures suitable for disputing and arguing and it aims towards rational demonstration, not rhetorical persuasion.[53]

Emphasising the distinction between rhetoric (understood to be the founding principle of literary composition) and logic (the founding principle of philosophical argument), Colombella in fact endorses the scholastic approach to Aristotle's text with an argument that recalls the most typical philosophical positions from late medieval *volgarizzamenti*. His assessment of the translated text, however, is unique for its critical

[50] *Ibid.*: 'acciò che non paia questa translatione più d'una oppinione che d'un'altra, m'è convenuto così propriamente ritrare come stanno le parole del texto' ('To avoid that this translation bear one opinion more than others, in some cases I followed the words as they are in the text'). Cf. Nicole Oresme's statement in his prologue to *Le livre de éthiques d'Aristote* in Menut (1940: 101): 'je ne ose pas esloingnier mon parler du texte de Aristote, qui est en pleuseurs lieux obscur, afin que je ne passe hors son intencion et que je ne faille' ('I do not dare distancing my words from the text of Aristotle, who is in many passages obscure; this I did in order not to betray his intention and to avoid mistakes').

[51] Modena, Biblioteca Estense Universitaria, MS Ital. 279, fol. 172r: 'chi la vuole intendere, vada agli expositori'.

[52] *Ibid.*: 'quella parte così detta è obscura et difficile molto, né si puote, così nel modo che tiene Aristotile, parlare con ornato rethorico piano et aperto' ('Those sections are obscure and very difficult, and, in Aristotle's style, it is not possible to speak in a rhetorically clear and straightforward way').

[53] *Ibid.*: 'el modo d'Aristotile è disputativo et argomentativo' ('Aristotle's style is disputative and based on logical arguments'); cf. Cartagena's similar statement in Griffiths, Hankins and Thompson (1987: 205–6): 'the man who wants to subordinate the strictest conclusions of the sciences to the rules of eloquence does not understand, when he is adding or subtracting words to create a suitable persuasive sweetness, that it is utterly foreign to the rigor of science'.

awareness, which well surpasses the commonplaces usually employed by
vernacular translators:

> Those who are willing to check whether I have translated well or not, should
> provide themselves with a correct and well studied passage, but they will
> find only a few passages of this kind. Moreover, before judging [my work],
> they should compare it with the source and then emend the translation
> where it needs to be emended.[54]

As this passage suggests, only a careful comparison between the source
text and the translated text will enable the reader to find mistakes and perhaps correct them. The terms employed by Colombella are worth stressing
since they appear to draw on the technical lexicon of philology. The verb
conferire, from the Latin *conferre*, for instance, refers to *collatio*, the critical
comparison between copies of the same text.[55] The verb *mendare*, however,
refers to the subsequent step of the philological process, the *emendatio*, the
emendation of the text.[56] The translation, then, is not simply conceived
by Colombella as a service text but, instead, as a potentially accurate and
faithful witness of the source and the result of a thorough study thereof.

Lastly, Colombella not only translated Aristotle's text, but also provided
each book of the *Ethics* 'with a table and summary of chapters ('la tavola
overo la sententia de capitoli') to make the subjects more easily accessible to the reader.'[57] While this was not an innovation in late medieval
manuscripts, Colombella's understanding of the practical function of
the table of contents is notable, for it confirms the authorial intentions
underpinning the paratext.[58] Indeed, these tables, opening each book of
the *Ethics*, are not bare lists of chapter headings but full summaries of the
contents of each book. Each 'tavola' offers an overview of the contents,
serving as a handy reference memorandum for the reader.

The 'tavola' of the second book illustrates the framing function of
Colombella's paratext:

> Book two has nine chapters, which cover the following topics:
>
> Virtues are neither natural nor against nature, but they are acquired through
> virtuous actions. Chapter 1.

---

[54] Modena, Biblioteca Estense Universitaria, MS Ital. 279, fol. 172r: 'Et però ciascuno che forsa vorrà
examinare se io ho ben translatato o non, priegho abbia un correpto et studiato texto, che ne troverà
pochi. Et prima che giudiche conferisca l'uno coll'altro, et poi mende ciò che è da mendare.'

[55] Rizzo (1973: 246–9).

[56] *Ibid.*: 249–50.

[57] Modena, Biblioteca Estense Universitaria, MS Ital. 279, fol. 2v.

[58] For an outline of the use of indexes in medieval and early modern manuscript culture, see Leonardi,
Morelli and Santi (1995).

There are no general rules about virtues that apply to all particular situations; virtues are corrupted by excess and defect. Chapter 2.

It says that evidence of possessing virtue is in being pleased or given pain by virtuous actions, and that virtue revolves around pleasure and pain. Chapter 3.

Not all those that perform virtuous actions are virtuous, and knowledge of virtue does not make one virtuous. Chapter 4.

It demonstrates that virtue is neither affection nor capacity, but habit of the soul. Chapter 5.

It infers by means of a deductive argument that virtue sits in the middle not in relation to things themselves, but in relation to man. Chapter 6.

It tells that virtues are in the middle between two vices, the one consisting in excess and the other consisting in defect. Chapter 7.

How the vice of excess is more contrary to some virtues, while the vice of defect is more contrary to other virtues, and for what reasons. Chapter 8.

It teaches the rules to find the virtuous mean, which is most difficult [to find]. Chapter 9.[59]

While indicating the content of each chapter, the index highlights the key concepts that Colombella believes should be learned from the *Ethics*. His treatment of the second book, with its focus on the notion of virtue, is particularly interesting in this respect. Without even entering the complexity of Aristotle's arguments, the reader can discern the basic ideas that inform Aristotelian moral philosophy: virtue as a habit; virtue as built through practice and not through theory (a statement that, by the way, coheres with Petrarch's preoccupation with the priority of the practice of virtue over its theoretical knowledge); virtue as a golden mean between vices at either extreme. As shown in similar examples from manuscripts across Europe, lay readers like Pancrazio sought 'clean' copies of texts, spared the overabundant explanations that characterised academic commentaries but

[59] Modena, Biblioteca Estense Universitaria, MS Ital. 279, fol. 19*r–v*: 'El secondo libro ha capitoli 9, ne' quali se contengono le seguente cose: Che le virtù non ci sono naturale né contra natura, ma per l'opere virtuose s'acquistar o. Cap. 1°. Che delle virtù non si può dare regola generale in tucte le cose particulare; et che elle si corronpono dalla soprabondanza et defico. Cap. 2°. Dice che 'l sengno d'avere virtù è dilectarse o tristarse nell'opere virtuose et che la virtù è circa la dilectatione et tristitia. Cap. 3°. Che non tuct che fanno l'opere virtuose sono virtuosi et che el sapere le virtù non fa l'uomo virtuoso. Cap. 4°. Pruova che la virtù non è passione né possanza, ma habito dell'anima. Cap. 5°. Deduce per ragione come la virtù sta nel mezzo non per rispecto delle cose in se stesse ma per rispecto dell'uomo. Cap. 6°. Narra come le virtù sono nel mezzo di due vitii, l'uno in soprabondanza, l'altro in difecto. Cap. 7°. Come ad alcuna virtù più è contrario el vitio che è soprabondanza, et alcuna p ù el vitio che è difecto et per che ragione. Cap. 8°. Insengna la regola di trovare el mezzo che è virtù dato che sia molto difficile. Cap. 9°.'

nonetheless equipped with some basic tools to facilitate the navigation of the work.[60]

Following the models of the Latin *accessus ad textum* and the *accessus ad auctorem* (and, in so doing, transposing these models into the vernacular), Colombella adds a short life of Aristotle to his introduction that outlines main biographical episodes and focuses on the meaning of the work's title, *Nicomachean Ethics*.[61] Aristotle is described as the chief philosopher of antiquity in a reference to Augustine's *City of God*, where Augustine criticises all the ancient philosophical schools except the Peripatetics. Augustine's reticence on Aristotle is interpreted by Colombella as his silent acknowledgement of Aristotle's compatibility with Christian doctrine.[62] Colombella's use of Augustine is nonetheless biased, for Augustine's discussion in the eighth and ninth books of the *City of God*, despite its minor criticisms of Platonic trends such as demonology, does not undermine his general promotion of Platonism as the philosophical school from antiquity closest to Christianity. The reference to Augustine as a symbol of the concordance of Aristotelianism with Christianity must instead stem from the theologian's training in Paris, where in the early fifteenth century similar views were popular.[63]

By explaining the history and meaning of the work's title, Colombella also provides details relevant to a comprehensive understanding of the work:

> [Aristotle] named one of his sons Nichomaco after his father, for whom he wrote the Ethics (although some people think he wrote the book for his father, while others say he wrote it for his father-in-law, also named Nichomaco). That is the reason why the work is entitled 'Libro de l'Ethica monostica nichomatia stragelica d'Aristotile peripathetico'. It is called 'Ethica' from 'Ethis,' that is, 'mos' and 'ycos,' that is, 'scientia,' which means

---

[60] An early fifteenth-century Spanish translator of Boethius not only provided his versions with rubrics and indexes at the opening of each book but also explained their function in the prologue to his work. Ruy López Dávalos, constable of Castile, had commissioned this work, explicitly requesting a 'clean' copy of the text, without academic features. The work is discussed by Lawrance (1985: 82–3). On the employment of paragraph headings, cf. *ibid.*: 82: 'E porque los títulos son claridad a la vía del proceder, e non se entreponga al texto cosa agena, en comienço de cada libro se porná una relación o argumento que señale algo de lo contenido en sus versos e prosas.'

[61] For an overview of Aristotle's biographies in the Greek, Arabic and Latin traditions, see Düring (1987). Colombella's *Life of Aristotle* clearly draws on the so-called *Vita Latina* (see the text *ibid.*: 151–8). As for the tradition of the *accessus ad auctorem*, see Copeland (1991: 66–76), with relevant bibliographical references.

[62] Modena, Biblioteca Estense Universitaria, MS Ital. 279, fol. 3r.

[63] An inspection of the most popular biographies of Aristotle that were circulating at the time did not allow me to find a precise source for Colombella's statement. I am grateful to Luca Bianchi for his helpful remarks on the passage.

science of habits, and it is called 'monosticha,' for it deals with those virtues relevant to one's own life. It is also called 'Nicomathia' from the names of his father, son and father-in-law, for it was to one of these that he dedicated the book. Finally, it is called 'Stragelica' from the name of Aristotle's birthplace.[64]

Despite the misspellings 'Nicomatia' and 'Stragiellicha' for 'Nichomacus' (Aristotle's son) and 'Stagira' (his birthplace), respectively, Colombella's brief explanation of the title aims to summarise the main object of Aristotle's treatise, the fulfilment of virtue.[65] More specifically, the etymology of the words 'ethica' and 'monosticha' draws on a tradition that stretches back to the scholastic interpretation of Aristotle: the explanation of 'ethis' as the original Greek term for 'mos', 'habit', is well established in etymological dictionaries, such as the *Derivationes Magnae* by Huguccio of Pisa.[66]

The etymological link between 'ycos' and 'scientia' (science, doctrine), however, draws on the study of Aristotelian texts. One might recall, in particular, the anonymous *Questiones super Librum Ethicorum Aristotelis* produced in late thirteenth-century Paris, which also provides a detailed discussion of the tripartite structure of moral philosophy ('monastica', 'yconomica', 'politica') identical to that which Colombella adopts in his own outline of Aristotle's moral corpus, as shown above. The prologue to the *Questiones*, 'Ethica dicitur ab ethi, quod est mos, et ycos, scientia, quasi scientia de moribus',[67] provides an etymological explanation for the title that probably stems from the *Auctoritates Aristotelis* and confirms

---

[64] *Ibid.*: fol. 3v: 'Ebbe un figliuolo tra gli altri el quale nominò del nome del padre, cioè Nicomacho, ad cui scripse el libro de l'*Ethica*, ben che alcuni dicono che lo scripse al padre, et altri che lo scripse al suocero, anche decto Nicomacho, onde el titolo di quello libro è questo: "libro de l'Ethica monostica nichomatia stragelica d'Aristotile peripathetico"; et è decta *ethica* ab *ethis* quod est *mos* et *ycos* quod est *scientia*, quasi scientia ci costumi; et *monostica* però che parla de le virtù pertinenti al vivere secondo sé solo; et *nichomatia* dal suo padre o dal figliuolo o dal suocero ad cui la scripse; et *stragelica* dal luogo ove nacque.'

[65] Similar misspellings were common in the textual tradition of the Latin *Ethics*; see, for example, Costa (2010: 130).

[66] Cecchini and Arbizzoni (2004: 397, s.v. 'ethis'): 'Ethis grece, latine dicitur mos; inde ethicus -a -um, idest moralis, et hec ethica -ce, idest moralitas vel scientia que tractat de moribus.'

[67] Costa (2010: 129–30). The meaning of both 'metaphysics' and 'logic' is also explained through the same reference to 'ycos' as 'scientia' in Duns Scotus' *Questions on the Metaphysics* (1, prologue: 'Et hanc scientiam vocamus metaphysicam, quae dicitur a 'meta', quod est 'trans', et 'ycos', 'scientia', quasi transcendens scientia, quia est de transcendentibus') and in Lambert of Auxerre's *Summa logicae* (1: 'Dicitur autem logica a logos quod est sermo, et ycos quod est scientia, quasi scientia de sermone'). Another example is in Peter of Auvergne, *Quaestiones super librum de caelo et mundo disputatae*, proem., 125–8, in Galle (2003: 12): 'bona moralia, quae triplicia sunt. Est unum bonum hominis in se et absolute et de illo determinatur in illa scientia morali sive in illa parte scientiae moralis quae dicitur monostica ve monosticalis. Et dicitur monostica a monos, unus, et ycos, scientia, quasi scientia docens se ipsum in actionibus suis regulare.'

Colombella's nuanced position.[68] The Augustinian Colombella is obviously familiar with the scholastic tradition, which would have played a major role in his education and which, in a way, is integrated into his project of *volgarizzamento*, one that appropriates ideas central to the coeval development of translation as a practice informed by strong methodological awareness.

As far as the extant documentation suggests, however, Colombella's endeavour did not enjoy great success, and his translation of the *Nicomachean Ethics* never circulated beyond Pancrazio's household. One could hypothesise that Pancrazio kept his beautiful and certainly expensive dedication copy in his library as a token of friendship and as a symbol of the virtues that his noble lineage embodied. A comparison here with the copious textual transmission of Alderotti's translation of the *Summa Alexandrinorum*, discussed in the previous chapter, is again striking – even more so when we consider that the only evidence of any sort of circulation of Colombella's *Ethics* results from the vernacular reception of the *Summa*.

A shortened version of Colombella's prologue, which includes the life of Aristotle but omits all references to the original dedicatee, appears at the beginning of the Italian version of the *Summa* in MS It. II.134 of the Biblioteca Marciana. The manuscript is a coherent compilation of moral philosophy assembled in 1473 by an unnamed scribe in which the *Summa* precedes an anonymous vernacular translation of Aristotle's *Economics* and a series of Latin excerpts from the pseudo-Aristotelian *Secret of Secrets*.[69] In a gesture that seems to highlight the authority of the alleged source, the *Summa* has the misleading title *Libri Etichorum sive moralium Aristotelis*. In both the *Summa* and the *Economics*, furthermore, all the rubrics and chapter headings are in Latin, while the body texts are in Italian, a characteristic that, along with the refined production of the manuscript and the presence of Latin excerpts from the *Secret of Secrets*, evokes a somewhat cultivated readership not totally separate from the world of Latinate learning. Lacking any other element that could enlighten the intellectual context of production of such a compilation, the manuscript nonetheless witnesses the fluidity of a linguistic culture that keeps alternating

---

[68] Galle (2003: 122), proposes the *Auctoritates Aristotelis* (*Anal. Prior.* 2, 24–5) as a source for the etymological link between *ycos* and *scientia*: 'In the *Auctoritates Aristotelis* it is said that *icos* is a probable proposition, a proposition that is known to be true in many cases.'

[69] Venice, Biblioteca Nazionale Marciana, MS It. II.134 [5212]; see the description of the manuscript in Frati and Segarizzi (1909–11 vol. 1: 280). The manuscript is structured as follows: the Italian translation of the *Summa Alexandrinorum* from fols.1*r*–47*v*, the Italian translation of Aristotle's *Economics* from fols. 48*r*–61*v* and the Latin excerpts from the *Secret of Secrets* from fols. 62*r*–65*v*.

between Latin and the vernacular, a linguistic space in which translation offers opportunities to mediate, reuse and innovate, to some extent. By combining the *Summa* with the *Economics* and the *Secret of Secrets*, the work also seems to stress the primarily practical dimension of moral philosophy that is at the core of the ethical preoccupations of lay readers, as is discussed in the following sections of this chapter.

One Generation Later

A similar overlap of cultural approaches characterises another work on the achievement of moral virtue, one produced approximately three decades after Colombella's translation of the *Ethics* and dedicated to another member of the Giustiniani family. In the mid-1460s, the Dominican Lazzaro Gallineta from Padua offered Bernardo di Niccolò Giustiniani a translation of the treatise *De virtutibus et vitiis* ('On Virtues and Vices'), then considered an original Aristotelian work. Bernardo di Niccolò Giustiniani (not to be confused with the more famous Bernardo di Leonardo Giustiniani, ambassador and humanist) belonged to the San Pantaleone branch of the family.[70] He held important offices for the Venetian Republic such as 'podestà' and 'capitano' at Crema in 1483, as well as 'savio di terraferma' in 1488, and died in Crete in 1500 while engaged in the campaigns against the Turks. Bernardo had been married to Suordamore Giustiniani, daughter of Pancrazio di Marco, the dedicatee of Colombella's translation of the *Ethics*.[71] Thus two members of the same patrician family, a family strongly concerned with political and mercantile affairs, had sponsored similar works. As mentioned earlier in this chapter, the two Venetians are representative of well-educated readers looking to develop a familiarity with the classics. For readers like them, the appropriation of classical models was central to a conscious process of self-fashioning based on the interplay of nobility, political influence and financial power.[72]

The author himself had a life not much different from Antonio Colombella's. Son of the schoolteacher Damiano of Pola, Lazzaro Gallineta entered the Dominican order at a young age and had his early training in Florence, where he became acquainted with local merchants, with whom he kept contact throughout his career. He then moved to Paris at least by

---

[70] On Bernardo the humanist, see Labalme (1969). On the San Pantaleone branch of the family, see Zago (2002: 270).

[71] Litta (1819–64: vol. 18 (1840), tables 5 and 7). See Refini (2013: 341), for a summary of the Giustiniani family's genealogy based on Litta.

[72] See Hopf (1859), Labalme (1969), Hale (1973) and King (1986).

1452 and obtained his degree in theology in 1460. Lazzaro then pursued an itinerant career that brought him first to London, back to Paris (in 1473) and finally to Padua, where he lived from 1475 until his death in 1490.[73] He enjoyed several opportunities to display his oratorical skills: he delivered Latin orations in Paris (in 1473), Rome (1483) and Venice (1487).[74]

Interestingly, whereas Colombella's experience seems quite impervious to the innovations of humanism, Lazzaro shows a much more versatile attitude towards the culture of the humanists. This stance is exemplified well in Lazzaro's translation of Leonardo Bruni's *Laudatio urbis Florentinae* ('Panegyric to the City of Florence'), which he wrote during his stay in London to pay homage to his Florentine acquaintances. As Lazzaro recalls in the preface to his translation, his time in Florence afforded him the chance to experience the kindness and hospitality of Florentine merchants, whom he praises as outstanding models of moral and civic virtue. Having recently received a copy of Bruni's *Laudatio*, whom he considers a great model of eloquence and wisdom, Lazzaro expresses his belief that the best way to show the Florentines his gratitude is to translate the text into 'our vernacular language, so that not only literate and educated men but also uneducated and simple ones will appreciate the excellence of the work'.[75] As we have seen, the link between discussions of one's own translation and appeals to vernacular readers of certain intellectual positions is commonplace. But Lazzaro's specific focus on the stylistic quality of Bruni's writing, which he considers a remarkable example of the rebirth of classical eloquence pursued by humanists, is worth highlighting.[76] Accordingly, Lazzaro presents his translation as an attempt to translate both 'text' and 'style', thereby contributing to the stylistic refinement of the target language.[77] The homage, then, is not simply to Florence, which is celebrated

---

[73] Gargan (1971: 131–4). See also Kaeppeli (1970 vol. 3: 69–70, nn. 2825–31).

[74] For details, see Gargan (1971: 131–4).

[75] Luiso (1899: 2): 'ammi parso cosa convenevole et degna, alquanto il mio ingiegno adoperarvi et traspuorlo nella nostra lingua vulgare, acciò non solo li huomini litterati et dotti, ma ancho li indotti et semplici possino il suo splendore et excellenzia cognoscere'. The translation of Bruni's *Laudatio* is in Florence, Biblioteca Riccardiana, MS 705, fols. 32*r*–67*v*; see Hankins (1997: 68 n.943).

[76] Luiso (1899: 2): 'Adomque a questi passati mesi vegnendomi innanzi uno egregio et elegantissimo trattato [che] già fece in latino messere Lionardo Aretino, huomo nei nostri seculi doctissimo et eloquentissimo …' ('Over the past few months I happened to read an excellent and most elegant treatise that Leonardo of Arezzo, one of the most erudite and eloquent men of our times, wrote in Latin').

[77] *Ibid.*: 3: 'non … restarò, quanto potria mia debolezza, fedelmente seguire l'ornato et copioso et pulitissimo stile del predetto messere Lionardo. Il quale, come chiaramente et ei confessa, tutto il suo ingegno in questa opera pienamente adoperò, quasi in questo trattato quantunque breve volesse lo extremo di sua virtù et elloquentia demonstrare' ('As much as my weakness will allow for, I will

in the *Laudatio* itself, cr even to the Florentine merchants but more
specifically to Florentine humanism as it was championed by figures like
Bruni.[78] Furthermore, by dedicating the vernacular version of the *Laudatio*
to the wealthy merchants with whom he was acquainted, Lazzaro gives
a fuller portrait of Florentine humanist culture, which, as we shall see in
Chapter 4, also interacted with vernacular readership.

The dedicatees of Lazzaro's translation of the *Laudatio* are the same
merchants with whom Lazzaro – who himself wrote poetry – exchanged
playful verses that illuminate his relationship with his readers. During his
stay in London, for instance, Lazzaro was involved in a poetical exchange
with the Florentine merchant and poet Giovanni Frescobaldi.[79] On the
outbreak of pestilence, Lazzaro moved to Greenwich and wrote a sonnet
to Frescobaldi, who had remained in London, inquiring about the disease.
Although the exchange does not reveal much about the actual relationship between the two, it nonetheless reveals some degree of familiarity,
shedding light on the kind of acquaintances authors such as Lazzaro were
interacting with.

A similar familiarity was probably also behind the dedication to Bernardo
Giustiniani of the annotated translation of the pseudo-Aristotelian treatise *On Virtues and Vices*, which Lazzaro likely composed between gradu-
ating from the Sorbonne and returning to Padua, for one of the three
manuscript copies, now at the Bibliothèque Nationale in Paris, is dated
1464.[80] A second copy, now at the Museo Correr in Venice, bears no date,
but further inspection indicates that it belonged to the same workshop
that produced the other copy. Palaeographic and codicological similarities
between the two manuscripts suggest a close chronological proximity.[81]

---

try to follow faithfully the elegant, rich and refined style of Leonardo. As he overtly affirms, he put
all his skills in this work, as if he wanted to show in such a small work the extent of his virtue and
eloquence').

[78] *Ibid.*: 'questa inclita et potentissima città dopo tanti secoli finalmente ha trovato il suo vero et non
ficto laudatore' ('This beautiful and powerful city, after many centuries, has finally found her true
and trusted singer of praise').

[79] For the poetical exchange with Giovanni Frescobaldi, see Florence, Biblioteca Medicea Laurenziana,
MS Redi 184, fol. 127v: 'Sonetto di maestro Lazzaro da Padova essendo a Granvicci [i.e., Greenwich]
fuggito la moría da Londra a Giovanni Frescobaldi, mercante Fiorentino dimorante a Londra,'
incipit *Fresco mio caro, qui fra miste lucciole*. See the texts in Cestaro (1914: 132–3); and Flamini
(1891: 674).

[80] Paris, Bibliothèque Nationale de France, MS Ital. 907 (hereafter Ital. 907). See the date on fol.
59r: 'Finis. MºCCCCLXIIII Londoniis'; see Kaeppeli (1970 vol. 3: 70).

[81] Venice, Museo Correr, MS Correr 15. See Kristeller (1963–97 vol. 2: 288) and Kaeppeli (1970 vol.
3: 70). A complete description of the Correr manuscript is available in Vanin (2013: 6–9); see also
Refini (2016a).

Furthermore, in all copies (including one now at the Vatican, which is independent from the production of the other two)[82] the work is dedicated to Bernardo, whose coat of arms appeared on the opening pages of the manuscripts in Paris and Venice [Figure 3.4].

The motto on the coat of arms, 'Imponit finem sapiens et rebus honestis' ('The wise man limits even honest things'), derives from Juvenal's *Satires* and summarises the Aristotelian notion of *medietas*.[83] By highlighting the golden mean as a distinctive feature of virtuous nobles, the motto resonates with the purpose of the treatise, which in both copies accompanies another text intended for a mercantile readership, the dialogue *De immortalitate animae* ('On the Immortality of the Soul') by the Genovese Dominican Jacopo Campora, written around 1432.[84] Three decades after its composition, Campora's dialogue (to which we shall return in Chapter 5) was repackaged and presented to Bernardo Giustiniani along with the newly translated treatise *On Virtues and Vices*. It is likely that whoever selected the two works for compilation – most probably Lazzaro Gallineta himself – found them complementary. Both give the mercantile reader easier access to philosophical themes: on one hand, the dialogue *De immortalitate animae* exemplifies the Christianised abridgments of Aristotle that were standard introductions to the Greek philosopher in this period while, on the other hand, the treatise *On Virtues and Vices* provides a basic summary of moral philosophy. The simple and clear structure of *On Virtues and Vices* would have appealed to readers seeking an overview of Aristotelian moral philosophy. Leaving aside the more demanding matters of the *Ethics*, it addresses virtues and vices with a strong focus on their impact on practical life.

Ethics for Beginners

Gallineta's annotated translation of *On Virtues and Vices* is introduced by a short dedicatory epistle to Bernardo Giustiniani and concludes with a

---

[82] The third copy of Lazzaro Gallineta's translation is included in a fifteenth-century miscellaneous manuscript, now Vatican City, Biblioteca Apostolica Vaticana, MS Ottob. Lat. 2105, fols. 17*r*–30*v*; see Kaeppeli (1970 vol. 3: 70).

[83] Though it has been cut off in Venice, Museo Correr, MS Correr 315, the Giustiniani coat of arms is still visible in Paris, Bibliothèque Nationale de France, MS Ital. 907, fol. 1*r*. The motto, from Juvenal, *Satires* 6.444, was often used as a philosophical maxim; see, for instance, Michel de Montaigne, *Essays* 2.28.

[84] Both manuscripts open with Jacopo Campora's *Trattato de l'anima*: Ital. 907, fols. 1*r*–52*v*; Correr 315, fols. 1*r*–55*r*. As will be discussed in Chapter 5, Campora's text was originally dedicated to the Venetian-born but London-based merchant Giovanni Marcanova and presents Aristotelian psychology in line with the Christian doctrine of the soul.

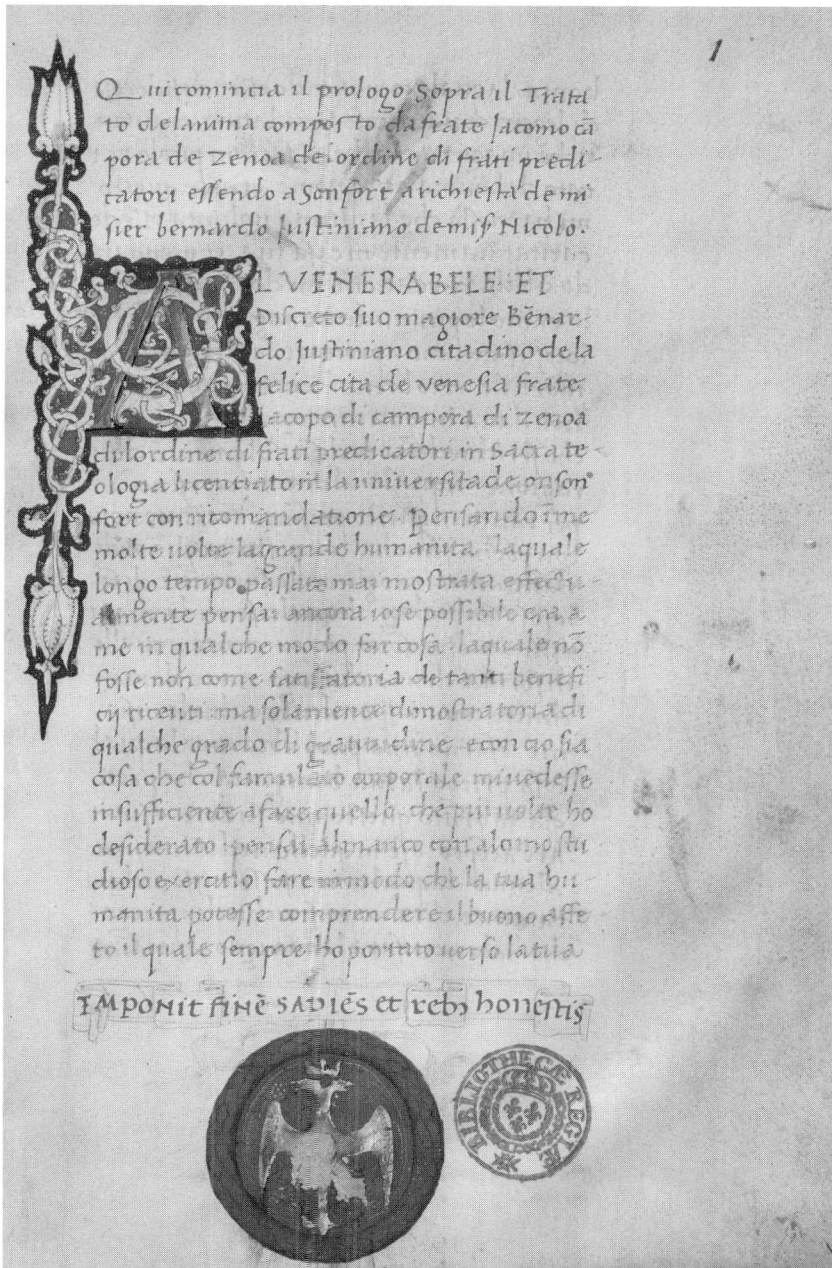

Figure 3.4 Paris, Bibliothèque Nationale de France, MS Ital. 907, fol. *1r*

succinct set of annotations. The structure of the paratext in the manuscripts Correr 315 and Ital. 907 is the same: according to humanistic standards, the layout is elegant with wide margins; the annotations follow the text, which is provided with cross-references.[85] By describing his ideal reader in his dedication, Gallineta reveals his chief objective with the work. He begins by indicating that his translation is based on a Latin version only recently produced by the humanist Niccolò da Lonigo, a detail that situates Lazzaro's own vernacular rendering under the aegis of contemporary Latin humanism.[86] The choice of a contemporary Latin version of *On Virtues and Vices* as the basis of his translation is consistent with Lazzaro's praise of humanist culture in the preface to his version of Bruni's *Laudatio*. It also explicitly relates his project to the wave of new Latin translations of Greek texts that Bruni himself had launched with his version of the *Ethics* and that would soon become a key feature of fifteenth-century humanism.[87]

While undoubtedly a 'minor' work when compared to other Aristotelian writings, *On Virtues and Vices* was very popular among humanists and saw several Latin translations. The Latin translation by Niccolò da Lonigo is lost, unfortunately, but the number of surviving humanist versions is significant, especially when compared to the medieval circulation of the text, limited to one mid-thirteenth-century Latin version attributed to Grosseteste.[88] The series of humanist translations originates in the early fifteenth century with Ciriaco d'Ancona, whose translation was still popular several decades later, when it was dedicated in one manuscript to Duke Federico da Montefeltro by one Nicolò Gerardini from Lendinara, philosopher and physician (1482).[89] The Greek humanist Georgius Hermonymus of Sparta authored another popular translation of the text, printed in Paris in 1478 and surviving in at least three manuscript copies, each addressed to separate dedicatees.[90] An additional version of the text was made by the renowned scholar Niccolò Perotti, who specialised in Latin translations of Greek works.[91] Perotti's version, a copy of which was also dedicated

---

[85] The Vatican copy of the work follows instead the common model of books with annotations on the margins all around the text. Quotations refer here to my transcription based on the Venetian manuscript.

[86] Mugnai Carrara (1978, 1991).

[87] On the importance of Latin translations of Greek works in the fifteenth century, see Cortesi (2007).

[88] As indicated by Brams (2003: 86), Grosseteste's *De virtutibus et vitiis* is not a direct translation of the pseudo-Aristotelian treatise but a reworking of the text; see also Schmitt (1979: 109–11).

[89] See Spadolini (1902), Garin (1947–50: 69); Cortesi and Maltese (1992) and Hofmann (2008: 41). I wish to thank Dr Paul Botley for sharing his expertise in the textual tradition of the treatise *De virtutibus et vitiis*.

[90] Kalatzi (2009: 103–4, 207–8, 214–15, 339–40).

[91] Garin (1947–50: 82) and Hofmann (2008: 41).

to Federico da Montefeltro (in 1474), was then printed in Fano in 1504. The circulation of the text continued in the sixteenth century, when, thanks to new translations by, among others, Ambrogio Leone, Alexander Chamaillardus and Simon Grynaeus, the interest of readers in the treatise only grew.[92]

The successful reception of these translations of *On Virtues and Vices* can be easily explained, for the work offered a succinct and effective discussion of the Aristotelian system of virtues and vices. Before its authorship began to be questioned, the short treatise was regarded as a compendium of moral philosophy made by Aristotle himself, thus preserving all the prestige of the author's name. As such, it appealed to humanists, who considered it as a sort of *prolegomenon* or *isagoge* ('introduction') to Aristotle's moral works. Translated into Latin by humanists, the text performed a function similar to Leonardo Bruni's *Isagogicon moralis disciplinae* ('Introduction to Moral Philosophy')(1420s), which, as will be recalled in the following chapter, was conceived as an introduction to moral philosophy for readers who could read Latin but were not academics. To these lay readers belong not only the dedicatee of Bruni's *Isagogicon*, the nobleman Galeotto Ricasoli, but also the various dedicatees of the Latin versions of *On Virtues and Vices* across Europe.[93]

Interestingly, Lazzaro Gallineta himself offered a copy of the treatise (apparently, a Latin version) to another prestigious dedicatee, Don Pedro, Constable of Portugal, widely known as an important political figure as well as an intellectual and literary author with significant ties to Italian humanism.[94] During Pedro's reign as king of Aragon (1463–66), Lazzaro sent him a manuscript of the treatise. While the manuscript is lost, a Latin letter of February 1466 from the king to the friar survives in which he expresses his gratitude for 'Aristotle's booklet on virtue', 'recently translated from Greek', that Lazzaro had dedicated to him.[95] The ambiguous phrasing suggests that the friar sent the king a Latin translation of the text, probably the same translation by Niccolò da Lonigo that Lazzaro used for his Italian version, though another, less plausible possibility is that he sent a copy of the Italian. In either case, the letter reveals that what particularly interested

---

[92] Leone (1525), Chamaillardus (1538) and Grynaeus (1539).

[93] As recalled above, Ciriaco d'Ancona's translation was dedicated to Duke Federico of Montefeltro, as was Niccolò Perotti's. Hermonymus' version was dedicated, on different occasions, to Tristan de Salazar, archbishop of Sens; John Shirwood, bishop of Durham; Engelbert of Clèves, count of Nevers. See Kalatzi (2009: 103–4).

[94] Martinez Ferrando (1942: 227, 231).

[95] Adão da Fonseca (1975: 377): 'Aristotelis De Virtute libellum quem nuper e greco traductum nostro nomini dedicasti libenter audivimus.'

Pedro was not the text itself but Lazzaro's dedicatory epistle, in which, as the letter details, the friar praised not only the king's own virtues but also those of the 'king of England and France',[96] a reference to the English king, Edward IV, whose sister, Margaret of York, was betrothed to Pedro (who died in 1466, before the marriage could take place). The evidence of Lazzaro's dedication of *On Virtues and Vices* to Pedro of Portugal leaves several unanswered questions about the occasion on which the theologian offered the work to the ruler as well as on his motivations for doing that, yet the episode nonetheless furthers our understanding of the translator's international connections.

With Lazzaro's vernacular rendering of the treatise *On Virtues and Vices*, the translation process moves one step further. The dedicatee, Bernardo di Niccolò Giustiniani, like his father-in-law Pancrazio before him, was part of the same lay readership which other dedicatees of the Latin versions of the treatise also belonged to. The translator references the dedicatee's social and intellectual status in his preface. Here the linguistic divide between 'literate' and 'illiterate' readers is not introduced in terms of any hierarchical difference between Latin and the vernacular. Instead, it presents the vernacular translation as a means to satisfy readers who, regardless of their language skills, wished to benefit from the study of virtue. The argument recalls the opening lines of the *Convivio* where Dante evokes the universal inclination to acquire knowledge.[97] Lazzaro's suggestion that his translation would be read primarily for the acquisition of virtue, however, shares the idea of language as a vehicle for moral enhancement that, following Petrarch, was at the core of contemporary humanist thought: 'I decided to translate [the text] into our vernacular and maternal Italian tongue so that not only literate and erudite intellectuals experienced in scholarship, but also anyone eager to acquire virtue will be able to benefit from it.'[98]

The public Lazzaro envisions comprises non-Latinate readers and is conveniently represented by Bernardo, who, as was typical of members of his rank, was likely to have basic knowledge of Latin still insufficient for reading philosophical texts in the original.[99] Bernardo, though, stands out for his nobility. Drawing on the same commonplace Colombella had employed for Pancrazio, Lazzaro emphasises the link between the

[96] *Ibid.*
[97] Dante, *Convivio* I.I.I. See Chapter 2, 62–3.
[98] Venice, Museo Correr, MS Correr 315, fol. 55v: 'deliberai quella redure ne la nostra volgare e materna lingua italica a ciò non solo i litterati e docti usati in li studii, ma anche qualunche de virtù studioso di quella possi pigliare alcun fructo'.
[99] On the unique aspects of Venetian humanism and the education of local patricians, see Labalme (1969), Gilbert (1979) and King (1986).

achievement of virtue and the noble origins of the dedicatee: 'since virtue is the worthiest ornament of noble and generous spirits, it is appropriate that I dedicate my translation to you: for just as your descent from the imperial house of the Giustiniani makes you most noble, so in reading this work you will be content to be no less elevated with respect to the nobility of your soul'.[100] Once the double meaning of nobility, genealogical and intellectual, is made clear, Lazzaro offers advice on how to cultivate it: 'You will house in your mind that virtue, which, strongly desired by any excellent man, is so difficult to find; furthermore, by looking at, and meditating on such virtue, you will recognize your own image mirrored in it.'[101]

Lazzaro further develops this point in the preamble to his commentary on the treatise. For him, the main purpose of Aristotle's *On Virtues and Vices* is to disclose the image of virtue ('la imagine de la virtù') thoroughly outlined in his main works, particularly in the *Nicomachean Ethics*.[102] Addressing an issue that had already engaged Antonio Colombella in the preface to his translation of the *Ethics*, Lazzaro indicates the unusual nature of the work he is bringing into the vernacular: the text is much shorter than the *Ethics*, and he therefore presents it as a brief summary ('picola summa') of moral philosophy with no obvious literary or poetical model. Instead of contrasting Aristotle with classical authors such as Cicero and Seneca, as had Colombella, Gallineta provides the reader with a thought-provoking remark that considers the 'modern' (i.e., vernacular) literary tradition: Aristotle's weighty and sententious style ('grave et sententioso') is not that of poets or historians such as the two 'modern vernacular authors' ('questi do' moderni vulgari') Petrarch and Boccaccio. The Aristotle of this treatise is a true moral philosopher ('vero philosopho morale'), whose main concern is outlining an achievable practice of life based on virtue ('ponendo quasi come una pratica a l'uomo virtuoso'), not the employment of poetical fiction and historical examples.[103] Here Aristotle systematically describes the virtues and vices, focuses on their interaction and treats their effects on human life. Thanks to this well-ordered project, readers can look into their own soul and, by discerning

---

[100] Venice, Museo Correr, MS Correr 315, fols. 55v–56r: 'e perché virtù è dignissimo ornamento d'ogni animo generoso e nobile, hami carso conveniente cosa mandarla et intitularla a vui: la quale sì come per generatione de la imperial casa Iustiniana discendendo seti nobillissimo, cussì non meno d'alteza e nobilità de animo splendido lietamente ricevereti'.

[101] *Ibid.*: fol. 56r: 'et ne lo albergo de la mente vostra alogereti quella che, da ogni excellente homo amata e desiderata, sì rara si trova; e spesso lei riguardando e considerando come in chiaro e purissimo spechio, cognoscereti la vostra imagine'.

[102] *Ibid.*: fol. 61v.

[103] *Ibid.*

which virtues they possess and which ones they lack, learn how to improve morally. The treatise thus functions as a handbook of moral philosophy with an immediate and practical impact: by learning to follow virtue and avoid vice, readers will attain the happiness that Aristotle set as the main goal for free and virtuous human beings.[104]

Confirmation of the belief in Aristotle's intended utility comes from Lazzaro's commentary, which immediately follows the text. To compensate for the concision of the treatise, the annotations provide readers with relevant references to other Aristotelian works that illustrate the description of virtues and related vices. Lazzaro's glosses inhabit an intermediate level between the short summary offered by the treatise *On Virtues and Vices* and the difficult text of the *Ethics*, although references to other sources are also present. To meet his audience's expectations, for example, the commentator expands on prudence, which is presented as the most useful of all the virtues described. Thanks to its main components – memory, experience and industriousness ('memoria, experientia e solertia') – prudence allows people to manage their everyday life wisely. Whereas Colombella's preface to the *Ethics* focused on intellectual speculation as the main goal of the virtuous, Lazzaro's approach to moral philosophy is much more practical.

The annotations devoted to prudence are highly significant: they focus on the necessity of learning through direct experience, a model of education and training particularly suitable for those engaged in political and economic affairs. It is not by chance that the commentator here explicitly refers to merchants: 'Prudence is attained thanks to the experience of many things: this is why, for instance, we see young traders sent by their fathers far away from their country in order to become wiser and more prudent through the direct experience of various matters.'[105] The picture envisioned by Lazzaro is not unusual in fifteenth-century mercantile society. As noted above, the young Pancrazio Giustiniani settled in Bruges and regularly wrote his father about his time abroad. In his own travels in London, as we have seen, and elsewhere in Europe, Lazzaro had the opportunity to connect with Italian merchants living abroad, thus experiencing the vibrant life of their communities.

---

[104] *Ibid.*: fols. 61*v*–62*r*: 'per le qual descriptioni ogni animo nobile e generoso può in se medesimo cognoscere qual possiede, o de qual ha bisogno e qual più abonda in lui, cioè virtù o vitio, e coregendo et emendando la vita, facilmente sequendo le virtù e schivando li vitii, può pervenire a quella felicità la quale Aristotile pone per fine ad ogni libero e virtuoso homo'.

[105] *Ibid.*: fol. 67*r*: 'prudentia, quella aquista et acresce per pratica et experientia di molte cose, come nui vediamo ioveni mercadanti esser da loro padri mandati fuora de la patria in paesi luntani a ciò che per pratica et experientia de molti fati se faciano più savii e prudenti'.

In his commentary on *On Virtues an Vices*, Lazzaro makes a striking comparison between the figure of Ulysses and the life of the fifteenth-century merchant:

> [This is] the kind of experience to which the Greek poet refers when he praises Ulysses at the beginning of the work entitled *Odyssey*. As the Latin poet Horace translates it, 'Dic mihi musa virum capte post tempora Troie qui mores hominum multorum vidit et urbes,' or in the vernacular: 'O Muse, sing for me, make me worthy to praise the man who after the fall of Troy came to see and to know many places and the many ways of men'.[106]

Ulysses, the classical hero that Dante identified as a controversial symbol of the thirst for knowledge is here presented as the ideal model for merchants eager to improve themselves.[107] Lazzaro holds that through the productive combination of experience, prudence and knowledge, merchants (ideally of patrician rank, as with Bernardo Giustiniani) can acquire moral excellence. If not already members of the aristocracy, these merchants can become noble by attaining virtue.

Perfecting the Merchant

Lazzaro Gallineta's reference to Ulysses summarises various developments crucial to the fifteenth-century vernacular reception of Aristotelian moral works within mercantile communities. In his dedication of the *Ethics* to Pancrazio Giustiniani, Antonio Colombella depicted him as an ideal example of patrician nobility, stressing both his willingness to read Aristotle's treatise and the relevance of contemplation to the moral ennoblement of lay readers. Lazzaro's motivations, however, shed light on the production of a text that, undoubtedly less ambitious than his predecessor's, seems to have been suitable for a readership more concerned with the *vita activa* than the *vita contemplativa*.[108] At the same time, Lazzaro's portrayal of the merchant who excels in virtue, knowledge and prudence does correspond to the new social and cultural status that merchants had been acquiring throughout the fourteenth and fifteenth centuries.

---

[106] *Ibid.*: fol. 67r–v: 'de la quale experientia, in laude di Ulixes Homero poeta Greco scrivendo l'opera intitulata Odissea, cominciò dicendo, come tradusse Oratio Flacco poeta latino, cioè: "Dic mihi musa virum capte post tempora Troie qui mores hominum multorum vidit et urbes," che in vulgare: "O musa d mi e fame dignamente laudare quel huomo il quale, dapuò Troia presa, vidi [sic] e prova [sic] molte cità: e molti costume de homeni."'

[107] On the implications of Ulysses in Dante's depiction, see, among others, Mercuri (1971).

[108] As for the actual circulation of these texts – and evidence of their different success – one might recall that only one copy of Colombella's translation is preserved today, while Lazzaro's is available in at least three manuscripts that we know.

Instructive evidence of this process comes, among other sources, from Benedetto Cotrugli's *Libro de l'arte de la mercatura* ('Book on the Art of Trade').[109] Written in 1458 by a well-established merchant who wishes to share his professional experience, the treatise circulated in manuscript before being printed in 1573 and again in 1602. Cotrugli's *Mercatura* pictures an exquisitely characteristic fifteenth-century situation, based primarily on the author's own career as a merchant and his first-hand knowledge of trading activities in Italian cities and abroad.[110] A native to Dubrovnik, where he was born around 1410, Cotrugli showed a juvenile passion for letters and philosophy, which, according to his own preface to the treatise, he had to abandon to take care of his family's trading business. We know that he studied law and his expertise in the field surfaces frequently in his work, as does his impressive record of experiences across the Mediterranean. Despite having no noble lineage, Cotrugli was assigned to prominent offices at the court of Naples, thus increasing his prestige in his birthplace as well. While his profile and career are somewhat exceptional, they testify to a trend in the development of mercantile culture and society that is by no means unique. From this point of view, both Venice (as we have seen in this chapter) and Florence (covered in the next) offer invaluable insights into the interplay of aristocratic traditions and trading activities.

The figure of the merchant traced by Cotrugli captures this transformation, where trade becomes a noble art, morally valuable and indispensable to the political life of the city. (Not surprisingly, he finds the embodiment of the ideal merchant in Cosimo de' Medici.)[111] In delineating the portrait of the perfect merchant, the author combines his direct experience of the world with a familiarity with both ancient and modern authors. In a gesture that would have perhaps pleased Machiavelli, Cotrugli argues that knowledge – specifically, practical expertise that aims to make effective decisions – stems from the combination of real-world experience and a solid education. This combination is believed to ensure a successful career in the art of trade, a field that Cotrugli aims to legitimise at the levels of

---

[109] Cotrugli's treatise on trade has been the object of several studies. In particular, see Tucci (1990) for the first scholarly edition of the text. The treatise has been recently the object of a new critical edition, Ribaudo (2016); for the English translation see Carraro and Favero (2017). On the significance of Cotrugli's text within the developments of humanist culture in both Latinate and vernacular contexts, see Refini (2013: 317–18), Cox (2016: 135–8) and Celenza (2018: 122–3).

[110] For a discussion of Cotrugli's life and career, see Luzzati (1984), Tucci (1990), Piotrowicz (2014) and Carraro and Favero (2017).

[111] Ribaudo (2016: 137).

the individual, the family and the whole community. The idea that trade is meant to grow honourably and without offending God or one's neighbour is thus presented in strictly Aristotelian terms, as the glue of society. Aristotle and Cicero provide Cotrugli with a compelling defence of trade:

> But trade, if properly cultivated and conducted, is not only useful but, more than that, quite vital to human operations, and therefore it is the noblest activity. On this subject, Cicero said: 'merchants are the resources of the state,' speaking of the better sort, expert and well-educated. For the same reason, Aristotle maintains that one of the principal and most necessary ornaments of the city is commerce, from which all other activities proliferate, as from a pure spring, until it deteriorates or fails.[112]

References to classical sources abound in the treatise and, among them, those to Aristotle stand out. Quotations from and allusions to the *Ethics*, the *Politics* and *On the Soul*, among other works, most often filtered through the reading of Thomas Aquinas, provide Benedetto with a philosophical framework, which enables him to showcase his culture and establish trade as a proper art.[113]

Two primary concerns inform the author's project: morals and language. To acknowledge the morality of merchants without sidestepping the controversial issue of wealth and the accumulation of riches, the author outlines a series of principles that merchants should adopt. These are discussed at the beginning of the third book of the treatise, devoted to the 'civic life of the merchant' ('de vita politica de lo merchante').[114] The concern for the common good, the desire to further the affluence of the family, the virtuous combination of private and public interests and, eventually, moral integrity are the main components of the perfect merchant's profile. An additional fundamental element that enables one to deal with all the others is what Cotrugli calls 'conversazione', which refers to both the ability to communicate with others and the ability to negotiate.[115] As such, Cotrugli's notion of 'conversation' (which applied to both the private and the public sphere) is reminiscent of the idea presented at the beginning of

---

[112] Carraro and Favero (2017: 25). See the Italian passage in Ribaudo (2016: 39): 'La quale mercatura, ben culta e drectamente observata, è non solamente comodissima, ma eciamdio necessarissima al governo umano, et *per consequens* nobilissima de le arte. De la quale parlando, Cicerone disse: "mercatores nervi sunt rei publice", parlando de li boni, periti et docti. Et però vuol Aristotele che uno de li precipui et necessari ornamenti de la città era la mercatura, de la quale dependeno le altre, come da fonte, dummodo che la non sia depravata o guasta.'

[113] For Cotrugli's Aristotelian quotations, see Ribaudo (2016: 47, 52, 54, 61, 72, 94, 116, 139, 140, 144, 152, 157, 171, 180, 182).

[114] *Ibid.*: 123–56.

[115] *Ibid.*: 126.

Brunetto Latini's *Tresor*, namely, that no human interaction takes place without language.[116] For this very reason, language is central to Cotrugli's definition of the art of trade. On one hand, language is the instrument that enables forms of communication and exchange; on the other hand, language is what makes people knowledgeable, distinguishing them from the ignorant populace.

Cotrugli twice addresses language: in his preface, where he explains his choice to write the treatise in Italian rather than Latin and again in the third chapter of the third book, where he discusses the education of merchants, which revolves around the centrality of the liberal arts. In the preface, Cotrugli acknowledges the superiority of Latin and explains that he nonetheless turns to the vernacular in order to reach a wider number of readers:

> I was uncertain which language I should adopt for my treatise, the Latin language or my maternal vernacular, and from this side and that came into my mind reasons pushing me in different directions now one way, now another. As far as Latin was concerned, I thought that it was a much worthier medium than the vernacular and would enable me to explain more elegantly what I needed to say in my treatise and give it a far greater polish. But then, considering the vernacular, I thought that, as I was writing my work for the benefit of merchants many of whom, for lack of education rather than any innate deficiency, would be inexpert in, or ignorant of, Latin, it was beholden on me to write in the language that was most commonly used and comprehensible to those merchants at whom the work was aimed.[117]

Cotrugli strongly stresses that the elegance of the Latin language cannot be equalled by the vernacular, thus taking a position that differs, at least in principle, from that of translators like Colombella and Lazzaro Gallineta, who publicly espoused the strength of the vulgar tongue.

He nonetheless supports his choice of Italian by turning to a simplified version of the *impedimenta* argument that we have seen at work in Dante's

---

[116] Brunetto highlights the centrality of language and rhetoric as instruments of social cohesion and interaction in *Tresor* 1.1–5; see Beltrami (2007: 4–15). See also my introduction to this volume, 9–10.

[117] Carraro and Favero (2017: 26). See also Ribaudo (2016: 39–40): 'stetti suspeso meco medesmo in che lingua io dovesse scrivere questa mia opera, o in lingua latina o in volgare et materna, et da l'una parte e da l'altra mi occoreva ragioni, le quali variamente me tiravano hor da una parte hor da l'altra; però che da la banda de lo scrivere latino mi occorreva la lingua latina essere multo più degna che la vulgare et potere molto più degnamente explicare quello che nel decto tratato mi occoreva et con multo magiore dignità scrivere la decta opera. Et per la parte de scrivere in volgare mi occoreva che io [ero] scrivendo l'opera per utele di mercanti, li quali per abusione d'esserno male alevati e non per difecto de l'arte, el più de le volte si trovano imperiti et ignoranti de le lectere.'

Convivio.[118] It is not due to 'innate deficiency' ('defecto de l'arte'), Cotrugli argues, that merchants do not read Latin; it is, rather, their lack of education that denies them access to the language of the ancients. The statement is of great interest for it demonstrates Cotrugli's very practical approach to the question of language alongside his concern over the education of merchants. They should ideally receive Latin education, but, since they do so only rarely, the vernacular serves as a helpful substitute. Cotrugli's decision to turn to the *volgare* is thus based on very practical reasons, not on the acknowledgement of the potential of the mother tongue.

What might seem a slightly conservative position on language, likely due to Cotrugli's attempt to fashion his work as a response to humanism, finds a more nuanced explanation in the third book of the treatise, in which the author treats the topic of education more explicitly. Here the author critiques the idea that merchants should not be concerned with learning.[119] On the contrary, according to Cotrugli, the perfect merchant should embody the prototype of the *homo universalis*, whose training in as many disciplines as possible would prove key to moral and economic success as well as to all forms of human interaction: 'in pursuit of delineating the perfect and complete merchant. I must exemplify the universal man, equipped with the capacity to understand and deal with all types of men'.[120] The core of the merchant's education should be the *trivium* (grammar, rhetoric, dialectic), which justifies its prioritisation of Latin instruction for reasons that are both ideological and practical: through instruction in grammar (i.e., Latin), the merchant will be prepared to handle official documents

---

[118] Dante, *Convivio* 1.1.2. See also the discussion of the passage here in Chapter 2, 63.

[119] Ribaudo (2016: 132): 'Et sono nientedimeno alcuni indocti et indisciplinatissimi homini, li qualli prorumpono a tanta insania che biasimano coloro i quali sanno alcuna cosa, et questi sono communamente li homeni ignoranti et vulgari, li quali, per doglia che si vegono inferiori de li altri homini, prorumpeno in insania et biasmano quelli li quali sanno, perché l'ignoranti tuti comunamente sono cativi, secundo la sentencia del Philosopho che disse: "Omnis ignorans malus". Et lo male è opposto a lo bene, lo quale è virtù, pertanto e' non ci è magiore guera, né inimicicia in questo mundo che da l'ignorante a lo savio, et da lo indocto a lo docto; et come l'aqua non sa, né può stare im pacie con lo fuoco, cosí lo docto con lo indocto'; 'Nonetheless there is no shortage of ignorant men, wholly without culture, who give themselves over to folly to the extent that they will criticise men of learning; and these are generally coarse and unlettered types, who, resenting their inferiority, espouse the idiocy of condemning the educated; in fact the ignorant are generally bad men, as the Philosopher said: "Every ignoramus is evil". And evil is necessarily opposed to good, which is virtue; thus in this world there is no war and no enmity greater that the ignorant bears towards the wise, or the uncultured towards the cultured. And just as water is ignorant of, and cannot co-exist with, fire, so the educated cannot mix with the uneducated'; Carraro and Favero (2017: 120).

[120] Carraro and Favero (2017: 117); see Ribaudo (2016: 130): 'Volendo instituire lo mercante perfecto e compiuto, mi bisognia fare uno homo universalissimo, dotato d'ogni facultà che possa intendere et comparere con ogni generacion di homini.'

and international communication, while rhetoric will also foster communication skills, both in Latin and in the vernacular, and logic will prove essential to good judgement.[121]

Needless to say, the other sciences also contribute, even if accessorily, to the merchant's readiness for the many challenges of that career. While mercantile culture since the thirteenth century had valued natural philosophy, as seen in the vernacular reception of works such as Aristotle's *Meteorology*, merchants also found great significance in the sciences that Cotrugli significantly defines 'in agibilibus mundi', those pertaining to the practical things of the world:

> And this is why, in addition to the already mentioned knowledge and the liberal arts the merchant must also have other practical knowledge of the world, such as one learns more through experience than any other way. Cosmography, for example, which is important for knowing how the world is made up and the names of the nations, regions, provinces and individual cities, but also to understand trading conditions and usages, tolls, the nature of all the merchandise and various things that are transported and exported from every part, because in ignorance of such things the merchant cannot know what is required for each season and place. And he must besides know distances, places, ports, landings, and especially sea charts to understand charters and insurance.[122]

Along with these disciplines the author includes cosmography and the art of navigation, thus presenting philosophical knowledge and practical experience as the necessary components of the ideal merchant.

The reference to navigation, a topic to which Cotrugli will later devote an entire treatise, brings us back to the image of the merchant as a modern-day Ulysses, which Lazzaro Gallineta had evoked in his commentary on the pseudo-Aristotelian treatise *On Virtues and Vices*.[123] The centrality of prudence as the quintessential virtue of the mercantile profession also

---

[121] Ribaudo (2016: 130).
[122] Carraro and Favero (2017: 121); see also Ribaudo (2016: 133): 'oltre le prenominate sciencie et arte liberali, e' l'è di necessario a lo mercante sapere altre sciencie *in agibilibus mundi*, le quali se imparano più per pratica che per altra via: et sono come la cosmographia, la quale è di bisogno non solamente sapere lo sito de l'orbe e lo nome de le patrie, regioni et provincie et terre particulari, ma è di bisogno eciamdio sapere le condicioni et li usi mercantili, et gabele di quele, et condicioni d'ogni robe et merchantie che si meteno et tragono d'ogni parte, però che, nol sapendo, non intende quello che ad ogni parte et in sue stagioni si convene. Et più li bisogna sapere le distancie, li siti, porti, spiagie, et multo bene la carta de lo navigare per sapere noligiare et asicurare; et tuto quello avimo dicto.' On the vernacular circulation of Aristotle's *Meteorology*, see Librandi (1995); more broadly, on the dissemination of scientific literature in the vernacular, Librandi and Piro (2006).
[123] On Cotrugli's treatise on navigation, see Falchetta (2009, 2012). For Gallineta's reference to Ulysses, see above, 121.

recalls Ulysses, as does Cotrugli's concept of universal knowledge needed to be a good merchant. Indeed, prudence and knowledge were considered to be fundamental to the classical characterisation of the hero, whose intellect excelled in both theoretical and practical matters. At the same time, Cotrugli's belief that the achievements of the perfect merchant depend on a universal knowledge appropriates one of the most enduring commonplaces of humanism: the idea of learning as the gateway to human perfection. His 'translation' of this humanist idea, however, outlines knowledge not merely as a theoretical object, but primarily as a practical form of wisdom. In so doing, he reiterates the virtuous combination of action and contemplation that informed the Aristotelian interests of merchants like Pancrazio and Bernardo Giustiniani, and which, by the way, will be crucial to developments in moral philosophy throughout the Renaissance.[124] In different ways, the vernacular translations dedicated to the Giustiniani merchants highlight the intellectual dimension of trade and, accordingly, identify prudence as the primary virtue of their trade. As Cotrugli sees it, given the unstable nature of the world, merchants should always be ready to calibrate their decisions and actions depending on their specific situation. His recommendations concerning prudence, which seem to fit Pancrazio's and Bernardo's experiences, promote the performing of good deeds as the surest guarantee to learn something from others at every opportunity. Hence the importance of reading ('such wisdom can be attained by reading widely, so I will remind you: whenever you have a spare moment, read') and of capable mentors.[125]

As we shall see in the next chapter, Cotrugli's instructions, which concern the philosophical education of the individual, echo the real (and well-documented) preoccupations of merchants with the moral education of their offspring. Shifting focus from Venice to Florence, we will see how merchants participated in the translation process not only through the collection and consumption of books, as with Pancrazio and Bernardo, but also through their active response to the translators. As noted above, this interaction makes readers an integral part of the process by which translation merges with reception. If the authoritative Aristotle championed by Petrarch's friends is indeed tamed in vernacular translation, which transforms moral philosophy to mostly worldly, practical issues, the cultural negotiations fostered by translators and their audience seem to restore the performative function of language embraced by Petrarch himself.

---

[124] On the interplay of action and contemplation in Renaissance philosophy, see Lines (in press).

[125] Carraro and Favero (2017: 117); cf. Ribaudo (2016: 129): 'questo può asequire legendo multe cosse, et però ti ricordo, sempre che tempo ti avança, legi'.

CHAPTER 4

The Philosopher, the Humanist, the Translator and the Reader

The Philosopher on the Campanile

The sculpture in the loggia of the Palazzo Ducale presenting Aristotle as an assertive lawmaker reminded Venetians that good laws are essential to good government. An even wider cluster of meanings – as well as a more dialogical attitude – is embodied in the image of Aristotle carved around 1437 by Luca Della Robbia for the campanile of the Florentine cathedral [Figure 4.1].

As stated by Giorgio Vasari, the sculptor was asked to complete the series of Andrea Pisano's fourteenth-century bas reliefs that illustrated, among other subjects, the sciences and the liberal arts. According to the 1568 edition of Vasari's *Vite de' più eccellenti pittori, scultori, e architettori* ('Lives of the Most Excellent Painters, Sculptors and Architects'), Della Robbia's five tiles represent grammar, philosophy, music, astrology and geometry. In the tile supposedly representing Philosophy Vasari identifies the two figures as Plato and Aristotle in a debate: the elder man to the right would be Plato, bearded and making an expressive gesture, and the younger man, pointing to the book he holds, would be Plato's pupil, Aristotle.[1] There is no way to know whether these identities were specified in the original iconographic program, and, in fact, there is some chance that Vasari's interpretation of the image was influenced by Raphael's later depiction of Plato and Aristotle in the School of Athens in the Vatican, where Plato points to the heavens and Aristotle points to the ground.[2] But Vasari's identification of the two debaters in the tile as the two greatest philosophers of antiquity was commonly accepted and seldom questioned.[3] Indeed, it indicates much about the emblematic value of the two philosophers as well as about

---

[1] Bettarini (1966–87 vol. 3: 50).
[2] The *School of Athens* was painted by Raphael between 1509 and 1511. See Hall (1997).
[3] See Pope-Hennessy (1980: 30–1, 231–3, and plate 30). An alternative interpretation is offered by Schlosser (1896: 73).

Figure 4.1 Luca Della Robbia, Philosophy, decorative tile,
Florence, Campanile of Santa Maria del Fiore, c. 1437

the notion of philosophy and philosophical practice that informed the culture of Renaissance Florence.

While perfectly inscribed within the medieval iconography of the liberal arts, Della Robbia's tiles significantly rephrase the trope.[4] Three

---

[4] On the traditional iconography of the liberal arts, see Stolz (2004).

of them highlight the discursive and communicative dimension of the arts: grammar presents a schoolteacher instructing two young boys, two men are captured in debate in the tile of Philosophy, and two 'confronting bearded figures' are busy in computation in the Geometry tile.[5] In each of these cases, the interaction between the figures is crucial to the representation, but the alleged depiction of Philosophy is surely the most vivid. The two men are actively involved in a dialogic exchange, the dynamism of which is enhanced by the stylistic features of the sculpture, in particular the garments and gestures. John Pope-Hennessy has suggested comparing Della Robbia's depiction of Philosophy to Leonardo Bruni's coeval humanist reshaping of Plato and Aristotle. While Pope-Hennessy's comparison – one more based on 'cultural' consonance than on 'factual' evidence – remains somewhat vague, it nonetheless evokes new trends across art, literature and philosophy that saw the classical past with new eyes.[6] Regardless of the iconographic intention behind Della Robbia's tile (either Philosophy broadly intended or, as proposed by Julius von Schlosser, Rhetoric in conjunction with Dialectic),[7] what matters here is that the observers were exposed to the representation of a dialogic act consistent with the forms and practices of knowledge that humanists such as Leonardo Bruni fostered. A combination of philosophy, rhetoric and dialectic, the practice of composing and circulating humanist dialogues would in fact become one of the main grounds for lively debates where ethics, language and the uses of both all intertwined.[8]

The humanist dialogic approach to philosophical inquiry does not, however, imply a sudden and uncontested change. The dialogic Philosopher portrayed by Della Robbia shared the Florentine stage with a more traditional figure, the Aristotle propagated by the scholastics, a stern embodiment of rigorous Dialectic more concerned with the packaging of faultless arguments than with the human interaction of the interlocutors involved in dialogical exchange: in short, the kind of Aristotle that Petrarch obliquely criticised in his invective *De sui ipsius et multorum ignorantia*, discussed in the previous chapter. This approach is exemplified by the portrayal of Aristotle in the chapter house of Santa Maria Novella where, in the *Trionfo di San Tommaso d'Aquino* ('Triumph of Saint Thomas Aquinas') painted by Andrea di Bonaiuto between 1365 and 1367 [Figure 4.2], the philosopher

[5] Pope-Hennessy (1980: 31).
[6] *Ibid.*: 231–2.
[7] Schlosser (1896: 73).
[8] On the humanist rebirth of dialogue, see Tinkler (1988) and Tateo (1993).

Figure 4.2 Andrea di Bonaiuto, Dialectic and Aristotle, detail from Triumph of Saint Thomas, Florence, Cappellone degli Spagnoli, Santa Maria Novella, 1365–7

sits at the foot of the personification of Dialectic as part of the cycle of the liberal arts.[9]

The difference between Andrea's Aristotle and Della Robbia's philosophers could not be more striking. In Santa Maria Novella, Aristotle figures prominently within a complex narrative illustrating the hierarchy of knowledge at the heart of the scholastic tradition. As a matter of fact, the core of the fresco is not Aristotle himself but, rather, his most pro- lific interpreter and the greatest glory of the Dominican order, Thomas Aquinas. Andrea di Bonaiuto's triumph of Aquinas, based on an icono- graphic program traditionally attributed to Jacopo Passavanti, summarises the stratification of layers that informs the reception of classical phi- losophy through later antiquity, both pagan and Christian, followed by the Arabic tradition and medieval interpretations.[10] Della Robbia's tile instead stages a different kind of narrative, in which the performative and dialogic function of philosophical inquiry is, or at least appears to be, relieved of the hierarchical structure informing Andrea's fresco.

Striking though the difference may be, it is misleading to read the two experiences as either unrelated or simply opposed. On one hand, various scholars have demonstrated that most humanists, especially those committed to the study and interpretation of Aristotle, relied heavily on the achievements of scholastic commentators.[11] On the other hand, scholars have also shown that, through their criticism of the humanists, fifteenth-century advocates of the scholastic tradition contributed widely to the interaction of 'old' and 'new' cultures and reading practices.[12] If the position of the various disciplines within the system of knowledge was one of the main issues at stake in the dispute, linguistic matters still played a primary role. Indeed, relationships among the languages (for

---

[9] See Dieck (1997: 79–104); and Poeschke (2005: 362–5). The iconographic typology of Aristotle corresponds to that embodied by the 'Aristoteles Dyalecticus' of the Palazzo Ducale in Venice; see Chapter 3 here, 86–7. It should be noted that the iconographic interpretation of Bonaiuto's frescos is debated. An alternative scholarly tradition identifies the man seated in front of the personification of Dialectics as Petrus Hispanus; according to this interpretation, Aristotle should be recognised in the man seated in front of another personification, possibly that of Philosophy, which appears on the left side of Thomas Aquinas' throne (see Dieck 1997: 98).

[10] On the Dominican preacher Jacopo Passavanti, see Auzzas (2014) and Corbari (2013: 29–35, 49–53, 92–5 and 107–48). On the more general context of Dominican preaching and its iconographic tra- dition, see Bolzoni (2002).

[11] See, for instance, the case of Marsilio Ficino as discussed by Di Dio (2016).

[12] The conflict and interaction between scholasticism and humanism have been discussed at length: see Kristeller (1939, 1944–45); more recently, see Hankins (2007b), Monfasani (2008, 2012) and Edelheit (2014); with a focus on the implications of such conflict in the domain of education, see Black (2001: 12–21).

example, Latin vs. vernacular, classical Latin vs. medieval Latin, one kind of vernacular vs. another) were at the core of the dispute, especially when addressed from the standpoint of their ethical implications.

As both the stern philosopher in Santa Maria Novella and the lively young man debating with Plato on the cathedral campanile, Aristotle was a key figure in the debates between humanists and traditionalists. In different ways, already evident in Petrarch, each camp considered Aristotle their own.[13] Accordingly, each group thought that the other had misappropriated the Philosopher and, with him, the whole system of Aristotelian knowledge. Both perspectives have been the object of thorough investigation, but the implications of their interaction and the common ground that they shared remain largely unexplored. In this chapter I argue that this interaction should be examined to better understand the ways in which humanism, through conflict and ambiguous forms of competition, came to permeate vernacular lay culture. I will first consider the ways in which the dynamics of the conflict between traditionalists and humanists seeped into vernacular literacy. I will then turn to the forms of translation and adaptation that fostered the appropriation of Aristotle by his vernacular readership. By exploring, in particular, Giovanni Rucellai's interest in Aristotle's moral philosophy and Bernardo Nuti's Italian translation of Leonardo Bruni's Latin version of the *Nicomachean Ethics*, I will focus on the active role played by readers in both 'translating' and 'receiving' Aristotle.

Fighting the Ancients

Given the multilingual dimension of fifteenth-century Florence, translation features as a prominent site of cultural interaction. Translation is not only the space where past and present meet, but also the tool with which the present engages in a cultural contest with the past. Bruni's *De interpretatione recta* ('On the Correct Way to Translate'), from around 1424 to 1426, stands out as the boldest outline of the humanist theories of translation.[14] Bruni claims that his Latin version of Aristotle's works restored the philosopher's

---

[13] See Marsh (2004); see also Chapter 3, 89–94, for my discussion of Petrarch's invective *De sui ipsius et multorum ignorantia*.

[14] See the Latin text of Bruni's *De interpretatione recta* in Baron (1928: 81–96); Viti (1996: 150–93). For the English translation, see Griffiths, Hankins and Thompson (1987: 217–29); for a more recent Italian annotated translation, see Baldassarri (2003: 193–217). On the role of Bruni within the definition of translation theories and practices in the Renaissance, see Baldassarri (2003: 93–103), Botley (2004: 41–62).

eloquence, perverted by earlier Latin translators. As is well known, Bruni's advocacy of Aristotle's eloquence is one of the weakest points of his discussion, for the Greek philosopher's style was not rhetorically refined in the sense Bruni intended, at least in those Aristotelian works that he had access to. Bruni, in fact, was not familiar with Aristotle's 'exoteric' writings – the ones that gained Cicero's praise of the philosopher's eloquent style – for he only knew Aristotle's 'esoteric' works, namely lecture notes taken by pupils and which were not supposed to be read outside the classroom. Yet the Ciceronian praise of the Greek philosopher's eloquence affected Bruni's vision of Aristotle as a whole. In other words, Bruni appropriated Cicero's comments on Aristotle's style, and this determined his reception of Aristotle's works and of what Greek eloquence should be.[15] Aside from Bruni's misunderstanding of Cicero's statement about the philosopher's eloquence, though, what truly matters in Bruni's argument is the utopian desire to appropriate the cultural values of the classical past as they had been shaped and performed by republican Rome.[16] This approach tends to entail the cultural priority of antiquity over contemporaneity, hence the primacy of (classical) Latin over the vernacular. With such a perspective, humanist translation was primarily concerned with bringing Greek texts into Latin; during this process, it paradoxically adopted a regressive attitude, wittingly rejecting concurrent developments within Latinate culture and in the vernacular context. Or, at least, so argued the 'traditionalist' counterpart with unbowed energy.

The humanist approach to the classics was nowhere hindered more than in Florence, where an intense quarrel between the 'ancients' and the 'moderns' fostered productive discussions about language and translation.[17] If it is true that the severe rejection of vernacular culture usually associated with the humanist movement in early fifteenth century Florence was less univocal than has been traditionally described, it is undeniable that some of the most outspoken representatives of humanism considered vernacular literature a byproduct of the decline that classical culture had gone through during the previous centuries. Just as outspoken, though, were

---

[15] Bruni's argument about Aristotle's eloquent style was based on Cicero's and Quintilian's authoritative opinions; for a discussion of this point, see Copenhaver (1988: 78–9); and, more recently, Celenza (2018: 86–7).

[16] See Griffiths, Hankins and Thompson (1987). On Bruni's statements on Aristotle's eloquence as a gesture towards the reassessment of the relationship between rhetoric and philosophy, see Botley (2004: 41–2).

[17] For an introduction to the literary debates between humanists and traditionalists in fifteenth-century Florence, see Lanza (1989).

the champions of the *volgare*, especially in matters concerning the 'three crowns': Dante, Petrarch and Boccaccio.[18]

Indeed, one of the strongest criticisms of the humanist advocacy of the ancients' superiority involved the function and value of translation. A well-educated notary and poet, learned in both classical and vernacular literatures, Domenico da Prato (c. 1389–c. 1433) addressed these issues in a short prose treatise written around 1420 to defend himself from the attacks of critics of vernacular poetry.[19] Domenico's self-defence recalls most of the arguments featured in previous controversies about language. One could think, for instance, of Dante facing similar critiques in his poetic exchange with the schoolteacher and protohumanist Giovanni del Virgilio, who disapproved of Dante's choice to write his poem in Italian rather than seeking the laurel with a Latin epic.[20] However, while Dante's reply to Giovanni, written in the form of a Latin eclogue, performs a sort of cultural and linguistic compromise, Domenico's self-defence spares no harsh tones.

The author's main argument is as follows: those who criticise the use of the vernacular do so unethically. Given that the vernacular *is* the mother tongue of the moderns, the humanists who exclude it from the domain of knowledge (which includes philosophy, science and poetry) foster an elitist and conservative understanding of learning; in so doing, they promote a cultural system that rejects the enhancement of virtue. Their notion of knowledge instead adheres to the assumption that the formal qualities of classical languages (Latin in particular) were enough to make men wise and virtuous. Domenico's self-defence paradoxically overturns Petrarch's criticism of the Aristotelians of Padua in his invective *De sui ipsius et multorum ignorantia*.[21] While, as shown in the previous chapter, Petrarch argued for eloquence and style as tools necessary to promote the moral enhancement of an individual, Domenico maintains that in the hands of humanists such as Leonardo Bruni and Niccolò Niccoli those tools (which prove as artificial as the ones they criticised) became detached from the true practice of virtue. What Petrarch found in the language and style of the ancients, Domenico finds in the language and style of the moderns. Before recalling Dante, his most relevant example, Domenico introduces

---

[18] McLaughlin (2005). On the 'humanist' reception of Dante in Florence, see Gilson (2005).

[19] For an overview of the career and works of Domenico da Prato, see Viti (1991). For a critical edition of his defence of the vernacular, see Gentile (1993: 67–73); see also Gilson (2005: 88–91).

[20] The exchange between Dante and Giovanni del Virgilio, which constitutes the collection of Dante's Latin eclogues, is the object of a recent thorough study that includes a revised edition of the text; see Albanese (2014).

[21] See the discussion of Petrarch's invective in Chapter 3, 89–94.

Petrarch himself into the defence, not the classicising Latin author but the confident vernacular poet. Both Dante and Petrarch were criticised for their choice to write in Italian ('perché vulgarmente scripse', 'because they wrote in the vulgar tongue'),[22] but, according to Domenico, the vernacular is more authentic than Latin and Greek, for that is the language instinctively spoken by the authors who use it.[23]

Domenico shows that the humanist critique of Dante – with its echoes of Leonardo Bruni's *Dialogi ad Petrum Paulum Histrum* ('Dialogues to Pier Paolo Vergerio'), particularly those Bruni attributes to Niccolò Niccoli – is unfair not only to the author of the *Divine Comedy* but also to modern readers, especially the young.[24] By discounting Dante for his alleged unfamiliarity with the classics, humanists also scorn contemporaneous intellectuals, who are led to believe that the grandeur of the ancients will never be equalled, let alone surpassed. Domenico presents language as a communicative tool, without accepting the idea of the inner superiority of certain languages over others. What counts in this perspective is the subject matter that language is able to transmit, not the language itself. Indeed, as Domenico argues, knowledge of many languages does not guarantee the mastery of virtue, a position that, as we shall see at the end of this book, is one of the premises of the linguistic discussions known as the *questione della lingua* ('debate on language').

Despite the roughness ('rozzezza') he attributes to his own writing, Domenico represents himself pursuing virtue and encourages young people to do the same. Rather than arguing the impossibility of paralleling the great achievements of antiquity, he invites the younger generations to strive for greater deeds:

> These most harmful men confuse the still unstable intellects of young students by saying: 'Who will equal Homer or Vergil in poetry? Who will be the new Solomon or Aristotle in philosophy? Who will parallel Demosthenes or Cicero in rhetoric and oratory? Who will be the new Aristarchus or Priscian in grammar? Who will equal Parmenides in dialectic?'; and so on

---

[22] Gentile (1993: 67–8).

[23] *Ibid.*: 68: 'Certo esso volgare, nel quale scripse Dante, è più auctentico e degno di laude che il latino e 'l Greco che essi hanno' ('For sure, the vulgar tongue, which Dante used, is more authentic and praiseworthy than their Latin and Greek'). On the discussion of the same topic by Biondo Flavio, see Marcellino (2016), with references to previous bibliography.

[24] Bruni's *Dialogi ad Petrum Paulum Histrum* have been the object of various interpretations, in particular due to the divergent opinions about the vernacular attributed to the character of Niccolò Niccoli. For an introduction to the text, see Griffiths, Hankins and Thompson (1987: 53–62); and the introduction in Baldassarri (1994). For recent discussions of the *Dialogi*, see Gilson (2005: 83–8, 92–3), Maxson (2013), Rizzi (2017: 91–113).

and so forth, saying the same about all the liberal arts and about the mechanical too, they argue that nothing can be done or said that has not yet been better said or done by the ancients.[25]

Domenico's ethical condemnation of the humanists is explicit. Their responsibility is stressed through an authoritative quotation from Aristotle's *Sophistical Refutations*: if 'one must trust those who teach', as Aristotle posits, then when young students hear an allegedly knowledgeable and wise teacher scorn all modern writings, they cannot help feeling humiliated. By constantly reminding their students that whatever the ancients did was better, teachers end up disheartening new generations.[26]

To support his critique of the humanist approach to learning, Domenico turns to a key example that, in his opinion, evidences the narrow-mindedness of his adversaries: the practice of translation. Given the humanists' criticism of the writings of all other authors, Domenico suggests looking at the works by the humanists themselves:

> What are the writings of these faultfinders, besides their loquacity? They should show them so that they are not the only judges of both themselves and the others. I have not yet seen any of their writings in historiography, philosophy, or poetry. One of them will reply scornfully: 'Haven't you read my translations of the Greek works of Aristotle and Plutarch that I made into Latin?'[27]

This polemic reference, of course, points to Leonardo Bruni himself, whose Latin versions of Greek authors were the flagship achievement of humanist

[25] Gentile (1993: 69): 'Or non confondono questi dapnosissimi huomini li animi non ancora fermi delli adolescenti e ricenti uditori, quando dicono: "Chi si farà Homero o Virgilio in poesia? Chi Solone o Aristotele in philosophia? Chi Demostene o Cicerone in rethorica e in orare? Chi Aristarco o Prisciano in gramatica? Chi Parmenide in dialectica?", e così di ciascuna arte liberale quanto di qualunque altra virtù natural così concludendo: ciò è non potersi alcuna cosa fare o dire sì bene che meglio non sia stata decta o fatta per li antichi passati.'

[26] *Ibid.*: 69: 'Odi Aristotele, quello che nel primo libro degli *Elenci* dice: "Ad colui – disse egli – che appara, bisogna credere". Adunque, se io novitio, dato l'animo mio ad la doctrina, udito te, reputato doctor e instructissimo, biasimare quasi tutte le moderne eloquentie e opere tanto poetiche quanto philosophiche, non debba invilire?' ('Listen to what Aristotle says in book 1 of *Sophistical Refutations*: "One who teaches," he says, "must be believed"'. For this reason, if I am a novice who devoted himself to learning, and I hear you – who are a renowned scholar and most erudite – blame almost all modern eloquence and writings, both poetical and philosophical, shouldn't I feel mortified?'). The Aristotelian reference is to Aristotle, *De soph. elen.* 1.2, 165b 3–4: 'he who is learning must take things on trust' (Forster 1955: 15).

[27] Gentile (1993: 69–70): 'Ma qual pertanto sono l'opere di questi tali spernitori fuori della loro loquacitade? Manifestinle ad altri che ad sé medesimi, acciò che soli essi non siano giudici e di loro e delli altri! Io non ho alcuna opera per ancora né historiographa, né philosophica, né poetica, veduta delle loro apparire. Alcuno di quelli risponderà disdegnosamente: "Tu non hai adunque lecte le traductioni che delle opere greche d'Aristotele e di Plutarco ho facte in latino?"'

translation theory and practice. Domenico does not deny Bruni's excellent skills in both Greek and Latin, but argues that he is not responsible for the merit of those works, for he did not author the originals:

> I do acknowledge that he knows Greek and Latin, but I do not praise him as the author of those works, which were made by others and of these little fame remains for him, despite the vain mention of his name in the rubrics [i.e., in the titles of the translations as they appear in the manuscripts]; indeed fame belongs to the authors of the works, not to their translators.[28]

Domenico's argument is intriguing, for it addresses an issue at the core of the relationship between the authorship of the work and the authorship of the translation.

He recalls that, while Bruni's translations circulated under the name of the translator himself, whose role is enhanced by the 'rubrics' in the manuscripts, previous translators kept a lower profile. The humanist claim to the authorial role of the translator, hence the acknowledgement of the translator's pivotal role in the dissemination of a given work, is labelled mere vainglory in Domenico's critique. The old translators instead hid their names behind those of the authors, revealing their unselfishness.[29] This attitude is exemplified by Jerome, whose translation of the Bible has been read by all, and yet no reader would consider him the author of the work.[30]

If the case of Jerome's Vulgate advances the discussion, even briefly, into the far more ambiguous territory of biblical translations, where the 'authorship' of the 'original' has a rather peculiar status, then the ethical dimension of Domenico's polemic harkens to earthlier concerns in the following section of his self-defence. The author again ridicules the humanist preoccupation with form rather than subject matter. Their despicable attitude, argues Domenico, is perfectly embodied by their passion for exquisitely produced books and, more specifically, for the so-called *littera antiqua*,

---

[28] *Ibid.*: 70: 'Lui commendo che sappi greco e latino, ma non per inventore delle opere, facte per altri, e di queste restargli pochissima fama, non obstante che per le rubriche in esso siano vanamente intitulate, imperò che la fama è delli inventori delle opere e non delli traductori.'

[29] *Ibid.*: 70: 'Né truovo per li passati che alcuna stima se ne facesse, né per essi, che anticamente tradussono tante e sì maravigliose opere quante e quali si leggono al presente, furono in altri intitulate che solo in quelli ad li quali s'appartenevano, occultando essi translatori li nomi loro, conciosiacosaché tali traductioni facevano caritativamente e non per vanità di pompa' ('I do not find that old translators were given any particular esteem, and it was not under their name that the many and glorious works that we read today circulated; rather, they were attributed to those to whom they belonged; indeed, translators hid their names, since they made those translations not for boastfulness, but inspired by generosity').

[30] *Ibid.*

the supreme humanist hand that Poggio Bracciolini and Niccolò Niccoli perfected following Petrarch's scribal experiments.[31] The latter is the direct target of Domenico's criticism: Niccolò is held as the boldest representative of a culture that seemed to spend more time and energy in recovering the ancients' supposed handwriting than in dealing with virtue itself.[32]

Domenico's criticism is clearly instrumental to his defence of the 'moderns': he exaggerates some features of the humanist movement to highlight the progressive drive of vernacular culture. From his point of view, the true 'enemies of philosophy' are those who value words more than things. By privileging the knowledge of ancient languages (for example Latin, Greek, Hebrew) over the use of the vernacular, they detach themselves from the real world. But Domenico does not dismiss the importance of language. He knows all too well that it is impossible to deal with things without using words, but he argues that it is sterile to use languages different than one's own. In the same vein, he describes Dante, Petrarch, Boccaccio and Coluccio Salutati as the authors who have best combined the quest for virtue with the poetical and philosophical use of their mother tongue.[33] If the reference to the three crowns is a commonplace, Domenico's mention of Coluccio Salutati (1331–1406) is of greater interest to this study, for it strikes right at the core of the humanist movement. By including a prominent member of the humanist circle such as Salutati among the authors scorned by the humanists themselves, Domenico draws a line between the intellectuals interested in the relationship between the study of literature and the practice of virtue and those unconcerned with it. He posits that when humanists criticise Dante and other vernacular authors for being unskilled in Greek and Latin, they are criticising those with both 'the intellectual wisdom and the speculative ability crucial to the real poetical genius'.[34] The humanists' resentment towards these authors

---

[31] See Ulmann (1960), Petrucci (1967) and Davies (1996).

[32] Gentile (1993: 71): 'L'altro dirà: "Io sono optimo cognoscitore d'un libro". Rispondo: "Sì, forse, se esso è ben legato; e questo sa fare uno bidello o un cartolaio". Ed ecco il sommo ingegno di questo tale biasimatore, ciò è di voler vedere una bella lectera antica, la quale non stima bella o buona se ella non è di forma antica e bene diptongata, e nullo libro per buono che sia gli piace, né degnerebbe di leggere non essendo scripto di lectera antica, correndo una giornata dietro ad una derivazione di vocabolo o ad uno diptonguzzo' ('The other will say: "I know books well". I reply: "You do, maybe, if they are well bound; and this is what stationers do well". Here it is the excellent intellect of such a faultfinder: he wants to see a beautiful ancient handwriting, which he does not consider beautiful or good if it is not of ancient shape and well diphthonged; no book is good, and he would not read any that is not written in ancient handwriting; for he spends entire days chasing an etymology or a little diphthong'). On the discussion of diphthongs, see Gombrich (1967).

[33] Gentile (1993: 71).

[34] *Ibid.*

is due simply to their own inability to help enhance the vernacular. Their ideas on language are just another facet of their dubious morality, and it is on the ground of ethics that Domenico closes his self-defence. On one hand, he compares the potential of the vernacular vis-à-vis classical languages to the spirit of Cicero's famous statement about the potential of Latin vis-à-vis Greek.[35] On the other hand, though, Domenico turns to an Aristotelian dictum in order to stress the ethical value of philosophical inquiry. No matter the language or languages with which one is conversant, priority should always be given to nurturing moral doctrine and practicing virtue throughout one's life: 'As Aristotle used to say, knowledge adorns us in prosperity and protects us in times of adversity'.[36]

The Humanist in the Middle

As has been shown, Domenico da Prato's self-defence has two unnamed but easily recognisable targets: Leonardo Bruni and Niccolò Niccoli. If Niccolò is traditionally considered the uncompromising representative of those humanists who distanced themselves from the vernacular world, Bruni embodies the inner conflicts of humanism vis-à-vis vernacular culture. In the aforementioned *Dialogi ad Petrum Paulum Histrum*, he articulates this conflict by explicitly addressing the relationship between Latinate and vernacular cultures. By giving a prominent voice to Niccolò, Bruni embodies the notion of humanism polemicised by Domenico da Prato, but he also provides space for an apology of the founding fathers of vernacular literature. As other scholars have noted, it is through Niccolò that the position expressed in the first dialogue is later nuanced in the second.[37]

The ambiguity of Bruni's position in the *Dialogi* reappears in his later vernacular biographies of Dante and Petrarch, where he acknowledges the relevance of the two poets to the cultural growth underway in his own time.[38] Bruni particularly stresses the civic inspiration of Dante, whose

---

[35] *Ibid.*: 71–2: 'non si ricordano del facundioso Tullio dicente nel primo libro *Delli fini de' beni e de' mali*: "Io sento, overo acconsento – disse elli –, e spesse volte l'ho admaestrato, la lingua latina non pur essere non bisognosa, ma molto più ricca che la greca' ('they do not remember what the eloquent Tullius wrote in book 1 of *On the ends of good and evil*: "I believe – he said – and I often showed that Latin is no less abundant, but even richer than Greek'); cf. Cicero, *De fin.* 1.10.

[36] Gentile (1993: 72): 'quello che spesso Aristotele usava di dire ... ciò è la doctrina essere nelle prosperitadi adornezza e refugio nelle adversitadi'.

[37] See Maxson (2013), Rizzi (2013); and, most recently, the thorough discussion of Bruni in Rizzi (2017: 91–113).

[38] Viti (1996: 537–60). For the English translation of Bruni's lives of Dante and Petrarch, see Griffiths, Hankins and Thompson (1987: 85–100); on Bruni's discussion of Dante in the *Dialogi*, see Gilson (2005: 83–8, 92–3).

lack of skills in classical Latin is undeniable, especially when compared to Petrarch and, even more so, to the humanists. The poet's personal experience as well as the political and ideological struggles he endured in an age of considerable turmoil are both aspects that, in Bruni's opinion, Boccaccio's pioneering biography had overlooked. Moreover, they are both crucial for any strictly Aristotelian portrayal of Dante. As Bruni puts it, 'man is a social animal, according to what the philosophers say'. Bruni's reference to one of the most frequently quoted passages from Aristotle's *Politics*, one which Dante himself quoted in the *Convivio*, corresponds to his wider ambitions to nuance the traditional promotion of solitary life as the ideal condition for students and intellectuals.[39] Bruni indeed advocates quite the opposite, using Dante's experience to show that political engagement and literary production inform each other in positive ways. The biography similarly highlights Dante's commitment to start a family as further proof that Dante conceived that communal welfare was maintained through bonds and responsibilities. As such, Dante follows illustrious predecessors like Cicero, Cato, Seneca and Varro, 'all great Latin philosophers' who 'had wives and children and carried out offices and duties in the Republic'.[40]

The 'philosophical' dimension of Bruni's portrayal of Dante, evoked by his comparison with the ancients, is then confirmed by Bruni's account of the quality of Dante's writing, his vernacular poetry in particular, poetry that is not frivolous but, rather, based on deep knowledge and learning. Though poor in Latin and ignorant of Greek, Dante far surpasses his vernacular predecessors, thus representing for Bruni the highest expression of literature in the *volgare*. Bruni's praise of Dante casts him as a humanist *avant la lettre*: by excusing Dante for his unrefined Latin – no fault of his but rather a product of the times – the biographer acknowledges the cultural and civic importance of his subject's human and literary experience. When compared with Niccolò's opinions in the first section of the *Dialogi*, the later *Vita di Dante* ('Life of Dante') stands out as a striking admission of Bruni's insistence on Dante's relevance to the humanist context.

Bruni's approach to Dante is inspired by the same agenda that also informs his appropriation of Aristotle. Just as Bruni 'rehabilitates' Dante in the eyes of the humanists and thus tries to wrest him from the traditionalists, so too does he aim to make Aristotle a hero of humanism by rejecting the ways in which scholasticism had moved the philosopher

---

[39] Aristotle, *Pol.* 1, 1253a. The same passage was referenced by Dante himself in *Convivio* 4.4.1.
[40] Griffiths, Hankins and Thompson (1987: 87); see the original passage in Viti (1996: 542); cf. Gilson (2005: 117, 123, 175).

quite far from the supposed original texts. Along with his translations of Aristotle's works, Bruni's reshaping of Aristotle (a process that inevitably offers us yet another transformation of the 'master of those who know') is best represented by his *Life of Aristotle*. Written in 1436 as part of a diptych that also includes the *Life of Petrarch*, Bruni's biography of Aristotle exemplifies his attempt to embed humanism into the philosopher's legacy.[41]

As recalled earlier in this chapter, Bruni's project is hardly 'philological' in the truest sense of the word, since his appropriation of the Greek philosopher is filtered through the Latin interpretations of Cicero, who deeply influences Bruni's understanding of both Aristotle's philosophy as well as his stylistic qualities.[42] On one hand, Bruni's detailed account emphasises the political and civic conscience that Aristotle demonstrated throughout his career, as both a counsellor of rulers and a teacher of princes, the most notable of whom is Alexander the Great. On the other hand, Bruni's need to substantiate the portrayal of the philosopher as a *vir bonus dicendi peritus* leads him to confront the common opinion about Aristotle's inelegant style. He refutes the claim with two arguments. First, what Latinate readers have been reading for centuries is not the authentic Aristotle, Bruni argues, but a tainted version of his works, the product of incompetent translators who have ruined the philosopher's eloquence. (Here Bruni repeats some of the points from his critique of the medieval translators of Aristotle in the preface to his version of the *Ethics*, later reaffirmed in the treatise *De interpretatione recta*.) Second, Aristotle's rhetorical skills and beautiful diction are assumed, as I have noted above, on the basis of Cicero's praise of the Greek philosopher's eloquence and on the evidence that Aristotle's own writings often treat both rhetoric and poetics.[43]

As this brief overview suggests, both Bruni's Latin *Life of Aristotle* and his vernacular *Life of Dante* portray a model of intellectual moulded on his own experience, one that combines civic duties, knowledge and literary skills. By conjuring Dante's Aristotelian cast and also arguing for Aristotle's consistency with the principles of humanism, Bruni closes the gap between the two figures and his own cultural milieu. Dante and Aristotle are both, in a way, 'translated' into terms that make them consistent with the humanist experience. In the case of Dante, it is the philosophical depth of the poet's work and biography that makes him a humanist. In the case of the Greek

---

[41] Viti (1996: 504–29); for the English translation of the text, see Griffiths, Hankins and Thompson (1987: 283–92).
[42] See above, 134.
[43] Griffiths, Hankins and Thompson (1987: 290).

philosopher, Bruni manages to appropriate the scholastic Aristotle only by translating him into the language of humanism.

Translation thus proves a powerful instrument of cultural appropriation that Bruni employs to achieve various ideological objectives. Not only does he translate the works of Aristotle into humanist-style Latin, supposedly restoring the 'eloquence' that medieval translators had ignored and altered, but he also attempts to make Aristotle the champion of humanist culture by abridging the core of his moral teachings for the benefit of readers outside the scholarly circles. In the case of this abridgment, 'translation' implies an operation of simplification and popularisation involving both Latin and the vernacular, as suggested by works by Bruni as diverse as the *Isagogicon moralis disciplinae* and the *Canzone morale*. Both works can be read as summaries aimed at disseminating philosophical ideas to audiences traditionally excluded from the sophistication of scholarly debates.

Probably written in the early 1420s, the *Isagogicon moralis disciplinae* ('Introduction to Moral Philosophy') addresses an audience of lay readers who, though conversant with Latin, are not professional scholars.[44] Bruni's translation here is not inter-lingual but intra-lingual. The humanist is not translating a philosophical text from one language into another, as from Greek to Latin, but, instead, he is translating the subject matter of classical philosophy (moral and Aristotelian thought, in particular) from the intellectual complexity of its original source into a format that can be more immediately grasped by the audience. As is the case with his biographies of Aristotle and Dante, Bruni's *Isagogicon* strives to relate the philosophical tradition to the everyday experience of his target audience. Indeed, along with a straightforward abridgment of some key topics in moral philosophy, including a summary of Aristotle's system of moral and intellectual virtues, Bruni strongly argues for the priority of the active over the contemplative life. While the excellence of contemplation goes unquestioned, Bruni argues that the active life is superior since it fuels the common good.[45]

---

[44] *Ibid.*: 267–82. Hans Baron proposed 1423 as the date of publication; see Vasoli (1972: 619). The kind of readership that Bruni had in mind for the *Isagogicon* is suggested by the dedicatee of the work, the Florentine aristocrat Galeotto Ricasoli (1365–1441).

[45] Viti (1996: 238): 'Enim vero, cum plures sint virtutes, ut diximus, constat alias ad otiosam vitam in contemplatione repositam, alias ad negotiosam et civilem esse aptiores … Utraque sane vita laudes commendationesque proprias habet. Contemplativa quidem divinior plane atque rarior, activa vero in communi utilitate prestantior'; see the English translation in Griffiths, Hankins and Thompson (1987: 282): 'Now of the many virtues we've discussed, some are clearly reserved to the contemplative life of retirement, while others are more suitable to the active civic life … Both kinds of life have their proper kind of esteem and merit. The contemplative life is, to be sure, the more divine and rare, but the active is more excellent with respect to the common good.'

Of course, Aristotle's *Ethics* proposes a different conclusion, describing philosophical contemplation as relevant to the highest human achievement,[46] but in Bruni's reshaping of the philosopher's paradigm, which is based on Bruni's direct experience as a civil servant, the public duties that involve intellectuals in civic life have become crucial to the fulfilment of one's virtue.

A similar concern with the abridgment of classical philosophy into humanist terms lies at the core of Bruni's *Canzone morale* (c. 1421), yet another example of his attempt to bridge the humanist culture of Latinate authors and contemporary vernacular readers.[47] Far removed from the speculative heights of philosophical literature in Latin, be it scholastic or humanist, the *canzone* brings us back to the tradition of vernacular philosophical poetry that Dante had encouraged in the *De vulgari eloquentia* and exemplified with his own *canzoni*. As recalled above, in Chapter 1, Dante holds that 'virtus', along with 'salus' and 'venus', is one of the few topics suitable for the highest among the vernacular poetic forms, the *canzone*.[48] Bruni's *canzone* addresses a question at the core of Aristotle's *Ethics*: what is happiness? To answer this, Bruni examines the various definitions of happiness propounded by the ancient philosophical schools and, after recalling the philosophers who identified happiness with honour and pleasure, he dwells on Socrates and Plato, who regarded virtue as the source of all happiness. But further divisions arise with the question of the ability of virtue to safeguard men from misfortune: the Stoics argued that virtue alone grants happiness while the Peripatetics, following Aristotle, specified that happiness lies not in virtue itself, but in virtuous actions. In the last stanza, Bruni endorses Aristotle's opinion by stressing the operational dimension of virtue, within which all the other threads of the inquiry seem to converge.

By composing a *canzone* on the topic of virtue, Bruni inscribes his own experience into a long-lasting tradition deeply rooted in the vernacular culture of Italy: Dante and, before him, poets like Guittone d'Arezzo and Guido Cavalcanti, among others, were committed to projects that considered poetry a vehicle suitable for philosophical discussions. If scholars are right to frame Bruni's *canzone* as nothing more than a summary

---

[46] The formulation of contemplation as the highest form of human life is central to Aristotle's *Nicomachean Ethics*; see book 10. On the place of contemplative life in the *Ethics*, see Reeve (2012) and Destrée and Zingano (2013).

[47] For the text of the *canzone morale*, see Baron (1928: 149–54). On Bruni's vernacular production in general, see Hankins (2006).

[48] Dante, *De vulgari eloquentia* 2.2.7; see Chapter 1, 24–5.

of the most important philosophical positions on happiness – one, more-over, with a clear preference for Aristotle's identification of happiness as the practice of virtue – they should not underestimate the role played by the poem at the crossroad of Latin and vernacular humanist practices.[49] Indeed, as we shall see later in this chapter, Bruni's *canzone* effectively connected the two cultures.

The Vernacular Reading List

Bruni's role in the mediation between Latinate and vernacular culture cannot be overstated, but, as we have seen, his approach to both clas-sical and contemporaneous literature remains largely based on the cultural premises of humanism. While widely shared within and beyond humanist circles, these premises encountered an educated lay readership, whose reading practices were often informed by very practical concerns. The complex relationship between humanism (including pre-existing humanist culture) and vernacular literary traditions is evident in the specific ways in which lay readers approached the classics, particularly masters of moral philosophy such as Aristotle, Cicero and Seneca. It would be nonetheless misleading to draw too sharp a line between the two approaches. Indeed, as the case studies discussed in this chapter show, it is through the grey zone of translation that some features of humanism penetrated vernacular culture.

One such case is the trope of advocating the reading of moral works that often informed private and public discussions about education for young Florentines. Most of the so-called *libri di ricordi* ('books of records') and *zibaldoni* ('notebooks') left by wealthy merchants from the fourteenth and the fifteenth centuries provide precise instructions about the books that young members of the family should study.[50] A prime example is the *Libro di ricordi* of Paolo di Giovanni Morelli (1371–1444), who recommends that his sons carry on reading approved authors even after having finished their schooling.[51] This routine will not only bring them knowledge of things earthly and divine but will also ensure them considerable pleasure and,

---

[49] Vasoli (1972: 626) labels Bruni's *canzone* a poetical abridgment of the same topics found in the *Isagogicon*. For a similar judgment, see Hankins (2006: 16).

[50] See Bec (1967, 1984) and Branca (1986, 1999). Other research on record-keeping pertaining to family and education, in books frequently meant to circulate within the household, includes Cicchetti and Mordenti (1985) and Ciappelli (1989).

[51] For biography on Morelli, see Pandimiglio (2012). The text of Morelli's *Ricordi* is edited in Branca (1969); excerpts of the text are also available in Branca (1986) and translated into English in Branca

above all, will guide them through life. Morelli prioritises the practical outcomes of his children's moral education, particularly its concern with activity:

> After you have completed your schooling, endeavor to study Vergil, Boethius, Seneca or other authors for at least an hour every day, as if you were still in school. This will result in great benefit to your mind: by studying the teachings of these authors, you shall know how you should act in your present life, both for the health of your soul and for the usefulness and honor of your body.[52]

If Morelli's claim about the importance of philosophical literature to the enhancement of individual virtue deploys arguments remarkably similar to the ones used by humanists, it is worth recalling that his catalogue of authors includes a non-classical writer, Dante, whom Morelli considers as relevant to moral education as Vergil, Cicero, Boethius and Aristotle.[53] When he references classical authors, Morelli is likely to have had in mind either the vernacular versions of their works (*volgarizzamenti*) or the many vernacular anthologies of ancient philosophers (titled as the 'detti' or 'sentenzie dei filosofi') so common among lay readers of the time. These anthologies, as we shall see, played an important role in the vernacular reshaping of Aristotle.[54]

Morelli's recommendations to his sons are even more remarkable when we remember that they illustrate a well-established trend. Indeed, as shown by Christian Bec and Vittore Branca, the production of *libri di ricordi* and *zibaldoni* in late medieval and early modern Florentine culture evidence the lively interaction between vernacular readership and the production of vernacular writings, both private and public, thus creating a particularly fertile ground for the reception of the classics.

The importance of such educational practices is further revealed by their early canonisation within contemporary philosophical literature. In this

---

(1999). On the authors read and taught in late medieval and Renaissance Florence, see Black (2001, 2007).

[52] Translated by Baca, in Branca (1999: 70). See the original in Branca (1969: 271): 'E di poi hai apparato, fa che ogni dì, un'ora il meno, tu istudi Virgilio, Boezio, Senaca o altri autori, come si legge in iscuola. Di questo ti seguirà gran virtù nel tuo intelletto: conoscerai, ispeculando, gli ammaestramenti degli autori, quello hai a seguire nella presente vita e sì in salute dell'anima e sì in utilità e onore del corpo.'

[53] Branca (1969: 272): 'Tu ti potrai istare con Boezio, con Dante e cogli altri poeti, con Tulio che t'insegnerà parlare perfettamente, con Aristotile che ti insegnerà filosofia' ('You can be with Boethius, with Dante and the other poets, with Tullio [i.e. Cicero], who will teach you perfect diction; with Aristotle, who will teach you philosophy'; transl. Baca in Branca 1999: 71).

[54] On the use of *sententiae* in education, see Black (2001: 320–4).

context, the encounter between lay readership and the humanist world proves particularly productive, as witnessed by works such as Leon Battista Alberti's *Profugiorum ab aerumna libri* ('On the Tranquillity of the Soul', 1442–43) and Matteo Palmieri's *Vita civile* ('Civic life', c. 1430). Both works belong to the Renaissance revival of the Ciceronian dialogue and stage conversations among prominent figures of the Florentine elite, chief among them Agnolo Pandolfini (1363–1446). A contemporary of Morelli's and a merchant renowned for his culture and interest in moral philosophy, Pandolfini was a highly influential political figure in early fifteenth-century Florence.[55] His appearances as a character in the dialogues of Alberti and Palmieri reiterate the educational pattern found in Morelli's *Libro* and focus specifically on Aristotle as the source of all philosophical knowledge. In Alberti's *Profugiorum libri*, the character of Pandolfini recalls his own learning experience in terms consistent with Morelli's instructions. After comparing the human being to a ship destined to leave its harbour but instinctively inclined to visit faraway lands, Pandolfini argues that the best way to prepare oneself for great deeds is the study of the authors, particularly Aristotle, whose writings lead men along the path of virtue:

> Brought to life like a ship, which is not made to rot in the harbour, but to cut through long routes at sea, we will always aim to gain praise through the accomplishment of great deeds. And it will be useful to impose ourselves some discipline in practicing virtue. I decided once to learn all that Aristotle wrote in philosophy. I called a few scholars and I forced myself to study with them two hours per day. That almost imposed duty made me more zealous than I would have been [if left on my own].[56]

That the merchant Pandolfini should promote his acquaintance with Aristotle indicates the desire to combine moral knowledge with its concrete application in life.

Such a desire is also at the core of Matteo Palmieri's *Vita civile*, in which the character of Pandolfini displays his philosophical expertise.[57] Though filtered through the fictional nature of the dialogue, which is largely

---

[55] For a recent biographical account of Pandolfini, see Plebani (2014). His importance to the social and cultural world of fifteenth-century Florence is highlighted by Vespasiano da Bisticci's biography; see Greco (1970 vol. 2: 261–84).

[56] Ponte (1988: 40): 'E noi, produtti in vita quasi come la nave, non per marcirsi in porto ma per sulcare lunghe vie in mare, sempre renderemo collo essercitarsi a qualche laude e frutto di gloria. E gioverà imporre a noi stessi qualche necessità di così essercitarci in virtù. Io deliberai un tempo riconoscere tutto quello che scrisse Aristotile in filosofia. Chiamai alcuni studiosi e a me imposi legger loro ogni dì due ore. Quella ascrittami quasi necessità mi fece assiduo più ch'io forse non sarei stato.'

[57] On Palmieri, see Mita Ferraro (2005).

inspired by Quintilian's *Institutio oratoria* and Cicero's *De officiis*, Palmieri's portrayal of Agnolo Pandolfini sheds light on the interconnections between lay readers and humanists. Palmieri details these connections and discusses their relationship to language and its uses. On one hand, Pandolfini's frequent references to Aristotle in Palmieri's dialogue, with almost verbatim quotations from the *Ethics*, effects a form of translation that selects philosophical content to be made available to vernacular readers; on the other hand, by crafting discussions explicitly about language, Palmieri contributes to the defence of the *volgare*. Indeed, the author frames his defence with a web of cultural and linguistic allusions that capture the conflict between scholastic and humanist Latin styles as well as the somewhat problematic status of the vernacular with respect to the Latinate tradition.

Palmieri's project presupposes that classical authors offer a model for the forms that civic life should take in his time. While such a position is scarcely innovative in the context of Florentine humanism, Palmieri's most original contribution to the discussion relates to his consideration of language. In the preface to his dialogue *Vita civile*, Palmieri justifies his choice to write in Tuscan by recalling that wide audiences are excluded from philosophy simply by not knowing Latin.[58] His preoccupation with the linguistic skills of his readers and his desire to disseminate the subject matter to new communities are motivations that, in the aftermath of Dante's discussion of language, were often used by the champions of the vernacular. But Palmieri's reshaping of Dante's arguments about the uses of the *volgare* is no mere repetition: he is not simply concerned with the philosophical and pedagogical use of the *volgare* as opposed to Latin in fifteenth-century Florence but first and foremost with the fundamental question of the capacity of the vernacular to communicate philosophical content. Palmieri's unapologetic defence of the vernacular is thus based on the assumption of the poor quality of the *volgare* used by many critics.

Echoing Dante's critique of Taddeo Alderotti, Palmieri chides the 'vernacularisers' ('volgarizzatori') who have produced inaccurate translations of the classics that embarrass their authors:

> Examining the authors that would be suitable to provide vernacular readers with satisfactory knowledge, I found but a few that could benefit the life

---

[58] Belloni (1982: 5): 'molti vedendone che, disiderosi di bene et virtuosamente vivere, sanza loro colpa, solo per non avere notitia della lingua latina, mancavano d'inumerabili precepti che molto arebbono giovato il loro buono proposito' ('I saw many people who, eager to live well following the path of virtue, without any fault of theirs and only because they did not know any Latin, lacked many precepts that would have benefited their purpose'; here, and in the following quotations, my transl.).

of virtuous people; of those that have been translated, however, many of those that were expressed in an elegant, instructive and noble Latin, have been corrupted by the translators' ignorance; most of those that are highly respectable in Latin, have been made ridiculous.[59]

Upon further inspection, Palmieri's argument adapts for a vernacular context the position of Leonardo Bruni and his humanist peers on the medieval Latin translators of ancient works. Vernacular translators have made the same mistake: by paralleling them with earlier Latin translators, Palmieri champions a humanist position that is not based on the privilege of one specific language but rather on the idea that any language, including the vernacular, can be used in either good (i.e., elegant) or bad (i.e., unrefined) ways.

If this proposition holds true for translators, it can also be extended to vernacular authors, who seem to be unable to communicate the good rules of civic life effectively. Dante, Petrarch and Boccaccio constitute a partial exception for Palmieri: while his judgement of the three crowns is favourable, he still considers that they are not without faults. Despite his greatness, Dante is often obscure and thus is more pleasing than instructive.[60] Petrarch's poetry is, on the contrary, too concise, only useful for those who are already knowledgeable about philosophy.[61] Boccaccio would have certainly counted among the finest authors of all time but for the lasciviousness of some of his tales.[62] To guarantee a link between morality and the vernacular, Palmieri commits to a project that combines a stylistically refined use of the vulgar tongue with moral instruction and philosophical clarity. Agnolo Pandolfini proves the ideal mouthpiece for a similar project.

---

[59] *Ibid.*: 'Examinando quali auctori fussino atti a potere dare a' volgari sufficiente notitia, ne trovai pochi da potere molto giovare alla vita de' virtuosi, però che alquanti ne sono volgarizati che in ne' loro originali sono eleganti, sententiosi et gravi, scripti in latino, ma dalla ignoranzia de' volgarizatori in modo corrotti, che molti ne sono da ridersene di quegli che in latino sono degnissimi.'

[60] *Ibid.*: 'Dante poeta ... in ogni parte tanto excelle qualunche altro volgare ... Ma pe' velami poetici è in modo oscuro ché, dove nonn-è grande ingegno et abondante doctrina, più tosto può dare dilecto che fructo' ('The poet Dante ... is more excellent than any other vernacular author ... Yet, because of his poetical veils, he is so obscure that, to readers who are not abundant in intelligence and doctrine, he gives more pleasure than learning').

[61] *Ibid.*: 6: 'Perché non sono materie diffusamente per aperto campo dilatate, in loro costrette, non molto giovano a chi non ha da sé materia abondante' ('Since subject matter is not widely diffused, expanded broadly, and is further confined in them, it is not of much use to those who are not already learned').

[62] *Ibid.*: 'volesse Iddio che i suoi libri volgari non fussino ripieni di tanta lascivia et dissoluti exempli d'amore, ché certo credo che, avendo così attamente scripto cose morali et precepti di ben vivere, non meriterebbe essere chiamato Boccaccio ma più tosto Crisostomo' ('I wish his vernacular books were

The connections between the various aspects of the Latinate world and the vernacular context that Palmieri is addressing are evident throughout the *Vita civile*. On one hand, the author outlines a cultural and educational model deeply rooted in the tradition of the liberal arts that humanism had revamped with a strong focus on the arts of discourse. On the other hand, Palmieri endeavours to mediate between Latin traditions and vernacular readers in order to produce a text that can meet the needs of his target readership. After praising grammar – that is, the study of Latin – as the gateway to individual refinement, Palmieri indicates philosophy as the overarching discipline, the study that encompasses all the others.[63] Without undermining the importance of natural philosophy, Palmieri emphasises moral philosophy as the discipline without which people could not live peacefully: the eventual ability to apply language to philosophical pursuits is what distinguishes humans from animals. His reflection fits in with a wider preoccupation over the cultural renewal promoted by humanism, which Palmieri seeks to transfer into the vernacular context. Particularly significant in this respect is Palmieri's critique of the scholastic approach to the study of philosophy, which derives from Leonardo Bruni's arguments. Indeed, Palmieri's insight into the decadence of so many disciplines over the preceding eight centuries, the liberal arts in particular, is one of the earliest endorsements in vernacular writings of the ideological divide between the Middle Ages and the Renaissance promoted by humanism. Bruni is explicitly credited with the rebirth of the long-neglected ancient style and made to symbolise a new epoch overcoming the alleged obscurities of medieval scholarship.[64]

Palmieri's account of Bruni leads to his promotion of a return to the classics able to cut through the many interpretive layers that have made them impenetrable. He envisions a translation process that builds on a direct connection between the audience and the sources. Rather than spending years in the study of confusing interpretations of the classics, vernacular readers should be able to converse with them directly:

> I truly believe that the time will come soon when it will be possible to learn philosophy and all other sciences by reading the most important authors

---

not so full of lasciviousness and dissolute examples of lust; in that case, having written so well about morals and good life instructions, he would not deserve to be called Boccaccio, but Chrysostom').

[63] *Ibid.*: 29.

[64] *Ibid.*: 44: 'Oggi veggiano per padre et ornamento delle lettere essere mandato nel mondo el nostro Leonardo aretino come splendido lume della eleganzia latina, per rendere agl'huomini la dolcezza della latina lingua' ('We see today that our Leonardo of Arezzo has been given to the world as father and ornament of letters, splendid light of Latin elegance, in order to bring back the sweetness of the Latin language').

more briefly and more perfectly than by going through the insoluble investigations of those, who claim to explain, but, in fact, make the well organized and composed authors of such high genius obscure.[65]

Palmieri's argument combines his harsh criticism of scholastic interpretive methods with a wider reflection on language, including strong opinions about traditional ways to teach Latin. To substantiate these, Palmieri suggests a comparison with the study of the vernacular: studying Latin according to the traditional methods, with which the simultaneous acquisition of language skills and philosophical content was often confusing, is as ineffective as learning to write vernacular poetry with poor poetic models.[66]

Palmieri's two-pronged opinion on the relationship between Latin and the *volgare* builds on his assumption that the cultural primacy of Latin does not prevent the vernacular from being used to reach those who were unable to read Latin but nonetheless wished to enhance their moral education. In that respect, Palmieri's critique of the 'traditionalists' as well as his strong belief in the potential of the vernacular offer one of the most effective examples of a trend that can be labelled 'vernacular humanism', despite the slipperiness of the term.[67] Delivered through the persona of Agnolo Pandolfini, this perspective seizes the cultural awareness that the mercantile class had been developing throughout the later Middle Ages and which benefited from the new stimuli offered by humanist culture.

Proactive Readership

The portrayals of Agnolo Pandolfini by Alberti and Palmieri are the fruit of fiction, but what we know about him makes their depictions convincing. His family ties – in particular, his relationship with his sister Caterina's son, the famous merchant and patron of the arts, Giovanni Rucellai (1403–81) – shed light on the culturally vibrant context of well-off merchants

---

[65] *Ibid.*: 45: 'Ma io bene credo essere non di lungi il tempo che dimonsterrà et philosophia et altre scientie potersi in su i principali auctori più brievemente et perfecte imparare, che non si fa in su le insolubili investigationi di quegl. che, dicendo volere exporre, obfuscano gli ordinati et bene composti auctori degli elevati ingegni.'

[66] Palmieri criticises the traditional teaching of grammar as a confusing blurring of the boundaries between the disciplines. On the intersection of grammar teaching and morals, see Gehl (1993).

[67] Compelling points about 'vernacular humanism' are made by Gilson (2005); see also Black (2001), Cornish (2010) and Rizzi (2017).

involved in the civic life of early fifteenth-century Florence. Pandolfini's penchant for philosophy was likely very influential in shaping his nephew's famous interest in the discipline. Rucellai was born to a wealthy family of Florentine wool merchants and occupied a significant political and cultural role during the complex period that brought the city under the control of the Medici family.[68] He held political posts under both Cosimo the Elder and Lorenzo il Magnifico, even if his personal relation to the Strozzi family, some of the Medici's strongest opponents, had earlier pushed him out of the political arena. In his youth, Rucellai worked under Palla Strozzi, whose daughter he married in 1428, staying closely connected to the interests of his father-in-law.[69] But if Palla Strozzi influenced Rucellai's career through his professional and political connections, Palla's wide knowledge and humanist education also had a strong impact on him. Indeed, throughout his life, Rucellai cherished the memory of his cultured father-in-law and followed his example by committing to both artistic patronage and personal erudition. Outstanding architectural projects such as the Palazzo Rucellai (1446–51) and the façade of Santa Maria Novella (1470), both designed by Leon Battista Alberti, confirm the long-lasting impact of Rucellai's patronage, which was part of carefully conceived cultural politics. Emboldened by his reacquired friendship with the Medici, Rucellai's agenda proved particularly effective when his son Bernardo was married to Cosimo's niece Nannina in 1461.[70]

Artistic patronage and new family bonds greatly shaped Rucellai's public persona while, on a more private level, his acquaintance with philosophy and moral concerns found an ideal space for reflection in his famous 'zibaldone quaresimale', a miscellaneous notebook and journal that he started keeping in 1457 during his stay in San Gimignano, where he and his family moved in order to flee an outbreak of plague in Florence.[71] The work is a heterogeneous collection of materials that Rucellai accumulated over the years, copied either by himself or others. The work includes historical accounts of the Rucellai family and information about Giovanni's

---

[68] The best introduction to the life and career of Giovanni Rucellai remains Perosa (1960); see also Kent (1981). On his role as a patron of the arts, see Kent (2000: 357–66). For a recent reassessment of Rucellai's biography, see Battista (2013).

[69] Battista (2013: XXVI).

[70] *Ibid.*: XXXIII.

[71] Alessandro Perosa's 1960 seminal study and partial edition of the *zibaldone* still offers invaluable insights into the work; see Perosa (1960). Thanks to the recent critical edition by Gabriella Battista (2013), scholars can now access a veritable goldmine of materials that enlighten the various components of Rucellai's culture.

household, notes on the history of Florence, select passages from classical and medieval authors, as well as a few writings commissioned by Giovanni himself.[72] The *zibaldone* was not meant for public circulation but addressed the younger members of Giovanni's family privately, with strong didactic purposes. Most of the materials in the volume show an interest in moral philosophy and Christian doctrine, providing a sample of the readings that informed the culture of a household such as Rucellai's. More importantly, the *zibaldone* gives us a sense of the preoccupations that guided Giovanni in the education of his children.

As is the case with the manuscripts copied by the Benci family recalled in Chapter 2, Rucellai's *zibaldone* not only offers a picture of the average culture of a well-educated merchant, but also challenges common assumptions about the interplay of cultural forces in Renaissance Florence.[73] In Rucellai's case, as with the Benci family, the presence of Aristotle and, more generally, the role of the Aristotelian tradition provide a productive lens through which the transformation of lay culture in the period can be reconsidered. Aristotle stands out as one of the philosophical authorities most frequently referenced throughout the miscellany, either through quotations from his works or through indirect references. With these, the *zibaldone* exposes a multifaceted process of reshaping that related Aristotle to the needs of the merchant family. Through this process, Aristotelian philosophy is adapted to Giovanni's concerns, which include the legitimation of wealth and various virtuous behaviours, from the very definition of morality to its applicability to contemporary mercantile society and its consistency with the mandates of Christian doctrine. (All these topics were, as also revealed by Cotrugli's treatise on trade discussed in Chapter 3, fundamental to contemporaneous mercantile culture and society.) The process of adaptation exemplified by Rucellai's *zibaldone* is not new: it belongs to a long tradition begun by Brunetto Latini and Dante, as indicated in Chapter 2. Yet Rucellai's monumental effort to collect moral instructions for his children is peculiar for its combination of uncritical acceptance of the tradition with the attempt to inquire into it.

A brief overview of the sources of the *zibaldone* is instructive of Rucellai's vision. In his almost regurgitative practice of building a series of moral teachings based on the authority of thinkers like Aristotle, Cicero and Seneca alongside biblical sources, Giovanni turns to the many collections of philosophical 'sentences' that circulated widely in both Latin and

---

[72] For a detailed outline of the content, see Perosa (1960) and Battista (2013: LIV).
[73] Cf. Chapter 2, 78, 80. On the Bencis, see Tanturli (1978).

vernacular versions. Florilegia such as Bartholomew of San Concordio's *Ammaestramenti degli antichi* ('Teachings of the Ancients') and the unattributed *Fiore di virtù* ('Flower of Virtue') provided the merchant with a nearly inexhaustible series of moral teachings that can be easily assimilated and disseminated.[74] Similarly, moral treatises such as those by Albertanus of Brescia (c. 1190–after 1253), Bono Giamboni (before 1240–c. 1292) and Geremia da Montagnone (d. 1320–21) functioned as 'translators' of philosophical statements that would have been easy to extrapolate and reuse in private editorial projects like Rucellai's. In all these works, the name of Aristotle appears frequently, often simply referred to as 'the Philosopher', and sentences that were originally authored by others were attributed to him. This is frequently the case with quotations from the Bible, which, through translation, adaptation and reuse, are often presented under the aegis of Aristotle's authority.

Rucellai's discussion of fortune offers an instructive example of the way in which his *zibaldone* draws freely from literary tradition, combining threads that are often difficult to disentangle. Though Aristotle is a prominent presence throughout the section, Rucellai's familiarity with him is usually filtered through vernacular go-betweens. When he quotes from Aristotle's *Physics* in his definition of 'caso' ('chance'), for example, he is instead relying on Boethius' *Consolatio Philosophiae* (5.1), which he knew through the Italian translation by Alberto della Piagentina.[75] But Rucellai does not seem to realise that Boethius' reference to Aristotle in the passage is misleading: in fact, while Aristotle talks generically about fortune in the second book of his *Physics*, the example of the farmer who accidentally

---

[74] The Dominican Bartolomeo of San Concordio (1262–1347) was a prolific author in both Latin and Italian. He compiled the *Documenta antiquorum*, a four-book treatise based on classical and Christian sources that he translated into Italian during his stay in Florence at some point after 1300 and dedicated to the Florentine banker Geri Spini; see Segre (1964). Without a modern critical edition of the *Ammaestramenti*, I have used the one by Manni (1734). The *Fiore di virtù* exists in multiple versions; for an overview of the work see Segre (1959). For the text of the *Fiore*, I have followed the edition by Gelli (1856).

[75] Battista (2013: 40): 'Ma Aristotelo, questo che tra 'l volgho è appellato caso, nella sua *Fisica* con ragione brieve e al vero prossimo difinì in questa forma, cioè: "Ogni volta che una cosa per cagione d'alcune cose si fa, e altro che quello che si pensa per alcune cagione aviene, caso si chiama, come se alcuno, lavorando il campo, tesoro truovi naschoso: questo per caso fortuito si crederrà esser venuto. Ma non è così per ciò che la prima cagione per la quale questo gli è avenuto, perché se 'l cultivatore del campo non avesse la terra cavata e se in quello luogho el tesoro non fusse stato nascoso non sarebbe stato trovato. Queste sono dunche le cagioni di quello che caso è appellato, la quale provenne da cagione insieme concorrenti e accidentali non per intentione dell'operante, inperciò che colui che 'l tesoro naschose non pensò che 'l fusse trovato, colui che 'l campo coltiva non pensava di trovarlo" ' ('What vernacular-speaking people usually call "chance", Aristotle defines in a clear and trustworthy way in his *Physics* as follows: "Every time something is done due to some cause, and the outcome is other than expected for some reason, this is chance; as if someone, digging a field, found

finds a treasure while digging his field comes from the *Metaphysics*.[76] In this case, the confusion produced by Rucellai's intermediate source (Boethius) is confined to works within Aristotle's corpus, but the Aristotelian example of the farmer is also the core of a cluster of references that, erroneously attributed to Aristotle, do not come from any of the philosopher's own writings. The formula 'Aristotle said' often introduces a statement that in reality has nothing to do with him, sometimes several at once: 'Aristotle said: mad are those who believe that fortune produces good or evil but praise wisdom. Also, he said that the wise masters the stars. And he added that adverse fortune can be resisted by staying well on guard: wise is the one who defeats fortune by means of virtue.'[77] The first sentence in this passage from Rucellai's *zibaldone* comes from the *Fiore di virtù*;[78] the second is a proverb frequently attributed to Ptolemy;[79] the third derives from Seneca's *Epistles*.[80]

Even more striking is the case of Rucellai's discussion of liberality, prodigality, wealth and poverty, a key issue in mercantile society. To tackle this, he brings together the authority of Aristotle by compiling passages of his supposed lessons to Alexander the Great known as the *Secret of Secrets* alongside the *Ethics* and a pseudo-Aristotelian dictum that, in fact, comes from the Bible. The quotation from the *Secret of Secrets*, primarily concerning the ways in which the ruler should display his generosity, was

a hidden treasure: this person will think that the finding is due to chance. But this is not the case, for if the farmer did not dig the field and if the treasure had not been hidden there, it would have not been found. These are the reasons behind what is called "chance", which stems from concurrent and accidental causes not because of the intention of whom is performing the action; indeed, the one who hid the treasure did not think that it would be found, and the farmer was not expecting to find it'; here, and in the following quotations, my transl.). Cf. the relevant passage from Alberto della Piagentina's translation of Boethius in Milanesi (1864: 232–3). As Perosa concedes with respect to other passages in the *zibaldone*, though Rucellai clearly had Alberto's translation of Boethius on his desk, it is hard to identify the specific version of the text he would have used. On the medieval and Renaissance reception of Boethius, see Black and Pomaro (2000), Nauta (2003, 2009) and Brancato (2012); specifically, on Alberto della Piagentina's translation, see Brancato (2000).

[76] Se Aristotle, *Physics* 2.4–5; and *Metaphysics* 1025a 14ff. The same example was quite popular in humanist literature; see Roick (2017: 142).

[77] Battista (2013: 46): 'Disse Aristotele: "Matto è colui che crede che la fortuna dia male o bene, ma la sapientia loda". Anchor disse che '. savio signoreggia le stelle. E più disse che col fare buona guardia si risiste all'avversa fortuna: "Savio è colui che vince la fortuna colla virtù"'.

[78] Cf. Gelli (1856: 51): 'Aristotle dice: ... è matto, chi crede che la ventura dia bene e male, ma la sapienza loda bene' ('Aristotle says ... mad are those who believe that fortune brings good and evil, but praise wisdom').

[79] The proverb about the wise mastering the stars reoccurs frequently in moral literature; see, for instance, Domenico Cavalca in Federici (1842: 132). In other contemporary sources such as Giovanni Cavalcanti's *Istorie fiorentine* it is attributed to Ptolemy: see Polidori (1838–39 vol. 1: 37).

[80] Seneca, *Epist.* 71.30: 'Sapiens quidem vincit virtute fortunam'. The Senecan derivation was indicated by Perosa (1960: 173).

probably taken from one of the several vernacular translation of the Latin text, which circulated widely throughout Europe, or from an anthology.[81] The fourth book of the *Nicomachean Ethics* provides Rucellai with a clear statement about liberality and prodigality, which he presents not through a direct quotation but in an abridged report of Aristotle's thought ('secondo Aristotele', 'according to Aristotle').[82] A subsequent, more general statement about poverty as a result of prodigality ('Aristotle said that poverty stems from prodigality and also that those who waste their riches will soon become poor') is also attributed to Aristotle in the *Fiore di virtù* without question.[83] Before reiterating the same concept shortly thereafter ('He said that he who is not moderate in spending, will soon be poor too'),[84] a more metaphoric statement with evident Christian nuances is also given as Aristotle's: 'Again he said: "A burning fire is extinguished by water, and charity extinguishes sin"' ('Anchor disse: Il fuoco ardente spegne l'acqua e la limosina spegne il peccato'). The biblical sentence, originally found in *Ecclesiastes* 3:33, probably came to Rucellai through the treatise *Dell'amore di Dio* ('On the Love of God') by Albertanus of Brescia.[85] Proverbs and sentences from the Bible are likewise given as Aristotle's throughout the work.

This overview of Aristotelian references in Rucellai's *zibaldone* shows that Aristotle is not only a direct source of moral instruction, but also a venerable *auctoritas* under whom disparate moral teachings can be packaged. In most cases, the confusion derives from the sources Rucellai copied without verification. On one hand, the ascription of biblical wisdom to Aristotle endows him with more familiarity; on the other, and in line with the Latin tradition of the 'sayings of the philosophers', Rucellai's use of his sources points towards a generally simplifying approach to the moral issues

---

[81] Battista (2013: 51).

[82] *Ibid.*: 'La liberalitade, cioè largheza, secondo Aristotele si è dare con misura a persone degne e bisognose, che quello che si dà a' non degni si perde, e dare a chi non à bisogno è come spandere acqua in mare, e chi dà più che non può si parte dalla virtù della largheza e discende nel vitio della prodigalitate, la quale, sicondo che si conta, nella somma de' vitii è a spendere quello che non è a spendere, non abbiendo alcun modo nelle sue spese' ('According to Aristotle, liberality, i.e., generosity, is to give with measure to people who deserve and need it; what is given to unworthy people, is lost; to give to those who do not need is the same as pouring water in the sea; who gives more than they can afford, falls from the virtue of liberality into the vice of prodigality, which, according to what people say, is to spend what one should not spend, without any measure in one's expenses'); cf. Aristotle's *Nicomachean Ethics* 4, 1–3.

[83] Battista (2013: 51): 'Disse Aristotele che della prodigalità discende povertà e chi spande le sue richeze oltra modo presto verrà in povertade.'

[84] *Ibid.*: 'Anchor disse che chi non observa misura nello spendere, suol presto inpoverire.'

[85] Rossi (1824: 18).

discussed. Accordingly, a constant and consistent thread that runs across the zibaldone is the productive intermingling of the layers that inform the compiler's method.

Along with the many 'Aristotle saids' in the *Fiore di virtù* and similar sources, another instructive example of the way in which Aristotle's thought is simplified and made accessible to the reader is the discussion of justice. While the section extends the biblical flair of the *zibaldone* by opening with Solomon's definition of justice (attributed to one Andronicus in the *Fiore di virtù*), the account soon turns to Aristotle.[86] In this case, though, by quoting from the *Fiore* the five reasons why justice perishes in the hands of tyrants ('Aristotele disse che la giustitia perisce ne' tyranni per cinque cagioni e regna ne' veri re e signori'), Rucellai is directly attributing to Aristotle what, in reality, is a summary of the discussion of the topic in Giles of Rome's *De regimine principum* ('On the government of princes', 1282). Given the unstable textual transmission of works such as the *Fiore di virtù*, it is difficult to say if the passage was already attributed to Aristotle in the manuscript from which Rucellai was copying (indeed, the passage is usually assigned to Giles of Rome in manuscripts of the *Fiore*).[87] The question here should not concern Rucellai's philological awareness, but instead whether it shows the conditions of permeability fostered by vernacular translation. While the Latin works of Giles of Rome had originally addressed a cultivated Latinate audience, vernacular translations of the *De regimine principum*, which, as recalled in my introduction, appeared both in France and Italy soon after the publication of the original Latin, reached wider communities of readers.[88] If the *volgarizzamenti* of the *De regimine principum* contributed to the dissemination of Aristotelian thought on politics and government, the *Fiore di virtù* marks a further advance in the process of popularisation of the work. By including materials from Giles of Rome alongside passages or abridgements of Thomas Aquinas, Albertanus of Brescia, Guillaume de Peyraut and others, the *Fiore* was largely responsible for the appropriation of philosophical and especially Aristotelian lexica by a vernacular readership. Much more successful than the ambitious intellectual program of Dante's *Convivio*, works such as the *Fiore di*

---

[86] Battista (2013: 89): 'Giustitia, secondo che disse Salomone, si è a dare a ciascuno igualmente la sua ragione' ('Justice, according to Solomon, is to equally give everybody their reason'). See also Gelli (1856): 'Giustizia, secondo Andronico, si è disporre egualmente la sua ragione a ciascuno' ('Justice, according to Andronico, is to equally confer everybody their reason').
[87] See Gelli (1856: 57).
[88] See Briggs (1999a, 1999b, 2003). For a focus on the Italian reception of Giles, see Papi (2015, 2016a). See also the recent edition of the 1283 Italian translation of the treatise, Papi (2016b).

virtù and Albertanus' moral treatises made their way into the libraries of wealthy families and merchants in particular and became fundamental to their culture.

The wide circulation of these works, together with concurrent developments of humanism, helped create the conditions for a hybrid form of lay philosophical culture in the *volgare*. Their presence in Rucellai's *zibaldone* witnesses this process of hybridisation at its best. As we have seen, the process is negotiated chiefly by translation, which is not only an instrument of interaction, but also the intellectual arena within which the status of the vernacular is defined in relation to the status of Latin. Furthermore, when readers – as is the case with the *zibaldoni* – become compilers if not writers themselves, the appropriation of the teachings is more dynamic (and less predictable) than the usual (and generally passive) assimilation entailed by the simple reading of, say, a collection of philosophical sentences. Such lively interaction is informed by the selection that reveals the specific interests of the compiler and by the written record of proactive forms of intellectual exchanges facilitated by the compiler himself. Exchanges of this kind usually stem from questions that the compiler of the *zibaldone* is not able to answer based on his readings.

This uncertainty is evident in Rucellai's concern over the question whether it is easier to do evil or good actions: 'I would like to know whether we [humans] are more inclined to do evil or good things.'[89] The question is raised in the earlier half of the *zibaldone*, where, as indicated by Alessandro Perosa, the merchant simply collects authoritative sentences on the question of evil, beginning with a passage from Aristotle's *Ethics*: 'Aristotle says in his *Ethics*, in the ninth chapter of the second book, that good can be done in one single way and evil can be done in many ways; for this reason, it is difficult and tiresome to be good while it is easy to be evil, hence men are more often evil than good.'[90] The passage in fact does not come from Aristotle's *Nicomachean Ethics* but from Taddeo Alderotti's Italian translation of the *Summa Alexandrinorum*.[91] Consistent with the overview given in Chapter 2, Rucellai's *zibaldone* confirms that Taddeo's compendium of

---

[89] Battista (2013: 189): 'E vorrei sapere dove noi siamo più inchinati o a ffare il male o il bene.'

[90] *Ibid.*: 'Dicie Aristotile nell'*Eticha* sua, nel secondo libro al nono chapitolo, che il bene si può fare solamente inn uno modo e che il male si fa in molti modi, et che perciò è grave chosa e fatichosa essere buono et lieve e agievole a essere reo et che però sono gli uomini più rei che buoni.'

[91] See the passage in Gaiter (1880: 43). In the *zibaldone*, Aristotle's authority is followed by a statement from Matthew's gospel ('the way to go to the damnation of hell is very broad and easy'); Battista (2013: 190): 'Disse Christo nel Vangelio di San Matteo che lla via d'andare a ddannazione dello inferno era larghissima e spaziosissima.' Cf. *Matthew* 7.13.

the *Ethics* remained the primary source for lay readers dealing with moral issues well into the fifteenth century.

Rucellai's approach to the question of good and evil becomes more complex in the subsequent section of the *zibaldone*, in which Giovanni, likely dissatisfied with the abstract character of the *sententiae*, records the opinions that he solicited from two experts in the field, the humanist Donato Acciaiuoli (1429–78) and the Dominican Giovanni Nanni (more widely known as 'Annio' or 'Annius') of Viterbo (1432–1502).[92] Alessandro Perosa has reconstructed the episode and its chronology, starting from a conversation Giovanni Rucellai had with his friend Donato in 1463 on whether it is easier to be good or evil. Shortly thereafter, Rucellai asked Annio to provide him with a written opinion on the same matter and had it copied in the *zibaldone*. After receiving Annio's account from Rucellai without knowing who authored it, Donato replied in August 1464 with his own opinion and sent it to Rucellai, who also had it copied in the *zibaldone*. (It is worth recalling that, while Donato wrote his opinion in the vernacular, he also kept a Latin version for his own records.) Rucellai gave Donato's original to Annio, who sent an additional response back that Rucellai sent on to Donato without copying it in his *zibaldone*. Even if we lack this last exchange, the two opinions recorded offer invaluable insights into the concurrent answers to which Giovanni was exposed.[93]

Both structured according to the scholastic format of the *quaestio*, in which students of philosophy provided arguments *pro* and *contra* before proving their own position, the essays of Donato and Annio reach contrary conclusions. Based on his reading of the medieval commentators of Aristotle, Aquinas in particular, Annio argues that for men, who are naturally inclined to use reason, good actions are easier to perform than evil ones. Donato instead offers a reading of the *Ethics* that aims to reveal Aristotle's supposedly original insight on the subject, according to which, as Donato puts it, it is easier to be evil than good. In typical fashion, Donato begins by criticising his opponent's misunderstanding of key terms like

---

[92] For an overview of Donato Acciaiuoli's life and works, see Bacchini (2016); for a sample of his philosophical writings, Kraye (1997: 47–58). On Annio of Viterbo, Grafton (1990) and Stephens (2004, 2010, 2011).

[93] See Perosa (1960: 164–5), for details on the dispute and a complete list of the manuscript witnesses of the texts, which are not limited to the copies made in the *zibaldone*, but also include original drafts by both Donato Acciaiuoli (the Italian version is in fols. 87r–94v of Florence, Biblioteca Nazionale Centrale, MS Magl. VI.162; the Latin is fols. 95r–101v) and Annio of Viterbo (Florence, Biblioteca Nazionale Centrale, MS Magl. II.IV.192, fols. 195r–197v). This manuscript also includes an autograph copy of the final version of Donato's letter (fols. 198r–208v) and Annio's second letter (fol. 209r, which was not copied in the *zibaldone*).

mos ('custom') before turning to medieval commentators, Giles of Rome in particular, to support his own interpretation.[94] By resorting to Giles and his contemporaries, he claims a return to Aristotle without renouncing the exegetical tradition on which his scholastic counterparts were also relying. As Perosa writes, Annio and Acciaiuoli embody two different approaches to the past, but, despite clear differences in both methodology and outcomes, they nonetheless participate in the same translation project promoted by their common acquaintance, Giovanni Rucellai, who facilitates the encounter between the two scholars and their disparate agendas. By asking Annio and Acciaiuoli to write their opinions, moreover, Rucellai fuels the interaction between concurrent (and not mutually exclusive) trends in the scholastic and humanist camps as well as their relationship to lay vernacular culture. Here we see humanistic ideas entering contexts traditionally linked to scholastic modes of learning and these scholastic contexts adapting themselves to and incorporating humanistic ideas.

From this point of view, the intersection of different linguistic layers acquires importance in the dispute between Annio and Acciaiuoli. Both scholars act as translators but in different ways. The attitude towards the practice of translation taken by the Dominican Annio, whose opinion is presented as squarely based on Aquinas' interpretation of Aristotle, is consistent with the tradition of the medieval *volgarizzamenti* (in which, by the way, the Dominican order had excelled).[95] In some cases, Annio paraphrases passages from Aristotle and introduces them with the same syntax with which philosophical sentences were introduced in *florilegia* and moral treatises ('according to the Philosopher …', 'as the Philosopher says …').[96] In other cases, Annio provides the quotation in Latin followed by a vernacular translation, thus introducing his audience to supposedly 'original' material to which lay readers seldom were exposed.[97] The source, though, especially when Annio is not quoting from memory, is

[94] This is the method used by Acciaiuoli in his Latin commentary on the *Ethics*; see Bianchi (1990); cf. also Field (1988: 212–22).

[95] For important remarks on the role of translation within the various cultural endeavours promoted by the mendicant orders, see Gehl (1994).

[96] Battista (2013: 198): 'Secondo el philosopho …', 'E però dice il philosopho …'.

[97] *Ibid.*: 199: 'E chosì s'intende il detto del philasapho nel sesto dell'*Ethica*: "Comfestim videntur a nativitate esse fortes et temperati et secundum alias virtutes dispositi", cioè dalla nativtà l'uomo si porta la disposizione alle virtù, intendi per corporal complexione', where the quotation is by heart ('This is the way to understand the philosopher's saying in book 6 of the *Ethics*: "Comfestim videntur a nativitate esse fortes et temperati et secundum alias virtutes dispositi", i.e., from birth men have their disposition to virtue, that is for bodily complexion'). *Ibid.*: 200: 'E 'l philosopho nel principio dell'*Etica*: "bonum est quod omnia appetunt", ogni cosa naturalmente vuole il bene' ('And the philosopher at the beginning of the *Ethics*, "bonum est quod omnia appetunt",

usually Thomas Aquinas rather than Aristotle himself. The detail reveals Annio's approach to the philosophical tradition, within which the notion of Aristotelian *auctoritas* is implicitly sanctioned by the authority of the scholastic exegesis.[98]

Donato's response adds another perspective to the dispute. In fact, beyond his specific contribution to the debate on good and evil, he also touches upon the social and linguistic implications of Rucellai's interest in philosophy. Whereas Annio's response gets straight to the point, Donato opens by recalling the occasion for his composition, particularly the pleasure he takes in talking to Giovanni Rucellai about philosophical matters. The statement evokes the familiarity between the merchant and the humanist:

> In 1458 I was serving as one of the *Priori della libertà* with you, Giovanni Rucellai, as you may recall. Having always loved and revered you as my own father for your virtues and many other reasons, I was delighted to be with you in that prestigious office, not only because I seemed to learn a lot from your prudence and advice, but also because of the great pleasure I took in talking to you. Having talked many times about morals, it happened that we proposed a question and you asked me whether it is more difficult to do good or evil actions.[99]

According to Donato, the question ('dubitatione') stemmed from one of the frequent conversations about moral topics ('ragionamenti di chose morali') that they enjoyed while serving in the same civic office. Donato satisfies now his friend's request by providing an articulate discussion of the matter and an accurate critique of the response of his unknown debater. If both texts reproduce the features of a Latin academic dispute in the vernacular, Donato frames his response with explicit references to both the context of the debate and the needs of his target audience, explaining

---

everything naturally desires what is good'), where the quotation of *Nicomachean Ethics* I, 1, 1094a 1 is quite close to the medieval translation.

[98] Battista (2013: 201): 'dice il philosopho nel fin del secondo e nel sexto dell'*Etica* che "virtus est circa difficile", "la virtù è fondata sopra la cosa malagievole". Adunque far il bene è malagievole' ('the philosopher says at the end of book 2 and in book 6 of the *Ethics* that "virtus est circa difficile", "virtue is based on difficult things". Hence the difficulty of doing good'). In this case, the translation follows Thomas Aquinas' own paraphrase of the passage (*Nicomachean Ethics* II, 9, 1109a 2) in his commentary, *In Eth. Nic.* IV. 1, 1120a 9; as indicated by Perosa, the reference to book 6 is generic.

[99] Battista (2013: 203): 'Essendo l'anno del mcccclviij de' Priori della libertà, insieme con voi, Giovanni Rucellai, come v'è noto e avendo sempre per le vostre virtù et per molte chagioni portatovi affectione e riverentia come a singular padre, mi fu gratissimo trovarmi di compagnia con voi in quello dignissimo magistrato, non solamente perché della prudentia e consiglio vostro mi pareva aquistare grandissimo fructo, ma etiam perché grande iocundità prendevo della vostra iocondissima conversaçione. E avendo insieme più volte ragionamenti di cose morali, acchadde che, proponendo noi una dubitatione, mi domendasti quale era più difficile, o bene o male operare.'

in one example that his response will follow the structure and sequence of arguments required by similar forms of academic disputation.[100]

Instead of merely relying on intermediaries, however, Donato promises to bring readers back to Aristotle, enacting the recommendations from the preface to Matteo Palmieri's *Vita civile*, where the author argued in favour of reading the classics without relying on obscure commentators. Even if Donato does refer to earlier interpreters, his approach privileges a direct engagement with the original source. The approach is particularly evident in his premise, which includes a thorough critique of his opponent's statement about the identification of *mos* (custom) with natural inclination. Annio's interpretation closely followed Aquinas' erroneous reading, itself based on a textual mistake already present in Robert Grosseteste's Latin translation of the *Ethics*, which projected an etymological link between morality and natural inclination.[101] Donato's reading of the Greek text dismantles that of Annio's and points out his mistake: custom and natural inclination are not the same, whence Donato's claim that morals are not naturally constructed but fostered by habit.[102]

By quoting from the original Greek and providing both a Latin and an Italian translation of the relevant passage, Donato argues not only in terms of interpretation but also in terms of method:

> This is explained clearly by Aristotle, excellent philosopher, in the second book of the *Ethics*; wishing to show that moral virtues are acquired through the habit of doing well, he said that this is indicated by the name itself of 'custom', which is just a little different from the name of 'habit'; this statement must be referred to the Greek text, which reads as follows: ἡ δ ἠθιχῆ ἐξ ἔδουζ περίγίνεται, ὅδευ καί τόύνομα ἔσχηχε, i.e., 'Moralis autem ex assuetudine fit, unde et nomen habuit tale'; these words in our vulgar tongue *de verbo ad verbum* [word for word] read as follows: 'Moral virtue is the product of habit, from which it had the name'. Here Aristotle shows that moral virtue is produced by habit, as suggested by the Greek name, which is similar and almost the same with the name for habit, and he does not distinguish between 'natural habit' and 'habit' generally speaking.[103]

As indicated by Perosa, Donato's Latin translation fuses those by Leonardo Bruni and John Argyropoulos, whose lectures on the *Ethics* Donato had

---

[100] *Ibid.*: 'sì chome si suole fare in simili quistioni' ('as is usual in this kind of debates'). *Ibid.*: 211: 'sì chome è consueto fare in simili disceptationi, si conchiude secondo la sententia nostra' ('as is typical of this kind of discussions, I conclude by stating my own understanding of the matter').

[101] *Ibid.*: 197.

[102] *Ibid.*: 204.

[103] *Ibid.*: 'E questo dichiara manifestissimamente Aristotile, sommo philosopho, el quale nel 2° libro dell'*Ethica*, volendo mostrare che le virtù morali si acquistano per la consuetudine del

attended in 1457–58. Donato rejects Annio's premise on linguistic evidence, a manoeuvre that implicitly advocates for the significance of language skills as a tool for philosophical interpretation. At the same time, for the sake of clarity, Donato explicitly provides his reader with a word-for-word Italian version of the passage ('le quali parole in nostro volgare *de verbo ad verbum* suonono chosì'), thus revealing the didactic purpose of his translation. In fact, the three-step translation of the passage – citing the Greek, translating it into Latin and translating the Latin into Italian – corresponds to Donato's wider commitment to the explanation of Aristotle's text, which he himself does most effectively. He knows that readers will need guidance through the sources: a plain translation would be insufficient, for the text would remain difficult, due both to the linguistic gap that separates the *Ethics* from a vernacular readership and to the many (often faulty) interpretations given by earlier scholars. Also, it is worth highlighting that the translation from Greek to Italian is done through the medium of Latin. The author is still 'thinking' in Latin and is still relying on a Latin conceptual world to express himself in Italian.

As recalled above, Donato is not entirely dismissive of his predecessors. In fact, he refers to (and quotes from) commentators such as Thomas Aquinas and Giles of Rome, whose commentaries on Aristotle's *Ethics* he holds in high regard. At the same time, he boldly indicates that the main divergence between his approach and his opponent's consists in their different relationship to the text of Aristotle.[104] While Donato claims to respect and champion the philosopher's actual opinion, he accuses Annio of having forced the meaning of the text to make it agree with his propositions. The humanist's claim is first and foremost a 'philological' one, based on the actual content of the text:

> Beyond the aforementioned things, and to further support our opinion, we can bring forward the authority of the great philosopher, Aristotle, who, in many places, resolves most clearly this question [by putting forward an argument that] agrees with my opinion. Impelled by such an authority, our adversary is adapting it as best he can … But I will bring forward Aristotle's

bene operare, disse di questo essere segno el nome del costume, che è pocho differente dal nome della consuetudine; la qual ragione e 'l quale segno si debba riferire al texto grecho che dice così: "ἡ δ ἠθιχῆ ἐξ ἔδουζ περίγίνεται. ὅδευ καί τόύνομα ἔσχηχε" Idest, "Moralis autem ex assuetudine fit, unde et nomen habuit tale" le quali parole in nostro volgare *de verbo ad verbum* suonono chosì: "La morale si genera per consuetudine, dunde ella ha avuto tale nome". Qui dimostra Aristotile che la virtù morale si faccia per consuetudine, segno ne è il nome che apresso i Greci è vicino et quasi coniuncto chol nome della consuetudine et non fa distinctione di costume naturale et di consuetudine.'

[104] For examples of references to Giles of Rome and Thomas Aquinas, see *ibid.*: 207, 213.

own text, which is so evident and clear that it cannot be in any way forced to have a different meaning. That said, our adversary must either confess that in this matter he knows more than Aristotle, or acknowledge that our opinion is true. To make it shorter, as said before, I will present the passages in our vernacular.[105]

To support his interpretation, Donato turns to the philosopher's authority ('l'auctorità del sommo philosopho Aristotile') and Aristotle's own text is in several instances marshalled to resolve the question most clearly ('apertissimamente'). The opponent, Donato argues, has instead been adapting ('adaptando') the philosopher's words to suit his purposes. To prove him wrong, the humanist provides Aristotle's text, the meaning of which is so clear that it cannot be distorted. By using the text as a sort of legal witness, Donato argues that his opponent will in response have only three options: acknowledge his mistake, claim an understanding that is better than Aristotle's (a paradoxical option that ironically refers to the opponent's alleged Aristotelian orthodoxy) or simply accept the truthfulness of Donato's interpretation ('la nostra sententia essere vera'). To facilitate his reader's experience, Donato anticipates the need to provide the relevant passages from Aristotle's text in Italian, thus fostering the cultural compromise that informs the relationship between academic discourse and vernacular readership in humanist Florence.

As the dispute between Annio of Viterbo and Donato Acciaiuoli confirms, Aristotle figures as one of the most significant philosophical authorities in Rucellai's *zibaldone*. The number of references to and quotations of Aristotle, be they genuine or spurious, make him an invaluable interlocutor and philosophical benchmark. Rucellai does not seem to have owned a copy of the *Ethics* for his personal use. His knowledge of Aristotle's moral philosophy is instead based on sources that function as mediators between the merchant and the Philosopher. In conversation with exponents of both scholasticism and humanism, Giovanni displays a flexible attitude towards philosophical knowledge that finds a particularly fertile ground in the shifting domain of vernacular culture. The

---

[105] *Ibid.*: 212: 'Ma oltra alle predette chose, per più confirmatione della sententia nostra possiamo anchora produrre l'auctorità del sommo philosopho Aristotile, el quale in più luoghi apertissimamente dicide questa quistione dando la sententia in mio favore, dalla quale auctorità strecta la parte adversa la va adaptando el meglio che può … Ma io produrrò e' testi proprii d'Aristotile e' quali sono tanto evidenti et sì manifesti che non si possono in alcuno modo tirare ad altro senso; et essendo così, bisogna che la parte adversa confessi o d'intendere di questa materia più di lui o la nostra sententia essere vera. Et per più brevità, come è detto di sopra, alleg[h]erò e' testi in nostra lingua vulghare.'

zibaldone thus proves a space for various stimuli as well as various genres. If Annio of Viterbo shows up next to Donato Acciaiuoli, the presence of poetry is no less indicative of Rucellai's wide-ranging reading experience: verses from Dante's *Divine Comedy* appear next to stanzas from Dante's rival, Cecco d'Ascoli, whose poem *Acerba* engaged in a harsh criticism of the *Comedy* based on Cecco's different ideas about poetry and knowledge.[106] Also, medieval poetry shares the floor with contemporary poetry, as indicated by the presence of Leonardo Bruni's *Canzone morale*, which Rucellai copied in a section of the *zibaldone* concerned with the definition of pleasure and supreme goodness.[107] As was recalled earlier in this chapter, the *Canzone morale* is a basic compendium of the various positions on happiness, with an evident penchant for the Peripatetic outlook. In Rucellai's manuscript, Bruni's poem is followed by a brief text that further summarises the various philosophical schools. In the form of few short *sententiae*, this recapitulation closes with Aristotle, according to whom 'the highest good lies in honesty and virtue'.[108] The concise statement offers a clear picture of Rucellai's purpose in collecting such a heterogeneous body of materials in the *zibaldone*, the somewhat dispersive variety of which can only be balanced by easily memorable instructions.

Owning the *Ethics*

Giovanni Rucellai's collection of ethical teachings is that of an enthusiastic reader of philosophy seeking effective forms of cultural interaction, both as a consumer (as is the case with his active role in fostering the dispute between Annio of Viterbo and Donato Acciaiuoli), and as an active mediator (as suggested by his preoccupation with instructing his children). While undoubtedly exceptional, Rucellai's experience is not an isolated case. Indeed, throughout the second half of the fifteenth century, vernacular culture played a significant role in the reception, appropriation and dissemination of classical philosophy, in particular Aristotle's *Ethics*. As shown in Chapter 2, medieval summaries of the *Ethics* such as Taddeo Alderotti's and Brunetto Latini's enjoyed steady popularity throughout the Renaissance.[109] Furthermore, as suggested by the case studies discussed

---

[106] Albertazzi (2002).
[107] Battista (2013: 77–82).
[108] *Ibid.*: 82: 'Aristotele nell'onestà e nella virtù pose il sommo bene.'
[109] See my discussion of the textual tradition of the *Summa Alexandrinorum* in Chapter 2.

in this book, vernacular readers were more at ease with abridgments and anthologies rather than with more complex works such as the *Nicomachean Ethics*. Yet some interest in the 'original' *Ethics* did emerge among vernacular readers in the second half of the fifteenth century, in part a result of the circulation of Leonardo Bruni's 1417 Latin translation. Even if Bruni's version never managed to replace entirely the standard Latin one used in universities, its impact was significant.[110] The number of manuscript copies and printed editions of Bruni's translation of the *Ethics* confirm its wide reception across Europe, which was certainly amplified by the controversy between Bruni and the Spanish scholar Alfonso de Cartagena, whose critique of the work fostered wide-ranging discussions about translation theory and practice.[111]

Curiously enough, another Spanish intellectual was at least partly involved in the vernacular reception of Bruni's *Ethics*, with a specific if accidental impact on Florentine readership. A close friend of the Italian humanist Giannozzo Manetti's, Nuño de Guzmán (died c. 1467–90) was the illegitimate son of Luis González de Guzmán, master of the military order of Calatrava.[112] He was raised under his mother's tutorship in Córdoba, where he received a good education but never learned Latin. In 1430, he travelled to Jerusalem and, on his way back, visited Italy before settling in Bruges at the court of Philip the Good, duke of Burgundy. He travelled again to Florence in 1439, where he became familiar with renowned librarian and bookseller Vespasiano da Bisticci, who later included a biography of Nuño in his collection of lives of illustrious men, *Le Vite*.[113] Nuño played an important role in fostering exchanges between Italian humanism and Iberian scholarship in the fifteenth century, and his specific interest in Aristotle corresponds to a wider preoccupation with the reception of Greek and Latin authors. Thanks to his Italian acquaintances, Nuño obtained numerous manuscripts of classical works, most of which in Italian translation.[114] As we learn from Vespasiano, who describes him as a wise and virtuous man, Nuño's knowledge of Italian was excellent

[110] See Griffiths, Hankins and Thompson (1987: 197–212, 255–67), Hankins (2000, 2003), Lines (2002: 81), Bianchi (2013) and Maxson (2018). On the importance of Bruni's translation in Florence outside scholarly circles, see Lines (2002: 181–220).
[111] On the textual transmission of Bruni's works, see Hankins (1997); on the *Ethics* controversy, see Baldassarri (2003: 93–103) and Botley (2004: 41–62).
[112] For Guzmán's biography, see Lawrance (2006). For more details on the Spaniard's life and cultural relations, see Russell and Pagden (1974) and Lawrance (1982).
[113] Greco (1970: vol. 1: 435–41).
[114] For details regarding the books that Nuño gathered thanks to his Italian connections, see Lawrance (1982: 67–9).

('even better than that of Tuscans') and, while in Florence, he had many
Italian-language books sent to Spain. In the Tuscan city, he would also
converse with Manetti (who collaborated with Nuño on two Latin works)
and Leonardo Bruni, and his expertise in many subjects and his accounts
of his travels delighted his friends.[115] Nuño's interest in Italian books did
not fade after his return to Spain. On the contrary, he continued to ask
for books to be sent to him, thus amassing a remarkable collection. As
Vespasiano records:

> He was so passionate about Tuscan letters that more than once he sent
> his men, at his own expense, to get books copied, and they waited in
> Florence until the books were ready. He requested several books to be finely
> translated from Latin into Tuscan, Tullius' *Tusculan Disputations*, *On the
> Orator*, Quintilian's *Declamations*, Macrobius's *Saturnalia*, and of many
> other works he made an outstanding library in this language, which, after
> his death in Seville, was dispersed.[116]

Among the manuscript copies that Nuño commissioned, two in par-
ticular witness his ties to Leonardo Bruni: the vernacular translation of
Bruni's *Cicero novus* and the Italian version of Bruni's Latin translation
of Aristotle's *Nicomachean Ethics*.[117] As far as Nuti's *volgarizzamento* of the
Ethics is concerned, the copy made for Guzmán is now MS 151 of the
Beinecke Library [Figure 4.3].[118]

The interest in this translation is consistent with the Spaniard's
humanist connections, in contrast to Antonio Colombella's translation
of the Grosseteste-Moerbeke version for Pancrazio Giustiniani, discussed
in the previous chapter. The importance of Nuti's translation can hardly
be overstated, since it contributed to the vernacular dissemination of the
Ethics in the Iberian peninsula. (Nuño de Guzmán himself authored a

---

[115] Manetti reworked notes by Nuño into humanist Latin on two occasions, the *Apologia Nunnii* (a
biographical letter sent to Nuño's father) and the *Laudatio Agnetis Numantinae* (a eulogy of Nuño's
mother). See Lawrance (1989).

[116] Greco (1970: vol. 1: 440–1): 'Tanto volto alle lettere toscane, che più volte mandò infino di Spagna
qui sua uomini propri, alle sua ispese, a fare trascrivere libri, et istetono in Firenze tanto che furono
finiti. Et fece tradurre più libri di latino in lingua tuscana con grande premio, le *Tusculane* di Tulio,
De oratore, le *Declamationi* di Quintiliano, Macrobio *De saturnalibus*, de più altre opere, fece in
questa lingua una dignissima librar a, le quale, prevento dalla morte in Sibilia, capitorono male.'

[117] Lawrance (1982: 66, 84).

[118] New Haven, Yale University, Beinecke Library, MS 151, fol. 1r: 'l'Ethica d'Aristotile tradocta di
greco in latino et di latino tradocta in volgare in Firenze ad petitione di messere Nugnio Gusmano
spagniolo' ('Aristotle's *Ethics* translated from Greek into Latin and from Latin into Italian in
Florence at the behest of the Spaniard Nuño de Guzmán'). For details on the manuscript, see De
Ricci (1935–40: 1, 651 n.216), Faye and Bond (1962: 35 n.51), Kristeller (1963–97 vol. 5: 278), Shailor
(1984–2004: 202–3) and Hankins (1997: 124 n.1704).

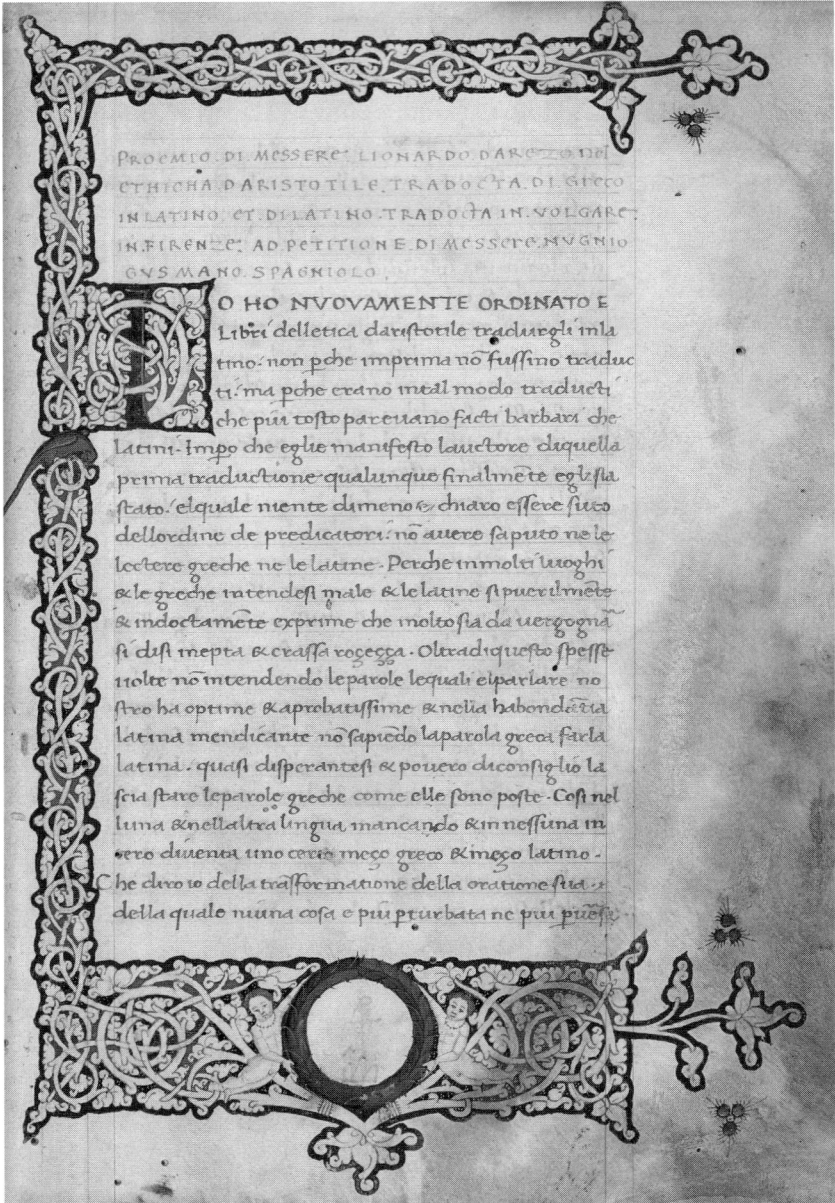

PROEMIO. DI. MESSERE. LIONARDO. DAREZZO. DEI
ETHICHA. DARISTOTILE. TRADOCTA. DI. GRECO
IN LATINO. ET. DI LATINO. TRADOCTA. IN. VOLGARE.
IN FIRENZE. AD. PETITIONE. DI. MESSERE. NVGNIO
GVS. MANO. SPAGNIOLO.

O HO NVOVAMENTE ORDINATO E
Libri delletica daristotile tradurgli inla
tino non pche imprima no fussino traduc
ti ma pche erano intal modo traducti
che piu tosto pareuano facti barbari che
latini. impo che eglie manifesto lauctore diquella
prima traductione qualunque finalmete eglsia
stato. elquale niente dimeno & chiaro essere suto
dellordine de predicatori no auere saputo ne le
lectere greche ne le latine. Perche inmolti luoghi
& le greche intendesi male & le latine si puerilmete
& indoctamete exprime che molto sia da uergogna
si dist inepta & crassa rozezza. Oltradiquesto spesse
uolte no intendendo leparole lequali elparlare no
stro ha optime & aprobatissime & nella habondatia
latina mendicante no sapiedo laparola greca farla
latina. quasi disperantesi & pouero diconsiglio la
scia stare leparole greche come elle sono poste. Cosi nel
luna & nellaltra lingua mancando & in nessuna in
uero diuenta uno certo mezo greco & mezo latino.
Che diro io della trasformatione della oratione sua
della quale niuna cosa e piu pturbata ne piu pros...

Figure 4.3 New Haven, Yale University, Beinecke Library, MS 151, fol. 1r

compendium of Aristotle's treatise that has been shown to have circulated widely both in manuscript and print.)[119]

However, along with the copy commissioned by Nuño and sent to Spain, Nuti's translation had a significant afterlife in Italy: several copies of the work were made in the fifteenth century.[120] Guzmán's copy does not give the translator's name, but a later witness of the text, MS Ashb. 493 of the Biblioteca Laurenziana, reports that the translation was done in Florence by Bernardo di Ser Francesco Nuti, whose activity as a schoolteacher and public servant is documented from the 1460s to the mid-1480s and whose name is familiar to readers of Marsilio Ficino's commentary on Plato's *Symposium*.[121] In fact, within the fiction of Ficino's dialogue, it is Bernardo who recites Plato's text for the scholars who had gathered to celebrate the Greek philosopher.[122] Bernardo was not only a friend of Ficino's, but also a close acquaintance of Cristoforo Landino's, as suggested by his several appearances in Landino's poems.[123] Though Ficino remembers Nuti as a 'Ciceronian', referring to his skilled oratory, he was more often recalled for his teaching activity. Humanists such as Pietro Cennini and Bartolomeo della Fonte studied under Nuti, whose teaching method is described in some detail by the latter in a nostalgic letter to his friend Bernardo Rucellai in 1513.[124] More recently, based on a comparison between the variant readings found in the manuscript copies of Nuti's *Ethics* and the schoolteacher's glosses on the *Aeneid* that survive in a codex written by Bartolomeo della Fonte, Alessandra Santoni has argued that the Aristotelian translation was likely related to Nuti's teaching activity – a theory that, if confirmed, would contribute to a better assessment of both the translator's

[119] Russell and Pagden (1974: 136), Lawrance (1982) and Valero Moreno (2015: 291–5). On the complex ways in which Guzmán's compendium relates to concurrent attempts to disseminate the *Ethics* in the Iberian vernaculars (particularly when compared to the popular *Compendio de la Ética Nicomaquea*, which circulated in various versions in the second half of the fifteenth century), see Cuenca Almenar (2017: XXV–XLV).

[120] A critical edition of Nuti's translation of the *Ethics* is currently in progress; for an overview of some of the most significant textual issues that characterise the manuscript tradition of the work, see the editor's preliminary study: Santoni (2017). I wish to thank Alessandra Santoni for her useful suggestions.

[121] On Nuti's activity as a schoolteacher, see Marchesi (1900: 14–24, 102–4 and 190–2). For a brief biographical overview and a list of manuscript sources, see Guerrieri (2006). See also Caroti and Zamponi (1974: 12 and 18–19), Verde (1973–76 vol. 3: 146), McCuaig (1982: 87–8), Tanturli (1988: 217, 230, 236–7) and Black (2007: 416).

[122] Raymond (1956: 136).

[123] Chatfield (2008: 1.11, 1.29 and 2.12). See the references to Nuti in earlier redactions of 1.10, 1.21 and 1.41.

[124] Marchesi (1900: 14–24, 102–4 and 190–2). For the letter by Bartolomeo della Fonte to Bernardo Rucellai of 1513, discussing Nuti's teaching method and ideas on imitation, see Daneloni (2011: 175–87).

endeavour and the patterns of circulation of Aristotle's *Ethics* in fifteenth-century Florence.[125]

The Beinecke copy of Nuti's translation of the *Ethics* that was commissioned by Nuño de Guzmán unfortunately does not provide a precise chronology for the work. Albinia de la Mare connected the illumination of the manuscript's first page to the style of miniaturist Gioacchino di Giovanni, better known as Gioacchino de Gigantibus, which suggests a date prior to the artist's departure from Florence in 1453.[126] While this hypothesis is in itself sound, a slightly later dating is suggested by a twin copy of the text, now MS It. II.1 in the Biblioteca Marciana in Venice, bearing the date 1464.[127] The manuscript is written by the same hand as the Beinecke copy and is clearly the product of the same workshop, almost certainly Vespasiano's. Given the similarity between the two manuscripts, it can be argued that the two were made at the same time. The decoration of the initials in the Venice manuscript is incomplete and the space for the initial rubric is left blank, thus omitting the reference to the patron. Since we know that Nuño was still alive in the late 1460s and that he continued to have manuscripts sent from Italy at that time, and since we lack any other material evidence, the chronology suggested by the Marciana manuscript is as acceptable as de la Mare's dating of the Beinecke copy that attributes the decoration to Gioacchino. In any case, both hypotheses cohere with the chronological and material evidence offered by the remaining manuscripts, which were produced over the following decades.

In fact, Nuti's translation had a significant circulation in the late fifteenth century. Beyond the Beinecke and the Venice copies, seven more manuscripts are extant, most of which are of Florentine making and illustrate the kind of readers who were interested in reading (or at least owning) Aristotle's *Ethics* in the vernacular. As we shall see, the text was particularly appealing to members of the city's elite, primarily wealthy merchants and aristocrats. One partial exception is the copy made for the king of Naples, Ferrante of Aragon, and decorated by miniaturist Cola Rapicano.[128] This beautiful copy, later given to the Escorial as a gift by King

---

[125] Santoni (2017: 220); Nuti's glosses on Vergil's *Aeneid* were transcribed by Bartolomeo della Fonte in what is now Florence, Biblioteca Riccardiana, MS Ricc. 152.

[126] Albinia de la Mare's expertise is reported by Shailor (1984–2004: 202).

[127] Venice, Biblioteca Nazionale Marciana, MS It. II.1 [4934]. For a detailed description of the manuscript, see Frati and Segarizzi (1909–11: vol. 1: 191); see also Hankins (1997: 214 n.2961) and Refini (2016b), with a reproduction of the first folio.

[128] El Escorial, Biblioteca de Real Monasterio, MS F.III.23. For details on the manuscript and bibliographical references, see Toscano (1998: 562–3).

Philip II of Spain, represents the gradual increase of interest in vernacular books informing the humanist court of Naples. The luxurious presentation of the manuscript, which recalls the style and format of similarly beautiful copies of Latin-language volumes in Ferrante's library, indicates that vernacular translations of the classics were acquiring a higher status than in previous periods.[129] The authorial role of the vernacular translator was nonetheless seldom brought to the forefront. As recalled above, only one of the nine copies of the text, MS Ashb. 493, mentions Bernardo Nuti as the translator. Indeed, the eight other manuscripts focus on the humanist who brought Aristotle to fifteenth-century Florence, Leonardo Bruni, whose name appears next to the philosopher's. By presenting the *Ethics* under the aegis of Bruni's name, the work is automatically branded as a humanist product, even if Bruni had no part in producing the vernacular text. The actual vernacular translator, Nuti, is not only overshadowed by the original author of the text, Aristotle, as was typically the case with medieval *volgarizzamenti*, in which the authorship of translators was systematically omitted, but it is also surpassed by the name of the Latin translator, Leonardo Bruni, who here acquires a veritable authorial role.[130]

If Bruni's reputation justifies the prominence given to his name in the presentation of this copy, his role is further enhanced by the fact that this manuscript edition of Nuti's vernacular translation preserves Bruni's prologue to the *Ethics* as well as his preface to Pope Martin V, to whom the Latin work was originally dedicated.[131] As is well known, it is Bruni's prologue to the translation that, along with the translation itself, triggered the controversy over the *Ethics* with Alfonso de Cartagena and others. By incorporating Bruni's prologue into the Italian translation, Nuti is, *de facto*, situating his own work within the theoretical frame outlined by Bruni, despite the differences in the vernacular audience and Bruni's Latinate readership. In this new context, there seems to be little relevance in Bruni's statements about his restoration of Aristotle's eloquence through a rhetorically refined Latin prose. Nuti's Italian translation, however, can be read as pursuing a double goal: on one hand, it contributes to the

---

[129] For similar examples, see the humanist copies of the Italian translations of the *Summa Alexandrinorum* by Taddeo Alderotti (Milan, Biblioteca Ambrosiana, MS C 21 inf., made for the Sforza family) and by Niccolò Anglico (Naples, Biblioteca dei Girolamini, MS CF 1.8, made for the Duchess of Andria): both discussed in Chapter 2, 84–5.

[130] On the typically anonymous status of translators in the medieval tradition of the *volgarizzamenti*, see Cornish (2011). The status of translators was even discussed by Domenico da Prato, as was seen earlier in this chapter, see 137–3.

[131] See the text of the two pieces in Baron (1928: 75–81). For an English translation, see Griffiths, Hankins and Thompson (1987: 213–17).

dissemination in the vernacular of Bruni's ideas about Latin; on the other, it makes Bruni's ideas on the relationship between Greek and Latin relevant to that between Latin and Italian.

In his version of the prologue, Nuti follows Bruni's phrasing very closely, as he does with the translation of the *Ethics* itself, though one small divergence shows that the translator adapts the text to his vernacular readers. Whenever Bruni refers to his Latin models, he calls them 'our authors' ('nostri auctores'), highlighting the continuity between antiquity and his present day that humanism emphasised.[132] Nuti consistently translates 'our authors' ('nostri auctores') as 'Latin authors' ('Latini', literally 'the Latin ones'): the alteration obviates the ambiguity that would arise from bringing the original phrasing into a non-Latin context while also informing the readers about the Latinate audience Bruni was addressing and the debates relevant to the world of humanists.[133] By highlighting the linguistic difference between the source and the target language, the translator makes Bruni's statements relevant to the vernacular world. Since the prologue talks about translation from Greek into Latin, the fact that the text is translated into the vernacular introduces another layer to the discussion, which Bruni had not considered: thanks to Nuti's translation, Bruni's commitment to show that the Latin of his contemporaries can be better than medieval Latin is transferred to the vernacular. The Italian translator replicates the Latin translator's gestures, implying that even Italian has the potential to express philosophical concepts effectively and with stylistic refinement.

Nuti's appropriation of Bruni's theoretical apparatus and his reiteration of Bruni's examples are particularly interesting parallels to the case of Antonio Colombella's translation of the *Ethics*, discussed in Chapter 3. Behind his confusion over the use of specific terms by medieval interpreters of the text, Bruni attacked the practice – standardised in medieval translations of Aristotle – of transliterating Greek words into the Latin alphabet instead of translating them into equivalent Latin terms. For Bruni, this operation not only proved the translator to be unskilled in both languages but caused endless obscurity. The problem characterised Colombella's translation of the *Ethics*, in which, as we have seen, the Greek terms transliterated by the medieval translator were simply adapted into a pseudo-vernacular form without being properly translated into actual vernacular words. The case is made by Bruni (and implicitly accepted by Nuti) in the preface, which

[132] Bruni refers to 'nostri auctores' on several occasions throughout the preface; see Baron (1928: 79, 80).
[133] New Haven, Yale University, Beinecke Library, MS 151, fols. 2v, 4r.

discusses the translation of Greek words such as *eutrapelia* (ἐυτραπελία) and *bomolochia* (βωμολοχία). Unhappy with the bare transliteration of the two terms that he found in the medieval translation of the *Ethics*, Bruni labels the translator a 'ferreus homo' ('man of iron') for his linguistic and stylistic stiffness. He also observes that Latin featured several words that could have been used to make the Greek terms understandable.[134] *Eutrapelia* (the quality of being skilled in conversation) could have been translated as 'urbanitas', 'festivitas', 'comitas' or even 'iocunditas'; *bomolochia* (scurrility) could be translated as 'scurrilitas'.[135] In his Italian translation of Bruni's preface, Nuti finds just as many synonyms in the vernacular: *eutrapelia* corresponds to 'urbanità', 'festività', 'piacevolezza' and 'giocondità' while *bomolochia* has the Italian 'scurrilità'.[136] Whereas Colombella opted for a conservative translation, reproducing in Italian the transliterations found in the source, Nuti adheres to a different approach to the translation process. Following Bruni's method, Nuti provides vernacular readers with words from their own idiom. In so doing, Nuti contributes to the expansion of the philosophical lexicon in the vernacular at once with smoothing out some of the asperities of the *Ethics* that made it challenging reading, especially for lay readers.

As suggested by the number of extant copies, Nuti's translation of the *Ethics* was more successful than Colombella's, which, as shown in Chapter 3, survives in only one manuscript. Even if the circulation of Nuti's *Ethics* pales in comparison to that of texts such as Taddeo Alderotti's translation of the *Summa Alexandrinorum*, Nuti's vernacular *Ethics* still satisfied the expectations of a sizeable audience that gradually overcame the boundaries between scholarly and lay cultures.[137] While Alderotti's work remained by far more accessible to lay readers than the *Ethics*, Nuti's vernacular translation was released at a moment when the interest in Aristotle's moral philosophy outside university classrooms was developing in interesting ways. Along with figures such as Giovanni Rucellai, who actively sought occasions to increase his knowledge in the field, several Florentines added Aristotle to their private libraries. In this regard, the extant copies of Nuti's translation of the *Ethics* are quite instructive. Even when they reveal nothing about scribes, owners and readers, they prove that the transmission of his translation intermingled with that of other works, thus entering the 'moral'

---

[134] Baron (1928: 78).
[135] *Ibid.*: 79.
[136] New Haven, Yale University, Beinecke Library, MS 151, fol. 2*v*.
[137] On the specificity of the Florentine reading public, see Lines (2002: 182–5).

horizon of fifteenth-century lay readership, in which classical philosophy and Christian doctrine were constantly interconnected. A good case in point is MS Pal. 24 of the Biblioteca Nazionale in Florence, a late fifteenth-century miscellaneous collection of moral works written in humanist cursive hand.[138] In this manuscript, the *Ethics* is followed by anonymous vernacular translations of John Chrysostom's *Treatise on the Compunction of the Heart*, a *Treatise on the Mass* attributed to Hugh of Saint Victor, and Augustine's *Sermons*. Even if the hand that copied the *Ethics* is not the one that copied the other works, the sequence of texts within the manuscript suggests that, in the eyes of vernacular readers, the *Ethics* could be read as a moral conduct book to be associated with works of Christian education, thus embodying the same status of medieval moral compendia.

More often, as with all the other witnesses of this work, Nuti's translation of the *Ethics* is not copied as part of a miscellany, but rather stands on its own as a single manuscript volume. In these cases, the text inevitably acquires a different, more autonomous status, as if Aristotle's prestige were restored. The Beinecke, Marciana and Escorial manuscripts discussed above are good examples of this practice, as is MS 1620 of the Biblioteca Riccardiana.[139] This elegantly written copy features outstanding decorations (including a full-page tondo announcing the title) that signal it as a luxury object, in which the lavishness of the artefact matches the status of the text. My consideration of the material aspects of the book is not secondary, for it offers insight into both the prestigious status of the text and the diverse vernacular audiences who consumed it. On one hand, when the work formed part of an unpretentious miscellany of moral writings, the reader can assume that its primary interest relies in the text itself; on the other hand, lavish copies, large in format and expensively decorated, suggest that the *Ethics* is first and foremost an 'object' to own, the luxurious shape of which indicates both its own importance and its owner's wealth. Not surprisingly, these deluxe manuscripts do not bear much evidence of use, but not all copies of the *Ethics* fall under this category.

Indeed, other Florentine manuscripts – usually of a cheaper make – illuminate the writing and reading practices of their owners. In this respect, the most interesting copies are those that explicitly direct us towards the mercantile context. The handwriting, often *mercantesca* or a hybrid of *mercantesca*

---

[138] Florence, Biblioteca Nazionale Centrale, MS Pal. 24. For a detailed description of the manuscript, see Gentile (1889–99: vol. 1: 25–6); and Hankins (1997: 64 n.878).

[139] Florence, Biblioteca Riccardiana, MS 1620. A detailed description of the manuscript is in Morpurgo (1900: 589–90); for the illuminated decorations, see D'Ancona (1914: 2).

and cursive humanist, is typical of cheaper manuscripts, which are largely unadorned or have limited decoration (coloured rubrics and initials). MS Magl. xxi.139 of the Biblioteca Nazionale is a good example of such a scribal activity.[140] Less elegant than the manuscripts previously mentioned, it is the only witness of Nuti's *Ethics* to be systematically annotated by a slightly later hand, possibly from the early sixteenth century, that gives some sense of the way in which the text was read. In fact, these marginal notes witness a reading activity that goes well beyond the common practice of adding catchwords in the margins: short rubrics are often provided for specific sections of the text, highlighting passages that caught the reader's attention.[141] On two remarkable occasions, this proactive reader finds missing segments in the vernacular text and integrates them by quoting from Leonardo Bruni's Latin translation.[142] While the anonymous reader is clearly no novice and possibly had some sort of training in Aristotelian philosophy, the careful reading of Nuti's translation in this manuscript demonstrates that the vernacular text was considered worthy of 'scholarly' attention, not just a second-best option for readers with no Latin.

In other cases, insights into writing and reading practices are offered by notes of possession and colophons rather than by annotations. Though this sort of evidence is certainly more superficial than annotations, the conclusions drawn from such explicit ownership notes, particularly when the copy was made for personal use, are nonetheless vital for situating the reception of the vernacular *Ethics* within a specific social and cultural milieu. One example (MS Ashb. 493 of the Biblioteca Laurenziana, written by Luigi di Giovanfrancesco de' Pazzi in February 1493) tells us that the *Ethics* was copied and owned by a famed Republican and anti-Medici militant at a particularly delicate moment in Florentine history following the death of Lorenzo il Magnifico, when the city was transitioning from the weak leadership of Piero de' Medici to the turbulence of the Republic under Savonarola.[143] One *ricordo* ('memory') of the 1494 descent of King

---

[140] Florence, Biblioteca Nazionale Centrale, MS Magl. xxi.139; the manuscript is only recorded by Hankins (1997: 58 n.784).

[141] In most cases, the anonymous annotator adds single words (e.g., lists of the virtues discussed at fols. 26v–27r); on other occasions, the annotator summarises concepts that are treated in the text by repeating key statements almost word for word; more rarely, simple manicules are added in order to highlight specific passages in the text.

[142] At the beginning of book 3, fol. 30r, for instance, when voluntary actions are discussed, a sentence that is missing in the text (but which was regularly present in the Beinecke copy of Nuti's translation) is added – along with a brief vernacular comment – as a marginal note.

[143] Florence, Biblioteca Medicea Laurenziana, MS Ashb. 493. A detailed description of the manuscript by Gianna Rao is available on the website *Manus OnLine* [manus.iccu.sbn.it], identification

Charles VIII of France into Italy is written on the last page of Luigi's copy of the *Ethics*, reminding us that the life and afterlife of a text are always, even if unexpectedly, part of history. Luigi's copy of the *Ethics* allows us into the study of a prominent political figure who held important offices during the years of the second Florentine Republic (1527–30). While it is no surprise that someone like Luigi di Giovanfrancesco would devote time and energy to studying the classics, his priority was certainly active politics.

The last two copies of Nuti's translation examined here invite us into the study of a different kind of wealthy Florentine, Bonaccorso di Filippo Adimari, who was less concerned with direct political engagement but very active as a scribe. As recalled in Chapter 2, Bonaccorso wrote a number of manuscripts, including several vernacular translations of classical works, and in 1445 he copied the text of Taddeo Alderotti's translation of the *Summa Alexandrinorum*.[144] In a manuscript he produced nearly twenty years later (MS Pal. 710 of the Biblioteca Nazionale in Florence),[145] in 1464, he returned to the *Ethics* through Nuti's translation of Bruni's version, which he copied again in 1467 (MS Magl. XXI.64 of the same library).[146] His case is of great interest, given that Bonaccorso (a member of a prestigious though somewhat impoverished Florentine aristocratic family) copied these texts for his own perusal and for the benefit of his descendants, as indicated by the colophon of MS Pal. 710:

> This book was written by Bonacorso di Filippo Adimari of Florence, for his own perusal and that of his friends and acquaintants, as someone who takes much pleasure in this sort of thing. It was begun and completed in December 1464. Leonardo of Arezzo's moral *canzone* follows; it defines what is happiness and of what it consists. Deo gratias. Amen.[147]

number CNMD\0000234025; see also Marchesi (1904: 137), Kristeller (1963–97 vol. 1: 89), De Robertis (1993: 224 n.11) and Hankins (1997: 50 n.643). On Luigi di Giovanfrancesco de' Pazzi, father of poet Alfonso de' Pazzi, see Masi (2015: 1–3).

144 Florence, Biblioteca Nazionale Centrale, MS Pal. 729. See Chapter 2, 26–8.

145 Florence, Biblioteca Nazionale Centrale, MS Pal. 710; detailed descriptions of the manuscript are in Gentile (1889–99: vol. 2: 258) and Bianchi (2003: 51 n.96, plate 50). See also Garin (1957: 409), Pasquini (1964: 546), Bénédictins du Bouveret (1965–82: 2304) and Hankins (1997: 65 n.893).

146 Florence, Biblioteca Nazionale Centrale, MS Magl. XXI.64; see Hankins (1997: 58 n.782).

147 Florence, Biblioteca Nazionale Centrale, MS Pal. 710, fol. 221r: 'Questo libro scrisse Bonacorso di Filippo Adimari da Firençe, ad istanza di sé et delli amici et conoscienti suoi, sì come huom che piglia sommo piaciere di simil cose. Cominciato et fornito del mese di diciembre in anno MCCCCLXIIII. Seguita questa morale fatta da messer Leonardo d'Areçço la quale difiniscie che è filicità et in che consiste. Deo gratias. Amen.' See also a similar colophon in MS Magl. XXI.64, fol. 211r, where the reference to the family is omitted, as the manuscript was probably copied for a separate reader: 'Questo libro scrisse Bonacorso di Filippo Adimari da Firençe in anno MCCCCLXVII. Seguita questa morale fatta da Mess. Lionardo d'Areço la quale determina che è felicità et in che consiste. Deo gratias che Yhē sempre sia laudato. Amen' ('This book was written by Bonacorso di

As far as the manuscript itself indicates, Bonaccorso's desire for his off-spring to read the book and keep it in the family was fulfilled: a later note of possession added by a younger member of the Adimari family, Bernardo di Paolino, informs us that the *Ethics* was given to him by Bonaccorso, who 'wrote it in this house' and who 'pushed [Bernardo] to study the text carefully and acquire virtue in youth'.[148]

To make this learning experience easier, Bonaccorso introduced a set of paratextual elements that frame the text, functioning as didactic tools. First, he added rubrics to the beginning of each book of the *Ethics* to facilitate perusal of the subject matter. In MS Magl. XXI.64, the rubrics are also transcribed in the table of contents that, copied at the beginning of the manuscript, provides the reader with a helpful overview of the work.[149] Second, Bonaccorso included a copy of Leonardo Bruni's *Canzone morale* at the end of the treatise in both manuscripts, making the connection between the poem and the *Ethics* explicit.[150] If the rubrics and the table of contents guide the reader through the treatise, the *Canzone* handily summarises the key topics discussed therein. As mentioned above, Bruni's poem provides readers with a generic and rather superficial definition of 'good' and 'virtue'. In Bonaccorso's manuscripts, the canzone performs the same summarising function as in Giovanni Rucellai's *zibaldone*, where it appears in the section devoted to the definition of 'good'. At the same time, by combining a philosophical treatise with poetry, Bonaccorso recreates a simplified version of the prosimetrum structure that combines prose and verse and that Dante, following Boethius' *Consolatio Philosophiae*, had revived with his *Convivio*. More than on the articulate structures of Boethius and Dante, though, Bonaccorso's juxtaposition of prose and verse seems to model itself on the format made popular by moral works such as the treatises of the Dominican preacher Domenico Cavalca (1270–1342).[151] In *Specchio di croce* ('Mirror of the Cross'), *Trenta stoltizie* ('Thirty Follies') and *Medicina del cuore* ('Medicine of the Heart'), Cavalca combined his

---

Filippo Adimari of Florence in 1467. Leonardo of Arezzo's moral *canzone* follows; it defines what is happiness and of what it consists. Deo gratias, may Jesus be forever praised. Amen').

[148] Florence, Biblioteca Nazionale Centrale, MS Pal. 710, fol. 221r: 'Questo libro intitolato Etyca di Aristotile è di Bernardo di Paolino Adimari el quale gli donò Buonacorso di Filippo Adimari scrivendo qui in casa nostra confortando detto Bernardo a studiarlo bene et imparare virtù [ma] in giovintù.'

[149] Florence, Biblioteca Nazionale Centrale, MS Magl. XXI.64, fol. [1]: 'Tavola del presente libro'.

[150] The text of the *canzone* appears in Florence, Biblioteca Nazionale Centrale, MS Pal. 710, fols. 221r–224r and MS Magl. XXI.64, fols. 211v–214r, respectively.

[151] For an overview of Domenico Cavalca's life and works, including his prosimeters, see Delcorno (1979).

skills as a populariser of Christian morals with his poetic abilities. In each work, the various prose sections are followed by poetical pieces, either sonnets or *sirventesi*, that help the reader memorise the subject matter. When considered within a similar tradition of works, Adimari's copies of the *Ethics* evidence the active role of the scribe in repackaging the text in correspondence with the reading habits of its new lay audience. If Nuti brings the *Ethics* to the vernacular reading public by translating it into Italian, Adimari too takes part in the translation process by further reducing the cultural distance between the original humanist project and contemporaneous vernacular readers.

By recommending that his children read and study the *Ethics*, Bonaccorso displays an attitude towards moral education that differs from Aristotle's instructions on the topic. As a matter of fact, Aristotle did not consider the study of moral philosophy suitable for the young, but instead he recommended it as a discipline to be acquired as an adult. As indicated in Chapter 1, moral education for youths in the Middle Ages was traditionally conveyed through the study of grammar.[152] This form of education, which derived its moral teachings from merging the classics with Christian doctrine, intended to provide young adults with the basics of moral philosophy, basics built on the acquisition of prescriptive norms rather than based on speculation proper (this, by the way, was the educational method that Matteo Palmieri criticised in the preface to his *Vita civile*).[153] While Aristotle's writings were studied in universities and religious schools, they also made their way through the popular forms of moral education thanks to various kinds of translation, including abridgments, compendia and, above all, anthologies like those of Giovanni Rucellai. Once the complexity of Aristotle's philosophy was tamed by popularisation, he could be easily considered an author for young readers as well. In a way, Adimari's statement reproduces the same approach to the study of moral philosophy behind the novella of Aristotle in the *Novellino*.[154] There, the philosopher recommended that his student develop virtuous habits at a young age, for only they can protect him from committing 'follies' later in life. As shown in Chapter 1, the novella 'translates' the Aristotelian idea of virtue as habit, an operation that, as we have seen in this chapter, also lay at the core of Giovanni Rucellai's philosophical concerns. At the same time,

---

[152] See my discussion of grammar in Chapter 1, 25–32. See also Gehl (1993).
[153] See 148–51 in this chapter.
[154] For the text of the novella, see Conte (2001: 116–17); see also Chapter 1, 35–6.

though, this 'editorial translation' inevitably reduces philosophical inquiry to issues of moral conduct. A similar mindset characterises the didactic function assigned to Aristotle in the Adimari household, where the copy of Aristotle's *Nicomachean Ethics* made in 1464 exhibited an analogous function to that performed by Bonaccorso's copy of Alderotti's translation of the *Summa Alexandrinorum* copied twenty years prior.

Examples such as these uncover the flexibility and instability of vernacular translation, a space that allows for various kinds of interaction between translators and readers. Both translators and readers take part in a process of reception that challenges common assumptions about the linear development and decline of cultural trends traditionally described in opposition. The experiences of Bonaccorso Adimari and Giovanni Rucellai reveal that forms of 'humanism' and 'scholasticism', 'innovation' and 'tradition' did indeed cohabit and that they did so in a vernacular universe. Even if the taming of Aristotle entailed forms of simplification, vernacular translation was nonetheless fuelled by a dialogic exchange between translators and readers. If translators were responsible for *translating* the sources, readers became translators in their own right by bringing those sources out to their peers, keeping the conversation alive. Indeed, as we shall see in the following chapter, such dialogic interaction – poignantly emblematised by Luca Della Robbia's tilework in the campanile of Santa Maria del Fiore – is more than a trope. By looking at the ways in which the textual transmission of two abridgments of Aristotelian philosophy (Luca Mannelli's *Compendium moralis philosophiae* and Jacopo Campora's *De immortalitate animae*) went through a process of constant reshaping, I will focus on the transformative power of reception and translation.

CHAPTER 5

Abridging the Philosopher(s)

Not Only Aristotle

One feature of the vernacular reception of Aristotle that runs across the various case studies discussed in this book is the diverse nature of such reception. What Charles B. Schmitt revealed about the Latin reception of Aristotle in the Renaissance – namely, his vision of a philosophical eclecticism that led him to use the plural 'Aristotelianisms' instead of the singular and monolithic 'Aristotelianism' – can certainly be applied to the ways in which Aristotle was read, received and appropriated in the vernacular.[1] Furthermore, the Aristotle that we see cross through the Middle Ages and Renaissance rarely stood on his own. While his status as philosopher par excellence was virtually uncontested, his legacy often merged with those of other authors, Christian or otherwise. The process, partly evident in the examples of translation and reception analysed in the previous chapters, becomes particularly prominent when translation functions as abridgment.

In abridging their sources for the benefit of their readers, translators often combined different authors, selecting materials from their works. The basic principle at the core of this kind of translation was the same that informed the coeval anthologies of philosophical *sententiae*. Yet, while collections of sayings such as the *Fiore di virtù* tended to accumulate data with no substantial editing on the part of the compiler, abridgments aimed to introduce readers to a specific topic (or even a given text) by presenting heterogeneous materials in structured ways.[2] Compendia of this kind, in which moral philosophy was usually combined with Christian doctrine, often took the form of treatises, thereby replicating the structure of works produced within the academic context. In other cases, authors

---

[1] See Schmitt (1973; 1983: 12–30). For the various philosophical threads involved in the Renaissance reception of Aristotle's *Ethics*, see in particular Lines (2002) and Lines and Ebbersmeyer (2013); cf. Blum (2012).
[2] On the relevance of anthologies of philosophical dicta to the vernacular reception of Aristotle, see Chapter 4, 156–7.

of compendia turned to the dialogical structure of simplified *quaestiones*, where the sequence of questions and answers (commonly asked and answered by a disciple and a master, respectively) both covered the subject matter at hand and functioned as an aide-memoire.[3] In both cases, authors performed the role of translators, connecting the sources to the targeted audience. At the same time, especially when a given compendium was received favourably and circulated widely, the mediation process continued far beyond the initial publication of the work. In fact, the afterlife of a text offers useful evidence of the active role played by its consumers in the constant reshaping of the text itself, a reshaping that often transforms the work into something very different from its initial condition. As the examples discussed in this chapter show, the process of translation entailed by the abridgment of philosophical sources did not result in an allegedly final product. Indeed, no product of this kind was 'final', for its textual transmission, far from being a process of mere reproduction, continued to transform it.[4] The very notion of translation thus uncovers a variety of nuances that are not limited to inter-lingual transfer and actually include all forms of adjustment proactively entailed by reception.

Such a fluid situation, which proved particularly fruitful for the vernacular abridgment of Aristotle, is illustrated by the circulation and reception of two works that, while very different from one another, were characterised by similar approaches to the classics: Luca Mannelli's *Compendium moralis philosophiae* ('Compendium of Moral Philosophy', c. 1350) and Jacopo Campora's dialogue *De immortalitate animae* ('On the Immortality of the Soul', c. 1430). Authored by members of the Dominican order, both works witness their authors' concern with the dissemination of a philosophical tradition deeply imbued with scholasticism. But their reception tells a story of cultural transformation that, once again, challenges traditional narratives about the conflicts between culture and language in the later Middle Ages and the early Renaissance. These works both feature Aristotle prominently and constantly refer to him as the source of all knowledge as well as the authority on philosophical questions ranging from the definition of happiness to the immortality of the human soul. While these questions occupied scholars in the universities and religious *studia*, and were addressed in sophisticated arguments based on the interpretation of Aristotle, lay readers sought out different answers, primarily concerned with problems that they could relate to their everyday life as

---

[3] The production of Latin compendia in the later Middle Ages is discussed in Grant (1996: 127–35).
[4] As recalled in my introduction, translation per se is never final; see also Martindale (1993: 100).

human beings.[5] Compendia such as Mannelli's and Campora's attempted to meet such expectations.

Aristotle is not, however, the only source that Mannelli and Campora aimed to *translate* in their works. Both authors display a wide knowledge of the exegetical tradition that accompanied the study of Aristotle in the Middle Ages, but they reinforce their reading of 'the master of those who know' by referring to classical and Christian philosophers such as Plato, Cicero, Seneca, Augustine and Jerome, as well as a variety of medieval authors. By doing so, they plunge the reception of Aristotle into a broad continuum that tones down clear-cut distinctions between the past and present, between 'old' and 'new' cultures.

Indeed, the two works are scarcely innovative in their content. They nonetheless provide precious insights into the ways in which philosophical discussions were repackaged and made accessible to audiences normally excluded from professional scholarship. By examining their transmission in manuscript and, as far as Campora's *De immortalitate* is concerned, in print, this chapter will also enlighten the transformative function performed by the vernacular reception of classical philosophy (Aristotle in particular) in a period of complex cultural transition.

One Step Backward

A prince sits on a throne, crushing a horrendous monster under his feet. With his right hand, the prince holds a sword, thus recalling the traditional iconography of justice. With his left hand, he holds a book – a symbol of wisdom and likely an allusion to the very volume where, on the first folio, this image is depicted, which is the same book that the prince is seen receiving from the hands of a Dominican friar in the illuminated initial higher up in the page [Figure 5.1].

As indicated by the incipit of Luca Mannelli's *Compendium moralis philosophiae* in MS Latin 6467 of the Bibliothèque Nationale de France, the prince is the dedicatee of the volume, Bruzio Visconti, whose political power is represented by the small-scale depictions of Milan and other Lombard cities in the decorative frame around the page.[6] The friar depicted

---

[5] The point was made by Schmitt (1983: 35–6) in his only reference to the vernacular spread of Aristotelianism in the Renaissance: 'Besides the books meant for classroom use or for the professor in his study, there were also others produced specifically for the private reader. Most of these were an intellectual cut below the academic level. A good number were written in the vernacular, others were simplified versions of Aristotle's crabbed and difficult writings.'

[6] Paris, Bibliothèque Nationale de France, MS Lat. 6467, fol. 1r. For details about the manuscript, see Dorez (1904: 19), Kaeppeli (1948: 244–6), Albertini Ottolenghi (1991: 57–8) and Zaggia (2015: 166).

Figure 5.1 Paris, Bibliothèque Nationale de France, MS. Latin 6467, fol. 1r

in the initial is the author of the work, the Florentine Luca Mannelli, who offered his *Compendium* to Bruzio in the early 1340s. A small caption on the lower edge of the page tells us that the monster being crushed by the prince is the allegorical personification of Pride ('Superbia'), clearly identified here as the most dangerous among the vices that a good ruler should defeat. Six other figures stand next to the victorious prince, three on each side: Valerius Maximus, Seneca and Aristotle on the left; Aquinas, Ambrose and Augustine on the right. Aristotle thus appears as one of the six authorities that ground Mannelli's work, which is presented at its very inception as a combination of classical philosophy and Christian doctrine.

The beautifully illuminated dedication copy of Mannelli's *Compendium* returns us to a time when Latin was the preferred language for a work dedicated to a prince. Bruzio Visconti was, after all, the same prince to whom Bartolomeo de' Bartoli had dedicated his own linguistically hybrid *Canzone delle virtù e delle scienze*, which I discussed in Chapter 1.[7] Even in the *Canzone*, despite the importance of its vernacular component, the scholarly and erudite dimension of the work was conveyed through the Latin language. In both cases, the prince (who was not only the son of the lord of Milan, Luchino, but also a bibliophile) was offered luxurious, illuminated manuscripts of moral works that he probably never read or, if he did, works from which he learned very little, as suggested by his rather mediocre political career. Far from being the 'ideal' ruler portrayed on the first page of Mannelli's *Compendium*, in reality Bruzio sought refuge in Bologna after his unlucky experience as *podestà* (chief magistrate) of Lodi. In Bologna, he plotted against his uncle Giovanni and was eventually exiled to the Veneto, where he died in 1357. More famous for his poetical exchange with Petrarch than for his political achievements, Bruzio was the type of prince who found himself at ease with the Latin culture of the time, a culture to which Mannelli himself belonged.[8]

Born in Florence between 1291 and 1296, Mannelli entered the Dominican order at a young age and pursued a brilliant ecclesiastic career.[9] In 1344, he was named bishop of the Greek diocese of Zituni. Only three years later, in 1347, in virtue of Mannelli's good relations with the Malatesta family, who were the lords of Rimini, he was made bishop of Osimo by Pope Clement VI. In 1358, Pope Innocent VI, also motivated by Manelli's connections,

---

[7] See Chapter 1, 26–30; see also Dorez (1904).
[8] See Kaeppeli (1948: 244–8); on Bruzio's poetical exchange with Petrarch, see Ricci (1947) and Zaggia (2015: 166–70).
[9] Cinelli (2007).

named him bishop of Fano, where Manelli died in 1362. Having spent much of his time in Avignon, Mannelli absorbed the vibrant culture of the papal city and was able to focus on erudite studies. Along with the *Compendium moralis philosophiae*, written at Bruzio's behest, Mannelli authored important Latin commentaries on Valerius Maximus and Seneca. Both the *Expositio Valerii Maximi factorum ac dictorum memorabilium libri IX* (c. 1340) and the *Tabulatio et expositio Senecae* (composed between 1349 and 1352) witness Mannelli's keen interest in classical authors whose works could be used as sources of moral instruction, an interest that resonated with Clement's project to establish a philosophical library where the Church Fathers and classical philosophers would be side by side.[10]

Indeed, as we have seen, these Church Fathers and classical philosophers do stand side by side on the first page of Mannelli's *Compendium*. In the preface to Bruzio the author defines himself as a 'frate' ('friar'), not yet a bishop. This suggests that the work was likely completed before 1344, a chronology further confirmed by the style of the illuminated decorations, which has been linked to the Bolognese school of the mid-1340s.[11] Written in Latin, the work is an instructive example of intra-lingual translation: Mannelli is not addressing someone unconversant with Latin, but instead someone who, despite a solid knowledge of Latin, is not a professional scholar, whence the need to 'translate' (and, to some extent, reduce) the subject matter from the technicalities of scholastic philosophy into a more accessible form. In this respect, the *Compendium* can be understood as a form of vulgarisation where the 'taming' of the source is not linguistic but conceptual in the first place.[12] As was the case with the *De regimine principum* by Giles of Rome, Mannelli's *Compendium* is offered to the dedicatee as a handy substitute for longer and more demanding readings to which the reader is too busy to commit. The function of the work is declared in Mannelli's dedication to Bruzio, where the relevance of moral philosophy to the prince is primarily based on the nobility of his lineage: if

---

[10] On Mannelli's commentary on Seneca, see Kaeppeli (1948), Mayer (2015: 278) and Hamilton (2014: 168–71).

[11] Paris, Bibliothèque Nationale de France, MS Lat. 6467, fol. 1r: 'Magnifico generoso domino ... Brucio Vicecomiti Frater Lucas ordinis praedicatorum bene valere et esse felicem'. On the stylistic features of the miniatures, see Mariani Canova (2005: 188). Mulas (2005: 152) recalls the Bolognese provenance of other illuminated manuscripts made for Bruzio, including copies of Augustine's *De civitate Dei*, Apuleius' *Metamorphoses* and Bartoli's *Canzone delle virtù e delle scienze*.

[12] The term 'vulgarisation' is used here in the sense suggested by Briggs (2003); see my discussion of the term in the introduction to this book, 11.

it is true that no happiness can be attained without virtuous deeds, it is moral philosophy that teaches us how to attain happiness and keep it.[13]

Not surprisingly, Mannelli's statement is supported by a reference to Aristotle, who gave instructions for the attainment of happiness in his *Nicomachean Ethics* ('Testis est Aristoteles Ethicorum primo ubi de felicitate inchoavit et ultimo ubi felicitatem consumavit').[14] In a gesture that recalls Petrarch's preoccupations about the fulfilment of virtue, Mannelli supports his Aristotelian reference with the quotation of a famous passage from Cicero's *Tusculanae disputationes*, where the human soul is compared to a field and philosophy to agriculture.[15] Just as the field needs to be carefully cultivated in order to bear fruit, so too does the soul require preparation in order to fulfil its potential. By turning to the Ciceronian notion of philosophy as the 'cultura animi' (literally, 'cultivation of the soul'), Mannelli aims to bridge the gap between the theoretical knowledge of moral philosophy and its concrete application. What Petrarch considered the coldness of Aristotle's scholastic legacy is thus revitalised by Mannelli under the aegis of Cicero. The pivotal presence of the Latin author in the *Compendium* is declared at the end of the dedication, where Cicero is mentioned alongside Aristotle and Aquinas: 'Whoever wishes to criticise this work should know that what I have conveyed in this work comes from Aristotle's *Ethics*, Cicero's *De officis* and *Tusculanae Disputationes* and Thomas Aquinas' *Summa Theologiae*'. By stating that he has added 'only a few considerations' of his own ('pauca de meis cogitationibus subiungens'), Mannelli minimises his authorial role and stresses his function as an intermediary between the sources and the reader.[16]

When one turns to the *Compendium* itself, the work quickly reveals its nature of philosophical compilation, where the *auctoritates* – always carefully referenced, often with precise quotations – are not, in fact, limited to Aristotle, Cicero and Aquinas. Other *auctores* include Vergil, Juvenal,

---

[13] Paris, Bibliothèque Nationale de France, MS Lat. 6467, fol. 1r: 'Qui alios nobilitate transcendunt et suorum progenitorum gloria illustrantur dignum est laude virtuosorum operum sine quo vera felicitas esse non potest ceteros superent ... morali phylosophie deserviantur ad felicitatem acquirendam et acquisitam conservandam' ('Those who are nobler than the others and enlighten the glory of their ancestors should surpass the others in being praised for their virtuous deeds, without which true happiness cannot be attained ... moral philosophy is needed to acquire happiness and, once it is acquired, to preserve it').

[14] *Ibid.*

[15] Cicero's passage, partly quoted and partly summarised *ibid.*: fol. 1r–v, is taken from *Tusculanae disputationes* 2.11–13.

[16] Paris, Bibliothèque Nationale de France, MS Lat. 6467, fol. 2v: 'quicumque hoc opus culpare voluerit, cognoscat quaeque in hoc opere expressi ab Aristotile ex libro Ethicorum, a Tullio ex libro de offitiis et Tusculanis questionibus, a Thoma ex prima et secunda secundae. Pauca de meis cogitationibus preter formam procedendi subiungens.'

Valerius Maximus, Sallust, Quintilian, Isidore of Seville and, above all, Seneca and Augustine. Mannelli's compilation, however, is an ambitious one, where the various *auctores* inhabit a wider structure that aims to offer an exhaustive treatment of moral philosophy. The work is clearly inspired by Aristotle's *Ethics*, which provides Mannelli with not only the philosophical subject matter but also a methodological frame to treat the topic adequately. Divided into three main parts, the *Compendium* begins by addressing the notions of virtue, passion and habit; it then proceeds with a detailed discussion of virtues and vices before closing with a section devoted to friendship.

While it is difficult to say whether Bruzio did actually read the *Compendium*, the afterlife of the work is of great interest to our study. In fact, the reception of Mannelli's work beyond the walls of Bruzio's library illustrates the dynamics that informed the increasing interest of lay readers in philosophical matters and, as we shall see, widens the breadth of the intersections of Latinate and vernacular cultures outlined in the previous chapters.

Two Steps Forward

As far as we know from its manuscript tradition, which is limited to the dedication copy, Mannelli's *Compendium philosophiae moralis* does not seem to have circulated widely. When one considers the vernacular reception of the work, however, significant differences emerge. One anonymous translation of the *Compendium* survives in five manuscripts written between the late fourteenth and the early fifteenth centuries. While the translation has been tentatively attributed to Mannelli himself, evidence for this claim is lacking.[17] It is nonetheless evident that the vernacular version proved much more successful than the Latin one. Once the text moved beyond Bruzio's household, it shed the courtly features that characterised its original commission as it entered private libraries belonging to patrons that would have also owned the other works discussed in my earlier chapters. More precisely, as suggested by a careful study of the five extant manuscripts, the vernacular version of Mannelli's *Compendium* went through a process of transformation that, without affecting the textual content of the

---

[17] For the hypothesis that the Italian translation was made by Mannelli himself, see Kaeppeli (1948: 247). The Italian translation is witnessed in the following manuscripts: Florence, Biblioteca Laurenziana, MS Acquisti e Doni 686; Biblioteca Nazionale Centrale, MS Pal. 581 and MS Pal. 649; Paris, Bibliothèque Nationale de France, MS Ital. 2235; and Vatican City, Biblioteca Apostolica Vaticana, MS Barb. Lat. 4031.

work, significantly altered the way in which it was presented to the reader. Interestingly enough, such a process highlighted the Aristotelian dimension of the text even more boldly than the original Latin version.

The oldest copy of the vernacular translation of Mannelli's *Compendium*, entitled *Compendio della filosofia morale*, is written in a *littera textualis* in a manuscript that cannot be dated more precisely than to the mid-to-late fourteenth century. Now MS Pal. 649 at the Biblioteca Nazionale in Florence, this copy identifies the author as 'il savio religioso de frati predicatori Frate Luca de Mannelli fiorentino' ('the wise member of the Order of Preachers, Luca Mannelli of Florence'), thus stressing the author's Florentine provenance.[18] As with all the other copies of the translation, this manuscript omits the preface to Bruzio Visconti that opened the original Latin version of the text. In so doing, the translation loses its connection to the initial dedicatee, repositioning itself as a text that, like Taddeo Alderotti's translation of the *Summa Alexandrinorum*, was free to circulate as a generic work of moral philosophy (as the *colophon* puts it, the work is 'd'utilità di chiunque ci leggerà di buon chuore e per essere vertudioso', 'of benefit to whoever will read with open heart and is willing to attain virtue').[19] One feature of MS Pal. 649 that witnesses the didactic purpose of the copy is the presence of a detailed index of the ninety-nine chapters that constitute the work. While the original Latin was not divided into chapters – the text being simply divided in three long sections – chapter division is common to all copies of the Italian translation. Along with the compilation of the index, the division of the text into short chapters is one of the ways in which the vernacular translation makes the text easier to navigate.[20]

Similar expedients made the work more palatable, as indicated by the material features of other copies, which suggest that the text circulated among lay readers of mercantile extraction. To this group of manuscripts belongs MS Pal. 581 of the Biblioteca Nazionale in Florence, written in the decades around 1400, characterised by a *mercantesca* handwriting with notarial elements.[21] In the manuscript, Mannelli's *Compendio* follows an epistle against marriage long attributed to Valerius Maximus.[22] Even if the

---

[18] Florence, Biblioteca Nazionale Centrale, MS Pal. 649; see Gentile (1889–99 vol. 2: 217–18) and Kaeppeli (1948: 247).

[19] Florence, Biblioteca Nazionale Centrale, MS Pal. 649, fol. 75r.

[20] The index or table of chapters appears *ibid.*: fols. 3r–4v.

[21] Florence, Biblioteca Nazionale Centrale, MS Pal. 581; see Gentile (1889–99 vol. 2: 147–8) and Kaeppeli (1948: 247).

[22] The 'Epistola a Rufino contro il prender moglie' (fols. 1r–5r) is a vernacular translation of the Latin epistle *Valerius ad Rufinum de non ducenda uxore*, attributed to the English writer Walter Map; see Gentile (1889–99 vol. 2: 147–8).

combination of the two texts is likely accidental, it nonetheless gives us a sense of the vernacular literature with which the *Compendio* was associated, which included moral works of classical philosophy and Christian literature. Another example of the circulation of the *Compendio* in a mercantile context is MS Acquisti e Doni 686 of the Biblioteca Medicea Laurenziana, written in 1419 by the Venetian merchant Bernardo Bragadin, who was detained in Florence due to a controversy in a commercial transaction.[23] Bragadin, who wrote other manuscripts during his stay in the *stinche* (prisons) of Florence to earn money to pay his Florentine creditors, was clearly writing under commission. This suggests that Mannelli's *Compendio* was indeed sought after in the book market, as is also indicated by the increasing interest of vernacular readership in the work during the early decades of the fifteenth century.

Two other manuscripts of the *Compendio* are instructive in this respect as they offer further insights into the cluster of implications that informed the transformative reception of the work. In MS Barb. Lat. 4031 of the Biblioteca Apostolica Vaticana, written in 1425, the *Compendio* is compiled by the same scribe alongside Alderotti's Italian translation of the *Summa Alexandrinorum*.[24] The pairing is of the utmost significance for two main reasons. First, consistent with the pattern of circulation described in my discussion of the textual tradition of the *Summa* in Chapter 2, the Vatican manuscript witnesses the enduring success of Alderotti's work. Second, and even more relevant to the present discussion, the manuscript confirms that vernacular readers considered Mannelli's *Compendio* comparable to a text like the *Summa*, which was itself an abridgment of Aristotle's *Ethics*. In a way, the two texts together offered an exhaustive survey of moral philosophy where the Aristotelian tradition was linked to the legacy of other philosophers whose moral teachings could also be easily appropriated by their vernacular readership.

The Aristotelian inspiration behind Mannelli's *Compendio* becomes even more explicit in MS Ital. 2235 of the Bibliothèque Nationale de France.[25]

---

[23] Florence, Biblioteca Laurenziana, MS Acquisti e Doni 686; see Kristeller (1963–97 vol. 4: 231 and vol. 5: 567), Kaeppeli (1970 vol. 4: 291), Fratini and Zamponi (2004: 53 n.48) and Cursi (2007: 109n177, 110n180). On Bernardo Bragadin's detention in Florence, see Christ (2012: 269). On the practice of copying manuscripts in prison, see Meneghetti (1992) and Cursi (2009); see also the case of a manuscript copy of Taddeo Alderotti's Italian translation of the *Summa Alexandrinorum* discussed in Chapter 2, 71–2.

[24] Vatican City, Biblioteca Apostolica Vaticana, MS Barb. Lat. 4031; see also Kaeppeli (1948: 247). The text of the *Summa*, entitled here *Hetica d'Aristotile*, is from fols. 1r–30v, the text of Mannelli's compendium from fols. 40r–105v.

[25] Paris, Bibliothèque Nationale de France, MS Ital. 2235. The manuscript results from a restoration of the original artifact, with pages that have been cut and reassembled. While the hand that copied the

In this mid-fifteenth-century copy, elegantly written in the style of humanist manuscripts with coloured rubrics and golden initials, the name of the author of the *Compendio* is omitted and the text is presented in a slightly different light. As per the incipit ('Incomincia um brieve tractato o compendio di philosophia morale sopra l'ethica d'Aristotile prencipe de philosaphi', 'Here begins a short treatise or compendium of moral philosophy based on the *Ethics* by Aristotle, the prince of philosophers'), the compendium is presented as being based on Aristotle's *Ethics*.[26] The new title privileges the Aristotelian component over the other philosophical threads that inform Mannelli's work. The reshaping of the *Compendio* also includes a further subdivision of the text, which here is divided into ten books so as to follow closely the structure of Aristotle's *Nicomachean Ethics*. The attempt to point out the connection between the *Compendio* and the *Ethics* has a twofold purpose: first, it enhances the prestige of the work by relating its content to Aristotle's authoritative treatment of moral philosophy; second, it aims to assimilate the *Compendio* into the contemporaneous production of philosophical works in the vernacular that, as we have shown, stemmed in various ways from the academic study of the philosopher.

Even if Mannelli's original project was conceived as a summary of moral philosophy in general, not as a specific summary of the *Ethics*, the Aristotelian inspiration of the work is evident from the preamble forward. Not only does it begin by recalling the centrality of virtue to any discussion of moral philosophy, but it also stresses the importance in philosophical study of an initial definition of terms, a methodological gesture reminiscent of Aristotle's way of proceeding in his treatise and other works:

> Given that I intend to write a short treatise on moral philosophy, it seems reasonable to me that I should begin with the definition of virtue, since the moral philosopher's aim is to possess virtue and act according to virtue. For this reason, this discipline is not taken to be mastered in theory, as is the case with speculative sciences. Rather, one studies it in order to act according to it, as Aristotle maintains in the second book of the *Ethics*. And since the end of moral philosophy is to live according to virtue, one must begin by [discussing] virtue, which cannot be explained better than by its

---

text is certainly a fifteenth-century one, the hand that wrote the title of the work on fol. 1r, dating it 1444, seems to be a different and possibly slightly later one.

[26] *Ibid.*: fol. 2r. The same phrasing is used in the title on fol. 1r: 'Brieve Tractato o Compendio di Philosophia Morale Sopra l'Ethica d'Aristotile Prencipe de Philosaphi. L'Anno di N.S. MCCCCXLIV.'

definition. In fact, a perfect definition includes all the features essential to the object defined.[27]

A strong focus on the practical dimension of moral philosophy is, as we have seen, a constant element in the vernacular reception of Aristotle. Lay readers like aristocrats and wealthy merchants were more interested in the applicability of philosophical teachings to real life than in abstract speculation. At the same time, works such as Mannelli's *Compendio* do not limit their discussion to prescriptive teachings. On the contrary, they attempt to articulate those teachings by giving them some sort of theoretical frame, always trying to find an effective balance between academic discourse and intellectual simplification.

Typical of this approach is the final section of the *Compendio*, where the author addresses the controversial question of the necessity of wealth for happiness, a topic that was of particular interest to the wealthy elites of the Italian city-states and which, as we have seen in the previous chapters, informed the reflections in the *zibaldoni* of rich merchants such as Giovanni Rucellai. Mannelli connects the topic to Aristotle's discussion of the final good in the first book of the *Ethics*, where the philosopher stresses the 'self-sufficiency' of happiness.[28] By giving the Aristotelian quotation a twist that is in fact foreign to the argument developed by Aristotle in the passage, Mannelli forces the text and uses it to endorse the idea that wealth helps in the pursuit of happiness. At the same time, by expanding on his source, he stresses the importance of 'moderation' in acquiring and managing wealth, which should always be used to benefit the community into which the individual belongs.[29] By recalling the natural sociable inclination of man

---

[27] Paris, Bibliothèque Nationale de France, MS Ital. 2235, fol. 2r: 'Volendo fare brieve Tractato della Philosophia morale parmi che ragionevolmente si debbia cominciare dalla diffinitione della virtù. Però che tucta la intentione del philosapho morale è di avere la virtù et virtuosamente operare. Onde questa scientia non si prende solo per saperla si come interviene delle scientie speculative. Ma acciò che saputola si possa adoperare secondo quella, sì come vuole Aristotile nel secondo de l'ethica. Et pero che 'l fine de la Philosophia morale è vivere virtuosamente convien cominciare dalla virtù. Et la virtù si puote per [niuno] meglio et più veracemente manifestare che per la sua diffinitione. Però che·lla perfecta diffinitione comprende in sé tutte le cose essentiale della cosa diffinita.'

[28] Aristotle, *Nicomachean Ethics* 1.7 1037b 7–14: 'the final good is thought to be self-sufficient. Now by self-sufficient we do not mean that which is sufficient for a man by himself, for one who lives a solitary life, but also for parents, children, wife, and in general for his friends and fellow citizens, since man is born for citizenship. But some limit must be set to this; for if we extend our requirement to ancestors and descendants and friends' friends we are in for an infinite series' (transl. Ross).

[29] The passage confirms the exegetical dimension of Mannelli's work, in which the translated (and slightly re-elaborated) source is often accompanied by the translator's commentary; see Florence, Biblioteca Nazionale, MS Pal. 643, fol. 72r: 'I beni temporali i quali son detti beni di fortuna si richegiono a la felicità sechondo Aristotele nel primo del *Ethica* dove dice così: "Il perfetto bene pare che per se medesimo sia sufficiente. Ma noi non diciamo che sia sufficiente per sé medesimo quelgli

('l'huomo naturalmente è civile e conversativo', 'man is, by nature, social and inclined to conversation'), Mannelli argues that wealth and riches are necessary to attain virtues like liberality, which lead to happiness.

Based on this assumption, the author discusses happiness and compares the active life to the contemplative. Adhering to Aristotle's opinion, Mannelli explains that the highest form of happiness is undoubtedly obtained through philosophical speculation, which, as a gateway to wisdom ('sapientia'), is the most perfect achievement of human intellect. At the same time, he shows that most people are bound to the practical dimension of everyday life, in which action is considered more useful than contemplation.[30] That said, Mannelli eventually defines moral philosophy as key to the pursuit of happiness in this earthly life. According to Mannelli, Socrates brought the discipline 'from the heavens to the city'; Plato continued his predecessor's philosophical inquiry; Aristotle made it perfect and taught it in the *Nicomachean Ethics*, on which the *Compendio* is primarily drawing.[31]

---

che vive solo e solitario, ma chi convive chon parenti, chon figliuoli, cholla moglie, cholgli amici e cho cittadini; però che l'huomo naturalmente è civile e conversativo. Ma questo si dee ponere in alchun termine". In queste parole pare che sia la intentione di Aristotele che l'uhuomo [*sic*] felice debbia avere sufficientia de beni temporali per sé e per choloro che appartenghono a lui. Ma questo dè essere in alchun termine, cioè che non si richiede che l'huomo felice abbia tante chose temporali che possa provedere a tucti parenti amici e cittadini, ma che possa provedere sechondo la conditione del suo stato' ('Wealth – i.e., the goods of Fortune – is necessary to one's happiness according to Aristotle in book 1 of the *Ethics*, where he says: "The final good seems to be self-sufficient. Now, we do not call self-sufficient a person who lives a solitary life, but someone who lives with parents, children, wife, and in general with his friends and fellow citizens, since man is by nature social and inclined to conversation. Yet, some limit must be set to this". In these words, Aristotle seems to be arguing that, in order to be happy, a person needs goods sufficient for himself and for those who belong to him. But some limit must be set to this: a happy man does not need to have goods enough to sustain all his relatives, friends, and fellow citizens, but only to be able to sustain them according to his status').

30 *Ibid.*: fol. 72*v*: 'nel x libro del Ethica il dittermina e dice che la felicità istà nell'operatione de le vertù morali cioè la felicità praticha et operativa. Ma la felicità spechulativa istà nell'operatione della vertù intelettiva la quale ee la sapientia' ('in book 10 of the *Ethics*, he explains that happiness resides in the practice of moral virtues, that is factual and practical happiness. But contemplative happiness resides in intellectual happiness, that is wisdom').

31 *Ibid.*: fol. 93*r–v*: 'A questa filicità mena et conducie la filosofia morale la quale si può avere in questa presente vita, la quale primamente chiamò Socrate da cielo et puosela nella prima mente et nella ciptà et nelle chase et costrinse gli uomeni a investigare et ricerchare della vita, de chostumi et delle cosse buone et ree; di questa filosofia disputò Platone sotilmente e per sua schritura lasciò memoria di sé e nobilitò; questa filosofia nel libro de l'*Ethicha* d'Aristotile confermò e dichiarò chon più efichaci et vere ragioni. Il quale singularmente seguito in questo libro' ('Moral philosophy leads to this kind of happiness that is attainable in this present life; Socrates brought it first from the heavens and placed it in God, in the city, in the households and led people to inquire about life, customs, good and evil; Plato discussed and ennobled such philosophy leaving memory of himself; Aristotle confirmed and explained this philosophy with more effective and truer arguments in the *Ethics*; in my own book I follow him closely').

Closing his work in a way that would have pleased Petrarch and Bruni, Mannelli addresses the reader by quoting from Cicero's praise of the civilising function of moral philosophy in the *Tusculanae disputationes*, where the discipline is described as an indispensable guide to both individual and common welfare – a welfare that, as Cicero puts it, is not only based on the practice of virtue but also on the use of language:

> Tullius addressed moral philosophy in the last book of the *Tusculan Disputations*, saying: 'O philosophy, guide of life, explorer of virtue and expeller of vice! Without you, what could the life of human beings be? You gave birth to cities; you gathered scattered human beings and got them to live together; you have united them first in joint habitations, next in wedlock. You have discovered law, you have been the teacher of custom. You have united people in the ties of common literacy and speech. We turn to you and look to you for aid and we entrust ourselves entirely to you'. If you, who are reading, ponder this statement, you will find in this booklet no small benefit.[32]

The transformation of Mannelli's Latin *Compendium moralis philosophiae* into a vernacular summary of Aristotle's *Ethics* brings to the surface elements of Mannelli's work that can certainly be labelled as pre-humanist, in particular the use of authors such as Cicero, Seneca and Augustine to support the predominantly Aristotelian content of the work. Of particular interest, though, is that this transformation takes place through vernacular translation. It is, in fact, in its vernacular version that the shape of the *Compendium* acquires an exquisitely humanist character (and is marketed as such), thus confirming the productive role played by vernacular translation as a catalyst of interaction between concurrent trends in fifteenth-century culture.

In the case of Mannelli's *Compendium*, the mediation process does include, as I have shown, inter-lingual translation (the Latin original is

---

[32] *Ibid.*: 93*v*: 'Questa filosofia chiamè Tulio ne l'ultimo libro delle *Questioni toschulane* et disse così: "O filosofia ducha della vita, trovatrice delle virtù, discaciatrice de vitii, che potrebe sanza te la vita degli uomini? Tu portasti la ciptà. Tu ragunasti gli uomini sparti et faciesti vivere in chonmpagnia. Tu primieramente gli achompagnasti nella habitatione delle chasse poi gli faciesti venire a matrimonio. Tu fosti trovatrice delle legi et maestra de chostumi. Tu faciesti participare gli uomini insieme per litere et per voci. Noi richorriamo atte et domandiamo da te adiutorio et atte ci diamo tutti"; la quale vocie et il quale detto se tu che leggi osserveray, troverray in questa operetta non pichollo utille'; see Cicero, *Tusculanae Disputationes* 5.2.5 in King (1927), 429: 'O vitae philosophia dux, o virtutis indagatrix expultrixque vitiorum! quid non modo nos, sed omnino vita hominum sine te esse potuisset? Tu urbes peperisti, tu dissipatos homines in societatem vitae convocasti, tu eos inter se primo domiciliis, deinde coniugis, tum litterarum et vocum communione iunxisti, tu inventrix legum, tu magistra morum et disciplinae fuisti: ad te confugimus, a te opem petimus, tibi nos, ut antea magna ex parte, sic nunc penitus totosque tradimus.'

properly *translated* into Italian). Other examples instead witness the broader and, to some extent, more ambiguous notion of *translatio* particular to the late medieval and early modern reception of classical philosophy. Indeed, the hybridisation of sources and argumentative devices that characterise compendia and abridgments enhances the notion of translation as a fluid field for the vulgarisation of philosophical discussions. Such a field proves very productive when (as indicated in the previous chapter) it involves the active participation of readers in the translation process. In most cases, the 'conversation' between translators and their readers is more metaphorical than real. There are instances in which, however, dialogue becomes a powerful instrument to facilitate the translation process. In such instances, the fictional frame of the dialogue deploys the overlapping of reception and translation in effective ways.

Ask the Theologian

London, 1432. The Venetian merchant Giovanni Marcanova (not to be confused with the coeval humanist of the same name) is hosting an acquaintance of his, the Genovese theologian Jacopo Campora.[33] The Dominican Campora is visiting the city from Oxford, where he has just obtained his degree in theology earlier that year. The advantages of dining with a theologian are not negligible. Making the most of his friend's skills, Giovanni asks him about a topic that would have been of interest to any Christian: the immortality of the human soul. Later, to thank his London-based friend for his hospitality, Jacopo decides to write down the conversation and offer it to Giovanni. The result is the dialogue entitled *De immortalitate animae*, which Jacopo sent to Giovanni from Bruges. The situation described by Campora in the prologue to the work, if not true in all its details, is undoubtedly realistic and consistent with similar forms of interaction between scholars and lay readers that I have discussed earlier in this book (e.g., the Giustiniani patrons in Venice and Giovanni Rucellai in Florence). From what we know about Marcanova's biography, the Venetian merchant was also a cultivated and highly esteemed man who, during his stay in London, was in touch with all sorts of travellers. He is, for instance, mentioned in the report of Pietro Querini's infamous shipwreck and following stop-over in London that was included in Giovan Battista Ramusio's *Secondo volume delle navigationi et viaggi*, where Marcanova is described as a most 'honourable and virtuous man', caring

---

[33] On the biography of Giovanni Marcanova, see Barile, Clarke and Nordio (2006: 21–135).

and heartwarming, all features that resonate with Campora's portrayal of the hospitable merchant.[34]

Despite the Latin title, the dialogue *De immortalitate animae* is written in the vernacular for vernacular readers not directly concerned with scholarly affairs. In his study of the library of Leonardo da Vinci, which probably included a copy of Campora's dialogue, Carlo Dionisotti discussed the nature of the work and its intended readership.[35] The scholar stressed the absolute pertinence of Campora's *De immortalitate animae* to a mainly non-Latinate readership, acquainted chiefly with vernacular literature and living outside the scholarly milieus of universities and religious *studia*. Conceived as a handy compendium of the Aristotelian doctrine of the soul and adapted to the expectations of Christian readers, Campora's work and its reception throughout the fifteenth century bring together several of the threads that we have been following across the previous chapters, particularly the choice of the vernacular as a medium crucial to the dissemination of philosophical topics, and the active involvement of vernacular readership in both translation and reception.[36]

Born in Genoa around 1400, Jacopo soon entered the Dominican Order and later studied theology at Paris and Oxford, where he obtained his degree in 1432. After a short stay in Flanders, his presence is documented in the Genovese convents of San Domenico and Santa Maria di Castello during the late 1430s. Campora was then appointed bishop of the Turkish town of Caffa (today Feodosya, Ukraine) in 1441. Following political troubles with the Genovese government, it is only thanks to his good relationship with the Curia in Genoa that his removal was avoided. After the appointment of a temporary replacement, Jacopo moved back to Central Europe, where he engaged in the promotion of a crusade against the Turks. As part of these efforts, he went to Graz in 1456, where he delivered an oration to the emperor Frederick III, urging him, on behalf of the Christian bishops, to make peace with Ladislaus I of Poland and unite against the infidels. Since

---

[34] Giovanni Marcanova is mentioned in the 'Viaggio del magnifico Messer Piero Quirino gentilhuomo vinitiano', included in Giovan Battista Ramusio's *Navigationi et viaggi*; see the relevant passage in Milanesi (1983 vol. 4: 75): 'Il gentilissimo et d'ogni virtù ornatissimo M. Zuan Marcanuova venendo a mia visitatione, perch'io non potevo andar fuori, similmente mi strinse con grande affetto et amorevolezza, mi abbracciò' ('The very kind and most virtuous Giovanni Marcanova came to see me, since I was not able to go out; he embraced me with affection').

[35] Dionisotti (1962: 185–8). For a brief discussion of Dionisotti's identification of one of the books listed by Leonardo on a leaf of the *Codex Atlanticus* with Campora's booklet, see Refini (2015: 67–8).

[36] For an overview of Campora's biography, see Zapperi (1974); for a list of works and manuscripts, see Kaeppeli (1970 vol. 2: 310–11). More recent discussions of *De immortalitate animae* are in Refini (2015) and Sgarbi (2016: 25–9).

a new bishop of Caffa was appointed in July 1459, it seems reasonable that Campora had died some time before this year.[37]

Campora's most recent biographer dismissed the dialogue *De immortalitate animae* as an unpretentious work of 'mere edification' and 'popularisation'.[38] While it is true that the text is scarcely original in its arguments – in fact, the author endorses a strongly orthodox view about the immortality of the soul, where all the ambiguities of Aristotle's own position are solved by turning to the Church Fathers and the medieval interpreters of the philosopher – the work is nonetheless interesting when studied from the standpoint of translation and, more precisely, the intermingling of 'vulgarisation' and 'vernacularisation'. Introduced as the reporting of a supposedly real conversation between Campora and Marcanova, the dialogue reveals Marcanova's interest in a topic (the immortality of the soul) that played a main role in the medieval reception of Aristotelian philosophy, originating intense debates that would engage scholars for centuries.[39] Vernacular culture was affected by such discussions, which principally concerned the interpretation of Aristotle's doctrine of the soul in agreement or disagreement with Christian theology.[40]

Accordingly, Campora's main aim is to reassure his interlocutor that the human soul is indeed immortal. Drawing on Aristotle's *On the Soul* and other works by the Greek philosopher, the Dominican provides the reader with a compendium of Aristotelian doctrine of the soul filtered through other philosophical sources such as Cicero, Seneca, Boethius, the Church Fathers and the medieval commentators of Aristotle. Divided into twenty-six short chapters, the text follows a strict structure based on a sequence of questions and answers that never result in the truly conversational style that will characterise the rebirth of classical dialogue in the Renaissance. In fact, Campora's dialogue has little to do with the Platonic and Ciceronian models; rather, it follows the format made popular in the Middle Ages by works such as the *Elucidarium* of Honorius of Autun.[41] This twelfth-century dialogue on morals and Christian doctrine, which stages a pressing interrogation between a disciple and an instructor, was read widely across Europe, both in the original Latin and in the many vernacular versions

---

[37] Zapperi (1974: 581–3).
[38] *Ibid.*: 583.
[39] Di Napoli (1963: 21–120). For an outline of the medieval and Renaissance reception of Aristotle's *De anima* through Alexander of Aphrodisias' controversial interpretation, see Kessler (2011: 2–24); on the medieval interpretation of the *De anima*, see also Kretzmann, Kenny, Pinborg and Stump (1982: 593–654).
[40] For an overview of the discussions about the soul's immortality in the Italian vernacular, see Sgarbi (2016).
[41] On the *Elucidarium*, see Lefèvre (1954).

that circulated in manuscript and, eventually, print.[42] Given its structure (simple and repetitive but livelier than the regular format of a treatise), the *Elucidarium* proved extremely effective in providing readers with a basic knowledge of the topics covered. Similarly, Campora's dialogue addressed the question of the immortality of the soul with a sequence of arguments that would satisfy the curiosity of the reader. Moving beyond general issues such as the definition of the soul, Campora develops specific topics more directly concerned with Christian doctrine (for instance, the resurrection of bodies after the Last Judgement), thereby offering one of the earliest vernacular accounts of the doctrine of the soul. A veritable example of *translatio* in the wide sense of transmission and reshaping of knowledge, Campora's *De immortalitate animae* let vernacular readers access a complex philosophical topic, which was usually discussed and approached almost exclusively by Latinate scholars. Before exploring the afterlife of the work, which is characterised by a rich textual transmission in both manuscript and print, and which offers an instructive example of the transformative function performed by reception, let us dwell on a fundamental feature of the work, namely the author's staging of his interaction with his targeted reader.

Pressing the Master

As recalled above, the treatise was originally conceived for a specific reader, the Venetian merchant Giovanni Marcanova. The author addresses Giovanni, who had asked him to explain the reasons for the immortality of the soul, as someone 'inclined to read and listen to speculative and authentic subjects', thus pointing out the dedicatee's interest in philosophical topics.[43] By presenting the treatise on the soul, the author both reminds the reader of his acquaintance with the dedicatee and also highlights the nature of the text that follows. Because of the brevity of their conversation on the topic, Jacopo is now providing Giovanni with a more detailed account of the human soul based on a thorough consideration of the relevant *auctores*, philosophers and theologians, whose opinions are summarised and discussed in light of the Christian doctrine of the soul.

---

[42] The work had a wide circulation in Italy, where it was translated both from the original Latin and, as was frequently the case, from an intermediary French version; see Degli Innocenti (1979, 1982).

[43] Unless stated otherwise, quotations from Campora's *De immortalitate* come from the 1472 *editio princeps* (Rome, Giovanni Filippo da Lignamine; the copy consulted is Paris, Bibliothèque Nationale de France, RES-R-211); translations are mine. Here, prologue, fol. 1r: 'La quale cognoscendo essere desiderosa di legere et audire cose speculative et autentiche.'

The genre of the compendium was widely employed as a tool for didactic purposes throughout the Middle Ages and the early modern period. What makes Campora's *De immortalitate* a less conventional work, as indicated above, is that it was written in the form of a dialogue. As its author explicitly states, the dialogic form, which does not involve a truly dynamic exchange between the interlocutors, is based on a schematic sequence of questions and answers and follows an exegetical model that combines a simplified version of the scholastic *quaestiones* and the didactic structure of works such as the aforementioned *Elucidarium*.[44] The presentation of the treatise as a dialogue is thus a pretext to frame it within a structure that remains univocal despite its two voices.

Yet, and herein lies one of the most significant aspects of the text, the merchant sometimes engages in a methodological discussion that helps better grasp some of the cultural components typical of vernacular readership and the vernacular interest in philosophical works. The author, in fact, has Giovanni voice some of the concerns that inform the ways in which a lay interlocutor of the time would respond to the vernacular dissemination of philosophical topics. From the outset, the merchant shows a strong awareness of the issues implied by the theme discussed. 'Even though we do believe by faith the human soul to be immortal, I would nonetheless like you to tell me the philosophical reasons for this', Giovanni requests, echoing the important distinction between faith, which requires no rational demonstration, and philosophy, which does.[45] The question, as Campora explains, is a difficult one and led many ancient philosophers to doubt the immortality of the soul. The reason for their mistake was their ignorance of the human soul's nature.

Following the Aristotelian principle according to which one must begin a philosophical investigation by defining its object (a principle that, as we have seen, was also the premise of Mannelli's *Compendium*) Campora decides to start with a definition of the soul:

> Giovanni, you are asking something about which many ancients have debated at length and have made big mistakes, strongly believing that the

---

[44] *Ibid.*: fol. 1v: 'Voglio ordinatamente richogliere le sententie di philosophi et di theologi, le quali secundo mia estimatione sonno più evidente; et quelle in forma de uno dialogo tra te domandante et me respondente redurle insieme et farne un piculo libro' ('I intend to collect the statements of philosophers and theologians that, in my opinion, are undeniable. I will present them as a booklet in the form of a dialogue between the two of us, one making questions and the other answering'). On the tradition of the *quaestio* as well as on its argumentative structure, see Marenbon (1987: 7–34).

[45] Campora (1472: fol. 1v): 'Et ben che per inviolabil fide noi crediamo l'anima essere immortale, niente de meno vorroei [*sic*] che me dicisti le ragioni philosophice questo persuadente.'

human soul is as mortal as the soul of beasts; they made this mistake because they ignored the real nature of the human soul. So, if one is willing to know about the immortality of the soul, one has to proceed in an orderly fashion, investigating the nature and characteristics of the soul: for it is not possible to discuss in a proper way something of which the definition is unknown. Indeed, as Aristotle says, definitions explain and reveal the essence of all things.[46]

Thus Campora's compendium opens under the aegis of Aristotelian method. The merchant, by acknowledging that the theologian is better trained than himself in the method of philosophical enquiry, listens to him quietly.[47] The way in which the master proceeds is well exemplified by the definition of the soul given in Chapter 2, where Campora begins by offering a summary of the Aristotelian notion of 'anima' as a tripartite principle:

> You should know that this term 'anima' is Greek and means 'principle that produces life'. For this reason, all things in which a vital operation is seen are said to have a soul. We thus see three kinds of vital operation – the first is concerned with growing and multiplying, as is seen in trees and plants; the second is concerned, beyond growing, with feeling and moving as is seen in terrestrial and aquatic animals; the third, beyond moving and feeling, is concerned with reasoning and understanding. Accordingly, it is clear that three souls exist: vegetative, sensitive and intellective or human.[48]

After this clear statement about the three kinds of soul that animate plants, animals and humans, which provides an easy summary of Aristotelian psychology, Giovanni asks his master to dwell on the human soul. Campora

---

[46] *Ibid.*: fols. 1v–2r: 'Iohanni tu domandi cosa circa la quale molti antichi grandamente dubitando sonno caduti in grande errore: et in tanto che egli hanno fermamente creduto l'anima humana essere mortale come quella de li animali bruti: et questo errore divenero per non cognoscere la natura de l'anima. Unde vogliando cognoscere la sua immortalità conviene ordinatamente procedere investigando la natura et le conditione de l'anima, però che mai non se può ben tractare de una cosa, se non si sa la sua diffinitione, però che, come dice Aristotile, la difinitione explica et declara lo essere d'ogni cosa.' The reference to the Aristotelian epistemological value of definitions is to Aristotle, *Topics* 7.2–5.

[47] Campora (1472: fol. 2r): 'Ma tu che sei più exercitato in sapere il modo di tractare questa materia incomincia da quella parte la quale ti parà più convenevole et io starò ad audire cum patientia' ('Since you are better trained than I am in the way in which this topic must be treated, please begin by the part that you deem most convenient and I will listen to you patiently').

[48] *Ibid.*: fol. 2r–v: 'Unde sapi che questo vocabulo anima è greco et è significativo de principio operante vita. Unde in ogni cosa dove si vede operatione vitale, quivi se dice veramente essere anima. Et però che noi vediamo tre operatione vitale – l'una solamente quanto el crescere et multiplicare, come se vede ne li arbori et ne le piante; l'altra ultra il crescere, sentire et moversi localmente, come ne li animali terrestri et aquatici; la tertia oltra el movere et sentire ragionare et intendere – et per tanto manifestamente se comprehende essere tre anime: la prima vegetativa, la secunda sensetiva et la tertia intellectiva o vero humana.'

complies by providing his interlocutor with a series of eight definitions, chosen from pagan and Christian philosophers, that highlight the main features of the human soul, namely its incorporeality and immortality.

Christian doctrine here is reinforced by classical philosophy: John Damascenus' definition of the human soul is given alongside the definition taken from the second book of Aristotle's *On the Soul*.[49] The Aristotelian reference gives Campora the opportunity to clarify key concepts of Aristotle's philosophy such as 'substance', 'accident', 'matter' and 'form', thus introducing the reader to the traditional philosophical lexicon that was at the core of scholastic philosophy. As a corollary, shorter statements combining philosophy and theology (and which evidence the variety of sources gathered in the work) integrate John of Damascus' and Aristotle's definitions of the human soul. From Plato and Seneca to Bernard of Clairvaux, Augustine and Remigius of Auxerre, Campora not only displays an impressive command of the topic, but he also witnesses the productive interaction of cultural traditions as diverse as classical philosophy, Christian theology and medieval exegesis.[50]

If Giovanni's role as an interlocutor is usually limited to advancing the treatise by asking simple questions to clarify what has been said, in a few cases he does engage in more active responses to Campora's arguments. For instance, in the fourth and fifth chapters, devoted to the union of the soul and the body, Giovanni challenges Campora's account by listing three objections, as if he were engaging in a *quaestio*.[51] After explaining that the vegetative and the sensitive souls are subject to the matter to which they are connected, Campora argues that the human soul relates differently to the human body. In fact, the soul is the principle that coordinates the body, making it perfect. Giovanni's objections reveal his ability to master what he has learned so far. Based on Campora's earlier definition of the soul as an 'incorruptible substance', the way in which soul and body relate to each other now raises a threefold question for Giovanni. Given that the soul is incorruptible, would it not be better joined to an incorruptible body? Given its immateriality, would it not be better united with a bodiless material than the human one? And given that the human soul is more perfect than the others, would it not correspond better to a body more perfect than the human one? The theologian acknowledges that the

---

[49] *Ibid.*: fol. 2*v*; compare John of Damascus, *De fide orthodoxa* 1.12; and Aristotle, *On the Soul* 2.4, 415b 8–12.
[50] Campora (1472: fol. 3*r–v*).
[51] *Ibid.*: fol. 6*r–v*.

merchant's objections are sound and need to be addressed carefully so as to free his mind from further difficulties.[52] He thus devotes his fifth chapter to providing a detailed answer that will introduce the interlocutor (as well as the reader) to the argumentative gestures typical of academic debates.

A long preamble about the place of humans in the order of the universe leads to a discussion of the relationship between the soul and the body. By turning to Aristotle and Augustine, Campora presents the imperfect nature of the body as essential to sense perception, without which no human experience could be processed by the intellect. Similarly, his subsequent chapter develops the discussion of the relationship between body and soul and particularly focuses on the changes in this relationship over time. Of great interest is Campora's reply to Giovanni's question about the qualitative enhancement that will come to characterise the soul over the years.[53] Does the soul improve as the limbs of the body get bigger? The theologian explains that changes in the shape of the body (e.g., physical growth) have no connection to the improvement of the soul, the transformation of which is instead due to the exercise of virtue. Here Campora bridges Aristotle's theory of the soul and his discussion of virtue as a habit in the *Ethics*:

> The reason that the soul's improvement is due to time is explained by Aristotle in book 3 of *On the Soul*, where he says that our soul arises as a tabula rasa, a tablet on which nothing is depicted; later, after much practice, it gains expertise, and many experiences require a length of time. Hence Aristotle says in the *Ethics* that it is impossible for a young person to be wise, the reason for this being that, in order to be virtuous, one needs to be accustomed to virtue and the virtuous habit is only preceded by many actions: in fact, one single action does not produce the habit of virtue, as one swallow does not make a summer.[54]

Campora's argument focuses on moral education as a long-term endeavour, within which the acquisition of virtue is not given through theoretical

---

[52] *Ibid.*: fol. 6v: 'Iohanni tu movi una bona difficultà: la quale, a ciò non facia scrupulo a la tua mente, te la [s]cioglirò' ('Giovanni, you are advancing a good objection: in order to avoid that it trouble your mind, I will solve it').

[53] *Ibid.*: fols. 8v–9v.

[54] *Ibid.*: fol. 9v: 'La ragione che questo megliorare viene per longeza di tempo, dice Aristotele nel terzo libro de l'anima, che l'anima nostra nasce come una tavola raxa, ne la quale non è depincto alchuna cosa; ma poi per molti exercitii essa si fa experta; et molti experimenti rechiedeno l[o]ngeza di tempo. Unde in lo libro de l'Ethica dice che gli è impossibile uno giovene essere savio; et dice la ragione che ad ciò che uno sia virtuoso conviene che esso sia ben habituado in le virtù: et l'habito virtuoso conviene precedere molti acti, però che uno acto non fa né genera l'habito de virtude, come una arundine non fa primavera.'

knowledge but through the continuous practice of virtuous actions. Interestingly, the statement provides yet another reshaping of the same teaching that was at the core of Aristotle's tale from *Il Novellino*, discussed in Chapter 1.[55] Both texts, though in different ways, appropriate the Aristotelian notion of virtue as a habit that needs to be built with tenacity and that is not simply dependent on nature or reason.

Campora's dialogue develops the argument by suggesting that the moral improvement of the individual follows a pattern similar to language acquisition. The merchant asks the theologian why infants do not speak at birth. The answer, once again, is based on Aristotle, more precisely, on the philosopher's theory of language as an artificial convention built on the premise that 'words are signifiers' produced by 'natural instruments' (i.e., the physical organs responsible for the articulation of sound and voice).[56] By comparing the bodily production of the voice to the way in which a musical organ produces sound, Campora explains that while bodily organs involved in the process are naturally suited to produce vocal sounds, the articulation of meaningful words is not natural but, rather, the result of an art (language) that needs to be learned and practiced at length. If language were natural, all humans would speak the same one.[57] The acquisition of language is implicitly compared to the acquisition of virtue: language skills improve over time as is the case with one's virtuous behaviour. At the same time, the focus on practice and exercise as the only ways to master language entails that, at least in principle, there is no ontological difference between one language and another. The statement is particularly resonant if one considers the context in which it is proposed, that is, a pedagogical dialogue meant to translate a set of notions from the Latinate tradition of scholastic philosophy into the vernacular.

Elsewhere the merchant acknowledges his perplexity at issues that require philosophical acuteness, for example, man's likeness to God, a topic about which Giovanni wishes to know more. To satisfy his interlocutor's request,

---

[55] See Chapter 1, 35–6.

[56] Campora (1472: fol. 9*v*): 'la parola si [è] una voce significativa: la qual procede da li naturali instrumenti'.

[57] *Ibid*.: fol. 10*r*: 'la parola non è naturale al huomo … et sapi che se 'l parlare fusse naturale come ho dicto, cussì come tutti li huomini hanno una simile propria passione, come ridire in segno d'alegreza, piangere in segno di tristeza, cussì harebbeno un modo di parlare; et serebbe una loquela de tutti li huomini del mondo. Ma el parlare è una arte che se impara per longo uso' ('Words are not natural to men … You should know that if speaking were natural, as I have said about men having the same passions – such as laughing for happiness and crying for sadness – so they would share the same way of speaking, and all men in the world would have the same language. But speaking is an art that is learnt through long practice').

Campora approaches a most difficult theological theme, the Trinity, and points out the necessity of summarising relevant theological works for Giovanni, who is not a trained scholar. Moving from the passage of *Genesis* 1:26, where it is said that God made man in his image after his likeness, theologians such as Ambrose, Hilary of Poitiers, Boethius, Richard of Saint Victor and Augustine developed 'most ingenious arguments and most subtle discussions' relevant to the topic. In order to make these difficult materials accessible to his reader, Jacopo aims to reduce them to a brief account.[58]

Here, the main purpose of the compendium is even more explicit. After listing his points about the correspondence of the human soul to the divine Trinity, Campora prompts his interlocutor to content himself with the summary provided, for it is not advisable for a 'Christian merchant' to face the 'deeper sea' ('questo basti per non intrare in più alto mare').[59] This phrasing recalls the 'open sea' ('alto mare aperto') towards which Ulysses sailed in Dante's account of the Greek hero's last journey[60] – a detail that, by the way, resonates with the iconic value of Ulysses as a model for young merchants in Lazzaro Gallineta's commentary on the pseudo-Aristotelian *On Virtues and Vices*, discussed in Chapter 3.[61] In Campora's dialogue, the kind of knowledge suitable for a merchant is determined by the theologian, who decides how to reshape the philosophical and theological doctrines to present to his interlocutor (and, ideally, to his reading public). Giovanni, on the other hand, does not accept such limitations.

Claiming his right to be an active interlocutor, Marcanova recommends that his friend expand on the doctrine previously abridged for him. Giovanni also suggests that speakers who interrupt themselves when the subject is difficult by accusing their audience of ignorance are in fact ignorant themselves; and it is worth noting that preachers are presented here as an example of this objectionable practice.[62] After the ironic reference to the ignorance of preachers (all the more remarkable when one remembers the author of the dialogue is a Dominican friar and hence a preacher himself), the merchant stresses his own intellectual skills: since

---

[58] *Ibid.*: fol. 12r: 'Et ben che li sancti doctori, come Ambrosio, Hilario, Boetio, Ricardo de Sancto Victore et Augustino habiano facto libri grandissimi in li quali tu puoi imaginare che tochano ingeniosissime ragioni, et subtilissime discussioni, niente di meno io te redurò tutto il fructo de la materia in breve sententia.'

[59] *Ibid.*: fol. 13r: 'Tu poi donque vedere quanto basta ad uno cristiano merchadante de la trinità divina et de la sua imagine et similitudine in l'anima humana.'

[60] Dante, *Inferno* 26.100 (Chiavacci Leonardi 1991–7: vol. 1: 784).

[61] See Chapter 3, 121.

[62] Campora (1472: fol. 13r–v).

he has understood the theologian's arguments so far, he will be able to follow them further. Campora's defence confirms his attempt to make the discussion suitable for his interlocutor: 'I worried I might exhaust you with overwhelming words; but, since you are willing to listen, I will tell you more'.[63] Even though Campora agrees to expound upon the argument, however, he warns Giovanni against the difficult challenge that he is going to face: 'listen carefully to what I am saying and raise your intellect, for I will address a most demanding topic', where the Italian phrasing ('alza lo intellecto che io intrarò alto') once again recalls Dante's use of the image of the sea as a metaphor for knowledge and, more specifically, for the unattainability of metaphysical knowledge.[64] The 'alto mare' ('open sea') recalls not only the intellectual challenges posed by Ulysses' journey but also Dante's reflection in *Paradiso* 19, where the inscrutability of the deep sea symbolises the limits of human knowledge.[65]

Further evidence of Giovanni's response can be found in chapters 15 and 16 of *De immortalitate animae*, which attest to the reader's reaction to authoritative sentences extracted from the philosophers of the past. To strengthen his account, Campora devotes the fifteenth chapter to the 'sentenie dei filosofi' (literally, 'sayings of the philosophers'). 'Before addressing the philosophical reasons [for the immortality of the soul], I will first deliver some quotations from philosophers and theologians', says Campora, whose method of developing the topic is deeply informed by the notion of intellectual authority.[66] Sentences from a variety of thinkers (Greek, Latin, Arab and Jewish) are quoted here at random and without critical intervention from the compiler, so as to better prove his argument. Citations of Aristotle, Macrobius, Galen, Porphyry, Isaac Israeli Ben

[63] *Ibid.*: fol. 13v: 'Io temea de affaticharti de parole. Ma puoi che tu hai piacere de audire mai non mi stancharò de dirtti'.
[64] *Ibid.*: 'Apri adonque le orechie et alza lo intellecto che intrarò in alto.'
[65] The point is made by the holy spirits that, shaped as a luminous eagle floating in the heaven of Jupiter, talk to Dante and solve his doubts about divine justice; see Dante, *Paradiso* 19.58–63 (Chiavacci Leonardi 1991–97 vol. 3: 534–5): 'Però ne la giustizia sempiterna / la vista che riceve il vostro mondo, / com'occhio per lo mare, entro s'interna; / che, ben che da la proda veggia il fondo, / in pelago nol vede; e nondimeno / èli, ma cela lui l'esser profondo' ('Thus, the vision granted to your world / may make its way into eternal justice / as deep as eyes may penetrate the sea. / From shore they well may glimpse the bottom, / but not once out upon the open sea, / and yet it is there, hidden in the depths'). As is well known, the image of the sea ('mare' or 'pelago', in Dante's words) is recurrent in the *Divine Comedy*, suggesting not only the poet's carefully crafted intra-textuality, but also confirming his preoccupation with the relationship between morality, knowledge and human limits; see, in particular, *Inferno* 1.23 and *Paradiso* 2.5 for occurrences of 'pelago' that are meant to symbolise Dante's own journey from damnation to salvation.
[66] Campora (1472: fol. 19r): 'Et avanti che io venga alle ragioni, recitarò prima certe sentenie de philosophi et de theologi.'

Solomon, Averroes, Ptolemy, Plato and Cicero follow each other according to a format similar to that of the several medieval vernacular anthologies usually entitled *Detti dei filosofi*, compilations based on the Latin model known as *Dicta philosophorum*.[67] The merchant's response is once again remarkable: 'according to the sayings of the philosophers, one can see that it is not reasonable to think of the soul as perishable. Nevertheless, I am eager to know arguments grounded in reason and not merely in authority.'[68] Dissatisfied with bare quotations from the philosophers, Giovanni shows a genuine interest in a rational demonstration of the immortality of the soul. Once again Campora accepts his interlocutor's invitation and integrates his discussion with truly philosophical arguments, choosing among those that he believes more 'palpable', where the employment of this word reiterates Jacopo's benevolent prejudice against Giovanni's intellectual skills.[69]

The exchange between the Dominican and the merchant, despite the fictional nature of the narrative frame, reveals much about the interplay of scholastic culture and vernacular readership. As we have seen, Giovanni Marcanova embodies the prototype of the cultivated early fifteenth-century layman.[70] Like the other merchants that we have encountered in this book (Pancrazio and Bernardo Giustiniani, Giovanni Rucellai, etc.), Marcanova probably had basic knowledge of Latin but not enough to read philosophical texts on his own. Eager to improve his education, he represents the ideal target of contemporary vernacular translation. Campora, on the other hand, takes on the task of the translator as it was conceived in the later Middle Ages and the early modern period: far from being an activity simply concerned with transferring a text from one language into another, translation implies a variety of interpretive options that depend on the type of readers being addressed. When the readership is not conversant with the tools of philosophical inquiry, for instance, it would be insufficient to merely translate a philosophical tract into the audience's language, for the text would in fact remain difficult and in a format that is unfamiliar. Commentaries, in their various forms, were the preferred choice in order to explicate a text, but they were often as demanding as

---

[67] On the vernacular fortune of the genre of the *dicta philosophorum*, see my discussion of the topic in Chapter 4, 146.

[68] Campora (1472: fol. 23*v*): 'Per questo che fino qui tu hai dicto, assai si può vedere la convenientia che l'anima sia incorruptibile; ma vorrei audire qualche argumenti fondati suso la ragione et non pur suso auctorità.'

[69] *Ibid.*: 'Molti philosophi per argumenti hanno provato questo; et de quelli argumenti metterone qui alchuni, li quali sonno più palpabili.'

[70] See Labalme (1969), Gilbert (1979) and King (1986).

the works they aimed to explain and they required a specific set of skills that were acquired in university. Furthermore, commentaries did not usually circulate outside scholastic and intellectual milieus. The compendia, which covered a given topic by gathering relevant materials from various sources, were more successful than commentaries, especially among vernacular audiences.

If Giovanni Marcanova's response to Campora's account within the fiction of the dialogue is revealing of the vernacular audience's expectations, the actual circulation of the work, as we shall see, illustrates several disparate attitudes that informed vernacular readership throughout the fifteenth century and, more specifically, demonstrates the active contribution of readers to the multifaceted reshaping of the text that characterised its reception in the period.

Transformative Reception

As the textual tradition of Campora's *De immortalitate animae* suggests, the dialogue was successfully received by the vernacular reading public. It has survived in sixteen manuscript copies and nine incunabula. Though not comparable to those of the Latin translations of Aristotle, these numbers are impressive for a minor work of this kind and are significantly larger than those of the other works examined in the previous chapters. Of the extant manuscripts, eight can be dated with some degree of precision: the oldest is from 1448, whereas the most recent dates from 1484, with a significant number of copies realised between the mid-1460s and the late 1470s, partly overlapping with the production of printed editions.[71] The *editio princeps* appeared in Rome in 1472 and was followed by three editions in the 1470s and another four in the 1490s.[72] The case becomes even more interesting when we consider that its diffusion is limited to the fifteenth century. There are neither later extant manuscript copies nor any sixteenth-century editions.

---

[71] The sixteen manuscript copies of Jacopo Campora's *De immortalitate animae* are: Amherst, Amherst College Library, B.3.5; Amsterdam, Bibliotheek van de Universiteit, III.F.34; Bergamo, Biblioteca Civica, MA 84 [Delta II 32] (dated 1448) and MA 283 [Delta V 2] (dated 1471); Bologna, Biblioteca Universitaria, It. 157 (dated 1479); Florence, Biblioteca Nazionale Centrale, Magl. xxxv.144; Biblioteca Riccardiana, 2104 (dated 1469); London, British Library, Add. 10691 and Add. 22325 (dated 1472); Milan, Biblioteca Ambrosiana, MS Y 59 sup. (dated 1484); Padua, Biblioteca del Seminario, 162; Paris, Bibliothèque Nationale de France, Ital. 907 (dated 1464) and Ital. 910; Venice, Biblioteca Nazionale Marciana, It. II.137 [5254] and Lat. XIV.295 [4348]; and Venice, Museo Correr, Correr 315 (c. 1464).

[72] Campora (1472, 1475, 1477, 1478, 1494, 1497a, 1497b, 1498a, 1498b).

As usual, chronological data intertwine with matters of geography in the production and consumption of books. In this respect, it is worth remarking that most of the manuscripts were written in northeastern and central Italy, whereas the situation with printed editions is quite different. The 1472 *editio princeps* of *De immortalitate animae*, as we shall see, was the first vernacular book ever printed in Rome by Giovanni Filippo de Lignamine, a printer chiefly concerned with the publication of Latin texts. Another edition was printed in 1478 by Ottaviano Salomonio in Cosenza, undoubtedly a minor location in the production of printed books but important as a place specialised in the printing of vernacular texts.[73] More widely, though, the circulation of Campora's booklet was guaranteed by Northern Italian printing presses based in Lombardy (Milan and Brescia) and, not surprisingly, in the Veneto (Venice and Vicenza).

In spite of a rather narrow chronological frame (1430s–90s), the high number of extant copies confirms a wide range of material and paratextual typologies. Scripts, formats, layouts, as well as the functions of specific copies, changed throughout the decades, testifying to the mobility of the text. A variety of solutions characterises manuscript copies and printed editions. For example, among the sixteen manuscripts, six are miscellanies of moral or religious works in Latin and vernacular and ten contain the text alone. In terms of formats and layouts, some of the copies follow late medieval models, while other copies are indebted to the new humanistic vogue.[74] An even wider variety of solutions informs the rich series of incunabula that were published since the 1470s. The 1472 *editio princeps* is an elegant folio printed in a clear and stylish Roman type, whereas among the following editions (with the exception of the large double-column print of Vicenza from 1477) small-format books prevailed. This is the case of the easy-to-handle Milanese and Venetian editions of the late 1490s, printed in either Roman or Gothic type.

The variation of social and cultural identities that informs the transmission and the circulation of the text is particularly well-documented by the editorial choices affecting the paratext and, more specifically, the dedications of the various copies. By inspecting these editorial choices, it is possible to follow the afterlife of Campora's work as well as the progressive transformation of its initial shape, chiefly informed by scholastic and medieval components, into a pseudo-humanistic product. The ways

[73] Addante (2001: 35–6).
[74] To this category belong the manuscripts now in Amherst, Amsterdam, Bergamo (MA283), London, Paris, Venice (Correr 315).

in which a text such as Campora's was received and understood by readers during the fifteenth century testify to the multiple implications of translation practices in a period more varied in its trends than has usually been acknowledged. Initially conceived as a personal gift to a specific reader, the dialogue soon became, as we shall see, a text to be appropriated and, in a way, reshaped by other readers.

The presence of the *De immortalitate animae* in miscellanies of moral and religious works gives us a sense of the educational purpose of the work. In MS 2104 of the Biblioteca Riccardiana in Florence, for instance, Campora's dialogue is part of a large miscellany of religious works, most of which are in Latin.[75] The anonymous scribe who copied it in 1469, according to the explicit, was also responsible for copying Petrarch's most famous canzone, *Vergine bella che di sol vestita* ('Lovely Virgin, who, clothed in glory'), immediately after the *De immortalitate animae*.[76] As is well known, the concluding poem of the *Canzoniere* describes the spiritual outcome of Petrarch's love for Laura. The pairing of the two works suggests that in the eyes of the compiler, Campora's dialogue was first and foremost a work of religious doctrine relevant to spiritual matters.

A similar pattern in the reception of the compendium is indicated by two large miscellanies now in Bologna and Venice. Both were compiled in the 1470s and enlighten the reading habits of their owners. While we do not know anything about the identity of who wrote or owned the manuscript in the first case (MS 157 of the Biblioteca Universitaria in Bologna), the long sequence of works copied by the same hand is instructive.[77] Here, Campora's dialogue on the immortality of the soul appears along philosophical works, like an anonymous Italian translation of Boethius' *Consolatio Philosophiae*, and pseudo-philosophical works such as the *Fiore di virtù*; to the same kind of works focused on morality belongs a pseudo-Aristotelian Latin epistle to Alexander. More directly concerned with Christian doctrine are vernacular works such as the *Lucidario* (an Italian translation of the *Elucidarium* of Honorius of Autun, mentioned above), treatises on the sacrament of confession, one *ars moriendi* and a series of 'sayings' about the soul that follow Campora's *De immortalitate animae*. As is typical of similar collections, works of prose are mixed alongside a

---

[75] Florence, Biblioteca Riccardiana, MS 2104, fols. 3r–52v; see also Bartolucci (1915: 536–8), Kristeller (1963–97 vol. 1: 216), Kaeppeli (1970 vol. 2: 310).

[76] Petrarch's *canzone* 365 is copied at fols. 53r–55v and is titled 'Cançone morale de Misser Francesco Petrarcha da Fiorença in laude de la gloriosa Madona Sancta Maria'.

[77] Bologna, Biblioteca Universitaria, MS 157; see also Zambrini (1868: 121–36, 251–72), Mazzatinti (1898 vol. 15: 149–54), Fantoni (1955–56) and Kaeppeli (1970 vol. 2: 310).

variety of writings in verse, mainly poems about the lives of Jesus, Mary and the saints.[78]

Even more interesting is the evidence provided by the Venetian miscellany written by the Camaldolese monk Mauro Lapi, a native of Florence who spent most of his life in the convent of San Mattia on the island of Murano, where he died in 1478.[79] A prolific writer and collector of other authors' works, Lapi did not limit himself to transcribing texts, but also interspersed them with his own thoughts. The large-format MS Lat. xiv.295 of the Biblioteca Marciana brings us into Mauro's workspace.[80] After a preamble that introduces the collection, a detailed index of the volume reveals the friar's interest in works of Christian doctrine and spiritual education. Indeed, Campora's *De immortalitate animae* is in good company. Among the many works copied in the volume, a group of vernacular translations stands out and includes writings by Dionysius the Aeropagite, Hugh of Saint Victor, Anselm of Canterbury and Bonaventure.[81] The miscellany, which includes many writings on pilgrimages to the holy places (a theme of great interest to Mauro), gives us some useful information about Campora's dialogue. In fact, this is the only witness of the *De immortalitate animae* to refer to the composition of the dialogue in Bruges. The initial rubric also highlights the fact that the work was composed not only for Marcanova but also for merchants in general.[82] As suggested by the fact that Mauro was acquainted with Marcanova (their relationship is confirmed by a letter from the merchant to the friar copied in Lapi's miscellany), the details provided by Lapi's copy of the *De immortalitate animae* appear veracious.

---

[78] For a detailed list of the works included in the miscellany, see the description of the codex by Zambrini (1868), mentioned in the previous footnote.

[79] The figure of Mauro Lapi is still awaiting a thorough study; information about his life, career and works are available in Farulli (1710: 110), Degli Agostini (1752: 435), Mittarelli (1764: 272, 286, 299; 1779: 224–6), Zurla (1806: 81–2) and Tola (1838: 260). See, more recently, Barile, Clarke and Nordio (2006: 103, 206).

[80] Venice, Biblioteca Marciana, MS Lat. xiv.295 [4348]; see also Kristeller (1963–97 vol. 2: 270). On the manuscript as part of the original library of the convent of San Mattia in Murano, see Barbieri (1997: 25–6).

[81] In the manuscript, Campora's *De immortalitate* (fols. 96r–119r) is copied after a series of vernacular works including Hugh of Saint Victor's *On Perfect Charity* (fols. 54v–56v), *On Human Life* by Anselm of Canterbury (fols. 56v–57v) and Bonaventure's *The Goal of Divine Love* (fols. 58v–91v).

[82] Venice, Biblioteca Marciana, MS Lat. xiv.295 [4348], fol. 94r: 'Qui di sotto sarà la tavola del libro dell'anima di frate Iacopo Capra [*sic*] Genovese in volgare, fatto a Bruggia a riquisitione di messer Giovanni Marcha Nuova in dialogo, cioè parllare di due. E ancora per gli altri mercatanti' ('The table of the vernacular book on the soul by Friar Jacopo Campora of Genoa follows below; made in Bruges, at the behest of Giovanni Marcanova in the form of a dialogue, that is with two interlocutors; it is done to the benefit of the other merchants too').

Even if we lack many details about the people involved in the production of these manuscripts, the scattered clues they offer confirm that Campora's dialogue remained a steady presence in the libraries of both religious and lay readers throughout the fifteenth century. Evidence for this assumption is offered by other examples that indicate the ways in which the work circulated and was appropriated. In this respect, a curious case is offered by two manuscripts that we have already discussed in Chapter 3: MS 315 at the Museo Correr in Venice and MS Ital. 907 at the Bibliothèque Nationale in Paris, where the dialogue is copied alongside the Italian translation of the pseudo-Aristotelian treatise *On Virtues and Vices* by the Dominican Lazzaro Gallineta from the mid-1460s.[83] In these manuscripts, both produced in the same workshop, the two works are dedicated to the Venetian merchant Bernardo Giustiniani, whose name replaces Giovanni Marcanova's as Campora's dedicatee and interlocutor.[84] The fact that in one of the two copies Gallineta's translation is dated 'London, 1464' offers a *terminus ante quem* for the composition of the manuscript and is consistent with the presence of both Giustiniani and Gallineta in London in the mid-1460s. Since Campora had died before 1459 and had no documented relationship to Giustiniani, a plausible hypothesis is that the dialogue was re-dedicated to Bernardo without the author's participation (possibly by the person responsible for the making of the two Giustiniani manuscripts).[85] In these copies of Campora's dialogue, the theologian no longer converses with Giovanni but instead with Bernardo: if the social context is unchanged (the professional profile of Bernardo is in fact comparable to Giovanni's), the text is repackaged for a new individual. The reshaping of Campora's compendium, which employs classical sources through the lens of medieval scholasticism, is also concerned with the material aspects of the text. The two Giustiniani copies are beautiful examples of humanist scribal culture, very different from other copies of the dialogue that, as I have already mentioned, follow the layout and format typical of medieval manuscripts.

Different concerns inform other copies of the dialogue. The small-format manuscript now at the Biblioteca del Seminario in Padua, for instance, omits all the circumstantial details to which both the prologue and the interlocutors' names had alluded.[86] First, the author and the dedicatee are

---

[83] See Chapter 3, 113–14.

[84] Venice, Museo Correr, MS 315, fol. 1r: 'Comincia il prologo sopra il tractato de l'anima composto da frate Iacomo campora di Zenoa de lordine de frati predicatori essendo a Sonfort. A rechiesta di Missier Bernardo Iustiniano de missier Nicolo.'

[85] On the presence of Bernardo Giustiniani in London around 1464, see Brown (1864: 113–14); and Caracausi and Jeggle (2014: 163); for details about Gallineta's biography, see Chapter 3, 111–13.

[86] Padua, Biblioteca del Seminario, MS 162.

here given fictional names, Cariophilo and Philide. Second, references to the author's acquaintance with the dedicatee are removed from the prologue. Last and in keeping with the entire project, the two names are replaced throughout the dialogue. As confirmed by the illuminated initial, which represents a blessing saint, the dialogue is presented as a devotional text aimed at reassuring the dedicatee (who here is, significantly, a woman) about the immortality of the soul. Furthermore, the two names suggest religious meanings. Cariophilo, in particular, recalls the Latin name for the carnation (*caryophyllum*), a flower that was usually employed as a Christian symbol for immortality and resurrection, but it may also refer to *charis*, the Greek word for grace, thus standing for 'the one who loves Grace'. On the other hand, the name Philide – which is not, in fact, a reference to the courtesan who tamed Aristotle! – is that of a female character from Greek mythology whose tragic story was narrated by Ovid in the *Heroides* and the *Remedia amoris*, among other works. The account of Phyllis' myth in the *Heroides* was interpreted as a moral allegory during the Middle Ages and the choice of the name for the interlocutor in the Paduan manuscript is likely to refer to this tradition.[87]

Another manuscript, now in the Biblioteca Ambrosiana in Milan, evidences the assimilation of the dialogue with a strain of popular, edifying literature meant mainly for private reading and Christian education.[88] In this case, the text is dedicated in 1484 to an unnamed woman by Giovanni, a member of the distinguished Picciolpassi family: according to the new preface introducing the dialogue, the work is suitable for women eager to read and ponder topics relevant to both moral issues and 'salvific' contemplation.[89] This example, along with the previous ones, testifies to the considerable manuscript circulation of the work within communities of vernacular readers chiefly concerned with moral and religious edification, much indebted to the long tradition of devotional literature that enjoyed a steady fortune throughout the Middle Ages.

An even more striking example of the continuity of this tradition during the Renaissance is the manuscript copy of Campora's dialogue offered to the duke of Ferrara, Ercole I d'Este, in 1472. The manuscript, recorded in the 1495 inventory of Ercole's library, later entered the Costabili Collection, and eventually was bought by the British Museum (now in the British

---

[87] For an account of the medieval reception of Ovid's *Heroides*, see Hagedorn (2004: 21–46).

[88] Milan, Biblioteca Ambrosiana, MS Y 59 sup.

[89] *Ibid.*: fol. 2*r*: 'persuadendori quella delectarsi et prendere piacere in legere et volere intendere le morale et fructuose cose apertinente a la salutiffera contemplatione'.

Library as MS Additional 22325).[90] Written on high-quality parchment by the scribe Giovanni Trotti and beautifully illuminated by the painter Giovanni Vendramin, the copy was offered to the duke as a most precious gift by the Palatine Count Naimerio dei Conti from Padua. Format, layout, handwriting and decorations follow the most exquisite humanistic fashion of the time and deserve special attention, for they clarify the nature of the editorial project pursued by Naimerio.[91] The manuscript opens with a full-page miniature representing the fight of the Greek hero Hercules against the monstrous Hydra of Lerna [Figure 5.2].[92]

The scene is framed by an architectural structure that hosts several decorative elements referring to the House of Este: the biblical motto of the Este family, *A Deo fortitudo mea*, modelled on *Psalms* 42:2 ('tu enim Deus fortitudo mea'), is engraved on the architrave; the ring with the diamond and the carnation, emblem of the dukes of Ferrara, stands out at the top of the aedicule. A Latin epigram, written in golden letters on the base under the main scene, offers a clear interpretation of the image: 'Since many times the shining victory obtained the palms against you, how do you benefit from being ferocious? The great God, never defeated, will gain the heights of the Mount Olympus, while you – sultry Echidna – will grieve at the fords of Lerna.'[93] The short poem addresses the Hydra and praises Hercules' enterprise: whereas the monster will be defeated, the hero will reach the realm of the Gods. Despite the obvious onomastic celebration of Duke Ercole, the choice of the subject for the miniature is probably meant to suggest further associations.[94]

Given that Campora's treatise concerns the immortality of the soul, the representation of Hercules fighting with the Hydra seems to be an allusion to the struggle of the human soul with the body. The reference to the hero's

[90] London, British Library, MS Add. 22325. See also Bertoni (1903: 236); and Kristeller (1963–97 vol. 4: 109).

[91] The name of the scribe, Giovanni Trotti, appears in the colophon: 'De immortalitate anime opusculum in modum dialogi explicit feliciter per me Johannem de Trottis die 4 aprilis 1472 scriptum' (London, British Library, MS Add. 22325, fol. 62r). As for the attribution of the opening miniature to Giovanni Vendramin, see Baldissin Molli (1999: 281–2) and Mariani Canova (2009: 346). On Vendramin, see Bentivoglio Ravasio (2004). For biographical details about Naimerio dei Conti, see De Ferrari (1983) and Martellozzo Forin (1999).

[92] The image is reproduced in Saxl (1953 vol. 3: 16).

[93] London, British Library, MS Add. 22325, fol. 1v: 'Candida cum totiens referat victoria palmas / in tua damna, tibi quid iuvat esse feram? / Ille deus summum petet insuperatus Olympum; / torrida Lernaeis flebis, Echidna, vadis.'

[94] On the Herculean imagery in Ferrara at the time of the Este, see Tuohy (1996). 'Echidna' is the Latin name of the Hydra; cf. Ovid., *Met.* 9.69, 158. As pointed out by one of the anonymous reviewers (whom I thank for the suggestion), Ovid's passages might be the source for the use of the term in the epigram.

ADEO FORTITVDO MEA

Candida cum toties referat uictoria palmas.
In tua damna tibi quid iuuat esse feram.
Ille deus summum petet insuperatus olympu.
Torrida lerneis flebis echidna uadis.

Figure 5.2 London, The British Library, MS Additional 22325, fol. 1*v*.
From the photographic collection of the Warburg Institute, London

ascension to Mount Olympus would confirm this interpretation, which was common in the humanistic and neo-Platonic reception of Hercules.[95] Both Cristoforo Landino and Marsilio Ficino interpreted the labours of Hercules allegorically.[96] By building on a tradition well represented by Boccaccio's *Genealogia deorum gentilium* and Coluccio Salutati's *De laboribus Herculis*, humanism made the Greek hero not only a symbol of Fortitude but also an ideal image of virtue, wisdom and moral strength.[97] Antonio del Pollaiolo's *Ercole e l'idra* (as well as the same painter's *Ercole e Anteo*) testifies to the relevance of this tradition within the Florentine context.[98]

In the very same years, the designer of the iconographic program for the miniature that opens the Este manuscript of Campora's *De immortalitate animae* was likely to have had similar ideas in mind. According to the Latin epigram, Hercules is capable of defeating the fierce nature of the monster. Indeed, what distinguishes the hero from the beast is the employment of reason. Whereas the Hydra responds to Hercules' violence with inexhaustible violence of its own, it is only thanks to Hercules' human intelligence that he manages to vanquish the monster; burning the neck stumps after decapitating each head of the Hydra, he prevents them from growing back. Interpreters of the myth understood fire as an image of Hercules' wit, thus stressing the intellectual component of the hero in opposition to the bodily and vicious nature of the beast.[99] Given that one of the main topics developed by medieval readers of Aristotle's *On the Soul* is the distinction between the human soul and the soul of animals, the choice of Hercules' fight with the Hydra as an image to introduce the treatise may also be an allusion to this symbolic meaning of fire.[100]

The imagery of fire, on the other hand, plays a pivotal role in the painted scene: the illuminator represents the hero and the monster surrounded by flames, thus introducing an interesting variation on Hercules' enterprise,

[95] On the humanistic interpretations of Hercules in Florence, see Ettlinger (1972) and Wright (1994). For the general humanistic reception of the ancient hero, see Rossi (2010). For other sources relevant to the Christian allegorisation of the Herculean myth, see Simon (1955), Jung (2002) and, for further bibliographical references, see Rossi (2010: 177).

[96] For relevant passages in Cristoforo Landino's *De vera nobilitate* and *Disputationes camaldulenses*, see respectively Liaci (1970: 107–9) and Lohe (1980: 32). Marsilio Ficino mentions the Hercules episode in a letter to Giovanni Nesi of 1477: see Ficino (1576: 775).

[97] See Giovanni Boccaccio, *Genealogia deorum gentilium*, 13.41, in Zaccaria (1998 vol. 2: 1283–4); for Coluccio Salutati, *De laboribus Herculis*, 3.9, see Ullman (1951 vol. 1: 191–205).

[98] Ettlinger (1972).

[99] Boccaccio, *Genealogia deorum gentilium*, 13.41, in Zaccaria (1998 vol. 2: 1283).

[100] The difference between the human soul and the soul of animals is discussed in chapter 10 of Campora's treatise: Campora (1472: fols. 14v–15v).

usually described as having taken place in a watery setting. The relevance of the scene to philosophical discussions involving both moral virtues and doctrine of the soul was part of a tradition that includes Ficino's interpretation of the Hydra as 'concupiscendi vis' and the sixteenth-century employment of the image to represent the superiority of virtue over human passions.[101] 'Affectus virtute superantur' or rather 'Vinconsi con vertù gli humani affetti', as stated by the motto of the typographer Anselmo Giaccarelli, who chose the fight of Hercules with the Hydra as his mark.[102] Still in the Ferrarese context, one might also recall that even the iconography of Ercole II d'Este would privilege the Hydra episode. The scene, which had been represented on a medal offered by Pope Leo X to the Este on the occasion of Ercole's birth in 1508, became the visual component of the duke's own emblem, as witnessed by Achille Bocchi's *Symbolicarum quaestionum libri*.[103]

If the miniature testifies to the new implications embodied by the gift, Naimerio dei Conti's dedication letter to Ercole I draws attention to the role of the Paduan aristocrat as the 'editor' of the text. When introducing the work, 'a small book on the immortality of the soul and its definition', Naimerio highlights the 'authentic, Catholic and speculative' nature of the treatise, an ideal reading for the duke, who is portrayed as eager to read and listen to 'Catholic and speculative matters'.[104] Of particular importance, though, is the way in which Naimerio presents himself, for he claims that he has 'arranged the text and addressed it to the duke in the Italian vernacular'.[105] The ambiguous phrasing suggests an active involvement of Naimerio in the edition of the text itself: if we did not know that the treatise is a work originally written in Italian by Jacopo Campora, we might be led to think that Naimerio was the vernacular translator of a Latin text. Yet by repackaging Campora's dialogue as a gift to the duke, Naimerio does

---

[101] Ficino (1576: 775).

[102] For details on Giaccarelli's activity, see relevant records in the *Cerl Thesaurus* (record identifier cnio0020899) and *Edit16* (record identifier CNCT 354).

[103] See Bocchi (1574: 194–5).

[104] London, British Library, MS Add. 22325, fol. 2*r–v*: 'Mi pervene a le mane una opereta de immortalitate anime e de la sua diffinitione la quale per essere cosa catholica et autentica et al mio picolo iudicio assai speculativa … maxime cognoscendo el sublime e generoso animo di quella consueta e desiderosa de legere et audire cose digne et presertim catholice e speculative.' As a confirmation of Ercole's interests in speculative issues, it is worth recalling here that he was also the dedicatee of Cristoforo Landino's Latin dialogue *De anima*; see Paoli and Gentile (1915–17) and Rüsch-Klaas (1993).

[105] London, British Library, MS Add. 22325, fol. 2*v*: 'Accomodarla et dirigerla cusì in materno nostro idioma alla excellentissima signoria tua.' On the place of vernacular literacy vis-à-vis Latinate culture in Ferrara, see Celenza (2004).

indeed play the role of the *translator* in a way that is specific to contemporaneous notions of *translatio*.

Similar trends, far from being limited to manuscript culture, inform the circulation of the work in print as well. Campora's *De immortalitate animae* was first printed in Rome in 1472 by the Sicilian publisher Giovanni Filippo de Lignamine.[106] It was the fourth text ever printed in the vernacular in Rome and the first vernacular text printed by Lignamine, who, as has been noted, specialised in the publication of Latin works. The printer published the treatise in two sets: whereas in most of the extant copies the text is printed along with Domenico Cavalca's *Pungilingua* and, along with the latter, is dedicated to the printer's uncle, the abbot Matteo de Marco, a single copy now in the Biblioteca Alessandrina in Rome, provides witness to an autonomous edition of the treatise with a dedication letter to Antonio Basso della Rovere, one of the nephews of Pope Sixtus IV, the main patron of Lignamine's printing activity.[107] Both versions of the 1472 Lignamine edition (a beautiful folio of humanistic inspiration) inform us of the audience that the printer is targeting: although usually concerned with Latinate and erudite readers, Lignamine is here offering these vernacular works to a different kind of public.

The dedication to Antonio della Rovere aims to comfort the dedicatee after his mother's death, thereby implying a sort of personal homage. The Latin preface to Matteo de Marco addresses instead the question of audience. Campora's and Cavalca's works are meant to be read not only by erudite scholars ('eruditissimi ingenii') but also, and foremost, by common and unlearned people ('mediocribus quoque et idiotis animis'). These texts in fact aim at instructing men with no scholarly knowledge as well as, 'if it is allowed to say so', women ('indoctis viris et si fas est tantum dicere mulierculis quoque ipsis').[108] By building on the commonplace that, following Dante's theory of language, portrays women as the ideal audience of vernacular literature, Lignamine points out the relevance of works like those by Cavalca and Campora to readers very different from the usual addressees of his other Latin publications.[109] Women were actually among the typical recipients of devotional and religious vernacular works chiefly

---

[106] See Capialbi (1941: 27–8, 96–8), Farenga (1979; 1983: 140–2) and Alaimo (1988).
[107] Rome, Biblioteca Alessandrina, Inc. 364. See the two prefaces in Capialbi (1941: 56–9 and 96–8).
[108] Campora (1472: fol. 1*r*).
[109] For Dante's statement about the relationship between women and the vernacular, see Chapter 2, 57–62; and see Refini (2017).

concerned with moral edification, which enjoyed a steady success in the book market throughout the late Middle Ages and the Renaissance.

Another example of the reception of Campora's dialogue consistent with the cultural trends described above is the 1477 edition, printed by Giovanni Leonardo Longo in Vicenza for the jurist Matteo Pigafetta.[110] In his preface to the printer, Pigafetta, who is directly involved in the publication of the book, presents the work as highly useful for devotional and speculative purposes. By providing a summary of the treatise, the patron highlights those components of Campora's dialogue that are relevant to a personal and meditative reading. According to Pigafetta, the work, which is rich in authoritative statements collected from philosophers, theologians and Church Fathers, would deserve to be written in 'golden letters'. The passage provides insight into the way in which the target audience would receive a similar text:

> If you have this work printed, as I am asking you to do, plenty of people will have the opportunity to discover their own nature. Within ourselves, in fact, lies the treasure through which – if we are eager to – we can make ourselves citizens of the Heavens. This treasure is the intellect, which is a certain kind of substance affected by reason and concerned with the government of the body. The intellect, when enlightened by wisdom, looks at its own cause and it knows itself. By doing so, it manages to perceive the soul that, once completely freed from human affections, is able – through its inner eyes focused on God – to contemplate divine happiness. When the soul is steady and blessed thanks to this subtle, inner sight, it willingly keeps God within itself and, with extraordinary faith goes towards its Creator, with whom the soul rests, having reached its goal. We miserable creatures will learn thus our own cause.[111]

Campora's *De immortalitate animae* is thus received as a handbook to guide Christian readers through the understanding of their spiritual nature in order to save themselves and gain access to Heaven.

---

[110] On the printing activity of Longo, see Faccioli (1796: 97–105); on Matteo Pigafetta, better known as the explorer Antonio's father, see *ibid*.: 72, 98–9.

[111] Campora (1477: fol. *v): 'Ma se la fareti imprimere, come io ve ne prego, darasse oportunità a molti che cognoscano l'esser sua. Imperò che dentro a nui è celato il thesauro col quale possemo, vogliando, farse citadini del cielo. Questo thesauro è l'animo el quale è una certa substantia participe de rason acomodata a governo del corpo. L'animo illustrato di sapientia risguardando el suo principio cognosce si medesmo, inde pervene a l'intelligentia de l'anima: la quale poi liberata in tutto da ogni condition humana con li proprii ochi interiori fissi nel lume de dio contempla tutti i soi gaudii et securità. Facta adoncha lei secura et cossì beata col veder sotile: volentiera allora tene ella sé et dio dentro da sé: et cum una certa incredibile fiducia se ne va nel suo creatore, ove se ripossa come a suo determinato fine. Imparemo adoncha, o miseri, la causa nostra.'

What was presented to the original dedicatee as a summary of Aristotelian doctrine of the soul becomes, by the end of the fifteenth century, a booklet with explicit devotional purposes. The Rome and Vicenza incunabula testify to the pertinence of Campora's dialogue within this tradition and it is noteworthy that both printers, as far as their vernacular productions are concerned, focused on devotional works. Lignamine, who inaugurated his short catalogue of vernacular printings with Campora and Cavalca, also published Bartolomeo Maraschi's *Libro de la preparatione a la morte* ('Book on the Preparation to Death', 1473). The record of vernacular books published by Longo in Vicenza is even more impressive in its consistency: there was not only Francis of Assisi's *Fioretti* ('Little Flowers', 1476), but also the *Vita di Gesù Cristo e della Vergine Maria* ('Lives of Jesus Christ and the Virgin Mary', 1477), the *Memoriale di confessione* of Galvano da Padova (1478) and an Italian translation of Johannes Climacus' *Scala Paradisi* (1478). To this list, one could add the presence of the Italian version of the *Elucidarium* of Honorius of Autun in the catalogues of printers such as Uldericus Scinzenzeler in Milan and Battista Farfengo in Brescia, who also printed Campora's dialogue.[112]

A final aspect of the afterlife and circulation of Campora's treatise is the progressive reshaping of the title. Whereas the manuscript tradition is quite consistent in preserving the Latin title, *De immortalitate animae*, the printed editions introduce significant elements of change. Only three of them follow the original 'De immortalitate anime in modum dialogi vulgariter', which clearly provides the readers with basic information on the topic (the immortality of the soul), the literary genre (a dialogue) and the language employed (the vernacular). The 1477 Vicenza edition translates the title *Dialogo de la inmortalità de l'anima*, making explicit two important components. First, the work is presented first as drawn from philosophers and theologians ('extrato de theologia et de philosophia'). Second, it is described as having been 'vulgarizato dal excellente philosopho maistro Iacomo Camphora da Zenova del ordene de li predicatori' ('vulgarised by the excellent philosopher-*magister* Giacomo Campora from Genoa, member of the Dominican order'), where the term 'vulgarizato' – according to the many implications of the verb *volgarizzare* – may be understood either as translated or written in the vernacular.[113]

---

[112] Scinzenzeler published the Italian translation (in fact, a shortened version) of Honorius' *Elucidarium*, entitled *Lucidario ovvero Dialogo del maestro e del discepolo* in 1481, 1496 and twice in 1499; Farfengo published the same work in 1492.

[113] For an overview of the implications of the verb *volgarizzare* in the Middle Ages and the Renaissance, see Folena (1991).

The ambiguity typical of the late medieval and early modern notion of translation (where, as we have seen, the distinction between proper translation and various forms of rewriting tends to be blurred) informs other editions of Campora's dialogue.[114] In particular, the 1497 Milan edition introduces a new title that highlights the philosophical claims of the treatise: *Loica vulgare e philosofia morale composta e traduta da duo valentissimi loici e grandissimi philosofi in dialogo.*[115] The treatise on the soul is presented here as a vernacular work on 'logic and moral philosophy' written and 'translated' by two 'most skilled logicians and moral philosophers in the form of a dialogue'. Once again, the phrasing is ambiguous, for the word 'traduta' may suggest either the act of translating from one language into another or the wider notion of textual transmission. The idea of transmission, on the other hand, as well as the dialogical nature of the work is evoked by the woodcut that appears on the frontispiece of the same edition [Figure 5.3]. Two men of different ages (the older seated, the younger standing) are engaged in discussion; between them stands the figure of a third man holding a book and wearing a turban, while a fourth person stands behind the seated elder. The scene captures, in a way, the dialogical dimension of Campora's work suggested by the newly crafted title on the frontispiece. Indeed, the three main figures wear robes and hats that recall the features of academic garments, thus staging what could well be interpreted as a scene of scholarly interaction.[116]

As was usually the case, however, especially for cheap prints of this kind, the printer reused a woodcut originally made for another publication. The conversation piece (probably chosen to allude to the dialogic nature of Campora's *De immortalitate animae*) comes from Scinzenzeler's own edition of Francesco del Tuppo's vernacular translation of the *Vita Aesopi* (*The Life of Aesop*), printed later that year.[117] The adventurous life of the Greek fabulist, a work that circulated widely throughout antiquity,

---

[114] For a discussion of translation as rewriting, see Forrai (2018).

[115] Campora (1497).

[116] The man wearing a turban recalls the way in which Aristotle himself was frequently represented during the Middle Ages. See, for instance, the illuminated initials in manuscript copies of Brunetto Latini's *Tresor* where Aristotle is represented as an Arab: London, British Library, MS Add. 30024 (late thirteenth century, France) and 30025 (early fourteenth century, France). On the iconography of Aristotle that, during the Middle Ages and the early Renaissance, included both Arabic and Jewish features, see Del Negro Karem (2011).

[117] Del Tuppo's translation is now available in a modern critical edition by Rovere (2017), which also provides a thorough discussion of the Renaissance reception of the text (see, in particular, *ibid.*: 1–90). For the original woodcut, see *ibid.*: fig. XII. I wish to thank Serena Rovere for sharing her expertise on Del Tuppo before the publication of her edition.

Figure 5.3 Jacopo Campora, *Loica vulgare composta e traduta da duo valentissimi loici e grandissimi philosofi in dialogo*. Milan, Ulrich Scinzenzeler, 1497, title page (Florence, Biblioteca Nazionale Centrale, Guicciardini 20.2.70)

had a successful revival in the Renaissance. A servant in the household of
the philosopher Xanthus, the ugly and clumsy Aesop stands out for his
wit on multiple occasions, proving much smarter than his master. The
original woodcut used by Scinzenzeler for the frontispiece of Campora's
dialogue refers to one of the many episodes of Aesop's life. Caught in an
unfavourable bet by one of his students, Xanthus (who has claimed to be
able to drink all the water in the sea) seeks Aesop's advice. Thanks to his
servant's shrewdness, he manages to get out of trouble. In the illustration,
Aesop stands on the left, behind the philosopher Xanthus, seated on a chair.
The student and another character – likely a scholar – stand before them.
While the situation is vaguely similar to the narrative frame of Campora's
dialogue (hence the effectiveness of the iconographic reuse), the overall
meaning of the original scene overturns the pedagogical interaction staged
by Campora. In the episode from Aesop's life, the source of philosophical
knowledge is not the 'professional' scholar (the philosopher Xanthus), who
is easily challenged by his students; rather, the 'true' philosopher is Aesop
himself, the ugly servant. Even if it is unlikely that readers of the 1497
Milan edition of Campora's *De immortalitate animae* would deconstruct
the image on the frontispiece, this specific iconographic reuse invites us to
reflect on the multi-layered process of transformation that characterised
the afterlife and reception of the work.

Something similar happened with Battista Farfengo's edition, printed
in Brescia in 1498, the last to appear of Campora's *De immortalitate
animae*. The frontispiece, where the work is entitled *Tractato de l'origine et
immortalità de l'anima in theologia e philosophia morale utilissimo, composto
per valentissimi homini in dialogo e vulgare* ('Treatise on the origin and
immortality of the soul, most useful in theology and moral philosophy,
composed by excellent men as a dialogue in the vernacular') features a regal
banquet [Figure 5.4]. In the image, which seems to be also reused from
another printing, as yet unidentified, a king and a queen stand in front of a
table laden with food and are surrounded by courtiers, including a bearded
man with a turban on the right.

A dog in the foreground is eating scraps that have fallen from the
table. The frontispiece omits the references to the lexicon of *translatio*
present in previous editions. (In fact, the work is said to be 'composto',
composed, and not 'tradotto', translated.) The illustration, however, accidentally mimics and inadvertently subverts the image of the banquet as
the source of knowledge, which was, for instance, at the core of Dante's
reflection on vernacular learning. Dante's *Convivio* aimed at bringing
crumbs of wisdom to those who were not admitted to the banquet. In

Figure 5.4 Jacopo Campora, *Tractacto de l'origine et immortalità de l'anima in theologia et philosophia morale utilissimo, composto per valentissimi homini in dialogo e vulgare*. Brescia, Battista Farfengo, 1498, title page (Rome, Biblioteca Angelica, Inc. 477)

Farfengo's frontispiece, it is the dog who makes the most of what falls from the table, likely a biblical allusion to the parable of the Gentile woman who said to Jesus, that even dogs are allowed to eat the crumbs fallen from the table.[118]

As is the case with many of the images that we have encountered in this book, the woodcuts on the frontispieces of Scinzenzeler's and Farfengo's editions of Campora's *De immortalitate animae* can be read in different ways. Of course, one could argue that the printers' decision to use those images did not entail the meanings that my own reading has taken into account. If it is likely that both printers simply recurred to ready-to-use blocks that they had in their workshops, it is undeniable that, as soon as the book is published with a given woodcut printed on the frontispiece, that image becomes part of the text. As such, it is received by readers and joins the unpredictable series of responses that constitute the reception of the work. But whether or not these frontispieces are partly misleading when compared to what readers will actually find in the book, they capture the transformative process fostered by translation and reception.

The cases discussed in this chapter show that the practice and notion of *translatio* were not limited to translations in the strict sense of the word, but engaged more widely with the cultural transmission and appropriation of earlier sources. Mannelli's *Compendium moralis philosophiae* and Jacopo Campora's *De immortalitate animae* are most interesting examples of this phenomenon, not only for the way in which the authors appropriate the Aristotelian tradition through a Christian lens but also because of the multifaceted process of reshaping that informed the afterlives of both works. The history of their material circulation throughout the fifteenth century shows how texts deeply rooted in the medieval tradition were received and appropriated by different sorts of readers, as well as adapted to different purposes. Both works offer examples of the ways in which, through translation, a given text is presented according to changing cultural circumstances. Their textual transmissions, furthermore, capture the dynamics at stake when translation and reception are considered as part of a process that, as recalled above, is never final.

---

[118] *Matthew* 15:26–8. I wish to thank David A. Lines for suggesting the biblical source.

Conclusion
The Spirit in the Crystal Bottle

With our last example, this study has reached the end of the fifteenth century, when, among other factors, the advent of print deeply affected the vernacular book market.[1] In particular, the afterlife of Campora's *De immortalitate animae* unveils the outcomes of the complex process of translation that fuelled the vernacular reception of Aristotle. Through the case studies discussed in this book, we have seen Aristotle mounted by the witty courtesan; revered as the 'master of those who know'; appropriated by aristocrats and wealthy merchants who wished to legitimise their status or simply desired to know more about moral and religious beliefs. Not only did the Philosopher remain steadily present in the academic cultures of the later Middle Ages and the early Renaissance, but he also came to interact with lay, primarily vernacular, readers outside academia. Translated, reduced, adapted, transformed, Aristotle embodied the very idea of knowledge that, in different and concurrent ways, vernacular audiences across Europe aimed to share and make their own.

The vernacular readings of Aristotle examined in this study tell a story made of readers interested in the subject matter of the philosopher's works, particularly moral philosophy in its relation to Christian doctrine. They also tell us about the ways in which both translators and their reading publics engaged with the wider cultural, ethical and political implications entailed by linguistic transfer. The playful 'taming' of Aristotle performed by the courtesan in the *Lai d'Aristote* (Chapter 1) captures the tension between the alleged authority of Latinate academia and the increasing demand for philosophical knowledge to be dealt with in the vernacular. At the same time, the almost proverbial prominence of Aristotle among the *auctoritates* of the past, powerfully represented by the many portrayals of the philosopher as a venerable scholar, functions as a unifying thread that runs across linguistic hierarchies in the period. Within such a context,

---

[1] Along with Eisenstein (1979), see Richardson (1994) for a specific focus on the Italian situation.

rich in conflicts of culture and language, Aristotle was made to speak vernacular. As suggested by the examples presented in this book, the process was all but linear. Indeed, these examples show that the interplay of translation and reception, which has been the primary concern of this study, is productive exactly because, through its workings, it questions the idea itself of linearity. In fact, the narrative drawn here is not so much about the ways in which vernacular readers went back to Aristotle; rather, it is about the ways in which vernacular readings of Aristotle expose the very making of the philosopher's non-linear reception. More than looking at nexuses of cause and effect, I have explored the coexistence of different approaches to (and uses of) translation. I have also examined the ways in which, through both conflict and constructive interaction, those approaches contributed to the vernacular appropriation of Aristotle. Imbued with stimuli as diverse as those concurrently elicited by scholasticism, humanism, the legacy of classical antiquity and the emerging claims of vernacular culture, the readings of Aristotle that I have discussed in this book invite us to think about translation and reception as the very conditions for any form of cultural appropriation.

With the visionary and ambitious project outlined in the *Convivio*, Dante attempted to create a dialogue between academic knowledge and lay readership without diminishing the intellectual status of philosophical inquiry. More successful than Dante's endeavour (even with Dante's own intended audience), Taddeo Alderotti's and Brunetto Latini's bestselling translations of the *Summa Alexandrinorum* helped disseminate abridged forms of Aristotelian philosophy that remained a continuous presence in the libraries of vernacular readers well into the Renaissance (Chapter 2). Concurrently, fifteenth-century attempts to make Aristotle's 'real' *Ethics* accessible to vernacular readership – either through complete translations of the treatise, as is the case with Colombella and Nuti, or through selective readings, as is the case with Gallineta and Rucellai – shed light on the proactive nature of the readers involved in the process (Chapters 3 and 4). In fact, along with eclectic works such as those by Mannelli and Campora (Chapter 5), the examples explored in this book show that reception triggers and includes its own making. In other words, this study reveals that translation and reception come to coincide with their objects, which, deeply rooted in an unattainable past, only exist when translated and received at given moments in time. The examination of such process also shows that, when considered as informing each other, translation and reception raise questions about the status of language. Indeed, throughout my five chapters, I have demonstrated that vernacular readings of Aristotle were made possible by (and contributed to) the gradual establishment of the vernacular itself as an instrument capable of receiving and disseminating the philosophical tradition.

As indicated by polemics such as those between the humanists and traditionalists of fifteenth-century Florence discussed in Chapter 4, all this did not come without controversy. As a matter of fact, prejudices about language persisted throughout (and well beyond) the time frame explored here. Yet, without lessening the specificity of later cultures of translation, the seminal role played by the cluster of issues addressed in this study is confirmed by its early canonisation. The linguistic and cultural tensions that have been at the core of this book were mythologised in a text that works particularly well as an epilogue to the present study: namely, the *Dialogo delle lingue* ('Dialogue on Languages') by the Paduan philosopher Sperone Speroni (1500–88), published in Venice in 1542.[2] Usually interpreted as one of the benchmarks of sixteenth-century translation theory, the dialogue has, in fact, a retrospective tone that is better understood when the work is read against questions such as the ones addressed in this study.

In order to support the idea of the ethical value of the vernacular, one of the interlocutors ('lo scolare', 'the student') reports a conversation that he overheard, involving the Mantuan philosopher Pietro Pomponazzi (1462–1525) and the Greek humanist Janus Lascaris (1445–1535).[3] The two interlocutors embody two opposite positions: Lascaris is shocked to hear that a renowned professor like Pomponazzi, who is teaching Aristotle's *Meteorology* at the University of Bologna, reads the commentary by Alexander of Aphrodisias not in Greek but in Latin translation. Pomponazzi shocks his interlocutor further by stating that he wishes he could read the Aristotelian commentator, as well as Aristotle himself, in the vernacular.[4] According to Lascaris, who follows Plato's linguistic thought, a text should always be read in its original language, a recommendation based on the idea of ontological connections between objects and their names.[5] As an Aristotelian, Pomponazzi argues instead that no

---

[2] See the text in Pozzi (1988). On Speroni more broadly, see Bruni (1967); on the *Dialogo delle lingue* specifically, see Mazzacurati (1977), Sorella (1999) and Cotugno (2019).

[3] Pozzi (1988: 320–31). On Lascaris, see Ceresa (2004); for an introduction to Pomponazzi, see Pine (1986).

[4] Pozzi (1988: 321).

[5] Lascaris supports his opinion by referring to Plato's *Cratylus*. See Pozzi (1988: 324–5): 'Diverse lingue sono atte a significare diversi concetti, alcune i concetti d'i dotti, alcune altre degl'indotti. La greca veramente tanto si conviene con le dottrine che a dover quelle significare natura istessa, non umano provedimento, pare che l'abbia formata; e se creder non mi volete, credete almeno a Platone, mentre ne parla nel suo *Cratillo*' ('Different languages are suitable for expressing different notions: some languages are able to express ignorant people's mind, some others fit in with erudite matters. Greek

language is 'natural', but all are the result of human conventions: as such, they are all equal.[6] In Pomponazzi's opinion, what matters is not eloquence or the alleged quality of a given language, but, rather, the communicability of subject matter. Instead of spending years in studying Greek, Latin and Hebrew, students should be trained to use their mother tongue to philosophise. Only by committing to philosophy from a young age will they be able to equal or even surpass the masters of antiquity.[7] By endorsing a position that recalls the anti-humanist polemic caused by the advocates of the *volgare* in early fifteenth-century Florence, Speroni's depiction of Pomponazzi aims to make a point about the use of language that proves even more radical than that of Domenico da Prato.[8]

Not only does Pomponazzi criticise the humanist devotion to Greek and Latin, but he also opposes the prominence of Tuscan among the Italian vernaculars, which he clearly perceives as yet another form of cultural dominance.[9] By idolising the literary language of Dante, Petrarch and Boccaccio, the supporters of the vernacular have *de facto* appropriated the humanists' conceptual approach to language, making Tuscan the new Latin. On the contrary, Pomponazzi's defence of the vernacular rejects the assumption that one given language needs to be stylistically refined, vetted and approved by self-proclaimed censors in order to be on par with those languages that, in virtue of their historical priority, have been already canonised. Vernacular languages ought instead to be

---

is so suitable for the expression of philosophical issues that it seems to be a creation of nature itself rather than a mere human convention: if you don't wish to agree with me, trust what Plato says about language in his dialogue *Cratylus*'; here and in the following citations, my trans.).

[6] Pomponazzi's reply to Lascaris' Platonic manifesto is blunt. See *ibid.*: 325: 'Più tosto vo' credere ad Aristotile e alla verità, che lingua alcuna del mondo (sia qual si voglia) non possa aver da sé stessa privilegio di significare i concetti del nostro animo, ma tutto consista nello arbitrio delle persone' ('I rather trust Aristotle when he says that no language has a sort of natural privilege in expressing our thoughts. Everything connected with language resides instead in human will').

[7] This argument too became a trope in debates over language and, more specifically, over the use of the vernacular and similar statements are found in works by Varchi and Piccolomini; see Refini (2009: 33–84).

[8] See Chapter 4, 135–40.

[9] Pozzi (1988: 322–3): 'noi altri moderni viviamo indarno gran tempo, consumando la miglior parte de' nostri anni … porto ferma oppenione che lo studio della lingua greca e latina sia cagione dell'ignoranzia, ché se 'l tempo, che intorno ad esse perdiamo, si spendesse da noi imparando filosofia, per avventura l'età moderna genererebbe quei Platoni e quegli Aristotili, che produceva l'antica. Ma noi … altro non facciamo diece e venti anni di questa vita che imparare a parlare chi latino, chi greco e alcuno (come Dio vuole) toscano' ('we modern people usually waste the best years of our lives … I thus believe that the study of Greek and Latin is the cause of our ignorance. If we spent more time in studying philosophy rather than learning Greek and Latin, our modern age would give birth to those Platos and Aristotles, whom the ancient times generated. We instead … spend ten or twenty years of our life in learning Greek, Latin and – as pleases God – occasionally Tuscan'). The terms and methodology that inform the controversy recall those that characterised the dispute between Ermolao Barbaro and Giovanni Pico della Mirandola; cf. McLaughlin (1996: 239–48).

preferred and used because of their immediacy, no matter their specific features. If Pomponazzi appears primarily concerned with the use of the vernacular in academia, his argument soon widens to include a broader reflection on the linguistic accessibility of knowledge. By arguing that Athenians and Romans were native speakers of Greek and Latin, respectively, as much as Italians are native speakers of their own vernaculars, Pomponazzi implies that the legitimation of the vernacular would lead to the dissemination of knowledge beyond the boundaries of academia.[10] The philosopher's statement worries Lascaris, who cannot help voicing a disquieting prospect:

> While you were talking like that, I was thinking about Aristotle's philosophy being written and discussed in Lombard among all sorts of miserable people such as porters, farmers, boatmen and others speaking with the strangest accents I have ever heard. In the meantime, I visualised in my mind mother Philosophy herself, wearing poor clothes from Romagna and complaining of Aristotle's disdain for her excellence. I imagined Aristotle as well, who denied having disregarded her and declared instead his love for her and that he had always treated her honourably in his writings. He stated to have been living as a Greek, not as an Italian from Brescia or Bergamo. That is why he wrote philosophical works in Greek. According to him, people thinking it different are undoubtedly lying.[11]

Speroni's account of Lascaris' response to Pomponazzi is, needless to say, ironically provocative. Not only does the humanist dread the event, obviously unlikely, that 'miserable people' would discuss Aristotle's philosophy in the streets, but he also pictures Lady Philosophy herself, poorly dressed, complaining about the debasement to which the vernacularisation of Aristotle has condemned her. Lascaris' vision recalls the tale from the *Novellino* that I have discussed in Chapter 1, in which the 'goddesses of science' appear in a dream to a philosopher 'who was much given to

[10] Pozzi (1988: 327): 'non pur a' dotti ma a' forsennati Ateniesi e Romani solea parlare eloquentemente Cicerone e Demostene, e era inteso da loro' ('Cicero and Demosthenes, who used to speak eloquently, did not address themselves just to erudite people: dull people among Athenians and Romans did understand them as well').

[11] *Ibid.*: 327–8: 'Mentre voi parlavate così, io imaginava di vedere scritta la filosofia d'Aristotile in lingua lombarda, e udirne parlare tra loro ogni vile maniera di gente, facchini, contadini, barcaroli e altre tali persone con certi suoni e con certi accenti, i più noiosi e i più strani che mai udissi alla vita mia. In questo mezo mi si parava dinanzi essa madre filosofia, vestita assai poveramente di romagnolo, piangendo e lamentandosi d'Aristotile che disprezzando la sua eccellenza l'avesse a tale condotta e minacciando di non volere star più in terra, sì bello onore ne le era fatto dalle sue opere; il quale, iscusandosi con esso lei, negava d'averla offesa giamai, sempremai averla amata e lodata, né meno che orrevolmente averne scritto o parlato mentre egli visse, lui esser nato e morto greco, non bresciano né bergamasco, e mentire chi dir volesse altramente.'

vulgarising science' to warn him of such a debasing practice.[12] If the trope is indeed the same, Lascaris' rephrasing of the bias against the use of the vernacular to discuss philosophical and scientific matters is supported by the tautological statement that, as a Greek, Aristotle wrote his works in Greek, hence the reader's necessity to master Greek in order to be able to read Aristotle. Lascaris' opinion entails the negation itself of translation as a tool for the transfer of knowledge, thus adding yet another layer to concurrent debates about translation theory and practice. In fact, Speroni's portrayal of Lascaris outlines a position that both fails to acknowledge the status of the vernacular and differs significantly from the strong belief in translation that had informed Latin humanism throughout the fifteenth century. Lascaris' rejection of Pomponazzi's defence of the vernacular is only one facet of a much more complex situation, one in which Greek humanism (the cultural weight of which had been increasing in Italy in the second half of the fifteenth century) was claiming its own space vis-à-vis Latin humanism.[13]

Only by considering these implications is it possible to grasp the striking contrast between the two interlocutors in Speroni's dialogue. On one hand, Lascaris embodies a position that is even more radical than the one expressed by humanists like Leonardo Bruni. According to the Greek scholar, the only way to access a text is to read it in its original language, as a given author's thought can only be fully appreciated in the language in which it was conceived. On the other hand, Pomponazzi radically overturns the idea that language per se matters. Indeed, Speroni makes Pomponazzi claim that language only matters as a tool for immediate communication, hence the crucial importance of translation as a way to overcome the difficulties posed by the variety of languages.[14] Lady Philosophy should not complain about people reading Aristotle in the vernacular. This does not diminish her prestige; rather, her being made vernacular makes her even more praiseworthy than before.[15] As Pomponazzi puts it, languages were created 'in order to let us communicate and reach the happiness which lies in knowledge itself, not in the mere sound of words'. Eventually, the philosopher continues, 'human beings shall write and speak in the way

---

[12] For the novella, see Conte (2001: 31–2); see also Chapter 1, 37–8.

[13] On the specificity of Greek scholarship within the larger picture of Renaissance humanism, see Ciccolella (2008) and Ciccolella and Silvano (2017).

[14] Similar positions are upheld by several sixteenth-century authors. Of particular interest with respect to the role of translation as a catalyst for the development of the vernacular is Alessandro Citolini's *Lettera in difesa della lingua vorgare* (Letter in Defense of the Vulgar Tongue, 1540); see Refini (2017: 55–7).

[15] Pozzi (1988: 328).

that is closer to nature, which means using the language they naturally learnt as children'.[16]

Pomponazzi's criticism of his opponent's views on language could not be harsher. Humanists such as Lascaris, he argues, believed that, in order to be good philosophers, it is enough to master Greek, 'as if Aristotle's soul, like a spirit in a crystal bottle, resided in the Greek alphabet and inspired them by means of Greek letters'.[17] By criticising the humanist veneration for the language of the ancients, Pomponazzi suggests that humanists (who vehemently attacked the notion of *auctoritas* embodied by the scholastic Aristotle) simply replaced one category of authority with another. Their belief in eloquence as the key to knowledge is, according to Pomponazzi, pointless, for many of them, despite their excellent expertise in the languages of the ancients, are incapable of mastering the philosophical subject matter of the authors on which they are lecturing. Furthermore, by rejecting the vernacular and, more specifically, vernacular translation, they prevent knowledge from being shared widely:

> I saw many [scholars] who, completely lacking in philosophical know-ledge and only trusting their language skills, dared to publicly lecture on Aristotle's books as if the field to which these works belong didn't matter. In their opinion, translations of Aristotelian works from Greek into the ver-nacular would be a waste of time … for they do not care to be understood by many people … When philosophers use the same language common people employ, sciences and philosophy will become of common know-ledge, since their value is not in words but in human intellects.[18]

Even if Speroni's characterisation of Pomponazzi cannot be taken at face value, the point made by Pomponazzi within the fiction of the dialogue

---

[16] *Ibid.*: 328–9: 'Le scritture e i linguaggi essere stati trovati … a utilità e commodità nostra, accioché … più facilmente conseguiamo la nostra propria felicità, la quale è posta nell'intelletto delle dottrine, non nel suono delle parole … così ora esser meglio che l'uomo scriva e ragioni nella maniera che men si scosta dalla natura; la qual maniera di ragionare appena nati impariamo e a tempo quando altra cosa non semo atti ad apprendere.'

[17] *Ibid.*: 330–1: 'Non altramente che se lo spirito d'Aristotile, a guisa di folletto in cristallo, stesse rinchiuso nell'alfabeto di Grecia, e con lui insieme fosse costretto d'entrar loro nell'intelletto a fargli profeti.'

[18] *Ibid.*: 331: 'molti n'ho già veduti a' miei giorni sì arroganti che, privi in tutto d'ogni scienza, confidandosi solamente nella cognizion della lingua, hanno avuto ardimento di por mano a' suoi libri, quelli a guisa degli altri libri d'umanità publicamente esponendo. Dunque, a costoro il far volgari le dottrine di Grecia parrebbe opra perduta … vana istimando la impresa dello scrivere e del parlare in maniera che non l'intendano gli studiosi di tutto 'l mondo … [S]e la forma delle parole, onde i futuri filosofi ragioneranno e scriveranno delle scienzie, sarà comune alla plebe, l'intelletto e il sentimento di quelle sarà proprio degli amatori e studiosi delle dottrine, le quali hanno ricetto non nelle lingue ma negli animi d'i mortali.'

witnesses a key moment in the vernacular reception of Aristotle that we have been following in this book.

Far from being a viable option at the time, the idea of turning to the vernacular in academic contexts was potentially disruptive (suffice it to recall Galileo Galilei's experience less than one century later).[19] Ascribed by Speroni to Pomponazzi, who was trained in the stronghold of scholastic Aristotelianism, the idea that knowledge should be dealt with in one's mother tongue challenged the academic establishment, both the traditional structures of universities and the classicising attitude of humanists, which, in different ways, contributed to keep the 'spirit' *in* the 'crystal bottle'. And yet, Speroni's depiction of Pomponazzi's desire to have philosophers use the language of 'common people' does share the preoccupations that were at the core of the case studies presented in this book. Since Dante's appeal to the targeted audience of the *Convivio* ('noble persons … princes, barons, knights and many other noble people, not only men but women, of which there are many in this language who know only the vernacular and are not learned')[20] and through the various examples that I have explored here, the main aim of vernacular literacy was not to let 'porters, farmers and boatmen' discuss Aristotle's works. Rather, the idea of accessing Aristotle in the vernacular (or, depending on the point of view, the idea of making him speak in the vernacular) hinged upon the attempt to avoid hypostatising the past so as to make it live in and be relevant to the present.

---

[19] On Galileo's commitment to the vernacular, see Celenza (2018: 401–4).
[20] Dante, *Convivio*, I.9.5.

Bibliography

Adão da Fonseca, Luís (ed.) (1975) *Obras completas do Condestável Dom Pedro de Portugal*. Lisbon, Fundação Calouste Gulbenkian.

Addante, Luca (2001) *Cosenza e i cosentini: Un volo lungo tre millenni*. Soveria Mannelli, Rubbettino.

Alaimo, Carmelo (1988) 'De Lignamine (Del Legname, La Legname, o Legname), Giovanni Filippo', *Dizionario Biografico degli Italiani* Vol. 36: 643–7.

Albanese, Gabriella (ed.) (2014) Dante Alighieri, *Egloge*, in *Opere. 2. Convivio; Monarchia; Epistole; Egloge*. Milan, Mondadori: 1595–783.

Albertazzi, Marco (ed.) (2002) Cecco d'Ascoli, *L'Acerba: Acerba etas*. Lavis, La Finestra.

Albertini Ottolenghi, Maria Grazia (1991) 'La biblioteca dei Visconti e degli Sforza: gli inventari del 1488 e del 1490', *Studi Petrarcheschi* Vol. 8: 1–238.

Alonso, Carlos (1977) 'Antonio de Recanati, O.S.A., obispo de Senigallia, 1447–1466', *Analecta Augustiniana* Vol. 11: 197–222.

(1982) 'Colombella, Antonio', *Dizionario Biografico degli Italiani* Vol. 27: 131–4.

Ardizzone, Maria Luisa (2016) *Reading as the Angels Read: Speculation and Politics in Dante's 'Banquet'*. Toronto, University of Toronto Press.

Ascoli, Albert Russell (2007) 'From *Auctor* to Author: Dante before the *Commedia*', in *The Cambridge Companion to Dante*, ed. Rachel Jacoff. Cambridge, Cambridge University Press: 46–66.

(2008) *Dante and the Making of a Modern Author*. Cambridge, Cambridge University Press.

Auerbach, Erich (1965) *Literary Language and its Public in Late Latin Antiquity and in the Middle Ages*. New York, Pantheon Books.

Auzzas, Ginetta (2014) 'Passavanti, Jacopo', *Dizionario biografico degli italiani* Vol. 81: 626–9.

Bacchini, Lorenzo Filippo (2016) 'Acciaiuoli, Donato', in *Encyclopedia of Renaissance Philosophy*, ed. Marco Sgarbi. Cham, Springer [https://doi.org/10.1007/978-3-319-02848-4].

Baker, Patrick (2015) *Italian Renaissance Humanism in the Mirror*. Cambridge, Cambridge University Press.

Baldassarri, Stefano U. (ed.) (1994) Leonardo Bruni, *Dialogi ad Petrum Paulum Histrum*. Florence, Leo S. Olschki.

(2003) *Umanesimo e traduzione: tra Petrarca e Manetti*. Cassino, Università di Cassino, 2003.

Baldissin Molli, Giovanna (ed.) (1999) *La miniatura a Padova dal Medioevo al Settecento*. Modena, Franco Cosimo Panini.

Baratto, Mario (1993) *Realtà e stile nel Decameron*. Rome, Editori Riuniti.

Barbieri, Edoardo (1997) 'Produrre, conservare, distruggere: per una storia dei libri e della biblioteca di S. Mattia di Murano', *L'Ateneo Veneto* Vol. 184, n.s. 35: 13–55.

Barile, Elisabetta, Paula C. Clarke and Giorgia Nordio (2006) *Cittadini veneziani del Quattrocento. I due Giovanni Marcanova, il mercante e l'umanista*. Venice, Istituto Veneto di Scienze, Lettere ed Arti.

Barolini, Teodolinda (1984) *Dante's Poets: Textuality and Truth in the Comedy*. Princeton, Princeton University Press.

Baron, Hans (ed.) (1928) Leonardo Bruni, *Humanistisch-philosophische Schriften*. Leipzig, B.G. Teubner.

Barrette, Paul and Spurgeon Baldwin (transl.) Brunetto Latini (1993), *The Book of the Treasure (Li Livres dou Tresor)*. New York, Garland.

Barsella, Susanna (2012) 'I *marginalia* di Boccaccio all'*Etica Nicomachea* di Aristotele (Milano, Biblioteca Ambrosiana A 204 Inf.)', in *Boccaccio in America*, ed. Elsa Filosa and Michael Papio. Ravenna, Longo: 143–55.

Bartolucci, Costantino (1915) 'Legenda B. Galeoti Roberti de Malatestis Tertii Ordinis S. Francisci (1411–1432)', *Archivum Franciscanum Historicum* Vol. 8: 532–57.

Batstone, William W. (2006) 'Provocation: The Point of Reception Theory', in *Classics and the Uses of Reception*, ed. Martindale and Thomas: 14–26.

Battaglia Ricci, Lucia (2001) 'Il commento illustrato alla "Commedia": schede di iconografia trecentesca', in *Per correr miglior acque: bilanci e prospettive degli studi danteschi alle soglie del nuovo millennio*. Rome, Salerno editrice: 601–39.

(2008) 'La tradizione iconografica della *Commedia*', in *Dante e la fabbrica della* Commedia, ed. Alfredo Cottignoli, Donatino Domini and Giorgio Gruppioni. Ravenna, Longo: 239–54.

Battista, Gabriella (ed.) (2013) Giovanni di Pagolo Rucellai, *Zibaldone*. Florence, SISMEL – Edizioni del Galluzzo.

Bausi, Francesco (1999) 'Gli spiriti magni. Filigrane aristoteliche e tomistiche nella decima giornata del *Decameron*', *Studi sul Boccaccio* Vol. 27: 205–53.

Baxter, Catherine Elizabeth (2013) '*Turpiloquium* in Boccaccio's tale of the goslings (*Decameron*, day IV, introduction)', *The Modern Language Review* Vol. 108, No. 3: 812–38.

Bec, Christian (1967) *Les Marchands écrivains: affaires et humanism à Florence (1375–1434)*. Paris, Mouton.

(1984) *Les livres des Florentins (1413–1608)*. Florence, Leo S. Olschki.

Belloni, Gino (ed.) (1982) Matteo Palmieri, *Della vita civile*. Florence, Sansoni.

Belloni, Luigi and Letizia Vergnano (1960) 'Alderotti, Taddeo', *Dizionario biografico degli italiani* Vol. 2: 85.

Bellosi, Luciano and Margaret Haines (1999) *Lo Scheggia*. Florence, Maschietto & Musolino.

Beltrami, Pietro, Paolo Squillacioti, Plinio Torri and Sergio Vatteroni (eds.) (2007) Brunetto Latini, *Tresor*. Turin, Einaudi.

Benedetti, Roberto (1988) 'Pulcerrime codex! Il ms. Correr 1493 (Roman d'Alexandre) del Museo Correr', in *Una città e il suo museo. Un secolo e mezzo di collezioni civiche veneziane*. Venice, Museo Correr: 123–42.

Bénédictins du Bouveret (eds.) (1965–82) *Colophons de manuscrits occidentaux des origines au XVIe siècle*. Fribourg, Editions universitaires.

Bentivoglio Ravasio, Beatrice (2004) 'Vendramin, Giovanni', in *Dizionario Biografico dei Miniatori Italiani: Sec. IX–XVI*, ed. Milvia Bollati. Milan, Bonnard: 982–7.

Bertelli, Sandro (2002) *I manoscritti della letteratura italiana delle origini. Firenze, Biblioteca Nazionale Centrale*. Florence, SISMEL – Edizioni del Galluzzo.

(2008) 'Tipologie librarie e scritture nei più antichi codici fiorentini di ser Brunetto', in *A scuola con ser Brunetto*, ed. Maffia Scariati: 213–53.

(2011) *I manoscritti della letteratura italiana delle origini: Firenze, Biblioteca Medicea Laurenziana*. Florence, SISMEL – Edizioni del Galluzzo.

Bertelli, Sergio, Nicolai Rubinstein and Craig Hugh Smyth (eds.) (1979–80) *Florence and Venice, Comparisons and Relations: Acts of Two Conferences at Villa I Tatti in 1976–1977*. Florence, La Nuova Italia, 2 vols.

Bertoni, Giulio (1903) *La Biblioteca Estense e la coltura ferrarese ai tempi del duca Ercole I (1471–1505)*. Turin, Loescher.

Best, Myra (2006) 'La peste e le papere: Textual Repression in Day Four of the *Decameron*', in *Boccaccio and Feminist Criticism*, ed. Thomas C. Stillinger and F. Regina Psaki. Chapel Hill, NC, Annali d'Italianistica: 157–69.

Bettarini, Rosanna (ed.) (1966–87) Giorgio Vasari, *Le vite de' più eccellenti pittori, scultori e architetteri nelle redazioni del 1550 e 1568*. Florence, Sansoni, 6 vols.

Biagi, Guido (1892) *Dante: illustrations to the Divine comedy of Dante, executed by the Flemish artist Jo. Stradanus, 1587, and reproduced in phototype from the originals existing in the Laurentian Library of Florence*. London, T. Fisher Unwin.

Bianchi, Luca (1990) 'Un commento "umanistico" ad Aristotele. L'*Expositio super libros Ethicorum* di Donato Acciaiuoli', *Rinascimento* Vol. 30: 29–55.

(1994) ' "Aristotele fu un uomo e poté errare": sulle origini medievali della critica al "principio di autorità"', in *Filosofia e teologia nel trecento: Studi in ricordo di Eugenio Randi*, ed. Luca Bianchi. Turnhout, Brepols: 509–33.

(2013) 'Renaissance Readings of the *Nicomachean Ethics*', in *Rethinking Virtue*, ed. Lines and Ebbersmeyer: 131–67.

Bianchi, Luca, Simon Gilson and Jill Kraye (eds.) (2017) *Vernacular Aristotelianism in Italy from the Fourteenth to the Seventeenth Century*. London, The Warburg Institute.

Bianchi, Simona (2003) *I manoscritti datati del fondo Palatino della Biblioteca Nazionale Centrale di Firenze*. Florence, SISMEL – Edizioni del Galluzzo (= *Manoscritti datati d'Italia*, 9).

Bianco, Monica (2003) 'Predicazione e letteratura nelle trascrizioni di Antonio da Filicaia', in *Letteratura in forma di sermone: i rapporti tra predicazione e letteratura nei secoli XIII–XVI*, ed. Ginetta Auzzas, Giovanni Baffetti and Carlo Delcorno. Florence, Leo S. Olschki: 233–54.

Black, Robert (2001) *Humanism and Education in Medieval and Renaissance Italy: Tradition and Innovation in Latin Schools from the Twelfth to the Fifteenth Century*. Cambridge, Cambridge University Press.

(2007) *Education and Society in Florentine Tuscany: Teachers, Pupils and Schools, c. 1250–1500*. Leiden, Brill.

Black, Robert and Gabriella Pomaro (2000) *La consolazione della filosofia nel Medioevo e nel Rinascimento italiano / Boethius's Consolation of Philosophy in Italian Medieval and Renaissance Education*. Florence, SISMEL – Edizioni del Galluzzo.

Blair, Ann (2010) *Too Much to Know: Managing Scholarly Information before the Modern Age*. New Haven, Yale University Press.

Blum, Paul Richard (2012) *Studies on Early Modern Aristotelianism*. Leiden, Brill.

Bocchi, Achille (1574) *Symbolicarum Quaestionum libri*. Bologna, Apud Societatem Typographiae Bononiensis.

Bolton Holloway, Julia (1986) *Brunetto Latini: An Analytic Bibliography*. London, Grant & Cutler.

(1993) *Twice-told Tales: Brunetto Latino and Dante Alighieri*. New York, Peter Lang.

Bolzoni, Lina (2002) *La rete delle immagini: Predicazione in volgare dalle origini a Bernardino da Siena*. Turin, Einaudi.

Boschi Rotiroti, Marisa (2015) 'Paolo di Duccio Tosi: un copista dantesco e non solo', in *Il collezionismo di Dante in Casa Trivulzio*. Milan, Biblioteca Trivulziana. (graficheincomune.comune.milano.it/GraficheInComune/bacheca/danteincasatrivulzio)

Botley, Paul (2004) *Latin Translation in the Renaissance: The Theory and Practice of Leonardo Bruni, Giannozzo Manetti and Desiderius Erasmus*. Cambridge, Cambridge University Press.

Botterill, Steven (ed. and transl.) (1996) Dante, *De vulgari eloquentia*. Cambridge, Cambridge University Press.

Bragantini, Renzo and Pier Massimo Forni (eds.) (1995) *Lessico critico decameroniano*. Turin, Bollati Boringhieri.

Brams, Jozef (2003) *La riscoperta di Aristotele in Occidente*. Milan, Jaca Book.

Branca, Vittore (ed.) (1969) Giovanni di Pagolo Morelli, *Ricordi*. Florence, Le Monnier.

(ed.) (1976) Giovanni Boccaccio, *Decameron*. Milan, Mondadori.

(ed.) (1986) *Mercanti scrittori: ricordi nella Firenze tra Medioevo e Rinascimento*. Milan, Rusconi.

(ed.) (1999) *Merchant Writers of the Italian Renaissance*. New York, Marsilio Publishers.

Brancato, Dario (2000) 'Appunti linguistici sul *Boezio* di Alberto della Piagentina', *Accademia Peloritana dei Pericolanti. Atti della Classe di Lettere, Filosofia e Belle Arti*, Vol. 76: 128–276.

(2012) 'Readers and Interpreters of the *Consolatio* in Italy, 1300–1550', in *A Companion to Boethius in the Middle Ages*, ed. Noel H. Kaylor and Philip E. Phillips. Leiden, Brill: 357–411.

Bray, Nadia and Loris Sturlese (eds.) (2003) *Filosofia in volgare nel Medioevo*. Louvain-la-Neuve, Fédération Internationale des Instituts d'Etudes Médiévales.

Brieger, Peter, Millard Meiss and Charles S. Singleton (1969) *Illuminated manuscripts of the Divine Comedy*. Princeton, Princeton University Press.

Briggs, Charles F. (1999a) *Giles of Rome's* De regimine principum. *Reading and Writing Politics at Court and University, c.1275–c.1525*. Cambridge, Cambridge University Press.

(1999b) 'Learned Commentaries for the Laity: Translators' Glosses on Giles of Rome's *De Regimine Principum*', in *Reading and the Book in the Middle Ages*, ed. S. J. Ridyard. Sewanee, University of the South Press: 65–77.

(2003) 'Teaching Philosophy at School and Court: Vulgarization and Translation', in Somerset and Watson (eds.), *The Vulgar Tongue*: 99–111.

Briggs, Charles F. and Peter S. Eardley (eds.) (2016) *A Companion to Giles of Rome*. Leiden, Brill.

Brook, Leslie C. and Glyn S. Burgess (eds.) (2011) *Henri de Valenciennes. The Lay of Aristote*. Liverpool, University of Liverpool [www.liverpool.ac.uk/media/livacuk/modern-languages-and-cultures/liverpoolonline/Aristote.pdf].

Brown, Rawdon (ed.) (1864) *Calendar of State papers and manuscripts, relating to English affairs, existing in the Archives and collections of Venice, and in other libraries of Northern Italy, vol. I, 1202–1509*. London, Longman, Green, Longman, Roberts, and Green.

Brownlee, Kevin and Walter Stephens (eds.) (1989) *Discourses of Authority in Medieval and Renaissance Literature*. Hanover, University Press of New England.

Brucker, Gene A. (1962) *Florentine Politics and Society*. Princeton, Princeton University Press.

(ed.) (1998a) *The Society of Renaissance Florence: A Documentary Study*. Toronto, University of Toronto Press.

(1998b) *Florence, the Golden Age, 1138–1737*. Berkeley, University of California Press.

Brugnolo, Furio (1997) '"Voi che guardate…". Divagazioni sulla poesia per pittura del trecento', in *Visibile parlare*, ed. Ciociola: 305–39.

Bruni, Francesco (1967) 'Sperone Speroni e l'Accademia degli Infiammati', *Filologia e letteratura* Vol. 13: 24–71.

(1990) *Boccaccio: l'invenzione della letteratura mezzana*. Bologna, il Mulino.

Buridant, Claude (1983) '*Translatio medievalis*: théorie et pratique de la traduction medieval', *Travaux de linguistique et de littérature* Vol. 21: 81–136.

Butler, Shane (ed.) (2016) *Deep Classics: Rethinking Classical Reception*. London, Bloomsbury Academic.

Callmann, Ellen (1974) *Apollonio di Giovanni*. Oxford, Clarendon Press.

Cambi, Matteo (2015) 'Sul più antico volgarizzamento di S. Girolamo (ms. Pisa, Biblioteca Cateriniana, 43', *Medioevi* Vol. 1: 141–68.

Campanelli, Maurizio (2014) 'Languages', in *The Cambridge Companion to the Italian Renaissance*, ed. Michael Wyatt. Cambridge, Cambridge University Press: 139–63.

Campbell, C. Jean (1997) *The Game of Courting and the Art of the Commune of San Gimignano, 1290–1320*. Princeton, Princeton University Press.

Campora, Jacopo (1472) *De immortalitate anime in modum dialogi vulgariter.* Rome, Johannes Philippus de Lignamine.

(1475) *De la immortalità del anima ellegantissimo dialogo vulgare ornatissimo.* Milan, Antonio Zarotto.

(1477) *Dialogo de la inmortalità de l'anima: extrato de theologia et de philosophia vulgarizato dal excellente philosopho maistro Iacomo camphora da Zenova del ordene de li predicatori.* Vicenza, Giovanni Leonardo Longo.

(1478) *De immortalitate anime in modum dialogi vulgariter.* Cosenza, Ottaviano Salomonio.

(1494) *Loica vulgare.* Venice, Guglielo da Trino.

(1497a) *Loica uulgare composta e traduta da duo ualentissimi loici e grandissimi philosofi in dialogo.* Milan, Ulrich Scinzenzeler.

(1497b) *Loica uulgare composta e traduta da duo ualentissimi loici e grandissimi philosofi in dialogo.* Milan, Ulrich Scinzenzeler.

(1498a) *Loica vulgare e philosofia morale composta, e traduta da duo valentissimi loici e grandissimi philosophi in dialago.* Venice, Manfredo Bonelli.

(1498b) *Tractato de l'origine et immortalità de l'anima in theologia e philosophia morale e utilissimo, composto per valentissimi homini in dialogo e vulgare.* Brescia, Battista Farfengo.

Candido, Igor (2015–16) 'Il "pane tra le favole" o del Convivio di Boccaccio: l'Introduzione alla Quarta Giornata', *Heliotropia* Vols 12–13: 51–85.

Capialbi, Vito (1941) *Memorie delle tipografie calabresi.* Tivoli, Chicca.

Caracausi, Andrea and Christof Jeggle (eds.) (2014) *Commercial Networks and European Cities, 1400–1800.* London, Pickering & Chatto Publishers.

Caracciolo Aricò, Angela (ed.) (2008) *Le schede dei manoscritti medievali e umanistici del Fondo E.A. Cicogna*, vol. 1. Venice, Centro di Studi Medievali e Rinascimentali.

Caroti, Stefano and Stefano Zamponi (1974) *Lo scrittoio di Bartolomeo Fonzio umanista fiorentino.* Milan, Il Polifilo.

Carraro, Carlo and Giovanni Favero (eds.) (2017) Benedetto Cotrugli, *The Book of the Art of Trade.* Basingstoke, Palgrave Macmillan.

Carré, Antónia and Lluís Cifuentes (2010) 'Girolamo Manfredi's *Il Perché*', *Medicina & Storia* Vol. 10: 13–58.

Casadei, Alberto (2013) *Dante oltre la Commedia.* Bologna, il Mulino.

Catalogue of the Valuable collection of Important Manuscripts, Formed by the Late Rev. Dr. Wellesley. London, Sotheby, 1866.

Cavazzini, Laura (ed.) (1999) *Il fratello di Masaccio: Giovanni di ser Giovanni detto lo Scheggia.* Florence, Maschietto & Musolino.

Cecchini, Enzo and Guido Arbizzoni (eds.) (2004) Uguccione da Pisa, *Derivationes.* Florence, SISMEL – Edizioni del Galluzzo.

Cecioni, Giorgio (1889) 'Il *Secretum secretorum* attribuito ad Aristotile e le sue redazioni volgari', *Il Propugnatore* Vol. 2 No. 2: 72–102.

Celenza, Christopher S. (2004) 'Creating Canons in Fifteenth-Century Ferrara: Angelo Decembrio's "De politia litteraria," 1.10', *Renaissance Quarterly* Vol. 57 No. 1: 43–98.

(2009) 'End Game: Humanist Latin in the Late Fifteenth Century,' in *Latinitas Perennis*, Vol. 2, *Appropriation and Latin Literature*, ed. Wim Verbaal, Yanick Maes and Jan Papy. Leiden, Brill: 201–42.

(2017) *Petrarch: Everywhere A Wanderer*. Chicago, The University of Chicago Press.

(2018) *The Intellectual World of the Italian Renaissance: Language, Philosophy, and the Search for Meaning*. Cambridge, Cambridge University Press.

Celenza, Cristopher S. and Kenneth Gouwens (eds.) (2006) *Humanism and Creativity in the Renaissance. Essays in Honor of Ronald G. Witt*. Leiden, Brill.

Ceresa, Massimo (2004) 'Lascaris, Giano', *Dizionario biografico degli italiani* Vol. 63: 785–91.

Cestaro, Benvenuto Clemente (1914) 'Rimatori padovani del sec. XV', *L'Ateneo veneto* Vol. 37 No. 1: 101–45, 155–203.

Cestaro, Gary P. (2003) *Dante and the Grammar of the Nursing Body*. Notre Dame, University of Notre Dame Press.

Chamaillardus, Alexander (1538) *Aristotelis De virtutibus libellus. Nunc primum et repertus et in lucem editus*. Paris, Christian Wechel.

Chartier, Roger (1994) *The Order of Books: Readers, Authors, and Libraries in Europe between the Fourteenth and Eighteenth Centuries*, transl. Lydia G. Cochrane. Stanford, Stanford University Press.

Chatfield, Mary (transl.) (2008) Cristoforo Landino, *Poems*. Cambridge, MA, Harvard University Press.

Chiamenti, Massimiliano (1995) *Dante Alighieri traduttore*. Florence, Le lettere.

Chiavacci Leonardi, Anna Maria (ed.) (1991–97) Dante Alighieri, *Commedia*. Milan, Mondadori, 3 vols.

Chiesa, Paolo (1987) 'Ad verbum o ad sensum? Modelli e coscienza metodologica della traduzione tra tarda antichità e alto medioevo', *Medioevo e Rinascimento* Vol. 1: 1–51.

Christ, Georg L.K.A. (2012) *Trading Conflicts: Venetian Merchants and Mamluk Officials in Late Medieval Alexandria*. Leiden, Brill.

Ciappelli, Giovanni (1989) 'Libri e letture a Firenze nel XV secolo: le "Ricordanze" e la ricostruzione delle biblioteche private', *Rinascimento* Vol. 29: 267–91.

Ciasca, Raffaele (1927) *L'arte dei medici e speziali nella storia e nel commercio fiorentino dal secolo XII al XV*. Florence, Leo S. Olschki.

Cicchetti, Angelo and Raul Mordenti (1985) *I libri di famiglia in Italia*. Rome, Edizioni di storia e letteratura.

Ciccolella, Federica (2008) *Donati Graeci: Learning Greek in the Renaissance*. Leiden, Brill.

Ciccolella, Federica and Luigi Silvano (eds.) (2017) *Teachers, Students, and Schools of Greek in the Renaissance.* Leiden, Brill.

Cinelli, Luciano (2007) 'Mannelli, Luca', *Dizionario biografico degli italiani* Vol. 69: 81–4.

Ciociola, Claudio (ed.) (1997) *Visibile parlare. Le scritture esposte nei volgari italiani dal medioevo al Rinascimento.* Naples, Edizioni Scientifiche Italiane.

Comparetti, Domenico (1997) *Vergil in the Middle Ages*, transl. E.F.M. Benecke, with a new introduction by Jan M. Ziolkowski. Princeton, Princeton University Press.

Conte, Alberto (ed.) (2001) *Il novellino.* Rome, Salerno editrice.

Copeland, Rita (1991) *Rhetoric, Hermeneutics, and Translation.* Cambridge, Cambridge University Press.

Copeland, Rita and Ineke Sluiter (eds.) (2009) *Medieval Grammar and Rhetoric: Language Arts and Literary Theory, AD 300–1475.* Oxford, Oxford University Press.

Copenhaver, Brian (1988), 'Translation, terminology and style in philosophical discourse', in Charles B. Schmitt, Quentin Skinner, Eckhard Kessler and Jill Kraye (eds.), *The Cambridge History of Renaissance Philosophy.* Cambridge, Cambridge University Press: 77–110.

Corbari, Eliana (2013) *Vernacular Theology: Dominican Sermons and Audience in Late Medieval Italy.* Berlin, De Gruyter.

Cornish, Alison (2000) 'A Lady Asks: The Gender of Vulgarisation in Late Medieval Italy', *Publications of the Modern Language Association of America* Vol. 115: 166–80.

(2011) *Vernacular Translation in Dante's Italy: Illiterate Literature.* Cambridge, Cambridge University Press.

Corrado, Massimiliano (2010) *Dante e la questione della lingua di Adamo.* Rome, Salerno editrice.

Cortesi, Mariarosa (2007) *Tradurre dal greco in età umanistica: metodi e strumenti.* Florence, SISMEL – Edizioni del Galluzzo.

Cortesi, Mariarosa and Enrico V. Maltese (1992) 'Ciriaco d'Ancona e il *De virtutibus* pseudoaristotelico', *Studi medievali* Vol. 33: 133–64.

Costa, Iacopo (ed.) (2008) *Le Questiones di Radulfo Brito sull'Etica Nicomachea.* Turnhout, Brepols.

(ed.) (2010) *Anonymi Artium Magistri Questiones super Librum Ethicorum Aristotelis (Paris, BNF, lat. 14698).* Turnhout, Brepols.

Cotugno, Alessio (2019) *La scienza della parola: Retorica e linguistica di Sperone Speroni.* Bologna, il Mulino.

Cox, Virginia (2003) 'Ciceronian Rhetorical Theory in the Volgare: A Fourteenth-Century Text and its Fifteenth-Century Readers', in *Rhetoric and Renewal in the Latin West 1100–1450: Essays in Honour of John O. Ward*, ed. Constant J. Mews, Cary J. Nederman and Rodney M. Thomson. Tournhout, Brepols: 201–25.

(2006), 'Ciceronian Rhetoric in Late Medieval Italy: The Latin and Vernacular Tradition', in *The Rhetoric of Cicero*, ed. Cox and Ward: 109–43.

(2016) *A Short History of the Italian Renaissance*. London, I.B. Tauris.

Cox, Virginia and John O. Ward (eds.) (2006) *The Rhetoric of Cicero in Its Medieval and Early Renaissance Commentary Tradition*. Leiden, Brill.

Crick, Bernard (ed.) (2003) Niccolò Machiavelli, *The Discourses*, translation by Leslie J. Walker, with revisions by Brian Richardson. London, Penguin Books.

Cuenca Almenar, Salvador (2017) *Compendio de la Ética Nicomaquea: divulgación filosófica a través de los romances ibéricos en el siglo XV*. Zaragoza: Prensas de la Universidad de Zaragoza.

Cursi, Marco (2007) *Il Decameron: scritture, scriventi, lettori: storia di un testo*. Rome, Viella.

(2009) ' "Con molte sue fatiche": copisti in carcere alle Stinche alla fine del Medioevo (secoli XIV–XV)', in *In uno volumine. Studi sul libro e il documento in età medievale offerti a Cesare Scalon*, ed. Laura Pani. Udine, Forum Edizioni: 151–92.

Dalmazzo, Claudio (ed.) (1845) *La prima deca di Tito Livio. Volgarizzamento del buon secolo*. Turin, Stamperia Reale.

D'Ancona, Paolo (1914) *La miniatura fiorentina, s. XI–XVI*. Florence, Leo S. Olschki.

Daneloni, Alessandro (ed.) (2011) Bartolomeo Fonzio, *Letters to Friends*. Cambridge, MA, Harvard University Press.

Darnton, Robert (1990) 'What Is the History of Books?' in *The Kiss of Lamourette: Reflections in Cultural History*. New York, Norton: 107–35.

Davies, Martin (1996) 'Humanism in Script and Print', in *The Cambridge Companion to Renaissance Humanism*, ed. Kraye: 47–62.

Davis, Natalie Zemon (1975) 'Women on Top', in *Society and Culture in Early Modern France: Eight Essays*, ed. Natalie Zemon Davis. Stanford, Stanford University Press: 124–51.

De Cesare, Raffaele (1956) 'Di nuovo sulla leggenda di Aristotele cavalcato', in *Miscellanea del Centro di Studi Medievali*. Milan, Vita e Pensiero: 181–247.

(1957) 'Due recenti studi sulla leggenda di Aristotele cavalcato', *Aevum* Vol. 31: 85–101.

De Ferrari, Augusto (1983) Conti, Nicolò (Come, de Comitibus)', *Dizionario Biografico degli Italiani* Vol. 28: 461–62.

D'Egidio, Angela (2015) 'How Readers Perceive Translated Literary Works: A Qualitative Analysis of Reader Reception', in *The Practice of Literary Translation: An Italian Perspective*, ed. David Katan. Lecce, Lingue e Linguaggi.

Degli Agostini, Giovanni (1752) *Notizie istorico-critiche intorno la vita, e le opere degli scrittori viniziani*. Venice, Simone Occhi.

Degli Innocenti, Mario (1979) 'I volgarizzamenti italiani dell'"Elucidarium" di Onorio Augustodunense', *Italia Medioevale e Umanistica* Vol. 22: 239–318.

(1982) 'La tradizione manoscritta dei volgarizzamenti italiani dell'"Elucidarium" di Onorio Augustodunense', *Studi Medievali* Vol. 23: 193–229.

De Jongh, Henri (1911) *L'ancienne faculté de théologie de Louvain au premier siècle de son histoire, 1432–1540*. Paris, Bureaux de la Revue d'Histoire Ecclésiastique.

De La Mare, Albinia (1982) 'Further Manuscripts from Holkham Hall', *Bodleian Library Record* Vol. 10: 327–38.

Delbouille, Maurice (ed.) (1951) *Le Lai d'Aristote*. Paris, Les Belles Lettres.

Delcorno, Carlo (1979) 'Cavalca, Domenico', *Dizionario Biografico degli Italiani* Vol. 22: 577–86.

Del Negro Karem, Marina (2011) 'A Conflation of Characters: The Portrayal of Aristotle and Averroes as Jews in a Venetian Incunabulum', in *Kunsttexte. de* Vol. 2 [edoc.hu-berlin.de/kunsttexte/2011–2/del-negro-karem-marina-1/PDF/del-negro-karem.pdf].

De Luca, Giuseppe (ed.) (1954) *Prosatori minori del Trecento: Tomo I; Scrittori di religione*. Milan, Ricciardi.

Del Soldato, Eva and Andrea Rizzi (2013) 'Latin and Vernacular in Quattrocento Florence and Beyond: An Introduction', *I Tatti Studies* Vol. 16 Nos 1–2: 231–42.

De Matteis, Maria C. (1970) 'Aristotele', in *Enciclopedia Dantesca*. Rome, Istituto della Enciclopedia Italiana, Vol. 1: 372–7.

Den Haan, Annet, Brenda Hosington, Marianne Pade and Anna Wegener (eds.) (2018) *Issues in Translation*. Special issue of *Renaissance Forum: Journal of Renaissance Studies* Vol. 14.

De Ricci, Seymour (1935–40) *Census of Medieval and Renaissance manuscripts in the United States and Canada*. New York, H.W. Wilson Company.

De Robertis, Teresa (1993) 'Breve storia del Fondo Pandolfini della Colombaria e della dispersione di una libreria privata fiorentina (con due Appendici)', in *Le raccolte della Colombaria*, I. *Incunaboli, con un saggio sulla libreria Pandolfini*, ed. Enrico Spagnesi. Florence, Leo S. Olschki: 79–314.

De Robertis, Teresa and Rosanna Miriello (2006) *I manoscritti datati della Biblioteca Riccardiana di Firenze*. III. *Mss. 1401–2000*. Florence, SISMEL – Edizioni del Galluzzo (= *Manoscritti datati d'Italia*, 14).

Destrée, Pierre and Marco Zingano (eds.) (2013) *Theoria: Studies on the Status and Meaning of Contemplation in Aristotle's Ethics*. Louvain-la-Neuve, Peeters.

Dibello, Daniele (2015) 'Convergenze di un dialogo anacronistico: Aristotele incontra Venezia', *Archivio Veneto* Vol. 10: 11–43.

Di Dio, Rocco (2016) '"Selecta colligere": Marsilio Ficino and Renaissance Reading Practices', *History of European Ideas* Vol. 42: 1–12.

Dieck, Margarete (1997) *Die Spanische Kapelle in Florenz: das trecenteske Bildprogramm des Kapitelsaals der Dominikaner von S. Maria Novella*. Frankfurt am Main, Lang.

Di Napoli, Giovanni (1963) *L'immortalità dell'anima nel Rinascimento*. Turin, Società Editrice Internazionale.

Dionisotti, Carlo (1962) 'Leonardo uomo di lettere', *Italia Medioevale e Umanistica* Vol. 5: 183–216.

  (1967) 'Tradizione classica e volgarizzamenti', in Carlo Dionisotti, *Geografia e storia della letteratura italiana*. Turin, Einaudi: 125–78.

Dod, Bernard G. (1982) 'Aristoteles Latinus', in *The Cambridge History of Later Medieval Philosophy*, ed. Kretzmann, Kenny, Pinborg, and Stump: 43–79.

Donato, Maria Monica (1988) 'Un ciclo pittorico ad Asciano (Siena), Palazzo Pubblico e l'iconografia politica alla fine del medioevo', *Annali della Scuola Normale Superiore di Pisa. Classe di Lettere e Filosofia* Vol. 18 No. 3: 1105–272.

    (1997) 'Immagini e iscrizioni nell'arte politica fra Tre e Quattrocento', in *Visibile parlare*, ed. Ciociola: 341–96.

    (2003) 'Il *princeps*, il giudice, il "sindacho" e la città: Novità su Ambrogio Lorenzetti nel Palazzo Pubblico di Siena', in *Imago Urbis: L'immagine della città nella storia d'Italia,* ed. Francesca Bocchi and Rosa Smurra. Rome, Viella: 389–407.

Doren, Alfred (1940) *Le arti fiorentine.* Florence, Le Monnier.

Dorez, Leone (1904) *La canzone delle virtù e delle scienze di Bartolomeo di Bartoli da Bologna.* Bergamo, Istituto Italiano d'Arti Grafiche.

Dorez, Léon and Germain Lefèvre-Pontalis (eds.) (1898–1902) *Chronique d'Antonio Morosini: Extraits relatifs à l'histoire de France.* Paris, Société pour l'histoire de France, 4 vols.

Düring, Ingemar (1957) *Aristotle in the Ancient Biographical Tradition.* Stockholm, Almqvist & Wiksell.

Eco, Umberto (1979) *The Role of the Reader: Explorations in the Semiotics of Texts.* Bloomington, Indiana University Press.

Edelheit, Amos (2014) 'Philosophy and Theology in an Oral Culture: Renaissance Humanists and Renaissance Scholastics', *Revue des sciences philosophiques et théologiques* Vol. 98: 479–96.

Eisenstein, Elizabeth L. (1979) *The Printing Press as an Agent of Change: Communications and Cultural Transformations in Early Modern Europe.* Cambridge, Cambridge University Press.

Eisner, Martin (2013) *Boccaccio and the Invention of Italian Literature: Dante, Petrarch, Cavalcanti, and the Authority of the Vernacular.* Cambridge, Cambridge University Press.

Ellero, Maria Pia (2012) 'Una mappa per l'inventio. *L'Etica Nicomachea* e la prima giornata del Decameron', *Studi sul Boccaccio* Vol. 40: 1–30.

    (2014) 'Federigo e il re di Cipro: Note su Boccaccio lettore di Aristotele', *Modern Language Notes* Vol. 129 No. 1: 180–91.

Ettlinger, Leopold D. (1972) 'Hercules Florentinus', *Mitteilungen des Kunsthistorischen Institutes in Florenz* Vol. 16: 119–42.

Faccioli, Giovanni Tommaso (1796) *Catalogo ragionato de' libri stampati in Vicenza e suo territorio nel secolo XV.* Vicenza, Giambattista Vendramini Mosca.

Falchetta, Piero (2009) 'Il trattato De navigatione di Benedetto Cotrugli (1464–1465). Edizione commentata del ms. Schoenberg 473 con il testo del ms. 557 di Yale', *Studi Veneziani* Vol. 57: 16–334.

    (2012) 'Benedetto Cotrugli et son traité *De navigatione* (1464–65)', *Historical Review/La Revue Historique* Vol. 12: 53–62.

Fantoni, Luciana (1955–56) *Il codice 157 della BUB. Tesi di laurea.* Bologna, Università degli Studi di Bologna, Facoltà di Lettere e filosofia.

Farenga, Paola (1979) '*In doctis viris … mulierculis quoque ipsis*: Cultura in volgare nella stampa romana?', in *Scrittura, biblioteche e stampa a Roma nel Quattrocento*, ed. Concetta Bianca, Paola Farenga, Giuseppe Lombardi, Antonio G. Luciani and Massimo Miglio. Vatican City, Scuola Vaticana di Paleografia, Diplomatica e Archivistica: 403–15.

(1983) 'Le prefazioni alle edizioni romane di Giovanni Filippo de Lignamine', in *Scrittura, biblioteche e stampa a Roma nel Quattrocento*, ed. Massimo Miglio, Paola Farenga and Anna Modigliani. Vatican City, Scuola Vaticana di Paleografia, Diplomatica e Archivistica: 135–74.

Farulli, Gregorio (1710) *Istoria cronologica del nobile ed antico monastero degli Angioli di Firenze*. Lucca, Pellegrino Frediani.

Fava, Mario and Domenico Salmi (1950) *I manoscritti miniati della Biblioteca Estense di Modena*. Milan, Electa: 119–20.

Faye, Christopher U. and William H. Bond (1962) *Supplement to the Census of Medieval and Renaissance Manuscripts in the United States and Canada*. New York, The Bibliographical Society of America.

Federici, Fortunato (ed.) (1842) *La Esposizone Del Simbolo Degli Apostoli di Fra Domenico Cavalca*. Milan, Giovanni Silvestri.

Fedi, Roberto (1987) 'Il regno di Filostrato: Natura e struttura della Giornata IV del *Decameron*', *Modern Language Notes* Vol. 102 No. 1: 39–54.

Fehlner, Peter Damian (transl.) (1992) in James Likoudis, *Ending the Byzantine Greek Schism: Containing the 14th c. 'Apologia' of Demetrios Kydones for Unity with Rome and St. Thomas Aquinas' 'Contra Errores Graecorum.'* New Rochelle, NY, Catholics United for the Faith.

Fenzi, Enrico (2008) *Petrarca*. Bologna, il Mulino.

Ficino, Marsilio (1576) *Opera*. Basel, Ex Officina Henricpetrina.

Field, Arthur (1988) *The Origins of the Platonic Academy in Florence*. Princeton, Princeton University Press.

Fioravanti, Giancarlo (ed.) (2014) Dante Alighieri, *Convivio*, in Dante Alighieri, *Opere. 2. Convivio; Monarchia; Epistole; Egloge*. Milan, Mondadori: 5–805.

Fish, Stanley (1980) *Is There a Text in This Class? The Authority of Interpretive Communities*. Cambridge, MA, Harvard University Press.

Flamini, Francesco (1891) *La lirica toscana del Rinascimento anteriore ai tempi del Magnifico*. Pisa, Nistri.

Flasch, Kurt (1995) *Poesia dopo la peste. Saggio su Boccaccio*. Rome, Laterza.

Folena, Gianfranco (1991) *Volgarizzare e tradurre*. Turin, Einaudi.

Forni, Pier Massimo (1996) *Adventures in Speech: Rhetoric and Narration in Boccaccio's Decameron*. Philadelphia, University of Pennsylvania Press.

Forrai, Réka (2018) 'Translation as Rewriting: A Modern Theory for a Premodern Practice', in *Issues in Translation*, ed. Den Haan, Hosington, Pade and Wegener: 23–40.

Forster, E.S. (transl.) (1955) Aristotle, *On Sophistical Refutations*. Cambridge, MA, Harvard University Press.

Fortuna, Sara, Manuele Gragnolati and Jürgen Trabant (eds.) (2010) *Dante's Plurilingualism: Authority, Knowledge, Subjectivity*. Oxford, Legenda.

Frati, Carlo and Arnaldo Segarizzi (1909–11) *Catalogo dei codici marciani italiani*. Modena, Ferraguti, 2 vols.

Frati, Lodovico (1909–23) *Indice dei codici italiani conservati nella R. Biblioteca Universitaria di Bologna*. Florence, Leo S. Olschki.

(1916) 'L'*Etica* di Aristotile volgarizzata da Taddeo di Alderotto', *Giornale storico della letteratura italiana* Vol. 68: 192–5.

Fratini, Lisa and Stefano Zamponi (2004) *I manoscritti datati del fondo Acquisti e Doni e dei fondi minori della Biblioteca Medicea Laurenziana di Firenze*. Florence, SISMEL – Edizioni del Galluzzo (= *Manoscritti datati d'Italia*, 12).

Freccero, John (1986) *Dante: The Poetics of Conversion*. Cambridge, MA, Harvard University Press.

Fulin, Rinaldo (1872) 'Saggio del catalogo dei codici di Emmanuele A. Cicogna', *Archivio Veneto* Vol. 4: 59–132, 337–98.

Gaiter, Luigi (ed.) (1880) *Il Tesoro di Brunetto Latini*. Bologna, Gaetano Romagnoli.

Galle, Griet (ed.) (2003) Peter of Auvergne, *Questions on Aristotle's De Caelo*. Leuven, Leuven University Press.

Galvani, Giovanni (1894) *Saggio di alcune postille alla Divina Commedia*. Città di Castello, S. Lapi.

Gargan, Luciano (1971) *Lo Studio teologico e la Biblioteca dei Domenicani a Padova nel Tre e Quattrocento*. Padua, Antenore.

Garin, Eugenio (1947–50) 'Le traduzioni umanistiche di Aristotele nel secolo XV', *Atti e memorie dell'Accademia fiorentina di scienze morali La Colombaria* Vol. 16: 55–104.

(1957) 'L'Etica a Nicomaco', *Giornale critico della filosofia italiana* Vol. 36: 409–10.

Gauthier, René Antoine (ed.) (1974) *Ethica Nicomachea*. Leiden, Brill.

Gehl, Paul F. (1993) *A Moral Art: Grammar, Society, and Culture in Trecento Florence*. Ithaca, Cornell University Press.

(1994) 'Preachers, Teachers and Translators: The Social Meaning of Language Study in Trecento Tuscany', *Viator* Vol. 25: 289–323.

Gelli, Agenore (ed.) (1856) *Fiore di virtù*. Florence, Le Monnier.

Gentile, Luigi (1889–99) *I codici Palatini*. Rome, Presso i principali librai, 3 vols.

Gentile, Roberta (ed.) (1993) Domenico da Prato, *Le Rime*. Anzio, De Rubeis.

Gentile, Sebastiano and Carlos Gilly (1999) *Marsilio Ficino e il ritorno di Ermete Trismegisto*. Florence, Centro Di.

Gentili, Sonia (2005) *L'uomo aristotelico alle origini della letteratura italiana*. Rome, Carocci.

(2015) 'L'edizione dell'*Etica* in volgare attribuita a Taddeo Alderotti: risultati e problemi aperti', in *Aristotele fatto volgare*, ed. Lines and Refini: 39–59.

Gilbert, Felix (1979) 'Humanism in Venice', in *Florence and Venice*, ed. Bertelli, Rubinstein and Smyth, 1:13–26.

Gilson, Simon (2005) *Dante and Renaissance Florence*. Cambridge, Cambridge University Press.

Giordano, Nora and Gabriella Piccinni (eds.) (2013) *Siena nello specchio del suo costituto in volgare del 1309–1310*. Pisa, Pacini.

Goldthwaite, Richard A. (1985) 'Local Banking in Renaissance Florence', *Journal of European Economic History* Vol. 14: 5–55.

(2009) *The Economy of Renaissance Florence*. Baltimore, Johns Hopkins University Press.

Gombrich, Ernst H. (1967) *From the Revival of Letters to the Reform of the Arts: Niccolò Niccoli and Filippo Brunelleschi*. London, Phaidon.

(1972) 'Aims and Limits of Iconology', in *Symbolic Images*, ed. Ernst H. Gombrich. London, Phaidon: 1–25.

Grafton, Anthony (1990) 'Invention of Traditions and Traditions of Invention in Renaissance Europe: The Strange Case of Annius of Viterbo', in *The Transmission of Culture in Early Modern Europe*, ed. Anthony Grafton and Ann Blair. Philadelphia, University of Pennsylvania Press: 8–38.

(1997) *Commerce with the Classics: Ancient Books and Renaissance Readers*. Ann Arbor, University of Michigan Press.

Grafton, Anthony, Glenn W. Most and Salvatore Settis (eds.) (2010) *The Classical Tradition*. Cambridge, MA, Harvard University Press.

Grant, Edward (1996) *The Foundations of Modern Science in the Middle Ages: Their Religious, Institutional and Intellectual Contexts*. Cambridge, Cambridge University Press.

Greco, Aulo (ed.) (1970) Vespasiano da Bisticci, *Le vite*. Florence, Istituto Nazionale di Studi sul Rinascimento.

Grendler, Paul F. (1989) *Schooling in Renaissance Italy: Literacy and Learning, 1300–1600*. Baltimore, Johns Hopkins University Press.

(2002) *The Universities of the Italian Renaissance*. Baltimore, Johns Hopkins University Press.

Griffiths, Gordon, James Hankins and David Thompson (1987) *The Humanism of Leonardo Bruni: Selected Texts*. Binghamton, NY, The Renaissance Society of America.

Grignaschi, Mario (1980) 'La diffusion du *Secretum Secretorum* (*Kitāb Sirr al-'asrār*) dans l'Europe Occidentale', *Archives d'histoire doctrinale et littéraire du Moyen Âge* Vol. 47: 7–70.

Groppi, Felicina (1966) *Dante as Translator*. Rome, Herder.

Grynaeus, Simon (1539) *Aristotelis De Virtutibus Libellus plane aureus, nuper quidem Graece inventus, iam vero primum per Simonem Grynaeum latinitate donatus*. Basel, Robert Winter.

Grzybowski, Jacek (2015) *Cosmological and Philosophical World of Dante Alighieri: The Divine Comedy as a Medieval Vision of the Universe*. Frankfurt am Main, Peter Lang.

Gualdo, Riccardo (ed.) (2001) *Le parole della scienza: scritture tecniche e scientifiche in volgare (secoli XIII–XV)*. Galatina, Congedo.

Guerrieri, Elisabetta (2006) 'Bernardus ser Francisci de Nutis', in *Compendium Auctorum Latinorum Medii Aevi (500–1500), II.3*. Florence, SISMEL – Edizioni del Galuzzo: 318.

Guerrini, Roberto (2003) 'Aristotele. Il grande pensatore. Il maestro. La guida. Il "profeta". La vittima del trionfo d'amore', in *La virtù figurata. Eroi ed eroine dell'antichità nell'arte senese tra Medioevo e Rinascimento*, ed. Marilena Caciorgna and Roberto Guerrini. Siena, Protagon: 35–42.

(2004) 'Da Taddeo di Bartolo a Beccafumi. Presenza e continuità del Buon Governo nell'arte senese', in *Il Buono e il Cattivo Governo: Rappresentazioni nelle Arti dal Medioevo al Novecento*, ed. Giuseppe Pavanello. Venice, Marsilio: 71–91.

Hagedorn, Suzanne (2004) *Abandoned Women: Rewriting the Classics in Dante, Boccaccio, and Chaucer*. Ann Arbor, University of Michigan Press.

Hale, John R. (ed.) (1973) *Renaissance Venice*. Totowa, NJ, Rowman and Littlefield.

Hall, Marcia (ed.) (1997) *Raphael's School of Athens*. Cambridge, Cambridge University Press.

Hamilton, Michelle M. (2014) *Beyond Faith: Belief, Morality and Memory in a Fifteenth-Century Judeo-Iberian Manuscript*. Leiden, Brill.

Hankins, James (1997) *Repertorium Brunianum. A Critical Guide to the Writings of Leonardo Bruni*. Rome, Edizioni di storia e letteratura.

(2000) *Renaissance Civic Humanism: Reappraisals and Reflections*. Cambridge, Cambridge University Press.

(2003) 'Translation Practice in the Renaissance: The Case of Leonardo Bruni', in *Humanism and Platonism in the Italian Renaissance*. Rome, Edizioni di Storia e Letteratura: 177–92.

(2006) 'Humanism in the Vernacular', in *Humanism and Creativity*, ed. Celenza and Gouwens: 11–29.

(ed.) (2007a) *The Cambridge Companion to Renaissance Philosophy*. Cambridge, Cambridge University Press.

(2007b) 'Humanism, Scholasticism, and Renaissance Philosophy', in *The Cambridge Companion to Renaissance Philosophy*, ed. Hankins: 30–48.

Hardwick, Lorna (2003) *Reception Studies*. Oxford, Oxford University Press.

Hastings, Robert (1975) *Nature and Reason in the 'Decameron'*. Manchester, University of Manchester Press.

Herrmann, Cornelia (1991) *Der "Gerittene Aristoteles". Das Bildmotiv des "Gerittenen Aristoteles" und seine Bedeutung für die Aufrechterhaltung der gesellschaftlichen Ordnung vom Beginn des 13. Jhs. Bis um 1500*. Pfaffenweiler, Centaurus-Verlagsgesellschaft.

Hofmann, Heinz (2008) 'Literary Culture at the Court of Urbino during the Reign of Federico da Montefeltro', *Humanistica Lovaniensia* Vol. 57: 6–59.

Hollander, Robert and Jean (transl.) (2000) Dante Alighieri, *The Inferno*. New York, Doubleday/Anchor.

(transl.) (2003) Dante Alighieri, *The Purgatorio*. New York, Doubleday/Anchor.

(transl.) (2007) Dante Alighieri, *The Paradiso*. New York, Doubleday/Anchor.

Hopf, Karl (1859) 'Giustiniani, Familie aus Venedig', in *Allgemeine Encyclopädie der Wissenschaften und Künste*, ed. Johann Samuel Ersch and Johann Gottfried Gruber. Leipzig, Johann Friedrich Gleditsch, 18: 290–303.

Hoshino, Hidetoshi (1980) *L'arte della lana in Firenze nel basso medioevo, il commercio della lana e il mercato dei panni fiorentini nei secoli XIII–XV*. Florence, Leo S. Olschki.

Hurtado Albir, Amparo (1990) *La notion de fidélité en traduction*. Paris, Didier Érudition.

Infurna, Marco (ed.) (2005) *Il Lai di Aristotele*. Rome, Carocci.

Iser, Wolfgang (1978) *The Act of Reading: A Theory of Aesthetic Response*. Baltimore, Johns Hopkins University Press.

Jacobson-Schutte, Anne (1980) 'Trionfo delle donne: tematiche di rovesciamento dei ruoli nella Firenze rinascimentale', *Quaderni storici* Vol. 15 No. 44: 474–96.

Janin, Hunt (2008) *The University in Medieval Life, 1179–1499*. London, McFarland.

Jung, Marc-René (2002) 'Hercule dans les textes du Moyen Âge: Essai d'une typologie', in *Rinascita di Ercole*, ed. Anna Maria Babbi. Verona, Fiorini: 9–69.

Kaeppeli, Thomas (1948) 'Luca Mannelli († 1362) e la sua *Tabulatio et expositio Senecae*', *Archivum Fratrum Praedicatorum* Vol. 18: 237–64.

(1970) *Scriptores Ordinis Praedicatorum Medii Aevi*. Rome, Ad S. Sabinae, 4 vols.

Kalatzi, Maria P. (2009) *Hermonymos: A Study in Scribal, Literary and Teaching Activities in the Fifteenth and Early Sixteenth Centuries*. Athens, Cultural Foundation of the National Bank of Greece.

Katzenellenbogen, Adolf (1961) 'The Representation of the Seven Liberal Arts', in *Twelfth-Century Europe and the Foundations of Modern Society*, ed. Marshall Clagett, Gaines Post and Robert Reynolds. Madison, University of Wisconsin Press: 39–55.

Kay, Sarah (2013) *Parrots and Nightingales: Troubadour Quotations and the Development of European Poetry*. Philadelphia, University of Pennsylvania Press.

Kempshall, Matthew S. (1999) 'The Life of Virtue: Giles of Rome's *De regimine principum*', in *The Common Good in Late Medieval Political Thought*. Oxford, Oxford University Press: 130–56.

Kennedy, William J. (2009) 'The Economy of Invective and a Man in the Middle (*De sui ipsius et multorum ignorantia*)', in *Petrarch*, ed. Kirkham and Maggi: 263–73.

Kent, Dale (2000) *Cosimo De' Medici and the Florentine Renaissance: The Patron's Oeuvre*. New Haven, Yale University Press.

Kent, Francis William (ed.) (1981) *A Florentine Patrician and his Palace*. London, The Warburg Institute.

Kessler, Eckhard (2011) *Alexander of Aphrodisias and his Doctrine of the Soul: 1400 Years of Lasting Significance*. Leiden, Brill.

King, Margaret (1986) *Venetian Humanism in an Age of Patrician Dominance.* Princeton, Princeton University Press.

Kirkham, Victoria (1993) *The Sign of Reason in Boccaccio's Fiction.* Florence, Leo S. Olschki.

(1995) 'Morale', in *Lessico critico decameroniano*, ed. Bragantini and Forni: 249–68.

Kirkham, Victoria and Armando Maggi (eds.) (2009) *Petrarch: A Critical Guide to the Complete Works.* Chicago, University of Chicago Press.

Kirshner, Julius (2015) *Marriage, Dowry, and Citizenship in Late Medieval and Renaissance Italy.* Toronto, Toronto University Press.

Kojève, Alexandre (2004) *La notion de l'autorité.* Paris, Gallimard.

Korning Zethsen, Karen (2009) 'Intralingual Translation: An Attempt at Description', *Meta* Vol. 544: 795–812.

Kraye, Jill (1993) 'The Philosophy of the Italian Renaissance', in *Routledge History of Philosophy, Volume IV, The Renaissance and 17th century rationalism*, ed. G.H.R. Parkinson. London and New York, Routledge: 15–64.

(ed.) (1996) *The Cambridge Companion to Renaissance Humanism.* Cambridge, Cambridge University Press.

(ed.) (1997) *Cambridge Translations of Renaissance Philosophical Texts. Volume I: Moral Philosophy.* Cambridge: Cambridge University Press.

Kretzmann, Norman, Anthony Kenny, Jan Pinborg and Eleonore Stump (eds.) (1982) *The Cambridge History of Later Medieval Philosophy.* Cambridge, Cambridge University Press.

Kristeller, Paul Oskar (1937) *Supplementum Ficinianum.* Florence, Leo S. Olschki.

(1939) 'Florentine Platonism and its Relations with Humanism and Scholasticism', *Church History* Vol. 8.3: 201–11.

(1944–45) 'Humanism and Scholasticism in the Italian Renaissance', *Byzantion* Vol. 17: 346–74.

(1963–97) *Iter Italicum. A Finding List of Uncatalogued or Incompletely Catalogued Humanistic Manuscripts of the Renaissance in Italian and Other Libraries.* London, The Warburg Institute; Leiden, Brill, 6 vols.

Labalme, Patricia H. (1969) *Bernardo Giustiniani: A Venetian of the Quattrocento.* Rome, Edizioni di Storia e Letteratura.

Lafleur, Claude and Joanne Carrier (1995) 'La Philosophia d'Hervé le Breton (alias Henri le Breton) et le recueil d'introductions à la philosophie du ms. Oxford, Corpus Christi College 283', *Archives d'histoire doctrinale et littéraire du Moyen Âge* Vol. 62: 359–442.

Lansing, Richard H. (transl.) (1990) *Dante's Il Convivio (The Banquet).* New York, Garland.

Lanza, Antonio (1989) *Polemiche e berte letterarie nella Firenze del primo Rinascimento (1375–1449).* Rome, Bulzoni.

Latini, Brunetto (1568) *L'Ethica d'Aristotile ridotta in compendio da Ser Brunetto Latini.* Lyon, Jean de Tournes.

Lawrance, Jeremy N. H. (1982) 'Nuño de Guzmán and early Spanish humanism: Some reconsiderations', *Medium Aevum* Vol. 51: 55–84.

(1985) 'The Spread of Lay Literacy in Late Medieval Castile', *Bulletin of Hispanic Studies* Vol. 62: 79–94.

(1989) *Un episodio del proto-humanismo español. Tres opúsculos de Nuño de Guzmán y Giannozzo Manetti*. Salamanca, Biblioteca Española del siglo XV.

(2006), 'Guzmán, Nuño de', in *Key figures in Medieval Europe: An Encyclopedia*, ed. Richard K. Emmerson and Sandra Clayton-Emmerson. New York, Taylor and Francis: 288–9.

Lazzi, Giovanna (ed.) (2001) *I colori del divino*. Florence, Polistampa.

Lefèvre, Yves (ed.) (1954) *L'Elucidarium et les Lucidaires*. Paris, E. de Boccard.

Leonardi, Claudio, Marcello Morelli and Francesco Santi (eds.) (1995) *Fabula in tabula: Una storia degli indici dal manoscritto al testo elettronico*. Spoleto, Centro italiano di studi sull'Alto medioevo.

Leone, Ambrogio (1525) *Eximii doctoris Ambrosii Leonis Nolani De nobilitate rerum dialogus. Eiusdem ex Aristotele translatum opus de virtutibus*. Venice, Melchiorre Sessa.

Levasti, Arrigo (ed.) (1924–26) Beato Iacopo da Varagine, *Leggenda aurea*. Florence, Libreria Editrice Fiorentina, 3 vols.

Liaci, Maria Teresa (ed.) (1970) Cristoforo Landino, *De vera nobilitate*. Florence, Leo S. Olschki.

Librandi, Rita (1995) *La Metaura d'Aristotile: volgarizzamento fiorentino anonimo del XIV secolo*. Naples, Liguori.

Librandi, Rita and Rosa Piro (eds.) (2006) *Lo scaffale della biblioteca scientifica in volgare, secoli XIII–XVI*. Florence: SISMEL – Edizioni del Galluzzo.

Lines, David A. (2001), 'Ethics as Philology: A Developing Approach to Aristotle's *Nicomachean Ethics* in Florentine Humanism', in *Renaissance Readings of the Corpus Aristotelicum*, ed. Marianne Pade. Chicago, University of Chicago Press: 27–42.

(2002) *Aristotle's 'Ethics' in the Italian Renaissance (ca. 1300–1650): The Universities and the Problem of Moral Education*. Leiden, Brill.

(2005) 'Sources and Authorities for Moral Philosophy in the Italian Renaissance: Thomas Aquinas and Jean Buridan on Aristotle's *Ethics*', in *Moral Philosophy on the Threshold of Modernity*, ed. Jill Kraye and Risto Saarinen. Cham, Springer: 7–29.

(2015) 'Latin and the Vernacular in Francesco Piccolomini's Moral Philosophy', in *Aristotele fatto volgare*, ed. Lines and Refini: 169–99.

(2019) 'When is a Translation Not a translation? Girolamo Manfredi's *De homine* (1474)', *Rivista di storia della filosofia* Vol. 30: 287–307.

(in press) 'Action and Contemplation in Renaissance Philosophy', in *Encyclopedia of Renaissance Philosophy*, ed. Marco Sgarbi. Cham, Springer [https://doi.org/10.1007/978-3-319-02848-4].

Lines, David A. and Alessio Cotugno (eds.) (2016) *Venezia e Aristotele (ca. 1454–c. 1600): Greco, latino, italiano*. Venice, Marcianum Press.

Lines, David A. and Sabrina Ebbersmeyer (eds.) (2013) *Rethinking Virtue, Reforming Society: New Directions in Renaissance Ethics, c.1350–c.1650*. Turnhout, Brepols.

Lines, David A. and Eugenio Refini (eds.) (2015) *Aristotele fatto volgare: tradizione aristotelica e cultura volgare nel Rinascimento*. Pisa, ETS.

Lisini, Alessandro (ed.) (1903) *Il costituto del Comune di Siena volgarizzato nel MCCCIX–MCCCX*. Siena, Tipografia sordomuti di Lazzeri.

Litta, Pompeo (1819–64) *Famiglie nobili italiane*. Turin, Basadonna.

Lohe, Peter (ed.) (1980) Cristoforo Landino, *Disputationes Camaldulenses*. Florence, Sansoni.

Lohr, Charles (1982) 'The Medieval Interpretation of Aristotle', in *The Cambridge History of Later Medieval Philosophy*, ed. Kretzmann, Kenny, Pinborg and Stump: 80–98.

Lorenzi, Cristiano (2013) 'Le orazioni *Pro Marcello* e *Pro rege Deiotaro* volgarizzate da Brunetto Latini', *Studi di filologia italiana* Vol. 71: 19–77.

Luiso, Francesco Paolo (ed.) (1899) *Le vere lode de la inclita et gloriosa città di Firenze composte in latino da Leonardo Bruni e tradotte in volgare da frate Lazaro da Padova*. Florence, Tipografia Carnesecchi e Figli.

Lusignan, Serge (1986) *Parler vulgairement: les intellectuels et la langue française aux XIIIe et XIVe siècles*. Paris, Vrin.

(1988) 'Nicole Oresme traducteur et la pensée de la langue française savante', in *Nicolas Oresme: tradition et innovation chez un intellectuel du XIVe siècle*, ed. Pierre Souffrin and Alain Segonds. Paris, Les Belles Lettres: 93–104.

Luzzati, Michele (1984) 'Cotrugli, Benedetto', in *Dizionario Biografico degli Italiani* Vol. 30: 446–50.

Luzzatto, Gino (1961) *Storia economica di Venezia dall'XI al XVI secolo*. Venice, Centro Internazionale delle Arti e del Costume.

Maffia Scariati, Irene (ed.) (2008) *A scuola con ser Brunetto: la ricezione di Brunetto Latini dal Medioevo al Rinascimento*. Florence, SISMEL – Edizioni del Galluzzo.

Malanima, Paolo (1979) 'Cerchi, Bindaccio', in *Dizionario Biografico degli Italiani* Vol. 23: 685–6.

Manenti, Giovanni (1538) *Col nome de Dio il Segreto de' segreti, le Moralità, et la Phisionomia d'Aristotile, dove si trattano e' mirabili ammaestramenti ch'egli scrisse al Magno Alessandro sì per il reggimento de l'Imperio, come per la conservatione de la sanità, et per conoscere le persone a che siano inclinate, ad esempio et giovamento d'ognuno accomodatissimi, fatti nuovamente volgari, per Giovanni Manente*. Venice, Giovanni Tacuino.

Manni, Domenico Maria (ed.) (1734) Bartolomeo da San Concordio, *Ammaestramenti degli antichi*. Florence, Manni.

Manni, Paola (2007) 'Il volgare toscano nella "Grammatichetta"', in *Alberti e la cultura del Quattrocento*, ed. Roberto Cardini and Mariangela Regoliosi. Florence, Polistampa, 2 vols: 2, 629–53.

Manno, Antonio (ed.) (1999) *Il poema del tempo. I capitelli del Palazzo Ducale di Venezia: storia e iconografia*. Venice, Canal & Stamperia.

Marazzini, Claudio (1993) 'Le teorie', in *Storia della lingua italiana*, ed. Luca Serianni and Pietro Trifone. Turin, Einaudi, Vol. 1: 231–329.

Marcel, Raymond (ed.) (1956) Marsile Ficin, *Commentaire sur le Banquet de Platon*. Paris, Les Belles Lettres.

Marcellino, Giuseppe (2016) 'Biondo Flavio e le origini del volgare: un riesame della questione (*De verbis* 108–111)', in *A New Sense of the Past: The Scholarship of Biondo Flavio (1392–1463)*, ed. Angelo Mazzocco and Marc Laureys. Leuven: Leuven University Press: 35–54.

Marchesi, Concetto (1900) *Bartolomeo della Fonte. Contributo alla storia degli studi classici in Firenze nella seconda metà del Quattrocento*. Catania, Niccolò Giannotta.

  (1903) 'Il compendio volgare dell'Etica aristotelica e le fonti del VI libro del *Tresor*', *Giornale storico della letteratura italiana* Vol. 42: 1–74.

  (1904) *L'Etica Nicomachea nella tradizione latina medievale. Documenti ed appunti*. Messina, Trimarchi.

Marenbon, John (1987) *Later Medieval Philosophy (1150–1350)*. London, Routledge & Kegan Paul.

Mariani Canova, Giordana (2005) 'La miniatura del Trecento in Veneto', in *La miniatura in Italia: Dal tardoantico al Trecento con riferimenti al Medio Oriente e all'Occidente europeo*, ed. Antonella Putaturo Donati Murano and Alessandra Periccioli Saggese. Naples, Edizioni scientifiche italiane: 164–76.

  (2009) 'La miniatura in Veneto', in *La miniatura in Italia: Dal tardogotico al manierismo*, ed. Antonella Putaturo Donati Murano and Alessandra Periccioli Saggese. Naples, Edizioni Scientifiche Italiane: 331–71.

Marsh, David (ed.) (2004) Francesco Petrarca, *Invectives*. Cambridge, MA, Harvard University Press.

Marsilli, Pietro (1984) 'Réception et diffusion iconographique du conte de "Aristote et Phillis" en Europe depuis le Moyen Age', in *Amour, mariage et transgréssions au Moyen Age*, ed. Danielle Buschinger and André Crépin. Göppingen, Kümmerle Verlag: 239–69.

Martellozzo Forin, Elda (1999) 'Conti palatini e lauree conferite per privilegio: L'esempio padovano del sec. XV', *Annali di Storia delle Università Italiane* Vol. 3: 79–119.

Martindale, Charles (1993) *Redeeming the Text: Latin Poetry and the Hermeneutics of Reception*. Cambridge, Cambridge University Press.

  (2006) 'Thinking through Reception', in *Classics and the Uses of Reception*, ed. Martindale and Thomas: 1–13.

Martindale, Charles and Richard F. Thomas (eds.) (2006) *Classics and the Uses of Reception*. Malden, Blackwell.

Martinez Ferrando, J. Ernesto (1942) *Tragedia del insigne condestable Don Pedro de Portugal*. Madrid, CSIC.

Mascheroni, Clara (1969) 'I codici del volgarizzamento italiano del *Tresor* di Brunetto Latini', *Aevum* Vol. 43: 485–510.

Masi, Giorgio (2015) 'Pazzi, Alfonso de', detto l'Etrusco', *Dizionario biografico degli italiani* Vol. 82: 1–3.

Maxson, Brian (2013) '"This Sort of Men": The Vernacular and the Humanist Movement in Fifteenth-Century Florence', *I Tatti Studies* Vol. 16, Nos 1–2: 257–71.

    (2014) *The Humanist World of Renaissance Florence*. Cambridge, Cambridge University Press.

    (2018) 'Bruni, Leonardo', in *Encyclopedia of Renaissance Philosophy*, ed. Marco Sgarbi. Cham, Springer [https://doi.org/10.1007/978-3-319-02848-4].

Mayer, Roland (2015) 'Seneca *redivivus*: Seneca in the Medieval and Renaissance World', in *The Cambridge Companion to Seneca*, ed. Shadi Bartsch and Alessandro Schiesaro. Cambridge, Cambridge University Press: 277–88.

Mazzacurati, Giancarlo (1977) 'Il "cortegiano" e lo "scolare" nel *Dialogo delle lingue* di S. Speroni', in *Conflitti di culture nel Cinquecento*, ed. Giancarlo Mazzacurati. Naples, Liguori: 141–82.

Mazzatinti, Giuseppe (ed.) (1898) *Inventari dei manoscritti delle biblioteche d'Italia. 8: Firenze (R. Biblioteca Nazionale Centrale)*. Forlì, Bordandini.

Mazzocco, Angelo (1993) *Linguistic Theories in Dante and the Humanists: Studies of Language and Intellectual History in Late Medieval and Early Renaissance Italy*. Leiden, Brill.

Mazzoni, Francesco (1985) *Il canto XI dell'Inferno*. Naples, Loffredo.

Mazzotta, Giuseppe (1986) *The World at Play in Boccaccio's Decameron*. Princeton, University of Princeton Press.

McCuaig, William (1982) 'Bernardo Rucellai and Sallust', *Rinascimento* Vol. 22: 75–98.

McElduff, Siobhán (2013) *Roman Theories of Translation: Surpassing the Source*. New York, Routledge.

McLaughlin, Martin (1996) *Literary Imitation in the Italian Renaissance: The Theory and Practice of Literary Imitation in Italy from Dante to Bembo*. Oxford, Clarendon Press.

    (2005) 'Latin and Vernacular from Dante to the Age of Lorenzo (1321–c. 1500)', in *Cambridge History of Literary Criticism*, ed. Minnis and Johnson, Vol. 2: 612–25.

Meneghetti, Maria Luisa (1992) 'Scrivere in carcere nel Medioevo', in *Studi di Filologia e Letteratura italiana in onore di Maria Picchio Simonelli*. Alessandria, Edizioni dell'Orso: 185–99.

    (2015) *Storie al muro: temi e personaggi della letteratura profana nell'arte medievale*. Turin, Einaudi.

Menut, Albert D. (ed.) (1940) Nicole Oresme, *Le Livre de Ethiques d'Aristote*. New York, Stechert.

Mercuri, Roberto (1971) 'Conosco i segni de l'antica fiamma', *Cultura Neolatina* Vol. 31: 237–93.

Migiel, Marilyn (2015) *The Ethical Dimension of the Decameron*. Toronto, University of Toronto Press.

Miglietti, Sara and Sarah E. Parker (2016) 'Editorial', *History of European Ideas* Vol. 42: 590–4.

Milanesi, Carlo (ed.) (1864) *Il Boezio e l'Arrighetto volgarizzamenti del buon secolo.* Florence, G. Barbèra.

Milanesi, Marica (ed.) (1983) Giovanni Battista Ramusio, *Navigazioni e viaggi. IV.* Turin, Einaudi.

Milani, Matteo (2001) 'La tradizione italiana del *Secretum Secretorum*', *La parola del testo* Vol. 5: 209–53.

(2006) 'Un nuovo tassello per l'edizione del *Segreto dei segreti*', *La parola del testo* Vol. 10: 291–318.

Minnis, Alastair and Ian Johnson (eds.) (2005) *The Cambridge History of Literary Criticism*, Vol. II: *The Middle Ages*. Cambridge, Cambridge University Press.

Mita Ferraro, Alessandra (2005) *Matteo Palmieri: una biografia intellettuale.* Genoa: Name.

Mittarelli, Giovanni Benedetto (1764) *Annales Camaldulenses ordinis Sancti Benedicti. Tomus Octavus.* Venice, Monasterii Sancti Michaelis de Muriano.

(1779) *Bibliotheca codicum manuscriptorum monasterii S. Michaelis Venetiarum prope Murianum.* Venice, Ex Typographia Fentiana.

Monfasani, John (2008) 'Criticism of Biblical Humanists in Quattrocento Italy', in *Biblical Humanism and Scholasticism in the Age of Erasmus*, ed. Erika Rummel. Leiden, Brill: 15–38.

(2012) *Bessarion Scholasticus: A Study of Cardinal Bessarion's Latin Library.* Turnhout, Brepols.

Monfrin, Jacques (1963) 'Humanisme et Traduction au Moyen Âge', *Journal des Savants* Vol. 3: 161–90.

(1964) 'Les traducteurs et leur publique au moyen âge', *Journal des savants* Vol. 4: 5–20.

Montanari, Fausto (1971) 'Limbo', in *Enciclopedia Dantesca*. Rome, Istituto della Enciclopedia Italiana: 651–4.

Morelli, Jacopo (1776) *I codici manoscritti volgari della libreria Nanniana.* Venice, Antonio Zatta.

Morpurgo, Salomone (1900) *I manoscritti della R. Biblioteca Riccardiana: manoscritti italiani.* Rome, Presso i principali librai.

Mostra di codici romanzi delle biblioteche fiorentine. Florence, Sansoni, 1957.

Mugnai Carrara, Daniela (1978) 'Profilo di Niccolò Leoniceno', *Interpres* Vol. 2: 169–212.

(1991) *La biblioteca di Nicolò Leoniceno. Tra Aristotele e Galeno: Cultura e libri di un medico umanista.* Florence, Leo S. Olschki.

Mulas, Pier Luigi (2005) 'La miniatura in Lombardia', in *La miniatura in Italia: Dal tardoantico al Trecento con riferimenti al Medio Oriente e all'Occidente europeo*, ed. Antonella Putaturo Donati Murano and Alessandra Periccioli Saggese. Naples, Edizioni scientifiche italiane: 147–55.

Muzzioli, Giovanni (ed.) (1954) *Mostra storica nazionale della miniatura, Palazzo di Venezia, Roma: catalogo.* Florence, Sansoni.

Najemy, John (1982) *Corporatism and Consensus in Florentine Electoral Politics, 1280–1400.* Chapel Hill, University of North Carolina Press.

Nanetti, Andrea (ed.) (2010) *Il Codice Morosini: Il mondo visto da Venezia, 1094–1433.* Spoleto, Fondazione Centro italiano di studi sull'alto Medioevo.

Nardi, Bruno (1955) 'Il canto XI dell'Inferno', in *Letture dantesche*, ed. Giovanni Getto. Florence, Sansoni: 191–207.

Natali, Antonio (ed.) (2012) *Bagliori dorati: Il Gotico Internazionale a Firenze 1375–1440.* Florence, Giunti.

Nauta, Lodi (2003) 'Some Aspects of Boethius' *Consolatio philosophiae* in the Renaissance', in *Boèce ou la chaîne des savoirs. Actes du colloque international de la fondation Singer-Polignac*, ed. Alain Galonnier. Louvain, Peeters: 767–78.

   (2009) 'The *Consolation*: the Latin Commentary tradition, 800–1700', in *The Cambridge Companion to Boethius*, ed. John Marenbon. Cambridge, Cambridge University Press: 255–78.

Newman, Karen and Jane Tylus (eds.) (2015) *Early Modern Cultures of Translation.* Philadelphia, University of Pennsylvania Press.

O'Connell, Daragh and Jennifer Petrie (eds.) (2013) *Nature and Art in Dante.* Dublin, Four Courts Press.

Olson, Kristina M. (2014) *Courtesy Lost: Dante, Boccaccio, and the Literature of History.* Toronto, University of Toronto Press.

Ong, Walter (1971) 'Latin Language Study as a Renaissance Puberty Rite', in *Rhetoric, Romance, and Technology: Studies in the Interaction of Expression and Culture.* Ithaca, Cornell University Press: 113–41.

Overmeyer, Sheryl (2015) 'Exalting the Meek Virtue of Humility in Aquinas', *The Heythrop Journal* Vol. 56: 650–62.

Pacca, Vinicio and Laura Paolino (eds.) (1996) Francesco Petrarca, *Trionfi, Rime estravaganti, Codice degli abbozzi.* Milan, Mondadori.

Padoan, Giorgio (ed.) (1994) Giovanni Boccaccio, *Esposizioni sopra la Comedia di Dante.* Milan, Mondadori.

Pandimiglio, Leonida (2012) 'Morelli, Giovanni', *Dizionario biografico degli Italiani* Vol. 76: 615–19.

Panofsky, Erwin (1955) 'Iconography and Iconology: An Introduction to the Study of Renaissance Art', in *Meaning in the Visual Arts: Papers in and on Art History*, Erwin Panofsky. Garden City, NY, Doubleday: 26–54.

Paoli, Alessandro and Giovanni Gentile (eds.) (1915–17) 'Cristoforo Landino, *De anima*', *Annali delle Università Toscane* Vols 34 (1915): 1–50; 35 (1916): 1–138; 36 (1917): 1–96.

Papi, Fiammetta (2015) 'Note filologico-linguistiche sul *Livro del Governamento dei re e dei principi* (*De regimine principum* di Egidio Romano)', *La lingua italiana* Vol. 11: 11–36.

   (2016a) 'Aristotle's Emotions in Giles of Rome's *De Regimine Principum* and in its Vernacular Translations (With a Note on Dante's *Convivio* III, 8, 10)', *Annali della Scuola Normale Superiore. Classe di Lettere e filosofia* Vol. 8 No. 1: 73–104.

(2016b) Il 'Livro del governamento dei re e dei principi' secondo il codice II.IV.129. Pisa, ETS.

Papio, Michael (transl.) (2009) *Boccaccio's Expositions on Dante's Comedy*. Toronto, University of Toronto Press.

Pasquini, Emilio (1964) 'Il codice di Filippo Scarlatti (Firenze, Biblioteca Venturi Ginori Lisci, 3)', *Studi di filologia italiana* Vol. 22: 363–580.

Patota, Giuseppe (ed.) (1996) Leon Battista Alberti, *Grammatichetta e altri scritti sul volgare*. Rome, Salerno editrice.

Pattini, Dante (2007) 'Manenti, Giovanni', *Dizionario Biografico degli Italiani* Vol. 68: 596–8.

Pegoretti, Anna (2015) 'Filosofanti', *Le tre corone. Rivista internazionale di studi su Dante, Petrarca, Boccaccio*, Vol. 2: 11–70.

Pelle, Susanna, Anna Maria Russo, David Speranzi and Stefano Zamponi (2011) *I manoscritti datati della Biblioteca Nazionale Centrale di Firenze*. III. *Fondi Banco Rari, Landau Finaly, Landau Muzzioli, Nuove Accessioni, Palatino Capponi, Palatino Panciatichiano, Tordi*. Florence, SISMEL – Edizioni del Galluzzo (= *Manoscritti datati d'Italia*, 21).

Pellegrin, Élisabeth (1955) *La bibliothèque des Visconti et des Sforza ducs de Milan, au 15. siècle*. Paris, Centre National de la Recherche Scientifique.

(1969) *La bibliothèque des Visconti et des Sforza ducs de Milan: supplement*. Florence, Leo S. Olschki.

Percival, W. Keith (1975) 'The Grammatical Tradition and the Rise of the Vernaculars', in *Current Trends in Linguistics*. Vol. 13, *Historiography of Linguistics*, ed. Thomas A. Sebeok. The Hague, Mouton: 231–75.

Perosa, Alessandro (1960) *Il Zibaldone quaresimale: pagine scelte*. London, The Warburg Institute.

Perrone, Giuseppina (2001) 'Il volgarizzamento del *Secretum Secretorum* di Cola di Jennaro (1479)', in *Le parole della scienza*, ed. Gualdo: 353–8.

Petrioli, Piergiacomo (1996) 'Aristotele e Fillide nella pittura senese del Trecento', *La Diana* Vol. 2: 209–30.

Petrucci, Armando (1967) *La scrittura di Francesco Petrarca*. Vatican City, Biblioteca Apostolica Vaticana.

(1969) 'Alle origini del libro moderno. Libri da banco, libri da bisaccia, libretti da mano', *Italia medioevale e umanistica* Vol. 12: 295–313.

(1995) *Writers and Readers in Medieval Italy. Study in the History of Written Culture*, ed. and transl. Charles M. Radding. New Haven, Yale University Press.

Petrucci, Livio (2007) 'Una scheda per Virgilio mago in Italia', in *Studi di filologia romanza offerti a Valeria Bertolucci Pizzorusso*, ed. Pietro G. Beltrami. Pisa, Pacini: 1253–84.

Picone, Michelangelo (2008) 'Le papere di fra Filippo (Intro. IV)', in *Boccaccio e la codificazione della novella: letture del Decameron*, ed. Michelangelo Picone. Ravenna, Longo: 171–83.

Pine, Martin L. (1986) *Pietro Pomponazzi: Radical Philosopher of the Renaissance*. Padua, Antenore.

Piotrowicz, Paulina (2014) 'L'ethos mercantile in *Il libro dell'arte di mercatura* di Benedetto Cotrugli', *Romanica Cracoviensia* Vol. 14: 305–12.

Pizzorno, Francesco (ed.) (1842–45) *Le deche di Tito Livio: Volgarizzamento del buon secolo*. Savona, Sambolino, 6 vols.

Plebani, Eleonora (2014) 'Pandolfini, Agnolo', *Dizionario biografico degli italiani* Vol. 80: 717–19.

Poeschke, Joachim (2005) *Itatian Frescoes, the Age of Giotto, 1280–1400*. New York, Abbeville Press.

Poggi Salani, Teresa (2001) 'La grammatica dell'Alberti', *Studi di grammatica italiana* Vol. 20: 1–12.

Polidori, Filippo Luigi (ed.) (1838–39) *Istorie fiorentine scritte da Giovanni Cavalcanti*. Florence, All'insegna di Dante, 2 vols.

Ponte, Giovanni (ed.) (1988) Leon Battista Alberti, *Profugiorum ab erumna libri*. Genova, Tilgher.

Pope-Hennessy, John (1980) *Luca Della Robbia*. Ithaca, Cornell University Press.

Porter, James I. (2008) 'Reception Studies: Future Prospects', in *A Companion to Classical Receptions*, ed. Lorna Hardwick and Christopher Stray. Malden, Blackwell: 469–81.

Pozzi, Mario (ed.) (1988) *Discussioni linguistiche del Cinquecento*. Turin, UTET.

Puoti, Basilio (ed.) (1843) *Il Catilinario ed il Giugurtino libri due di C. Sallustio Crispo volgarizzati per Frate Bartolommeo da San Concordio*. Naples, Nella Stamperia del Vaglio.

Purnell, Frederick (1977) 'Hermes and the Sybil: A Note on Ficino's *Pimander*', *Renaissance Quarterly* Vol. 30 No. 3: 305–310.

Rackham, Harris (transl.) (1956) Aristotle, *The Nicomachean Ethics*. Cambridge, MA, Harvard University Press.

Ragni, Eugenio (1966) 'Benci, Tommaso', *Dizionario biografico degli italiani* Vol. 8: 201–3.

Rapisarda, Stefano (2001) 'Appunti sulla circolazione del *Secretum Secretorum* in Italia', in *Le parole della scienza*, ed. Gualdo: 77–97.

Raymond, Marcel (ed.) (1956) *Marsile Ficin. Commentaire sur le Banquet de Platon*. Paris, Les Belles Lettres.

Rebhorn, Wayne A. (transl.) (2013) Giovanni Boccaccio, *The Decameron*. New York, Norton.

Reeve, C. D. C. (2012) *Action, Contemplation, and Happiness*. Cambridge, MA, Harvard University Press.

Refini, Eugenio (2009) *Per via d'annotationi: le glosse inedite di Alessandro Piccolomini all'Ars poetica di Orazio*. Lucca, Pacini Fazzi.

    (2013) 'Aristotile in parlare materno: Vernacular Readings of the *Ethics* in the Quattrocento', *I Tatti Studies* Vol. 16: 311–41.

    (2015) 'Shifting Identities: Jacopo Campora's *De immortalitate anime* from Manuscript to Print', in *Remembering the Middle Ages in Early Modern Italy*, ed. Lorenzo Pericolo and Jessica Richardson. Turnhout, Brepols: 67–80.

(2016a) 'Jacopo Campora, *Tratato de l'anima*', in *Venezia e Aristotele*, ed. Lines and Cotugno: 40–1.

(2016b) 'Bernardo di Ser Francesco Nuti, *Etica d'Aristotele tradotta*', in *Venezia e Aristotele*, ed. Lines and Cotugno: 42–3.

(2017) 'By Imitating Our Nurses: Latin and Vernacular in the Renaissance', in *The Routledge History of the Renaissance*, ed. William Caferro. London, Routledge: 46–61.

Reusens, Edmond (1881–1903) *Documents relatifs à l'histoire de l'Université de Louvain, 1425–1797*. Louvain, Chez l'auteur.

Rhodes, Peter John (1981) *A Commentary on the Aristotelian Athenaion Politeia*. Oxford, Oxford University Press.

Ribaudo, Vera (ed.) (2016) Benedetto Cotrugli, *Libro de l'arte de la mercatura*. Venice, Edizioni Ca' Foscari.

Ricci, Pier Giorgio (1947) 'Il Petrarca e Brizio Visconti', *Leonardo* Vol. 16: 337–45.

Richardson, Brian (1994) *Print Culture in Renaissance Italy: The Editor and the Vernacular Text, 1470–1600*. Cambridge, Cambridge University Press.

Richter Sherman, Claire (1995) *Imaging Aristotle: Verbal and Visual Representation in Fourteenth-Century France*. Berkeley, University of California Press.

Rizzi, Andrea (2013) 'Leonardo Bruni and the Shimmering Facets of Languages in Early Quattrocento Florence', *I Tatti Studies* Vol. 16: 243–56.

(2017) *Vernacular Translators in Quattrocento Italy: Scribal Culture, Authority, and Agency*. Turnhout, Brepols.

Rizzo, Silvia (1973) *Il lessico filologico degli umanisti*. Rome, Edizioni di Storia e Letteratura.

Rodolico, Niccolò (1898) *Dal comune alla signoria. Saggio sul governo di Taddeo Pepoli in Bologna*. Bologna, Zanichelli.

(ed.) (1955) Marchionne di Coppo Stefani, *Cronaca fiorentina*. Bologna, Zanichelli (= *Rerum Italicarum Scriptores* 30.1).

Roick, Matthias (2017) *Pontano's Virtues: Aristotelian Moral and Political Thought in the Renaissance*. New York, Bloomsbury.

Rossi, Bastiano (ed.) (1824) *Tre trattati di Albertano giudice di Brescia*. Brescia, Venturini.

Rossi, Luca Carlo (ed.) (2010) *Le strade di Ercole: itinerari umanistici e altri percorsi*. Florence, SISMEL – Edizioni del Galluzzo.

Rotili, Mario (1972) *I codici danteschi miniati a Napoli*. Naples, Libreria scientifica editrice.

Roux, Brigitte (2008) 'Les auteurs du *Trésor*', in *A scuola con Ser Brunetto*, ed. Maffia Scariati: 13–33.

(2009) *Mondes en miniatures: l'iconographie du Livre du Trésor de Brunetto Latini*. Geneva, Droz.

Rovere, Serena (2017) *L'Esopo napoletano di Francesco Del Tuppo*. Pisa, ETS.

Rubinstein, Nicolai (1958) 'Political Ideas in Sienese Art: The Frescoes by Ambrogio Lorenzetti and Taddeo di Bartolo in the Palazzo Pubblico', *Journal of the Warburg and Courtauld Institutes* Vol. 21 Nos 3–4: 179–207.

Rüsch-Klaas, Ute (1993) *Untersuchungen zu Cristoforo Landino, De Anima*. Stuttgart, Teubner.

Ruskin, John (2007) *The Stones of Venice II: The Sea Stories*. New York, Cosimo Classics.

Russell, Peter and Anthony R. D. Pagden (1974) 'Nueva luz sopre una version española cuatrocentista de la Etica a Nicomaco: Bodleian Library, Ms. Span. D.1', in *Homenaje a Guillermo Guastavino*. Madrid, Asociación Nacional de Bibliotecarios, Archiveros y Arqueólogos: 125–46.

Ryan, W.F. and Charles B. Schmitt (1982) *Pseudo-Aristotle the* Secret of Secrets. *Sources and Influences*. London, The Warburg Institute.

Salwa, Piotr (1991) *Narrazione, persuasione, ideologia: una lettura del Novelliere di Giovanni Sercambi, lucchese*. Lucca, Pacini Fazzi.

Sanguineti, Edoardo (1982) 'La novelletta delle papere nel Decameron', *Belfagor* Vol. 37: 137–46.

Sanson, Helena (2011) *Women, Language and Grammar in Italy, 1500–1900*. Oxford, Oxford University Press.

Santoni, Alessandra (2017) 'Per l'edizione critica del volgarizzamento dell'*Etica d'Aristotele*: primi sondaggi sulle varianti', in *Storia, tradizione e critica dei testi: Per Giuliano Tanturli*, ed. Isabella Becherucci and Concetta Bianca. Florence: Pensa MultiMedia Editore, Vol. 1: 219–29.

Saxl, Fritz (1953) *Catalogue of Astrological and Mythological illuminated Manuscripts of the Latin Middle Ages* London, The Warburg Institute.

Scarpino, Cristina (2015) 'Notizie intorno all'*Etica d'Aristotele* tradotta in volgare da Nicola Angelico', *Zeitschrift für romanische Philologie* Vol. 131 No. 3: 714–53.

Schlosser, Julius (1896) *Quellenbuch zur Kunstgeschichte des abendlandischen Mittelalters: ausgewählte Texte des 4. bis 15. Jahrhunderts*. Vienna, Graeser.

Schmitt, Charles B. (1973) 'Towards a Reassessment of Renaissance Aristotelianism', *History of Science* Vol. 11: 159–63.

  (1979) 'Aristotle's *Ethics* in the Sixteenth Century: Some Preliminary Considerations', in *Ethik im Humanismus*, ed. Walter Rügge and Dieter Rutke. Boppard: 87–112.

  (1983) *Aristotle and the Renaissance*. Cambridge, MA, Harvard University Press.

Segre, Cesare (ed.) (1959) *La prosa del Duecento*. Milan, Ricciardi.

  (1964) 'Bartolomeo di San Concordio', *Dizionario biografico degli italiani* Vol. 6: 768–70.

  (1995) 'I volgarizzamenti' in *Lo Spazio Letterario del Medioevo. 1. Il Medioevo Latino, vol. 3: La ricezione del testo*, ed. Guglielmo Cavallo, Claudio Leonardi and Enrico Menestò. Rome, Salerno editrice: 271–98.

Sgarbi, Marco (2016) *Profumo d'immortalità: controversie sull'anima nella filosofia volgare del Rinascimento*. Rome, Carocci.

Shailor, Barbara A. (1984–2004) *Catalogue of Medieval and Renaissance manuscripts in the Beinecke Rare Book and Manuscript Library, Yale University*. Binghamton, NY, Medieval and Renaissance Texts and Studies, 4 vols.

Sheridan, James J. (transl) (1980) Alain of Lille, *The Plaint of Nature*. Toronto, Pontifical Institute of Mediaeval Studies.

Simon, Marcel (1955) *Hercule et le Christianisme*. Paris, Les Belles Lettres.

Sinicropi, Giovanni (ed.) (1995) Giovanni Sercambi, *Novelle*. Florence, Le Lettere, 2 vols.

Siraisi, Nancy (1981) *Taddeo Alderotti and His Pupils: Two Generations of Italian Medical Learning*. Princeton, Princeton University Press.

Skinner, Quentin (1986) 'Ambrogio Lorenzetti: The Artist as Political Philosopher', *Proceedings of the British Academy* Vol. 72: 1–56.

  (1999) 'Ambrogio Lorenzetti's Buon Governo Frescoes: Two Old Questions, Two New Answers', *Journal of the Warburg and Courtauld Institutes*, Vol. 62: 1–28.

  (2002) *Visions of Politics*. Cambridge, Cambridge University Press, 3 vols.

Smith, Susan L. (1995) *The Power of Women. A Topos in Medieval Art and Literature*. Philadelphia, University of Pennsylvania Press.

Somerset, Fiona and Nicholas Watson (eds.) (2003) *The Vulgar Tongue: Medieval and Postmedieval Vernacularity*. University Park, PA, Pennsylvania State University Press.

Sorella, Antonio (ed.) (1999) Sperone Speroni, *Dialogo delle lingue, edizione condotta sull'autografo*, Pescara, Libreria dell'Università.

Spadolini, Ernesto (1902) 'Un'opera inedita di Ciriaco d'Ancona', *Le Marche* Vol. 2: 179–85.

Stahl, William H. and Evan L. Burge (1971–1977), *Martianus Capella and the Seven Liberal Arts*. New York, Columbia University Press, 2 vols.

Staley, Edgcumbe (1906) *The Guilds of Florence*. London, Methuen & Co.

Stäuble, Antonio (1991) '*Parlar per lettera': il pedante nella commedia del Cinquecento e altri saggi sul teatro rinascimentale*. Rome, Bulzoni.

Stephens, Walter (2004) 'When Pope Noah Ruled the Etruscans: Annius of Viterbo and his Forged Antiquities, 1498', in *Studia Humanitatis: Essays In Honor of Salvatore Camporeale*. Supplement to *Modern Language Notes Italian Issue* Vol. 119: 201–23.

  (2010) 'Annius of Viterbo', in *The Classical Tradition*, ed. Grafton, Most and Settis: 46–7.

  (2011) 'The *Antiquities* of Annius of Viterbo: A Misinterpreted Genealogical Forgery', *Revista de Historiografía* Vol. 15 No. 8: 58–65.

Stock, Markus (ed.) (2016) *Alexander the Great in the Middle Ages: Transcultural Perspectives*. Toronto, University of Toronto Press.

Stolz, Michael (2004) *Artes-liberales-Zyklen: Formationen des Wissens im Mittelalter*. Tübingen, Francke.

Storer, Edward (transl.) (1925) *Il novellino. The Hundred Old Tales*. London, Routledge.

Storost, Joachim (1955) *Zur Aristoteles-Sage im Mittelalter*, in *Monumentum Bambergense. Festgabe für Benedikt Kraft*. Munich, Kösel Verlag: 298–348.

  (1956) 'Femme chevalchat Aristotte', *Zeitschrift für französische Sprache und Literatur* Vol. 66: 186–201.

Tanturli, Giuliano (1978) 'I Benci copisti: vicende della cultura fiorentina volgare tra Antonio Pucci e il Ficino', *Studi di filologia italiana* Vol. 36: 197–313.

(1988) 'La cultura fiorentina volgare del Quattrocento davanti ai nuovi testi greci', *Medioevo e Rinascimento* Vol. 2: 217–43.

Tanzini, Lorenzo and Sergio Tognetti (eds.) (2012) *Mercatura è arte: Uomini d'affari toscani in Europa e nel Mediterraneo tardomedievale*. Rome, Viella.

Tardelli, Claudia (ed.) (forthcoming) Francesco da Buti, *Commento alla Commedia*. Rome, Salerno editrice.

Tateo, Francesco (1993) 'Il dialogo da Petrarca agli umanisti', *Quaderni petrarcheschi* Vol. 9–10: 537–54.

Tavoni, Mirko (1984) *Latino, grammatica, volgare: storia di una questione umanistica*. Padua, Antenore.

(ed.) (2011) Dante Alighieri, *De vulgari eloquentia*, in *Opere. 1. Rime; Vita nova; De vulgari eloquentia*. Milan, Mondadori: 1067–547.

(ed.) (2013) *Dante e la lingua italiana*. Ravenna, Longo.

Taylor, Paul (2008) 'Introduction', in *Iconography without Texts*, ed. Paul Taylor. London, The Warburg Institute: 1–10.

Tinkler, John F. (1988) 'Humanism and Dialogue', *Parergon* Vol. 6: 197–214.

Tola, Pasquale (1838) *Dizionario biografico degli uomini illustri di Sardegna. Volume secondo*. Turin, Chirio e Mina.

Toscano, Gennaro (ed.) (1998) *La Biblioteca Reale di Napoli al tempo della dinastia Aragonese. La Biblioteca Real de Nápoles en tiempos de la dinastía Aragonesa*. Valencia, Generalitat Valenciana.

Tucci, Ugo (1973) 'The Psychology of the Venetian Merchant in the Sixteenth Century', in *Renaissance Venice*, ed. Hale: 346–78.

(ed.) (1990) Benedetto Cotrugli, *Il libro dell'arte di mercatura*. Venice, Arsenale.

Tuohy, Thomas (1996) *Herculean Ferrara: Ercole d'Este, 1471–1505, and the Invention of a Ducal Capital*. Cambridge, Cambridge University Press.

Tylus, Jane (2015) *Siena: City of Secrets*. Chicago, Chicago University Press.

Ullman, Berthold Luis (ed.) (1951) Coluccio Salutati, *De laboribus Herculis*. Zurich, In Aedibus Thesauri Mundi.

(1960) *The Origin and Development of Humanistic Script*. Rome, Edizioni di Storia e Letteratura.

Valero Moreno, Juan Miguel (2015) 'Formas del Aristotelismo Ético-Político en la Castilla del siglo XV', in *Aristotele fatto volgare*, ed. Lines and Refini: 253–310.

Vanin, Barbara (2013) *I manoscritti medievali in lingua volgare della Biblioteca del Museo Correr*. Padua, Antenore.

Varvaro, Alberto (ed.) (1957) Antonio Pucci, *Libro di varie storie*. Palermo, Presso l'Accademia.

Vasoli, Cesare (1972) 'Bruni, Leonardo, detto Leonardo Aretino', *Dizionario biografico degli Italiani* Vol. 14: 618–33.

Venuti, Lawrence (ed.) (2000) *The Translation Studies Reader*. London, Routledge.

(2012) *Translation Changes Everything: Theory and Practice.* Hoboken, Taylor and Francis.

(2017) *The Translator's Invisibility: A History of Translation.* London, Routledge.

Verde, Armando (1973–1976) *Lo studio fiorentino. 1473–1503. Studi e ricerche.* Pistoia, Memorie Domenicane, 5 vols.

Verdier, Philippe (1969) 'L'iconographie des arts libéraux dans l'art du moyen âge jusqu'à la fin du quinzième siècle', in *Arts libéraux et philosophie au moyen âge. Actes du quatrième congrès international de philosophie médiévale.* Paris, J. Vrin: 305–55.

Viti, Paolo (1991) 'Domenico da Prato', *Dizionario Biografico degli Italiani* Vol. 40: 661–3.

(ed.) (1996) *Opere letterarie e politiche di Leonardo Bruni.* Turin, UTET.

Vivanti, Corrado (ed.) (2000) Niccolò Machiavelli, *Discorsi sopra la prima deca di Tito Livio.* Turin, Einaudi.

Von Leyden, Wolfgang (1958) 'Antiquity and Authority: A Paradox in the Renaissance Theory of History', *Journal of the History of Ideas* Vol. 19: 473–92.

Wagner, David L. (ed.) (1983) *The Seven Liberal Arts in the Middle Ages.* Bloomington, Indiana University Press.

Walker, Leslie J. and Brian Richardson (transl.) (2003) Niccolò Machiavelli, *The Discourses.* New York, Penguin.

Wallace, David (1991) *Giovanni Boccaccio, Decameron.* Cambridge, Cambridge University Press.

Waquet, Françoise (2002) *Latin or the Empire of a Sign*, transl. John Howe. London, Verson.

Wartenberg, Imke (2015) *Bilder der Rechtsprechung: Spätmittelalterliche Wandmalereien in Regierungsräumen italienischer Kommunen.* Berlin, De Gruyter.

Watson, Andrew G. (1979) *Catalogue of Dated and Datable Manuscripts c. 700–1600 in the Department of Manuscripts: The British Library.* London, British Library, 2 vols.

Weijers, Olga (1988) 'L'appellation des disciplines dans les classifications des sciences aux XIIe et XIIIe siècles', *Archivum Latinitatis Medii Aevi* Vols 46–7: 39–64.

Wilkins, Ernest H. (transl.) (1962) *The Triumphs of Petrarch.* Chicago, University of Chicago Press.

Williams, Steven J. (1994) 'Prima diffusione dello pseudo-aristotelico "Secretum Secretorum" in Occidente: corte papale e corte imperiale', in *Federico II e le scienze*, ed. Pierre Toubert and Agostino Paravicini Bagliani. Palermo, Sellerio: 459–74.

(2003a) 'The Vernacular Tradition of the Pseudo-Aristotelian *Secret of Secrets* in the Middle Ages: Translations, Manuscripts, Readers', in *Filosofia in volgare nel medioevo*, ed. Bray and Sturlese: 451–82.

(2003b) *The Secret of Secrets: The Scholarly Career of a Pseudo-Aristotelian Text in the Latin Middle Ages.* Ann Arbor, University of Michigan University Press.

Witt, Ronald G. (2000) *In the Footsteps of the Ancients: The Origins of Humanism from Lovato to Bruni.* Leiden, Brill.

Wright, Alison (1994) 'The Myth of Hercules', in *Lorenzo il Magnifico e il suo mondo*, ed. Gian Carlo Garfagnini. Florence, Leo S. Olschki: 323–39.

Zaccaria, Vittorio (ed.) (1998) Giovanni Boccaccio, *Genealogie deorum gentilium*. Milan, Mondadori, 2 vols.

Zacour, Norman P. and Rudolf Hirsch (1965) *Catalogue of Manuscripts in the Libraries of the University of Pennsylvania to 1800*. Philadelphia, University of Pennsylvania Press.

Zaggia, Massimo (2007) 'Codici milanesi del Quattrocento all'Ambrosiana per il periodo dal 1450 al 1476', in *Nuove ricerche su codici in scrittura latina dell'Ambrosiana*, ed. Mirella Ferrari and Marco Navoni. Milan, Vita e Pensiero: 331–84.

(2015) 'Culture in Lombardy, ca. 1350–1535', in *A Companion to Medieval and Early Modern Milan: The Distinctive Features of an Italian State*, ed. Andrea Gamberini. Leiden, Brill: 166–89.

Zago, Roberto (2002) 'Giustinian, Nicolò', *Dizionario Biografico degli Italiani* Vol. 57: 270–1.

Zambrini, Francesco (1868) 'Descrizione di codici manoscritti che si conservano nella R. Biblioteca dell'Università di Bologna', *Il Propugnatore* Vol. 1: 121–36, 251–72, 384–97, 506–16.

Zamuner, Ilaria (2005) 'La tradizione romanza del Secretum Secretorum', *Studi Medievali* Vol. 46: 31–116.

Zanichelli, Giuseppa Z. (2006) 'L'immagine come glossa. Considerazioni su alcuni frontespizi miniati della *Commedia*', in *Dante e le arti visive*, ed. Maria Monica Donato, Lucia Battaglia Ricci, Michelangelo Picone and Giuseppa Z. Zanichelli. Milan, Unicopli: 109–48.

Zapperi, Roberto (1974) 'Campora, Giacomo', *Dizionario biografico degli italiani* Vol. 17: 581–3.

Zhou, Wangyue (2013) 'Literary Translation From Perspective of Reception Theory: The Case Study of Three Versions of *Na Han*', *Studies in Literature and Language* Vol. 7 No 2: 19–25.

Ziolkowski, Jan (1985) *Alan of Lille's Grammar of Sex: The Meaning of Grammar to a Twelfth-century Intellectual*. Cambridge, MA, The Medieval Academy of America.

Zurla, Placido (1806) *Il mappamondo di Fra Mauro camaldolese*. Venice.

Index

.